REGULATING CONTRACTS

HUGH COLLINS

UNIVERSITY PRESS

This book has been printed digitally and produced in a standard specification
in order to ensure its continuing availability

OXFORD
UNIVERSITY PRESS

Great Clarendon Street, Oxford OX2 6DP

Oxford University Press is a department of the University of Oxford.
It furthers the University's objective of excellence in research, scholarship,
and education by publishing worldwide in

Oxford New York

Auckland Cape Town Dar es Salaam Hong Kong Karachi
Kuala Lumpur Madrid Melbourne Mexico City Nairobi
New Delhi Shanghai Taipei Toronto
With offices in
Argentina Austria Brazil Chile Czech Republic France Greece
Guatemala Hungary Italy Japan South Korea Poland Portugal
Singapore Switzerland Thailand Turkey Ukraine Vietnam

Oxford is a registered trade mark of Oxford University Press
in the UK and in certain other countries

Published in the United States
by Oxford University Press Inc., New York

Oxford is a registered trade mark of Oxford University Press
in the UK and in certain other countries

Published in the United States
by Oxford University Press Inc., New York

ISBN 0-19-925801-5

Preface

A YEAR or more ago I commenced a short essay to answer a question which had been intriguing me as a lawyer interested in the law of contract. I wondered what lawyers might learn from the insights provided by empirical studies of contractual practices. I was sceptical that lawyers might learn anything useful, because contract law has traditionally been much more engaged with positioning itself with respect to the ruling political theories of the age. As I pursued this question, however, I became persuaded that lawyers could profit from these empirical studies. The essay became longer as I tried to draw out the implications, especially by exploring the insight that the law thinks about contractual relations in ways which differ from the framework in which the parties to the contract themselves perceive their relations.

As the essay evolved, it became apparent that in fact I was attempting to bring together three discordant academic discourses—economics, sociology, and law,—each of which contained its unique insights and misperceptions about contractual behaviour and the construction of markets. The ambition of the essay became more challenging, as I sought to construct a genuine interdisciplinary approach, in which the whole range of social sciences could be brought to bear on the topic of regulating contractual relations. This approach requires asking the question what each discipline may learn from the others. Instead of a one way street flowing from social science to law, it became a tripartite conversation, between sociology, economics and law. Each discipline instructed and criticised the others. By the time this dialogue had been pursued to the limits of my imagination and the publisher's patience, the short essay had turned into the present tome.

I hope that the outcome will profit readers from a broad range of social sciences. Economists may discover convincing evidence that contractual behaviour cannot be adequately be explained by reference solely to self-interested materialistic behaviour. Sociologists may realise that subtle economic accounts of rational conduct may explain far more behaviour in the construction of markets than they might have expected. Lawyers can learn from both, but also explain that the design of regulation is both a complex task and one which has implications for contractual behaviour.

Nevertheless, my original interest in what lawyers may learn from the (other) social sciences remains the key ingredient in each chapter. Legal regulation is regarded as an instrumental activity, which creates rules, standards, and enforcement mechanisms in the pursuit of particular

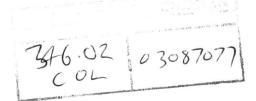

purposes. Lawyers may learn from the social sciences what kinds of purposes can be pursued productively by legal regulation and how those objectives can best be achieved. Or, to put the point the other way round, lawyers can learn how legal regulation can easily become counter-productive, ineffective, and inefficient. Contract lawyers have not bothered much with these issues in the past, being content rather to attempt to describe principles of good conduct based upon political and moral theory, and then to assume that rules with these purposes have their intended effects. I hope that this book assists in the reorientation of the way in which contract lawyers think about the problems which they address.

I would like to thank the many friends and colleagues with whom I have discussed themes of this book, some of whom have also commented on earlier draft chapters. I thank especially Tim Murphy for discussions about social theory, Julia Black for her insights into regulation, financial markets, and public law, and Colin Scott for his help with respect to consumer law and regulation. Simon Roberts has taught me a great deal about dispute settlement and encouraged scepticism about the utility of lawyers in that regard. I have also benefited from discussions with Christian Joerges about the general topic of private law and particularly European developments. Eric Schanze helped me understand ways in which the discourses of institutional economics and legal doctrine might be fruitfully combined. Anna Edwards provided patient research assistance as the direction of my investigations shot off at unforeseen tangents.

Two colleagues at the LSE have been especially helpful in a more general way. Nicola Lacey has provided essential support in leading me to believe that the project has been worthwhile. Above all, Gunther Teubner has been a patient teacher and an inspiration on innumerable occasions.

H.C.

London School of Economics
January 1999

Contents

Part 4 Distributive Tasks of Regulation

Table of Cases

Table of Legislation

United Kingdom

European Directives

USA

Other Jurisdictions

Part 1
Introduction

1
The Tasks for Regulating Contracts

Making contracts is a routine practice. We purchase goods in a shop, buy a ticket for a bus ride, cash a cheque in a bank, or take a job. These everyday actions occur without much detailed reflection or circumspection. Life would become almost impossible, if we had to ponder and inspect the risks every time we made a contract. But the risks of betrayal or disappointment are nearly always present. I purchase a book from a shop. I run the risk of disappointment: the book may lack any interesting insights, some pages may be missing, or the spelling may be atrocious. The shopkeeper takes the risk of betrayal: the money that I give in payment may be counterfeit, or my cheque may bounce. Despite a wide range of possible risks, however, the transaction runs smoothly, with only trivial precautions to guard against betrayal or disappointment. I do not insist upon reading the book before purchasing it. The shopkeeper does not insist upon his bank account receiving an irrevocable credit before parting with possession of the book. The stakes may be low in this simple purchase compared to other transactions such as a contract of employment or a multimillion-dollar investment, but the risks are nearly always present.

The willingness to run these risks may be described as trust. A high degree of trust enables us to discount such risks almost entirely and to get on with the business of making contracts. This trust becomes habitual in modern societies, in the sense that it is a widespread and taken-for-granted feature of social interaction. Despite the individualism or atomism of modern societies, we are bound together by this type of social solidarity in which trust enables the myriad of contractual relations that make up the complex division of labour to occur. Modern society rests upon the realization of the possibility of trust between strangers. One of the central puzzles for social theory is how this degree of trust can be accomplished, that is, how trust becomes routine.

The study of the social bonds that enable the construction of modern society has always represented an important theme in the social sciences. The idea of an enforceable contract was central to the tradition of liberal political theory and its schemes of political association described as a Social Contract. The significance of contractual relations was also a principal focus in the writings of the most influential social theorists, including Marx, Durkheim, and Weber. These theorists tended to view the law as a direct reflection of the nature of social relations in modern societies. They regarded the law as essential to the construction of social and economic bonds. The prominence of the law governing contracts in the intellectual discourses of lawyers was believed to correspond to the real nature of social relations and the significance of contract in sustaining social bonds. For example, in Durkheim's discussion of his contrast between the 'mechanical solidarity' of traditional societies and the 'organic solidarity' fundamental to the social order of modern societies, he concludes by observing:

> We know under what external forms these two types of solidarity are symbolized, that is to say, what the body of juridical rules which corresponds to each of them is. Consequently, in order to recognize their respective importance in a given social type, it is enough to compare the respective extent of the two types of law which express them, since law always varies as the social relations which it governs.[1]

Political economy or economics has also employed the idea of contract as its description of the character of the division of labour and market relations. In political economy, it is the legally enforceable contract, buttressed by state sanctions, that describes and enables social order to be preserved, despite the disintegration of social ties required by the increasing division of labour.

In all these works, a persistent and dominant strand in explanations for the establishment of those bonds of trust that underpin a market economy identifies the law as a crucial component. This explanation holds that the presence of laws against betrayal and disappointment, enforced by courts armed with powerful state sanctions, enables trust to become widespread. People take the risks of contractual relations, because they can always rely upon the implicit threat of punishment by a state sanction against defaulters. On this view, it is not so much trust that enables transactions between strangers to occur, but rather an extensive system of sanctions that can be imposed against those who breach the rules of the game. Trust is built upon insurance.

In this common account of the constitution of modern societies, the law plays a pivotal role. The regulation of contractual behaviour by courts as agencies of the state provides the system of rules and sanctions, which enables the necessary degree of trust between strangers to be constructed. It follows that societies that lack this type of legal system in which economic relations are facilitated by the systematic application of the Rule of Law must lack the vital element that permits a complex division of labour. This absence of law provokes a fundamental handicap in the

---

[1] Durkheim, E., *The Division of Labor in Society* (New York: Free Press, 1933) (originally published 1893) 131–2.

competition for prosperity and the construction of social order. This influential view about the significance of law guides, for example, the conditions of support by the World Bank for developing economies.[2]

The classics of the social sciences examined the idea of contract largely at the level of theoretical speculation and casual observation. In recent years, however, scholars have engaged in detailed empirical studies of contractual behaviour, the historical and social origins of markets, and the social effects of the legal regulation of contracts. The central puzzle set by these studies concerns an apparent contradiction. On the one hand, most political, economic and social theory suggests that in a market economy the law of contract comprises a fundamental mechanism of social order. Lawyers too, in their emphasis upon the fundamental position of the law of contract within the legal system, hold that this legal regulation provides the crucial cement in sustaining the social system. On the other hand, the evidence from empirical studies of contractual behaviour indicates the marginal and sometimes socially disintegrative effects of the law of contract. Consumers who purchase defective products almost never vindicate their legal rights in the courts. If I am dissatisfied with the book I have purchased, I will not go off to court, but return to the shop, make a complaint, and in all likelihood be offered an exchange or a refund. Businessmen seem not to be concerned about the legal validity of their transactions, do not insist upon their legal rights, and when a dispute requires adjudication they avoid the ordinary courts like the plague. If the shopkeeper does not receive full payment for the book that I have purchased, perhaps because my cheque has bounced, the shopkeeper is most unlikely to bring a legal action for debt, but will certainly refuse to trade with me in the future. There is also evidence that whole swathes of the most vibrant parts of the economy such as the financial and banking sectors function entirely within their own regulatory system that renders the law almost irrelevant.

Can these insights be reconciled? Can we explain how the law of contract is both fundamental to the social system, and yet almost irrelevant to most daily market practices? How far, if at all, do laws and legal institutions contribute to the construction of habitual trust? These questions define a recurrent theme of this book. Yet this work is not intended primarily as an exploration of social theory. There is a second theme, which compels a much more detailed investigation of the system of legal regulation of contracts.

This second theme may be defined by the following question: what form and content of legal regulation enables the legal system to perform its functions in supporting the market system most effectively and efficiently?

---

[2] World Bank, *World Development Report 1997: The State in a Changing World* (Oxford: Oxford University Press, 1997).

Even if we discover that law only plays a marginal role in the establishment
of habitual trust, that conclusion leaves open the possibility that the law
could be improved so that it might provide better assistance. We can
engage, therefore, in a critical and normative enquiry with respect to the
law of contract. The general question becomes what kind of law is best
suited to this task of regulating markets and contractual forms of association, and how might its success be measured and evaluated? In particular,
we can ask what kinds of laws and legal institutions are good for commercial transactions, and what sorts of legal regulation are efficient and
effective in retail sales to consumers? Would it be better in these two cases,
for instance, either to impose clear mandatory rules enforced by powerful
regulators employing state sanctions, or to permit the parties to a transaction to regulate themselves, and to create their own system of private
justice through mediation and arbitration? We should not assume, however, that law has any positive contribution to make in these fields; any
'juridification' of social practice by the imposition of legal norms and
processes should be assessed on the empirical evidence as to its merits.[3]
This investigation of the best kind of law proceeds beyond a consideration
of the forms of rules and the nature and competence of legal institutions. It
includes as well a more detailed examination of the legal rules and
principles, the intricacies of legal discourse that channel legal regulation.

Although we shall discuss many legal doctrines regarding contracts, it
should be clear that this book does not provide a text about the law of
contract. Lawyers write treatises that construct a systematic analysis of the
legal rules and principles. They try to make sense of the law, to render it a
coherent and consistent discourse for the allocation and vindication of
rights and obligations. We will be adopting a more external point of
view, one which is always more interested in the interaction between the
law and the social practices which it regulates. Of course, we cannot avoid a
consideration of how the law thinks about these practices or how its
regulatory objectives are defined and implemented. On the contrary, in
order to grasp the nature of the dynamic interaction between law and the
social practice of making contracts, we need to understand both how the
law thinks about its role and how the participants who make contracts
understand the meaning of their social interaction. Nevertheless, the
questions that we have posed cannot be answered exclusively from a legal
point of view. The character and effects of legal regulation must be examined from an external vantage-point, one which appreciates the distinctive
qualities of legal discourses, yet which seeks also to measure critically that

---

[3] Teubner, G., 'Juridification: Concepts, Aspects, Limits, Solutions', in G. Teubner (ed.),
*Juridification of Social Spheres: A Comparative Analysis in the Areas of Labour, Corporate,
Antitrust and Social Welfare Law* (Berlin: Walter de Gruyter, 1987).

system of knowledge about the world against other systems drawn from the whole range of the social sciences.

Such an approach is not entirely novel. Various types of economic analysis of contractual practices and legal regulation have been employed to answer these questions. We can learn a great deal from the models of social interaction suggested by an analysis based upon a rational, utility-maximizing, individual. But these models must be tested against the empirical evidence available in order to ascertain the extent of their validity and their weaknesses. Furthermore, economic analysis tends to ignore how the legal system itself thinks about its regulatory tasks and methods, a dimension which is important to any critical assessment of the potential efficacy and efficiency of legal regulation. Economic analysis must therefore be treated as a heuristic device, not a comprehensive method for obtaining answers to our questions.

The word 'regulation' has already cropped up several times, and a caution needs to be expressed at this point regarding its meaning. I use it as a generic term to describe any system of rules intended to govern the behaviour of its subjects. Law provides one type of regulation, but it is only one of many types of social regulation such as custom, convention, and organized bureaucracies. The term regulation is often used in a much narrower sense to describe a distinctive set of techniques used by states to control the operations of markets. In this narrow sense, regulation concerns the work of specialized agencies (regulators) vested with the power to control distortions of competition in the market (market failures), to protect participants in markets, and to guard against undesirable external effects of markets such as pollution. I am content to pick up on this resonance of the word regulation when considering the legal system as a form of regulation, provided it is understood that we should not presuppose that specialized regulatory agencies and codes are the sole type of legal mechanism. The private law of contract enforced by the ordinary courts is equally a form of legal regulation. The interesting questions are rather whether the different forms of legal regulation pursue similar objectives such as the prevention of market failure, and which one of the different legal techniques and agencies proves more successful in achieving its objectives.

My expansive conception of the idea of regulation is needed in order to grasp a third theme underlying this book. Legal regulation of contracts thinks about its activities in two radically different ways. The fundamental contrast lies between private law and welfare regulation. By the close of the nineteenth century (and often much earlier) modern legal systems evolved a distinctive method of regulating contracts described as part of the private law of obligations. The private law of contract was usually embodied in codes that comprised a set of general principles applicable to most contractual relations. These codes of private law were conceived by the legal system as fundamental to the legal order, a pre-political statement of basic rights and obligations in civil society, which was linked inextricably to the cultural and political identity of nation states. These private law systems provide the substance for the systematic treatises on the law of contract described above. At the same time, however, every legal system also engaged in more detailed regulation of particular types of contractual practices for explicit instrumental purposes. This discourse of legal regulation adjusted the private law of rights and obligations for such purposes as fairness and distributive justice, alleviation of market failures, restrictions on the exercise of private power, and other welfare goals.

The simultaneous presence of these two forms of legal discourse could be managed for a time by the closure of the discourses. Specialists in private law ignored the impact of regulation upon their elaborate schemes of entitlements, and the regulatory lawyers suppressed the implications of their radical challenge to the nineteenth-century legal order. By the close of the twentieth century, however, these techniques used for the avoidance of the clash of legal discourses no longer provide a persuasive account of legal regulation. Is it convincing, for instance, to insist upon the continuing validity of the private law principle that the law should not assess the fairness of contracts, when we can observe so many examples of legal regulation apparently introduced for precisely that purpose, such as minimum wage laws, fair rent controls, limits on interest rates in credit transactions, and restrictions on unfair terms in consumer contracts? My argument is that legal systems are in a process of transition from the dominance of traditional private law regulation to one where welfarist regulation increasingly provides the basic discourse of the legal regulation of contracts. How the law thinks about contractual practices is therefore undergoing a reconfiguration.

These observations are again not entirely novel, but their implications have not been adequately explored. Once legal discourse reorients itself towards the instrumental reasoning of welfarist regulation, it must observe closely the consequences of regulation in order to ascertain whether the objectives are being achieved. The trajectory of legal evolution alters from the private law discourse of seeking the better coherence for its scheme of principles to one of learning about the need for fresh regulation by observations of the consequences of present regulation. Information about the world, especially market practices, has to be gathered and reconstituted in a form which enables the legal discourse to adjust its own internal operations and regulatory outcomes. Within this new form of legal reasoning, what the law actually does, its social and economic effects, becomes crucial to the dynamic operations of the legal system. The empirical evidence of the effects of legal regulation gathered together in this book therefore

becomes not merely some interesting information, a mere external observation, but rather the evidence becomes central to the process of legal
reasoning itself. The legal system translates this information into its own
internal operations where it provides the crucial evolutionary dynamic.

It will be tempting for lawyers who are steeped in the traditions of the
private law discourse about contracts to regard this book as a set of
external observations. Such a reading is possible: a sociological and
economic study of legal regulation of contracts. Yet this third theme of
the book insists that such a reading would misconceive my project. The
sharp contrast between external observation and the internal operations of
the legal system becomes untenable in a legal discourse of welfarist regulation that presupposes that it must interact with its external environment.
What were once regarded as 'non-legal reasons', that is reasons which were
strictly speaking irrelevant to the legal discourse, such as the effects or
policies of private law, become central reasons for the legal discourse, at the
core of its motivation. It is not my view that legal discourse collapses or
degenerates into a political or economic discourse, for it still understands
its environment within a distinctive framework of reasoning. My argument
is merely that the growing dominance of welfarist regulation in the legal
discourse requires the legal system to regard information about its environment, such as the effects of a particular regulation, not as irrelevant to its
reasoning process, but rather as an intrinsic and inseparable part of it.

The title of this book, *Regulating Contracts*, tries to capture the unfamiliar, interdisciplinary terrain that it occupies. We examine regulation in
all its forms, processes, and systems. Legal regulation merely comprises one
system applied in the space established by contractual practices.[4] Other
systems of regulation may comprise institutional structures of self-
regulation by the participants, or may involve other external institutions
such as trade associations. Similarly, the concept of contract in the title
does not refer to the legal conception alone, but refers more broadly to
social relations that acquire a distinctive set of meanings and dynamic that
are commonly described as contractual. In the next chapter, I try to clarify
the threads that are common to those contractual practices. They involve, I
suggest, a distinctive set of meanings attributed to a variety of types of
human association.

In Part 2, I develop the argument that a new configuration of laws
regulating contracts is evolving. The most important strand in this argument suggests that out of the collision between private law and public
regulation a new style of legal discourse about contracts emerges. The

---

[4] Shearing, C. D., 'A Constitutive Conception of Regulation', in P. Grabosky and
J. Braithwaite (eds.), *Business Regulation and Australia's Future* (Canberra: Australian
Institute of Criminology, 1993).

new regulation is a type of hybrid, which retains many of the characteristics of private law, yet at the same time produces new capacities and evolutionary trajectories. My discussion is divided into two chapters. Chapter 3 describes the characteristics of traditional private law and how this form of legal discourse has been subject to productive disintegration. The fourth chapter examines the new capacities and evolutionary trajectories of the modern style of regulation. These chapters rely upon an unfamiliar shift in the paradigms of legal thought in which not only is private law understood as a regulatory technique, but also the negotiation of terms by the parties is also understood as a method of self-regulation.

Part 3 of the book examines the general issue of the role of legal regulation in the construction of markets. It is assumed that a basic task for regulating contracts must be to contribute to the formation of contractual relations and markets. Yet it is not assumed that law plays a vital role in this task. The principal question is rather what role can law usefully play? The investigation opens in Chapter 5 with an examination of the part played by legal regulation in the construction of trust and sanctions, which, it is argued, are together the indispensable foundations of markets. Building on that investigation, in Chapter 6 we examine how contractual behaviour interacts with legal regulation. The most interesting issue is what conclusion should we draw from the evidence that parties to contracts tend not to employ the institution of a legally enforceable contract as part of their rational behaviour towards transactions and each other. In the next chapter we turn our attention to the work of lawyers in the construction of contractual relations. Lawyers think of their primary role as one of planning contractual relations, that is devising the self-regulation of the business relation. We examine the obstacles to the performance of this role and question its importance in the construction of markets.

Building on those observations about the way the law both supports and obstructs the construction of trading relations, Chapter 8 draws together the threads of the argument with respect to the question of what kind of regulation of contracts will best support markets. The argument challenges the conventional wisdom that a clear, formal set of rules defining the entitlements of the parties to the contract best serves the interests of business. My argument is that the advantages of formalism in legal reasoning are normally overstated, and that calculability of legal entitlements requires rather more open textured rules and other techniques for contextualizing the dispute. The final chapter in this part of the book considers the role played by law in the construction of specialized commercial markets such as stock exchanges and financial instruments such as money. In these markets, it is suggested, the meaning of contract differs because the relation becomes a thing in itself. Legal regulation has to transform its understanding of contractual relations in order to provide support for these commercial transactions. The task of legal regulation in these markets also differs sharply due to the interposition of self-regulating intermediate institutions.

Part 4 of the book considers the distributive impact of contractual relations and legal regulation. Market transactions alter initial allocations of endowments. In regulating this activity, the law necessarily channels the distributive patterns achieved through trading. Markets function as the principal distributive mechanism in modern societies, with only marginal adjustments effected by the instruments of the state such as taxation and welfare benefits. The rules governing contracts steer these distributive outcomes of markets by controlling the power of the parties to devise their own self-regulation. These concerns of distributive justice have many aspects and not all will be considered here.

The selected topics begin with the control of the construction of discretionary power relations through contracts. We examine the reasons for the construction of relations of domination and subordination through contracts in three diverse contexts: consumer purchases under standard form contracts, the employment relation and other types of agency, and in networks of contracts that amount to inchoate organizations. In each context, we consider the possible objectives of regulation, and how those objectives might be accomplished efficiently and effectively. It is argued that the objective should not be simply to attempt to combat relations of domination, but rather to improve the efficiency of these types of contract by revising their structures and their market contexts.

The next chapter examines the regulation of unfairness in contracts in the strict sense of an imbalance between the performances required by each party under the contract. I challenge two popular views that instances of unfairness in contracts are illusory and that effective legal regulation to combat (the supposed non-existent) problem of unfairness is either impossible or counter-productive. The chapter develops the argument that the modern type of regulatory discourse evolving through private law has the capacity to produce effective regulation designed to combat instances of unfairness in contracts.

The discussion turns in the next chapter to the related problem of disappointments arising from poor quality in goods and services. Although no one doubts that poor quality sometimes occurs, the question of whether any type of regulation can prevent disappointments is more contested. In particular, private law is often regarded as ineffective in imposing reasonable standards of quality. This chapter is therefore devoted to a close examination of how private law can achieve the capacity to achieve efficacious and efficient styles of regulation of quality.

In Chapter 13 we take a slight diversion, in order to consider the distinct topic of the regulation of contracts used by governments for the delivery of public services. Although these contracts provoke many of the distributive issues already considered, such as relations of domination, unfairness, and poor quality, they also present particular difficulties for adequate self-regulation by the parties. The principal question that interests us is what kind of legal regulation can best assist governments in the use of markets to deliver services to the public.

Finally, Chapter 14 regards the problem of dispute settlement as a task for regulating contracts that raises distributive issues. The principal difficulty here is to decide what are the 'goods' that we seek to redistribute through regulation. Is the 'good' one concerning the ability to vindicate the rights established by self-regulation, or is the 'good' rather the procedural right of access to justice. My argument is that the redistribution of neither of these 'goods' should be the prime task of regulation. Instead, regulation should be aimed at a fairer distribution of the 'good' of self-regulation of disputes, that is the 'good' of settlements.

A concluding chapter reviews some of the theses presented during the book. It also contains some reflections on methodology and questions for future research.

2

The Meaning of Contract

Before examining any regulation of contracts, we should devote some time to the idea of a contractual relation itself. This relation plainly differs from other types of human association, such as those found between friends, neighbours, members of a club, and between members of a family. Such an investigation of the social institution of contract presents a considerable problem, because the idea of contract possesses a confusing surplus of meanings.

We use the idea of contract in numerous contexts: from a commonplace purchase of goods from a shop, to abstract theories of the foundations of political obligations in modern societies, the Social Contract. Furthermore, each conception or use of the idea of contract can be examined from a variety of perspectives or discourses, including morality, politics, economics, and law. We can ask of both the shop purchase and the hypothetical Social Contract: is the bargain fair, just, efficient, or binding?

Even within a particular discourse such as law, we discover a rich variety of themes and emphases about contracts. The practising lawyer identifies the key function of contracts as the planning of an economic relation. The legal scholar views the rules of contract law as a particular source of private law obligations. The socio-legal scholar perhaps considers contract law as a tool for the regulation of economic and social transactions. Finally, the judge treats contracts as creating binding rules of law between the parties, breach of which provides a justification for the imposition of state sanctions.

This multiplicity of contexts and meanings signifies that the idea of contract is used not only to describe a key economic institution in a market economy, but also to express more generally a central form of human association in modern society. In this chapter, I attempt to distil some key themes in the meaning of contractual relations to the participants, and how the dominance of contracts as an organizing principle of human association in modern society defines the meaning of social life.

How Contract Thinks About Association

A contract creates a relationship between people. It comprises a distinctive type of human association. What distinguishes a contractual relation from other forms of association, such as links of status, kinship, friendship, and membership of a community or an organization? Some caution is required in answering this question, because contract is such an abstract idea that many kinds of relationship such as marriage or an exchange of gifts between friends can be perceived, at the price of some distortion, as contractual. My contention is, however, that a paradigm meaning can be attributed to the idea of contract.

Philip Selznick has identified four core features of this paradigm meaning of contract.[1] Like the classical social theorists, he discovers these features by an examination of legal doctrine. First, he emphasizes the point that contracts comprise a voluntary relationship between individuals, rather than the obligations which arise involuntarily by virtue of membership of a group or family. This is the traditional legal distinction between contract and status, or between contract and domestic relations. Second, a contract implies a limited commitment. A contract forms an impermanent, precise set of undertakings, rather than an open-ended diffuse set of commitments as in friendship or marriage. A third element consists of mutuality, the idea that contracts represent a species of social order based upon exchanges, which is a largely self-enforcing system founded on self-interest and reciprocity. Finally, contracts are bounded relationships in that the obligations which the contract creates usually affect only the parties to the agreement, rather than imposing obligations and commitments upon a broader social group. In short, contractual relations conceive of patterns of human association as individualized and confined, rather than collective and indeterminate.

This valuable analysis seems to me to remain too closely attached to the legal perspective upon the meaning of contracts. It tracks closely the traditional private law doctrinal categories: the formation of contracts by consent or agreement; the determination of the content of the obligation by reference to the terms of the contract; the idea of mutuality expressed by the doctrine of consideration in the Common Law or *causa* in Civil Law systems; and the doctrine of privity of contract (or relative effect) that determines the bounded quality of the relation. Legal doctrine no doubt can provide insights as to the meaning of social institutions, for it is produced by observation of those social practices. At the same time, legal analysis provides a selective and partial view of social institutions that is generated for the purpose of conducting the law's own internal operations for regulating contracts.

When we try to distance ourselves from the legal conception of the meaning of contractual relations, we can observe that contracts establish

---

[1] Selznick, P., *Law, Society and Industrial Justice* (New York: Russell Sage Foundation, 1969), 52–62.

a discrete communication system between the individuals. Whatever their prior relationship, a contractual agreement constitutes a distinct and isolated specification of particular undertakings. The contract may be made between friends, for example, who already have diffuse expectations of loyalty and support established through previous interactions including exchanges. A contract marks a distinct communication between the friends, which is not governed solely by the ties of friendship, but which establishes its own discrete normative context. My friend, the professor of Roman Law, agrees to sell me his bicycle for £30. The agreement marks a severable transaction between us, with a fixed price and object, within a finite time. The contract has no effect on our other social interactions such as buying a round of drinks or commenting on a draft article. Indeed, even if the bicycle turns out to be unsatisfactory in some respect, the bonds of friendship will not be deeply affected by the disappointment. My expectations from the contractual relation will be confined to the promise and the implicit obligation of the seller to provide goods free from defects. The contractual relation creates new, more specific expectations, but simultaneously it tends to exclude the surrounding normative context in the evaluation of whether those expectations have been fulfilled or disappointed.

Furthermore, unlike other social interactions which may create diffuse expectations for the future, such as the formation of a friendship or the making of a gift, a contractual relation empowers the parties to create their own distinct understanding of how this particular relationship should proceed. A gift may create the expectation of reciprocity and a sense of obligation, but the content of the exchange remains indeterminate and the expectations diffuse. In contrast, an agreement usually contains a detailed specification of the normative standards which should apply to this aspect of a relationship. A contractual relation shares some features with other types of exchange relations that create the bonds of human association that make up society.[2] But contractual relations differ from other species of exchange, because they establish a discrete relation between people, an isolated exchange with its own point of reference.

I call the contract a form of communication system because this phrase emphasizes the point that the contract 'thinks' about the relation between people in a particular way. It functions in human interaction as a distinctive way of understanding relationships. The contract constructs an image of the human association that reduces its complexity to the elements and trajectories that have significance within the contractual framework. The contract thinks about events, for instance, by examining human actions and words within a narrow time-frame; the prior pattern of the social

---

[2] Blau, P. M., *Exchange and Power in Social Life* (New York: Wiley, 1964).

relation between the parties and their sentiments of trust and loyalty are irrelevant to this construction of knowledge. The contract thinks, for instance, about a promise, whether it was made, what the promisor intended by the commitment, and whether the promise has been kept. This construction of the event ignores most of the context in which the promise was made, how it fitted into a prior relation between the parties, how it affects other people, and how performance of the promise serves the interests and aspirations of the parties. 'Contract strains against the idea of the person.'[3]

These observations about the meaning of contract suggest that the paradigm can be identified not through an examination of the typical features of the legal discourse concerning regulation of contracts, but rather from a consideration of how contract, viewed as a discrete communication system, views the characteristics of its distinctive form of human association. Four characteristics of the meaning of contractual association stand out in this approach.

(1) The association marked by a contract consists of isolated or discrete commitments, which have an exclusionary force in practical reasoning, so that these commitments tend to displace other normative standards derived from the social context of the contractual relation, including other forms of association such as friendship and status. Contract therefore reduces the complexity of human association, rendering social relations susceptible to management and reconstruction.

(2) The commitments identified by a contract tend to be temporary and specific. Contract therefore reasons about associations in such a way that they can either be completed (the money is exchanged for the goods) or broken (no payment is made). Association is therefore understood by contract as finite in duration, and always susceptible to dissolution.

(3) Contract thinks about association as a personal bond between the parties to the agreement, so that it neither imposes obligations on others nor confers any rights on third parties. This personal bond is a private relationship between individuals rather than a social undertaking towards a community.

(4) Contract thinks about association as an artificial and almost infinitely malleable construction, the product of a voluntary choice by individuals.

The way in which the contract thinks about the relation is not the same as the way in which the law of contract thinks about the same events. Both

---

[3] Selznick, P., n. 1 above, 62.

communication systems construct their own knowledge of the world within their own criteria of relevance. It is quite possible, for instance, for two people to believe that they have entered a contractual relation, and permit that framework to provide a normative guide to their behaviour, even though in law the events do not count as a contract at all. The differences between the two communication systems will be of great interest to us here, but for the time being we concentrate upon the contractual relation rather than legal reasoning.

Contractualization of Social Life

As a paradigm of types of human association, a contract resists or excludes claims for social solidarity. It favours instrumental relationships formed voluntarily by individuals containing precise undertakings. As a concept to be employed for interpreting the meaning of social relationships, it appealed immensely to liberal political theory because of its emphasis upon individual choice and the denial of the significance of imposed obligations arising from involuntary social relationships.

For social theorists in the nineteenth century who studied the structure of modern societies with their novel market economies, the idea of contract represented the hallmark of modern social relations. Maine famously observed that this transition of 'progressive societies' was marked by a move from 'status to contract'.[4] About the same time, however, Marx decried the 'commodification' of social life achieved by contractual relations, for they reduced all aspect of human association to an instrumental transaction for a specified exchange of items of market value.[5] Durkheim observed that contractual relations constituted the heart of social ties in modern society, a position he described as 'organic solidarity' in order to distinguish these loose, devolved ties formed by contract from the closer bonds of kinship and feudalism.[6] Max Weber described modern society as a 'contractual society',[7] and a study of the evolution of the law of contracts comprises the bulk of his sociology of law. In the nineteenth century, the idea of contract was embraced as a convincing interpretation of most social relations, and many welcomed this style of social relation as a liberating reconstitution of society.

The dominance of contractual relations in social life was partly eclipsed

---

[4] Maine, H. S., *Ancient Law* (London: John Murray, 1861), 170.

[5] Marx, K., *Capital,* i (Harmondsworth: Penguin/New Left Review, 1976), ch. 1(4).

[6] Durkheim, E., *The Division of Labor in Society* (New York: Free Press, 1933) (originally published 1893).

[7] Weber, M., *Economy and Society* (G. Roth and C. Wittich, eds.), (Berkeley: University of California Press, 1978), ii, 669.

for most of the twentieth century as a result of the development of two patterns of social organization. First, as a result of the development of productive relations within organized large firms, economic relations were expressed not only through contractual undertakings but also through bureaucratic relations. Second, slightly later and no doubt in imitation of private enterprise, the state assumed the functions of economic steering and welfare roles, and these tasks were performed typically through bureaucracies.

These trends have been reversed to some extent in recent years. Within private industry, vertical disintegration of productive relations has been the management aim, in order to bring the discipline of the market to bear on production as far as possible. The public sector quickly followed suit. The moves towards privatization of former state-owned industries, the breaking up of state-run monopolies, and the introduction of 'quasi-markets' into expenditure on health, defence, and education also signal the replacement of bureaucracy at least in part with contractual relations.

It is important to notice that these recent types of contractual relations in production and government often do not fit easily into a simple model of a discrete exchange such as a sale of goods, with limited commitments for a finite period. These new contractual relations often outline a long-term relation with indeterminate obligations in order to permit flexibility and co-operation. Within these contractual relations, there emerges increased scope for the deployment of discretionary power, and as a consequence the contractual undertakings will be less sharply differentiated from other kinds of open-ended commitments based on social and business relations. We will explore these differences from the paradigm meaning of contract further. But the contrasts are not so sharp as to detract from the observation that the shift towards contractualization in social life is perhaps one of the most potent symbols of political and business culture at the close of the twentieth century.

The contemporary resurgence of faith in contracts, or rather the advocacy of a particular conception of contracts derived from the study of markets in economics, springs from a number of sources. The success of markets in performing the task of efficient satisfaction of consumer wants is no doubt the major justification for the contractualization of social relations. Provided that a competitive market can be created or simulated by introducing categories of buyers and sellers, or purchasers and providers, then market pressures toward competitiveness should improve efficiency, thereby increasing the satisfaction of consumers and citizens alike. This theory explains, for example, why public services have become increasingly approximated in their organization and financing to private contractual provision of services. Viewed in this light, any limit upon contracts and markets, such as a prohibition of the sale of education, health care, parts of the body, or arrangements for prostitution, is likely to impede the efficient satisfaction of wants, and is therefore to be regarded as undesirable without a strong countervailing justification. Yet there are even deeper reasons for the strength of the current faith in markets.

One attraction of markets is their seductive claim that they avoid any governmental choice with respect to the pattern of the distribution of wealth in society.[8] The stock of goods that a person possesses depends upon a myriad of market transactions rather than any conscious human agency which engineers a particular distributive pattern based upon such criteria as merit or privilege. The invisible hand of market forces as a distributive mechanism has the apparent attraction that it requires no political justification for its outcomes. The government can absolve itself from responsibility, and simply claim that poverty and wealth are the result of market choices by individuals. Once again this thesis strongly supports the absence of limits to markets, for those limits will necessarily interfere with this neutral mechanism for the distribution of wealth. This conventional view is misleading, however, for the legal constitution and regulation of markets does entail decisions regarding issues of distributive justice. The legal system only supplies selective enforcement of transactions, so that insofar as legal regulation has the capacity to steer contractual relations, it influences distributive outcomes.[9]

Perhaps the deepest attraction of markets and contracts as institutions for organizing and co-ordinating social life is that they provide a solution to a problem of loss of confidence in institutionalized structures giving direction to persons' lives. The preference for markets is symptomatic of a scepticism with respect to any claim to know best how social relations should be organized, what standards they should observe, and, perhaps, a fear that any institutionalized power of control over social relations will be abused and employed to destroy individuality. By permitting contractual relations to flourish, the state effectively delegates to individuals as many choices as possible as to the nature of the social relations into which they may enter. Instead of determining in advance the reciprocal obligations in cohabitation, for instance, the law leaves the partners to select their own property settlement and distribution of assets and responsibilities. This scepticism about the role of institutionalized direction of social standards thus gives considerable impetus to the extension of contractual relations.[10]

Linked to this strategy of delegation comes a profession by government

---

[8] Hayek, F. A., *Law, Legislation and Liberty*, ii (London: Routledge and Kegan Paul, 1982), 65–9; Nozick, R., *Anarchy, State, and Utopia* (Oxford: Blackwell, 1974), 159.

[9] Collins, H., 'Distributive Justice Through Contracts', *Current Legal Problems* 45(2) (1992), 49.

[10] Collins, H., 'The Sanctimony of Contract', in R. Rawlings (ed.), *Law, Society, and Economy* (Oxford: Oxford University Press, 1997) 63, 75.

that this contractualization treats citizens with greater respect. By being granted control over their own lives through the extension of individual choice, citizens are treated like adults. Of course, individuals then become responsible for their choices, rather than being steered and protected by a paternalistic government. In its extreme form, this appeal to the metaphor of contract appears to deny the responsibility of the state for any welfare role. In the case of unemployment, for instance, instead of the individual being regarded as the hapless victim of business cycles and global competition wars, the claimant for public assistance is portrayed as the author of his predicament, having chosen to exercise his contractual powers irresponsibly by pricing himself out of a job. The state will not provide welfare support now unless the claimant enters a new contract, the 'Job Seeker's Agreement', under which the claimant agrees to mend his ways by making numerous serious job applications.[11] The contractual metaphor can be employed in this way by the state to achieve simultaneously both a new legitimacy for government based upon its respect for the individual, and a new type of bureaucratic control that appears a much tougher instrument for the purpose of disciplining and punishing errant citizens.[12]

Meaning of Contractual Relations

These developments in the structures of social life that I have described as a process of contractualization cut much deeper into the meaning of social relations than Karl Marx supposed in his theory of commodification. Marx perceived that in a market economy nearly everyone sold his or her labour power in order to live. This was true both of the wage labourer and the manager of a business. In selling labour power, the market determined what people produced. As a consequence, individuals were alienated from their productive capacity, their originality, their drive to find meaning in their lives.[13] For Marx, this state of alienation was the true evil of capitalism, not just the vast inequalities of wealth and power that it produced. With the benefit of hindsight, we can perhaps argue that Marx exaggerated the degree of alienation produced by the labour contract for many people. At the same time, by concentrating his attention on the labour contract, I think he missed some of the most important dimensions of the meaning of social relations once they are reduced to contracts. In his later work, Marx sought

---

[11] Job Seekers' Act 1995, ss. 1, 9; Fulbrook, J., 'The Job Seekers' Act 1995: Consolidation with a Sting of Contractual Compliance', *Industrial Law Journal* 24 (1995), 395.

[12] Harlow, C., and Rawlings, R., *Law and Administration*, 2nd edn. (London: Butterworths, 1997), 140.

[13] Marx, K., 'Economic and Philosophical Manuscripts', in L. Colletti (ed.), *Early Writings* (Harmondsworth: Penguin/New Left Books, 1975), 322–34.

to generalize his insight in his theory of commodification. He observed that in a market system everything, including human labour, was evaluated like a commodity, that is, it was measured solely by reference to its market value. The effect of this 'commodification' of social life was to render worthless those features of human aspirations to which a market value could not be ascribed. Important human aspirations such as to achieve meaning in one's life through work, to establish friendships, to be a member of a community, to enjoy family life and the rewards of parenthood, all of these were systematically devalued by a capitalist or market society, because little or no financial value could be attached to them. The result of this tension between the valuations of a market society and human aspirations Marx described as 'commodity fetishism'.[14] But I think that this analysis still fails to grasp the full dimensions of the contractualization of social relations.

Here I shall attempt to rectify that weakness by examining how contractual relations attribute significance to particular dimensions of social relations. The point is that the use of contracts or contractual metaphors in this process of the contractualization of social relations is not merely a way of understanding those social relations, but serves to structure those social relations for the participants. Particular meanings are attributed to those social relations, which in turn provide reasons for action that steer those relations in specific directions. In short, if a social relation is conceived of as contractual, then people tend to exhibit contractual behaviour within it and towards it. Four dimensions of the meaning of contractual relations are especially important.

Valuation of Conduct

Contracts circumscribe the valuation of conduct. As a discrete communication system, contracts purport to measure conduct narrowly by reference solely to the terms recorded for the transaction. The terms purport to set the exclusive point of reference, which inevitably confines or truncates the perception of the obligations owed between the parties.[15] This perception creates the possibility of a conflict between the agreed bargain and the reasonable expectations of the parties. These expectations contain informal understandings based upon the surrounding social relation regarding co-operation, give-and-take, and dealing in good faith. If a friend asks for help, then the response of 'what will you do for me in return' represents a contractual valuation of conduct, which contradicts the expectation of willing support based upon friendship. In some long-term business

---

[14] Marx, K., n. 5 above, ch. 1(4).
[15] Goodrich, P., *Languages of Law* (London: Weidenfeld, 1990), 154.

relations a strict insistence upon the terms of the contract will be regarded as a form of opportunism,[16] for this valuation of conduct contradicts the basis of the relation in good faith conduct which establishes a business reputation for fair dealing. Diffuse obligations of support, co-operation, reciprocity, and sharing, become harder to establish, with the effect that the dynamic and meaning of the social relation becomes altered. The problem becomes most striking in agency relations, such as employment, where the more that the employer seeks to control the employee's discretion about how to define and carry out tasks, the less the employer can call upon diffuse obligations of loyalty and professionalism to further the interests of the employer's business.[17]

Currency of Exchange

Contracts also establish social relations with a currency of exchange which is quantifiable and measurable. This currency permits the introduction of what Max Weber called formal rational economic behaviour into any type of social relation contained in a contract.[18] The question asked about the relation is whether it increases the wealth of the parties or whether it satisfies their preferences. Other questions about the contribution of the relation to the meaning of the lives of the parties are rendered irrelevant, because they cannot be incorporated into the contractual measurement of success. In this vein, for instance, non-pecuniary losses such as vexation and disappointment caused by breach of contract cannot be the basis of a legal remedy in damages because they cannot be quantified.[19] Similarly, to view an invitation to dinner with a friend as a contract would suggest that the value of the invitation can be reduced to a monetary price, whereas the point of the invitation is to reinforce the ties of friendship that are not the product of formal rational economic behaviour. The insertion of contracts into such relations as friendship does not destroy those relations, but it does introduce a particular form of valuation of behaviour within its discrete communication system, which may tend to exclude other types of measurement such as loyalty and trust.[20]

[16] Beale, H., and Dugdale, T., 'Contracts Between Businessmen: Planning and the Use of Contractual Remedies', *British Journal of Law and Society* 2 (1975) 45, 47.

[17] Fox, A., *Beyond Contract: Work, Power and Trust Relations* (London: Faber, 1974).

[18] Weber, M., n. 7 above, 85, 669.

[19] e.g. *Addis v Gramophone Co Ltd* [1909] AC 488, HL (unpleasant dismissal of employee); *Watts v Morrow* [1991] 1 WLR 1421, [1991] 4 All ER 937, CA (disappointed expectation of acquiring a trouble-free holiday home).

[20] Radin, M., 'Market-Inalienability', *Harvard Law Review* 100 (1987), 1849; Mack, E., 'Dominos and the Fear of Commodification', in J. W. Chapman and J. R. Pennock (eds.), *Markets and Justice* (New York: Nomos 31, New York University Press, 1989) 198; Duxbury, N., 'Do Markets Degrade?', *Modern Law Review* 59 (1996) 331.

It is this dimension of contractual relations that approximates most closely to Marx's theory of commodification. Marx believed, of course, that it would be possible to overcome this state of alienation, if a market society could be replaced by a Communist society, though he possessed no solution to the problem of finding an alternative to a market system for the efficient co-ordination of production and distribution. A more realistic alternative to the construction of a solution to the problem of the reduction of social life to formal economic rationality is rather to confine the operations of markets in social life, and to promote alternative systems of valuation and currencies of exchange.[21]

Atomization

A third feature of contractualization consists in the atomization of social relations, so that the effects of a transaction upon other people are regarded as irrelevant or externalities. The discrete communication system of the contract constructs obligations owed between the parties, but it does not give others any power to influence the content of those obligations, and nor does it give others any rights to enforce the contract. For instance, if one employee of a business receives high pay, which compels the business to dismiss another for lack of funds, the connection between these two decisions is rendered opaque by the separation of contractual relations. Similarly, a business contract to supply an industrial product may have considerable impact on the local community, for it may create jobs and pollute the local environment, but the wishes and expectations of the local community play no part in the determination of the contractual relation (in the absence of other forms of direct state intervention). Contracts, as a form of social relation, therefore, juxtapose themselves against ties of community or bonds of social solidarity.

The legal system, especially when performing its governmental regulatory role, can obstruct the atomization of contractual relations. Legal reasoning may examine contractual behaviour of individuals within the framework of perceiving them as members of a class, such as consumers, landlords, or employees, and then seek to interpret and regulate the relation in ways that serve the interests of the class as a whole. A particular consumer may, for example, be prepared to purchase a car which may prove unsafe if the price is sufficiently low, but the legal system can invalidate this choice, both because it is not in the general interest of consumers to purchase unsafe products, and because of the probable externalities, that is, the risk of injuries to other persons such as pedestrians. In the language of economics,

---

[21] Walzer, M., *Spheres of Justice: A Defence of Pluralism & Equality* (Oxford: Blackwell, 1983).

the objective of the law is to compel the parties to internalize the costs of externalities into their transaction. This strategy of challenging the atomization of social relations invariably creates a tension within legal discourse. On the one hand, the private law of contract aspires to support the discrete communication system represented by the contract, but on the other, it is tempted to control the operations of the market system in order to reduce the harmful externalities which it produces.

Discretionary Power

Finally, contractualization permits the formation of a particular type of power relation. Although the imagery of freedom of contract presents an egalitarian picture of two people negotiating the terms of their agreement, in practice many contracts constitute the opportunity for one party to create unilaterally a system of rules and governance structures for the relation.[22] The standard form of consumer contract imposed on a 'take it or leave it' basis by businesses represents only the tip of an iceberg of these governance structures. Contracts can incorporate whole regulatory systems such as staff handbooks, works rules, railway by-laws, and quality assurance procedures.[23] These codes simulate the form of an agreement, but they really represent the exercise of discretionary economic power by one party to the contract over the other backed up by a system of economic sanctions specific to that relation, such as the discipline of the employee or the disqualification of a contractor. Contracts therefore create 'governance' structures, which are private in the sense that they are only indirectly supported by state power. Markets and hierarchies are therefore not opposites, as they are sometimes presented, but rather markets create their own hierarchies through contracts.

These four features of contractual relations as a form of social relation— the valuation of conduct in delimited terms, the measurement by a precise currency of exchange, the externalization of social effects, and the establishment of private governance structures—reveal that the decision to delegate to individuals the power to construct their own social relations through the market mechanism is not such a neutral choice as it may appear at first. In the case of cohabitation agreements, for instance, we can welcome the empowerment to the parties concerned of being able to shape through contracts how their relation should be constructed. They

---

[22] Kessler, F., 'Contracts of Adhesion—Some Thoughts About Freedom of Contract', *Columbia Law Review* 43 (1943), 629; Slawson, D., 'Standard Form Contracts and Democratic Control of Lawmaking Power', *Harvard Law Review* 84 (1971), 529.
[23] Macneil, I., 'Bureaucracy and Contracts of Adhesion', *Osgoode Hall Law Journal* 22 (1984), 5.

may wish, for instance, to pool all their property, or alternatively to keep their financial affairs strictly apart with no assumption of maintenance obligations towards a partner. By permitting contracts to be made between the parties on such matters, the law facilitates this power of choice to construct social relations.[24] At the same time, the practice of entering contracts, with or without legal recognition, permits individuals to reduce the complexity of social life by selecting certain precise obligations as priorities, and then to discount other more diffuse social expectations. A social worker who makes a 'contract' with a client in difficulty helps the client by identifying priorities in a complex social world with many competing claims for attention.[25] But it should be recognized that the contractualization of social relations will usually have the tendencies described above of emphasizing the values of preference satisfaction and a monetary currency of exchange between the parties. If we wish to insist, for example, that cohabitation arrangements should entail more open-ended commitments of sharing, reciprocity, and loyalty, then we will discover that the intrusion of contracts subverts this goal.

Embeddedness

Although I have described contractual relations as a discrete communication system with its special criteria of relevance and measurement, it is plain that contracts always function in particular social contexts. The contexts may differ radically, from the simple consumer purchase of apples at the market stall to an elaborate joint venture agreement between multinational companies to design and manufacture an advanced technology fighter jet. These various contexts influence the meaning of the contractual relations, or how the contract thinks about events and relations. This influence between contract and context is often described by the insistence that contractual relations always remain 'embedded' in the social practices and norms from which they arise.[26] But what does embeddedness mean, how does this influence occur, and how does this affect the way contracts think about events and relations?

The concept of embeddedness can be understood as the way in which contract thinks about its relation to other normative frameworks that may

[24] Olsen, F. E., 'The Family and the Market: A Study of Ideology and Legal Reform', *Harvard Law Review* 96 (1983), 1497; Dalton, C., 'An Essay in the Deconstruction of Contract Doctrine', *Yale Law Journal* 94 (1985), 997, 1095.

[25] Nelken, D., 'The Use of "Contracts" as a Social Work Technique', *Current Legal Problems* 40 (1987), 207.

[26] Granovetter, M., 'Economic Action and Social Structure: The Problem of Embeddedness', *American Journal of Sociology* 91 (1985), 481.

influence the conduct of the parties. One example might comprise conventional moral standards of behaviour. These conventions may discourage force, fraud, and cheating during the course of negotiations and performance of transactions. These standards can be incorporated into the way in which the contract thinks about relations and events by translating them into its own narrow frame of reference. The contract may think that its concentration upon voluntary undertakings implicitly excludes promises obtained by lies or coercion. The moral standard that one should not lie or threaten others with violence becomes translated into the contractual understanding of the events as a determination that a voluntary undertaking was not given in the circumstances. These conventional moral standards often play a significant role in guiding how the contract thinks, but only by their insertion and translation into the contract's own discrete system of communication. As well as these conventional moral standards, two other sources of norms provide much more significant and specific 'interferences' with contractual reasoning.[27]

The first source of normative standards that supplement and qualify the discrete contractual communication system derives from conventions of the market. Reliance upon conventions is crucial to the operation of markets, since they provide a vital supplement which is usually taken for granted in ordinary transactions. In the sale of a newspaper, for instance, the purchaser assumes that the newspaper is complete and not missing some pages, and the vendor assumes that the normal retail price will be paid in the local currency. These assumptions and expectations must arise from a normative framework established by convention during routine market practices. There is no need to specify these details of the transaction, because they 'go without saying'. They are conventional standards, which are implicitly incorporated into the agreement. In the simple transaction of the sale of the newspaper, all that the parties need to specify is the precise newspaper to be purchased. Beale and Dugdale describe these conventions as the 'unwritten laws' that are accepted by both sides to the transaction, but which are rarely incorporated formally into the written contract.[28]

For commonplace transactions or repeated business deals between familiar trading partners, the conventions may be sufficiently replete for the parties to dispense with discussion about all but the most central topics such as the price and the specification of the goods to be exchanged. The 'unwritten laws' in the Beale and Dugdale study appear quite dense in these business relations between engineering firms of a locality. For example, the parties observe customarily the rule that the seller is only responsible for cost of

---

[27] Teubner, Gunther, 'How the Law Thinks: Toward A Constructivist Epistemology of Law', *Law & Society Review* 23 (1989), 727, 745.
[28] Beale, H. and Dugdale, T., 'Contracts between Businessmen: Planning and the Use of Contractual Remedies', *British Journal of Law and Society* 2 (1975) 45, 59.

repairs to defective products, not the cost of a new product or any consequential loss.[29] This rule, which differs from the law, appears to rest upon a convention in that sector. Similarly, the presence of a convention seems to be a better explanation of the practice of tipping in restaurants than a more general moral standard. In contrast, the conventions may be thin in international business transactions, where the parties are unfamiliar with each other's trading customs. Even here, however, some conventions will apply, such as the assumption that the seller owns the goods and can transfer good title. The density of the incorporated conventions may differ, but they always supplement the discrete communication represented by the contract.

The normative orientation of the parties in respect of market conventions will be directed primarily towards the customs of the local market, or the standards of the particular trade or business in which they are engaged. These are the key standards, because it will be by reference to those standards that reputation will be judged. In the construction business, for example, general contractors and subcontractors will conduct themselves towards each other by reference to the local customs of the trade, so that their reciprocal commitments will be coloured and defined not only by their explicit negotiations but also by the routine practices and expectations in that line of business. For some specialized markets, such as stock exchanges, an institutional framework may exist both to promulgate rules to govern transactions and to police observance of those rules.

To say that contractual relations are embedded in market conventions therefore points to how the contract thinks about relations and events by drawing upon unexpressed normative standards in order to render the finite commitments of contractual undertakings more determinate. The market convention is translated by the scheme of contractual thought into a richer description of the content of obligations created by the voluntary relation. The convention is presupposed by the parties in their dealings with each other. When the events are considered within the framework of contractual thinking, the conventions are translated into articulate expansions and limitations upon the undertakings. The custom of the trade becomes an implied promise or term of the contract. This technique of incorporation within contractual reasoning is very different, however, from the interference posed by the second source of norms that is often described by the term 'embeddedness'.

The second source of normative context that is often described by the term 'embeddedness' derives from the identity and past relations of the parties to the contract. Expectations of trustworthy behaviour may be based upon the identity of the other person as a friend, a fellow member

---

[29] Ibid. 56.

of a kinship group or business association, or a person sharing ties of ethnicity or religion. Similarly, the history of satisfactory dealings between the parties gives rise to expectations of trustworthy conduct that goes beyond the strictly measured contractual undertakings. Not every contractual relation will be established within such a context. No doubt the degree of embeddedness has been reduced in modern society compared to traditional, agrarian communities where nearly all contracts were made face to face with members of the local community. To some extent modern social institutions can replace this source of embeddedness by producing reliable qualifications by which to establish the identity of the other contracting party, such as the qualification of being a professional doctor or lawyer which carries with it expectations of skill and competence in providing a service.[30]

This type of embeddedness grounded in personal relations is extremely important, as we shall see later, in the construction of market relations. But it differs fundamentally from conventional moral and market standards in the way in which it reacts with contractual thinking. In many respects this type of embeddedness represents the antithesis of contractual thinking. It invokes obligations based on solidarity rather than voluntary undertakings; it recognizes groups as a form of human association rather than being composed of a collection of separate undertakings; and it resists strict and finite measurements of social obligations. Embeddedness in personal relations based upon history and social ties tends rather to exclude contractual thinking, to treat it as an inappropriate and dysfunctional understanding of events and relations. In this context, the interference between contractual thinking and norms based upon ties of solidarity is one of conflict and competition, with each communication system providing opposing valuations of conduct.

When two individuals enter a contract, therefore, they create a discrete communication system, which serves to specify some particular undertakings that the parties commit themselves to observe. At the same time, it focuses the relationship by implicitly excluding any other expectations which have not been included in the reciprocal undertakings. The contractual frame of reference prises the relation out of its context of personal relations, and insists upon narrow criteria of relevance and significance of events. But the communication system of contract is never entirely closed, for it incorporates a set of standards drawn primarily from the conventions of the local market or particular trade which flesh out the full content of those undertakings. The legal system, to which we now turn, is charged with the task of evaluating and regulating contractual behaviour in the light of this complex normative matrix.

---

[30] Giddens, A., *The Consequences of Modernity* (Cambridge: Polity Press, 1991), 21–9.

Part 2
The New Regulation

3
The Discourses of Legal Regulation

The legal system observes contractual relations with a view to determining its own central question of whether sanctions should be deployed against one or both parties. Sanctions such as financial compensation may be ordered, for example, if one party has broken an undertaking in a legally enforceable contract, or has broken a legal rule such as a prohibition against fraudulent statements governing the bargaining process. In order to reach such determinations, modern legal systems have created a doctrinal system that is known as the private law of contract. These doctrines specify the general conditions for the creation of legally enforceable contracts, the rules governing the bargaining process, the tests for determining whether a breach of these legal obligations has occurred, and a system of sanctions for breach of these obligations. In addition to the private law of contract, modern legal systems also contain a substantial body of further regulations, which may conveniently be described as public law regulation. These regulations overlay and derogate from the private law of contract in the contexts where they apply. They tend to target particular types of contract such as consumer purchases, or particular types of market practice such as advertising. What will interest us most in this chapter is the interaction between these two kinds of legal regulation.

The legal systems of advanced industrialized countries share similar discourses of private law. Although the precise content of the legal concepts and rules governing contracts differs, these legal systems conform to a general pattern of determinations of which agreements will be enforced, the types of sanctions imposed, and the rules governing the bargaining process. Apart from the different languages in which these rules are expressed, perhaps the most noticeable difference lies not in the content of the rules but rather in their formal sources and the methods of legal reasoning used in order to elaborate legal doctrine. In this respect a contrast can be drawn between Codified systems and Common Law systems based upon adjudication and precedent. Under a Codified system, at least in principle, the Civil Code provides a comprehensive statement of the rules governing contracts. Legal reasoning must reach its determinations by means of an elaboration and application of the Code. In Common Law systems, however, the law must be derived from prior court decisions, which provide authoritative precedents or statements of the applicable legal rules and principles. Although these differences in the formal sources of the legal rules lead to some sharp contrasts in legal technique, I suggest that in devising and developing legal doctrine each legal system must reconcile a similar body of competing normative considerations. These considerations derive from a wide range of political, moral, and pragmatic sources. Our first task is to examine these divergent sources and to reveal how they cause major tensions in the fabric of legal doctrine.

Having explored the complexity of these normative considerations, we then examine the practice of legal reasoning more closely. Despite the wide range of normative sources which shape legal doctrine, the traditional doctrinal reasoning of private law displays a narrow, technical ambience. Private law reasoning will be described as highly self-referential and closed. We consider how this self-referential and closed system of legal reasoning copes with the task of regulating contractual behaviour.

As part of this investigation of private law reasoning, we consider next how a distinctive branch of legal doctrine known as the law of contract has emerged and sustains itself. Since Roman times, the law of contract has been located as a part of the private law of obligations. We examine the construction of this system of classification and its implications for legal reasoning in private law.

The chapter concludes by examining the forces that appear to be leading to a collapse of the distinctive properties of the private law of contract as a regulatory system governing social conduct. The pattern of closure and self-reference exhibited by private law has been subjected to a series of subversive attacks. As a consequence, the integrity of the doctrinal system has been eroded, but at the same time, I shall argue that the productive potential of private law as a regulatory instrument has been enhanced.

Normative Complexity

Our first and perhaps elementary observation about the private law of contract stresses its normative complexity. The body of rules, principles, and concepts that comprise the private law of contract have their immediate source in authoritative legal materials such as Codes, statutes, and precedents. These positive statements of the law express interpretations and decisions about fundamental normative standards appropriate for the law of contract. Legal rules invariably rest on interpretations of other normative standards. One such standard, for instance, might be the moral idea that promises ought to be kept, which might then be translated into a positive legal rule. Usually, however, the transition from normative standard to a particular legal rule does not permit a simple transposition, and indeed, no legal system has ever simply adopted a legal rule requiring that all promises should be kept. Instead, the content of the law depends upon a rich dialogue with a variety of normative standards drawn from politics, morality, economics, public policy, conventions, and values internal to the legal system.

These normative standards often compete and present incommensurable values. The process of translation is carried out by legal doctrinal writers, judges, and legislators, who may be viewed as being engaged in a dialogue both with the background normative standards and the legal system itself. With respect to the private law of contract, three crucial sources of normative standards should be stressed: theories of political obligation, doctrinal integrity, and market conventions.

Political Obligation

Since the application of sanctions by the state comprises the practical outcome of the application of legal doctrine, private law responds to the governing political theories about the appropriate occasions for the use of state power and the type of sanctions which can be employed. Because the law of contract converts a social arrangement into a potential instrument for the application of sanctions backed by the force of the state, the legal system must ensure that this application of state power conforms to appropriate principles of justice, including due respect for liberty, equality, and solidarity. The dialogue represented by legal doctrine can therefore be understood in part as a specialized branch of theories of justice and political obligation relating to the formation of binding associations between citizens.

The key consideration of respect for the liberty of the individual points in several directions that provide the basic shape of the private law of contract. Respect for liberty leads to a requirement that the additional social obligations represented by a contract should not be imposed by the state without the voluntary consent of the individual. Respect for freedom leans the law heavily in favour of granting to individuals the power to enter binding commitments on any subject that they might choose. Finally, respect for liberty curtails the kind of remedies which may be required for breach of contractual obligations, so that in effect an individual can usually escape a commitment on the payment of a suitable level of compensation. In a more ambiguous way, the idea of freedom also supports the whole practice of enforcing contracts, for it may be argued that by providing the facility to enter binding commitments, the state expands worthwhile opportunities for its citizens.

As well as liberty, however, another key consideration in the formulation of legal doctrine has always consisted of a concern to ensure the justice of legal obligations created by contracts. The state seeks to refrain from

promoting injustice, and in legal doctrine this objective becomes interpreted as a justification for restraints upon freedom of contract. Private
law places limits on the enforceability of agreements, in order to constrain
power relations created by contracts and to upset exploitative bargains. In
a similar ambiguous way, the idea of justice also supports the enforcement
of binding commitments, for it may be urged that justice requires compensation for losses resulting from misplaced reliance upon agreements with
others.

These strands of liberty and justice provide a crucial normative source
for legal doctrine. The implications of these ideals are, of course, controversial. At one time the principle of justice may be paramount, so that
courts refuse to enforce what they regard as unfair bargains, and at another
time the principle of liberty may become dominant in the determination of
legal doctrine, so that freely undertaken obligations are regarded as
necessarily just. These variations correspond to broader intellectual movements, so that disputes about legal doctrine can often be interpreted as
derivations from larger ideological disputes about the sources of political
obligation and justice.[1]

There have been many interesting attempts to link the law of contract to
moral standards as well as political ones. It is suggested, for instance, that
the moral principle that promises ought to be kept has helped to determine
the content of the law of contract.[2] Although it would be rash to deny any
influence of moral principles in the formulation of the law of contract, this
influence seems to me to have been far weaker. Theories which seek to forge
such a link always fail to provide a plausible account of legal rules, because
they cannot explain why the moral principle is not followed faithfully. The
explanation for this failure is surely that to justify the application of a state
sanction the legal system must find conduct that is not simply immoral but
which causes injustice of a kind that ought to be remedied by the state.

Doctrinal Integrity

The authority of law in modern societies depends in part on the perception
that it achieves a system of governance according to the ideal of the Rule of
Law. This ideal is generally interpreted to require consistency in the
application of law and the ability to justify the content of the law by
rational argument. These considerations exert a force on the development
of legal doctrine, since they require that its elaboration of the law of
contract should be presented as a coherent system of rules, based upon
principle, without arbitrary distinctions. Legal scholarship perceives its

[1] Atiyah, P. S., *The Rise and Fall of Freedom of Contract* (Oxford: Clarendon Press, 1979).
[2] Fried, C., *Contract as Promise* (Cambridge, Mass.: Harvard University Press, 1981).

central task to provide the rational elaboration of a coherent doctrinal
system of law. Due no doubt to the economic importance of contractual
relations in a market society, scholarship in the law of contract has been
usually rich and profound.[3]

The extent to which the objective of rationalization of law places
constraints upon its evolution is controversial, for the patterns of legal
doctrine may also be explained by reference to the promotion of particular
political ideologies,[4] or the result of pressure from interest groups.[5] For
example, a problem confronting legal systems in the twentieth century was
how to regulate exclusion clauses in standard form consumer contracts.
Businesses frequently inserted terms into their contracts which minimized
their obligations in the event that goods proved defective or services were
performed carelessly, thereby leaving the consumer with no redress under
the law. The courts typically rejected the possibility of striking down these
exclusion clauses on the ground of unfairness, because such a rule would
conflict with the fundamental contractual principle that the parties should
be free to select the terms of their transaction. Such decisions might also be
explained by the courts exercising an ideological preference for free
markets over consumer protection,[6] but the requirement of doctrinal
coherence certainly raised a formidable obstacle in the way of occasional
judicial attempts to help consumers by deleting unfair exclusion clauses.

Private law discourse is only loosely linked to standards outside its own
system of communications. General ideals of freedom and justice serve to
define the principal features or basic principles of the private law of contract,
but the details of regulation are generated within legal discourse by reference
to the internal demands of the law for legitimacy through coherence and
consistency. The general ideal of freedom of contract insisted, for instance,
that contractual obligations should be based upon consent or agreement.
However, the detailed rules of offer and acceptance, which legal doctrine
developed in order to render the idea of consent more precise for the purposes
of determining the application of legal sanction, were guided in their particular rules by the rigorous pursuit of doctrinal integrity.

Market Convention

Yet private law could not develop in complete isolation from one crucial
normative dimension of social practice in markets. The law could not

---

[3] Gordley, J., *The Philosophical Origins of Modern Contract Doctrine* (Oxford: Clarendon
Press, 1991).   [4] Atiyah, P. S., n. 1 above.
[5] Friedman, L. M., *Contract Law in America* (Madison: University of Wisconsin Press,
1965); Horwitz, M. J., *The Transformation of American Law, 1780–1860* (Cambridge: Harvard
University Press, 1977).
[6] Adams, J. N. and Brownsword, R., 'The Ideologies of Contract', *Legal Studies* 7 (1987) 205.

ignore conventional understandings of when binding commitments have been made, when they have been broken, and where unfair market practices have been deployed. Shoppers in Britain, for example, expect that once they have paid for goods then they have acquired ownership, and that if the goods prove defective, they can return them and receive a replacement or their money back. The legal system needs to achieve close concordance with this conventional expectation, if it seeks to provide support for routine transactions. Given that these conventions may seldom be expressly articulated, and given that they will vary between different types of markets and trades, this task presents the law with a formidable task of discovery and interpretation of information. The parties themselves through their contractual agreement specify many of their reciprocal undertakings, but these specifications will only incompletely describe their expectations. These expectations will also be discovered in the norms derived from the embeddedness of their relation, both in the sense of their personal relationship and their implicit reference to market convention. When pursuing the task of providing support for market transactions, in its application of state sanctions, legal regulation cannot ignore these conventional understandings.

The important point to notice is that a market convention may not be easy to reconcile with a political theory for the imposition of obligations by the state. A reconciliation will be especially troublesome when the political theory has received a refined and systematic articulation through legal doctrine. A market convention, for instance, may ascribe a binding obligation before a final agreement has been reached, when perhaps protracted negotiations have been conducted or one party has made a firm offer which the other acted upon. Whereas liberal political theory may be reluctant to justify the imposition of state-enforced obligations at this stage without evidence of a clear agreement, the business expectation based upon convention may be that some obligations have arisen.[7] Legal doctrine may then be faced with the choice of either denying any legal force to the market convention on which the business expectation is grounded, or engaging in a process of reconstruction of doctrine. This reconstruction might take the form of the development of new categories for the ascription of legal responsibility, as has happened in the Common Law with the development of the reliance-based liability of promissory estoppel.[8] The new legal doctrine then may restore concordance between the market convention and the doctrinal rules by discovering binding voluntary obligations prior

---

[7] Weintraub, R. J, 'A Survey of Contract Practice and Policy', *Wisconsin Law Review* (1992) 1, 28.

[8] e.g. *Hoffman v Red Owl Stores Inc.*, 26 Wis. 2d 683, 133 NW 2d 267 (1965); *Crabb v Arun District Council* [1976] Ch 179, [1975] 3 All ER 685, CA; *Waltons Stores (Interstate) Ltd. v Maher* [1987–88] 164 CLR 387 (High Ct.).

to the formation of an agreement. In another instance, however, doctrinal coherence may demand that the legal system should ignore an established market convention for the sake of its own integrity. A convention in a particular trade or a business relationship may permit an 'order' for goods to be cancelled within a reasonable period of time. Doctrinal coherence may insist, nevertheless, that once an agreement has been concluded by the placing of an order and its acknowledgement, a legally binding contract should be found. The only way to avoid the divergence of legal regulation from market convention in such instances is for the court to interpret the events in an improbable manner. By suggesting that the order was not intended to be binding, but merely part of exploratory negotiations (an 'invitation to treat', as common lawyers say), a court can defer the moment of contractual responsibility in law for the sake of achieving concordance between market convention and legal outcomes. The task of reconciling doctrinal integrity with market convention (or the embeddedness of contractual relations) can therefore be achieved either through reconfigurations of private law doctrine or by reprocessing information about events in ways that trigger a different outcome under the doctrinal rules.

The argumentation of lawyers in the private law of contract seeks to reconcile these competing normative considerations of political principle, doctrinal integrity, and market convention. Legal reasoning does not inhabit some objective, omniscient meta-space, which provides it with a privileged vantage-point. The legal system uses the doctrinal concepts and rules which it inherits as part of the tradition of legal reasoning. Legal reasoning then refines or elaborates legal doctrine in a series of transitory, only partially successful, reconciliations of the competing pressures on its evolution. The two evolutionary mechanisms of reconstructing private law doctrine and producing unexpected interpretations of events supply the legal system with its techniques for reconciling the demands of integrity based upon political principle with the need to respect the embeddedness of contractual relations in market conventions and business expectations.

Self-reference and Closure

These techniques of reconstructing legal doctrine and reinterpreting events reveal some key features of traditional private law discourse. This discourse understands the world in its own terms and draws inferences according to its own operational rules. It is a technical discourse, not a general discussion of the issues, taking into account all the background considerations explicitly. The resulting communication system can be described as both self-referential and closed.[9]

Private law discourse is self-referential in the sense that it evolves its own doctrinal concepts of what counts as a legally enforceable contract and its own rules governing the bargaining process. In turn, these concepts and rules are further defined by more detailed legal concepts and rules. As this communication system achieves ever greater complexity in its operational rules, it distances itself from the foundational normative criteria such as the political ideal of freedom of contract. The rules of private law may be described as autonomous in the sense that they can be deployed for the most part independently of other normative systems such as morality and custom.

The doctrinal concepts are closed in the sense that that they direct the legal examination of the facts of a dispute with strict criteria of relevance. Some facts will be relevant to legal reasoning, because they need to be established in order to satisfy the legal rule, whereas others will be irrelevant to the legal enquiry. In the case of a fraudulent statement, for instance, the law requires proof that the statement was false, not merely misleading, confusing, or exaggerated. This definition of the factual condition that triggers the rule restricts the relevant evidence; it narrows the enquiry. The legal issue is not whether someone was in fact misled, or entered into a transaction which was not beneficial as the result of a mistake, but whether it can be proved that the statement which induced the transaction was false. The legal analysis confines or closes the enquiry into the events or circumstances of a transaction. This closure enables private law reasoning to reduce the complexity of events, so that it can insist upon finite limits to the information to be considered prior to reaching a conclusion about the application of a legal sanction. All communication systems achieve this reduction of complexity to some extent, but my contention is that private law, and the law of contract in particular, pushed its device of closure to extremes.

We can illustrate these features of self-reference and closure in private law by considering the application of the rules common to most legal systems which determine when and if the parties have reached an agreement. Every legal system with European origins adopts the elaborate and interrelated concepts of 'offer' and 'acceptance'. These concepts define the legal concept of agreement and function to determine the moment of legal responsibility.[10] In order for a legal agreement to be formed, there must be an offer and an acceptance. Legal doctrine then defines an offer by

---

[9] In this section I am developing ideas suggested by Gunther Teubner, see Teubner, G., *Law as an Autopoietic System* (Oxford: Blackwell, 1993).
[10] Zweigert, K., and Kotz, H., *An Introduction to Comparative Law*, 2nd edn. (Oxford: Clarendon Press, 1987), 2, ch. 3.

distinguishing it from an 'invitation to treat', such as a tender, and a 'counter-offer'; and it defines an acceptance by rules which require an unequivocal, communicated consent to the same terms as those contained in the offer. The legal rules are not exactly the same across legal systems, so that what counts as an offer, how long an offer persists, and what counts as an acceptance differ in material ways.

Lawyers are aware that these concepts of offer and acceptance are not self-applying. The court must make a determination as to whether in law the facts reveal an offer and an acceptance. Lawyers are also aware that the legal reasoning often displays instrumental qualities: a court that is intent upon protecting a weaker party may find a contract by determining that an offer and an acceptance occurred on the basis of ambiguous conduct of the parties. Equally the courts can defer the moment of contractual responsibility for instrumental purposes such as the protection of consumers.[11] The concepts of offer and acceptance are therefore not descriptions of facts, but conclusions of law about the facts.

When a court confronts an issue of whether a contract has been formed by an agreement, it employs this system of self-referential rules with an apparently autonomous logic. The facts are analysed in order to determine whether or not there was an 'offer' which was 'accepted'. In a typical English decision, *Gibson v Manchester City Council*,[12] the question was whether a tenant had entered into a contract to purchase his house from the Council. The answer depended in law on whether the correspondence between the parties included an offer and an acceptance. Mr Gibson had written to the Council enquiring about the price of a purchase. The Council had written back saying that it *'may be prepared to sell'* for a fixed sum, and instructed him to complete a form in order to make a *'formal application to buy your council house'*. Mr Gibson returned the form, but sought a reduction of the price, which was refused. He then agreed to the Council's price in a subsequent letter. There was no doubt that the parties had reached agreement on the principal terms of the sale, though minor matters still needed to be sorted out. The Council had ceased to maintain the property, and Mr Gibson had effected some minor improvements. Yet the House of Lords (the highest appeal court) concluded that there was no agreement in law. The Council's letter stating that it 'may be prepared to sell' was not an offer, but merely an invitation to Mr Gibson to make an offer. Even if it had been construed as an offer, Mr Gibson had rejected it by seeking to offer a lower price, which was a counter-offer, not an acceptance. In addition, the form sent by Mr Gibson described itself as an 'application to buy' rather than an acceptance of an offer, so it could not

[11] Collins, H., *The Law of Contract*, 3rd edn. (London: Butterworths,1997), 159–65.
[12] [1979] 1 WLR 294, [1979] 1 All ER 972, HL.

be construed as an acceptance. Lord Diplock summarized the conclusion
in these terms:

My Lords, there may be certain types of contract, though I think they are exceptional, which do not fit easily into the normal analysis of a contract as being
constituted by offer and acceptance; but a contract alleged to have been made by
an exchange of correspondence between the parties in which the successive
communications other than the first are in reply to one another is not one of these.
I can see no reason in the instant case for departing from the conventional approach
of looking at a handful of documents relied on as constituting the contract sued on
and seeing whether on their true construction there is to be found in them a
contractual offer by the council to sell the house to Mr Gibson and an acceptance
of that offer by Mr Gibson . . .

My Lords, the words italicised seem to me . . . to make it quite impossible to
construe this letter as a contractual offer capable of being converted into a legally
enforceable open contract for the sale of land by Mr Gibson's written acceptance of
it. The words 'may be prepared to sell' are fatal to this; so is the invitation, not, it be
noted, to accept the offer, but 'to make formal application to buy' on the enclosed
application form.

This example of legal reasoning illustrates its closure and self-referential
reasoning in several ways. The fact that both parties believed that they had
an agreement and had acted upon it in minor respects is not relevant to the
investigation of whether there was an agreement in law. The crucial issue in
the legal reasoning is whether there was an offer and an acceptance, which
according to the legal definitions of these concepts turns on a construction
of the documentary evidence alone. This limited body of evidence is used to
determine the intention of the parties, so that any expressions in these
documents that negate an intention to be bound immediately override any
contrary indications from conduct and the apparent expectations of the
parties. The narrow focus of the enquiry upon the documents and their
expressions of intent flows directly from the framing of the issue in terms of
an offer and an acceptance, for the legal definitions of these concepts
require an unconditional willingness to be bound on the terms proposed.
The important consideration from the point of view of Mr Gibson, that he
had carried out work to improve the property because he reasonably
believed that he had reached an agreement with the Council, is regarded
as an irrelevant fact under the rules of law which exclude such evidence of
detrimental reliance.

The exact state of mind of the Council, as a corporate body, was harder
to determine. The language employed in the letters appears to be carefully
worded, so that it avoided a binding commitment during the negotiations.
This aspect of the correspondence suggests that legal advisors had been
employed in the drafting of the letters in order to retain the council's
freedom of action. Although other staff of the council might not have

appreciated that in law the negotiations were still at a very preliminary stage, the drafters of the letters may well have understood this implication. Knowledge of the self-referential legal rules and their implications for the closure of the legal enquiry serves as an important advantage to parties involved in contractual negotiations. The technical discourse of the law is therefore not neutral in its application: those people with superior legal knowledge can gain advantage by performing actions that trigger favourable legal consequences.

These features of the private law system of contract that describe its self-referential operational rules and tight closure rules with respect to information from the social practices being regulated can be discovered no doubt in other communication systems. Although not unique in its methods, private law became intensive in their application. Its self-referential system of rules became a paradigm example of formal, autonomous legal reasoning, the subject from which law students learned the mysteries and skills of legal analysis. Its closure rules with respect to information about social practice became so tight that market conventions and expectations could be ignored. Whether or not a particular rule made any 'commercial sense' did not seem to matter much; the important thing was that the integrity of the doctrinal system was preserved. This combination of qualities of self-reference and closure have been described as the formalism of private law.

My argument will be that formalism in private law is a phenomenon that is disintegrating rapidly. In particular, the closure rules come under increasing pressure, which in turn serves to undermine the integrity of the self-referential rule system. Before examining why these changes are taking place, and how they affect the productive capacity of private law for regulating contracts, we should consider a particular aspect of the self-referential system that both explains how private law manages to reduce the complexity of events, and also points to a source of the disintegration of the formalism of private law.

The Doctrinal Classification System

As a category of legal thought, the private law of contract is familiar to every lawyer as part of the earliest stages of training. It seems to be a fundamental part of any modern legal system in a society where wealth is produced in a market economy. Furthermore, the category of contract appears to be a distinctive and discrete part of the law, for it is concerned with the voluntary creation of additional obligations, whereas most branches of the law such as criminal law and public law normally impose mandatory obligations on citizens and public officials. Here I want to spend a few moments to consider the significance of the doctrinal classification of contract within a self-referential legal discourse. My objective is to demonstrate how this private law classification both assists and obstructs the productive regulation of markets and contractual relations. This line of argument also forces us to examine the origins and evolution of this doctrinal category not only as a product of discourses that are internal to the legal system, but also as the product of group identity and negotiation between social groups.

The part of the legal system known as the law of contract represents a self-referential sub-system within the category of the private law of obligations. The law of obligations as a category includes the other subsystems of the law of tort (or delict) and the law of unjust enrichment (or restitution). The common thread in the law of obligations is the idea that certain legal duties arise between citizens, which, if broken, give rise to a secondary obligation (the sanction) to pay compensation or take some other kind of corrective remedial step. The legal duties range broadly over obligations not to cause personal injury, to damage property, to break valid contracts, and many other instances. It was a Roman law idea that the law of obligations could be subdivided. The major division was between obligations arising from contracts and those arising from wrongs, though it was recognized that not every event giving rise to a legal obligation could be fitted into this dual structure.[13] Modern legal systems tend to prefer a fourfold classification, which adds to contract and tort the category of unjust enrichment, and a further miscellaneous category.

The importance of these categories within the law of obligations lies in the way that they organize and foreclose legal reasoning. Once a particular situation has been classified as falling into a particular category, such as contract, then the rules of that subsystem will be applied to the exclusion of others. This process of legal reasoning should be appreciated as a valuable way of reducing the complexity of events, so that legal reasoning can apply its closed and self-referential reasoning in order to produce a legal result such as a determination that a sanction should be imposed. The initial determination that the event under dispute raises an issue within a particular category such as contract permits the event to be analysed exclusively by the rules of the subsystem of contract. The rules of the subsystem render certain aspects of the events as the relevant facts, and then the legal consequences of those facts can be determined by subsuming them under the operational rules of the subsystem. Thus, if the initial determination is that the event falls within the category of contract, the subsystem will insist that only those facts relevant to the question of whether a valid contract

---

[13] Gaius, Institutes, 3.89–91; Justinian, Institutes, 3.13. See Birks, P., 'Definition and Division: A Meditation on Institutes 3.13', in P. Birks (ed.), *The Classification of Obligations* (Oxford: Clarendon Press, 1997), 1.

has been breached should be considered by legal reasoning. If those facts fail to satisfy the requirements of the operational rules, such as the requirement that the parties should have reached an agreement, then the conclusion must follow under the operational rules that no contractual obligation has been broken, so that no sanction should be imposed. Legal classifications are therefore important features of law as a system of knowledge that is employed in the government of society. They enable lawyers to simplify complex social events, and then to reach legal conclusions by the application of the rules of a discrete subsystem.

How do these legal classifications, such as the law of contract, originate? In their inception the classifications probably represent pragmatic attempts to organize legal materials in convenient ways for the efficient government of society and for the instruction of lawyers in the details of legal doctrine. But some classifications, such as the law of contract, owing to their longevity and central importance in the government of market economies, have had attributed to them a source of deeper moral principles that guide the institutions of society. In the case of the law of contract, for instance, the classification may be linked to a moral idea that promises or agreements ought to be kept. Alternatively, the special quality of the classification of contract may be perceived in the distinctive consensual basis for the determination of the content of the obligation. These perceptions of links to background moral considerations elevate the classifications of legal knowledge to fundamental moral guides of the legal system, rather than their remaining convenient and pragmatic tools of a particular knowledge system aimed at government of the community. Some classifications such as the law of contract become vested with a hallowed character, so that criticism of the utility of the classification in particular instances is perceived not only as an attack upon the legal system as a whole, but also a challenge to the underlying moral principles of society. Gilmore's proclamation of the death of the classification of contract on the ground that it no longer provided a convenient organizing category for legal knowledge was therefore greeted with shock and horror, as well as provoking valiant attempts to defend the utility of the classification.[14]

Legal classifications are not only sustained by their mythical origins but also by social action. Within the legal profession, specialist groups emerge which claim expert knowledge in particular classifications of law. Just as the natural sciences become subdivided into professional groups, such as physicists, chemists, biologists, and so forth, so too lawyers aspire to mastery of particular classifications such as contract, public law, and European law. Membership of the specialist group can be established by

---

[14] Gilmore, G., *The Death of Contract* (Columbus, Ohio: Ohio State University Press, 1974).

formal associations, such as groups of scholars in a learned society, or membership of a specialist practising lawyers association. Informal association through teaching, writing, or practising in a particular field on a recurrent basis is also possible. Having asserted this specialist knowledge of a legal subsystem, then the group claims a privileged insight into its principles and its appropriate field of application. The scope of the classification then rests upon the customary practices of the specialist group, the matters which they regard as being within their area of expertise. This conventional basis for the classification may defy any logical analysis of the differences between sources of legal rights and obligations. In the Common Law world, for instance, the specialist groupings often divide their spheres of competence on the basis of an old jurisdictional division in the courts between common law and equity, so that by convention the classification tends to exclude sources of obligations derived originally from one of the jurisdictions. As a result, the law of obligations in the common law world is often described with scant attention being paid to equitable sources of obligations. The conventional basis for the classification also places obstacles in the way of attempts to link the classification system to underlying moral principles. What is conventionally regarded as a contractual issue, and therefore handled by the operational rules of contract law, may prove either narrower or broader than the extent of moral principles regarding promises or the consensual basis of obligations. The law of contract may regulate some situations where the presence of consent is at best a legal fiction, and equally may decline to regulate some consensual agreements on the ground that they are more conveniently handled by another subsystem such as the law of trusts or company law. The conventional basis for the legal classification system finally has the effect that it permits differences to arise between legal systems. Whereas in one legal system an issue may be classified as contractual, in another it may be regarded as a matter or delict, unjust enrichment, or even public law.

From this sociological perspective, therefore, the classification of the law of contract is important, not because it represents some immutable category of legal thought based upon some fundamental moral ideals of the community, but because it provides a valuable tool for managing complexity in social events which is sustained and defined by the conventional practices of lawyers.[15] It must be observed, however, that the conventional classifications can also serve to obstruct coherent and effective regulation of social events. The initial determination that a particular subsystem such as the law of contract applies to a particular event has the effect of limiting the operating rules of private law which the courts apply

---

[15] Collins, H., 'Legal Classifications as the Production of Knowledge Systems', in P. Birks (ed.), n. 13 above, 57.

to the event to those contained within the classification. In turn, these operating rules further foreclose the factual considerations regarded as relevant to the legal determination.

We can illustrate this process and the blindness which it produces by considering an example of the implication of terms into contracts. The legal issue in *Liverpool City Council v Irwin*[16] was whether there was an implied term in a lease for an apartment in a high-rise block that the landlord should take reasonable care to keep in 'reasonable repair and usability' the common parts of the premises such as stairways and halls. Having classified this issue as one of contract, because there was an agreement for a lease, the operational rules of the private law of contract required that the court should try to elucidate the content of the agreement between the parties in order to determine whether or not they had agreed implicitly that the landlord should undertake the alleged obligation. This classification sets the court off on a trajectory of determining the scope of the implicit agreement by reference to the alleged intentions of the parties and the market conventions which they may be assumed to have presupposed in their agreement. The classification of contract prevents the court from framing the issue in different terms, such as a rule to promote the safety of occupants and visitors. A concern to impose efficient levels of safety constitutes one of the central objectives of the law of tort or delict, another branch of private law. But the law of tort was not relevant to the problem once the issue had been classified as contract, so that private law regulation was precluded from drawing on the insights and resources of this different category. In order to overcome this obstruction to productive learning from other doctrinal subsystems in private law, it is true that private law sometimes entertains startling reclassifications of events, such as transforming a tort issue into a problem regulated by contract law.[17] It is also possible to insert regulations from other classification systems surreptitiously, as in cases where tort regulation is presented as a source of implied terms in contracts. For example, in a contract of employment that confers a discretionary power upon the employer to determine the hours of work, a court will impose a duty derived from tort regulation that the power must be exercised consistently with the health and safety of the employee, but this duty is presented as an implied term of the contract in order to fit within the doctrinal classification system.[18] Legal classifications such as the law of contract are both valuable in the way they assist in managing complexity, but they also obstruct productive cross-fertilization of ideas and values within the legal system.

---

[16] [1977] AC 239, [1976] 2 All ER 39, HL.

[17] Collins, H., 'Productive Learning from the Collision Between the Doctrinal Subsystems of Contract and Tort', *Acta Juridica* (1997) 55.

[18] *Johnstone v Bloomsbury Health Authority* [1992] QB 333, [1991] 2 All ER 293, CA.

Returning to the decision in *Liverpool City Council v Irwin*, however, it must be observed that none of these private law classifications look capable of grasping adequately the crucial problem of distributive justice faced by legal regulation. What had happened was that a local public authority had decided to create cheap housing and to minimize the costs of upkeep by delimiting its obligations towards the comfort and safety of the tenants through a standard form contract. The distributive issue raised is whether this use of self-regulation by a government body acting as a contractor was a reasonable way to exercise its statutory powers to provide affordable housing in the community. The court upheld the presence of the alleged implied term in the contract despite the difficulty that the clear intention of the standard form contract had been to minimize the landlord's obligations. Perhaps the court in fact grasped the regulatory issues of distributive justice and the controversial exercise of contractual power (self-regulation) by a public body, though the judges did not expressly make any reference to it.

The Collision of Private Law with Public Regulation

Whatever interpretation one places on the motives of the judges in *Liverpool City Council v Irwin*, the issues presented in the dispute lead us conveniently to our principal argument in this chapter. The contention is that the private law system of contract described above is disintegrating under the impact of a collision with public law regulation. Indeed, the integrity of the doctrinal system established by self-reference and closure has been unable to withstand the impact of several different forces. Perhaps the most obvious force that challenges the traditional doctrinal system of the private law of contract springs from the increasing variety of contractual practices. We shall consider the nature and extent of this subversive force more closely in subsequent chapters. Here we confine our attention to the deep and systematic challenge to the integrity of the private law system posed by the advent of extensive economic and social regulation. The presence of this public or welfare regulation in the field of contractual practices compels a dialogue between it and the traditional private law. The outcome of this collision of discourses consists of a reconfiguration of private law reasoning.

One of the great achievements of the nineteenth-century doctrinal systems of contract law was that they evolved a level of abstraction or generality that permitted the regulation and enforcement of a great variety of contractual undertakings. Instead of the legal system only recognizing a finite list of nominate contracts, such as the standard transactions of sale, loan, hire, and bailment (looking after goods belonging to another), the general law of contract had the potential to observe within its closure rules a vast array of transactions. In the common law, for instance, the general rules for the formation of contracts only required there to be an agreement for consideration, and these terms were described at a sufficient level of abstraction to encompass most consumer transactions and commercial business arrangements. Not every business arrangement could be included in these abstract rules, however, so even at the zenith of private law of contract we can observe special rules for commercial transactions, such as the Bills of Exchange Act 1882, and the Commercial Codes of civil law systems. Nevertheless, the abstraction and generality of private law usually enabled courts to encompass most novel transactions within its regulatory system. It empowered parties with the discretion of freedom of contract in the sense of freedom to choose the terms of their contracts. Using this discretionary power, they could adjust the legal framework to the content of their economic arrangements, rather than having to adjust their transaction to the requirements of the law. This discretion supported the capacity of participants in markets to exploit the potential benefits arising from an intensification of the division of labour.

The main problem with the abstraction and generality of the private law system was that it lacked mechanisms for differentiating in its regulation between different kinds of contracts. The familiar story of the control over exclusion clauses in consumer contracts illustrates this weakness. Freedom to choose the terms of contracts empowered the parties to select an efficient allocation of risks. They could decide, for instance, who should bear the loss arising from the goods proving unsatisfactory in a sale of goods. In a commercial transaction between two businesses, this freedom to allocate risks could reduce costs by permitting the parties to place the risk on the party who could avoid or cover the loss at the least cost. When these principles were applied, however, to consumer transactions, the effect was that businesses took advantage of small print in standard form contracts in order to place the risk of loss upon the consumer, without the consumer usually being aware of this allocation and without a commensurate price reduction. In order to respond to this potential abuse of freedom of contract, private law systems needed to evolve a differentiation between different types of contract, so that some controls over the allocation of risks in consumer standard form transactions could be developed.

Yet such an evolution ran counter to the generality of private law systems, so that the development of special consumer protection was always blocked. In English law, the courts tried to overcome the problem by the doctrine of 'fundamental breach'. Under this idea, the court could argue that some breaches of contract were so fundamental that any allocation of risk contained in the standard form contract was irrelevant. In the case of a consumer purchasing a car that lacked a working engine, for

instance, the court could argue that the breach of contract was so fundamental that the term of the contract which placed this risk on the consumer
was irrelevant to the events which had occurred.[19] Another, perhaps more
cogent way of expressing this line of reasoning, was to declare that an
exclusion clause could not be attributed a meaning that contradicted the
fundamental purpose of the transaction, as in the case of a sale of goods
where the exclusion clause placed the risk that the seller did not own the
goods on the buyer. Yet ultimately the higher courts rejected these
doctrinal developments, because they could not be reconciled with the
requirements of generality of the private law system.[20] In a commercial
context, these kinds of allocation of risk could constitute a fair and
efficient transaction between the parties, so the application of the doctrine
of fundamental breach was inappropriate.[21] In the absence of the capacity
of private law to create a differentiation for consumer sales, the general
rules had to reject the possibility of a doctrine of fundamental breach.

The story of exclusion clauses in consumer contracts ends with legislative intervention in most jurisdictions. Legislation could displace the
generality of the private law doctrinal system with a differentiated treatment of consumer contracts, employment contracts, and so forth. The
legislation empowers a court to invalidate (according to the terminology
of the jurisdiction) unreasonable, unfair, unconscionable, or abusive
exclusion clauses in a consumer standard form contract. The lesson to
be learned from this story is that the price of the advantages obtained
from the generality of private law systems was the incapacity to develop
an adequately differentiated system of regulation of contracts. The
system could only maintain its integrity by resisting the normative
complexity and variety of instrumental policy concerns provoked by
the extension and complexity of contractual practices into every aspect
of social life.

The legal system responded to these inadequacies of private law by the
introduction of differentiated economic and social regulation of contractual practices. As this regulation increased in scope, so private law regulation became excluded from more and more fields of contractual
undertakings. This phenomenon caused scholars to wonder whether the
private law of contract had any importance except as a set of default
regulations that applied in the absence of more specific controls. Yet
much more interesting than this attenuated role for the private law of

---

[19] *Karsales (Harrow) Ltd v Wallis* [1956] 1 WLR 936, CA.
[20] *Photo Production Ltd v Securicor Transport Ltd* [1980] AC 827, [1980] 1 All ER 556, HL.
[21] e.g. *Harbutt's 'Plasticine' Ltd v Wayne Tank and Pump Co.* [1970] 1QB 447, CA; see,
Adams, J. N., 'Unconscionability and the Standard Form Contract', in R. Brownsword,
G. Howells, and T. Wilhelmsson (eds.), *Welfarism in Contract Law* (Aldershot: Dartmouth,
1994) 230.

contract was the impact of this social and economic regulation on the discourses of private law themselves.

The presence of social and economic regulation confronted private law with the challenge of restoring its integrity by including the welfare regulation within its normative domain. The regulation of consumer contracts, for instance, was not dismissed as irrelevant to the normative orientation of private law, but rather private law sought to reconfigure itself in order to place this regulation within its discourses as far as possible. Similarly, the extensive introduction of types of price controls, such as a minimum wage, fair rents, and controls over usurious interest rates in consumer credit transactions posed a challenge to the private law stance that it did not test or examine the fairness of transactions. Although private law could have ignored this challenge as wholly irrelevant, it could instead seek to reorganize its doctrines in order to permit challenges to unfairness in egregious cases. The norms underlying the social and economic regulation could be fitted into vague private law doctrines that qualified freedom of contract, such as abuse of rights, unconscionability, and good faith. Once reinvigorated by this dialogue with social and economic regulation, these doctrines could then be applied to fields of contractual practice outside those covered by this regulation in a way which permitted much more complex and differentiated regulation.

As an illustration of this outcome of the collision between private law and social and economic regulation, consider the private law regulation of transactions involving wives acting as sureties for their husband's business debts. In a typical case, a man seeks a loan from a bank in order to provide capital for his business ventures. The bank grants the loan on condition that it is secured by a valuable asset, which is often the matrimonial home that is owned jointly with the businessman's wife. Under pressure, misinformation, or simply a sense of loyalty, the wife agrees to mortgage her home, which is then lost as a result of the mismanagement and collapse of her husband's business ventures. The factual pattern can differ slightly, as when the surety is the father, child, or employee of the debtor. The common element is that the surety transaction escapes consumer protection legislation, for the main loan is between a bank and a business. On the other hand, the position of the family member is often similar to a consumer due to the lack of reliable information and the subtle pressure produced by family ties to agree to the transaction. Private law reasoning could respond to this situation by insisting that the parties to a commercial transaction should protect their own interests and that the law should support the validity of loans made by banks by enforcing them in the absence of wrongdoing by the bank. But in fact private law reasoning has developed a more differentiated approach through which it can observe the special predicament of the surety in these circumstances and place obligations upon the bank to ensure that the surety makes a fully informed and carefully considered decision without pressure. In English law, this development has been achieved by suggesting that the bank will usually have constructive notice of the problem of pressure or misrepresentation, that is the bank is deemed to know of the problem.[22] This is a fiction, that is an invented fact, which is required by the internal operations of the private law system in order to trigger the application of an exception to unrestricted freedom of contract. The bank is then subjected to a duty to take reasonable steps to ensure that the family surety has received independent advice, and the failure to take sufficient steps results in the mortgage becoming voidable or unenforceable under the doctrine of undue influence. A similar line of reasoning enables the German courts to invalidate such transactions. Under article 138 of the civil code (the BGB) the law does not permit love and gratitude to be commercialized in the interests of third parties, so that protection to family members who act as sureties will be afforded when they suffer grave economic hardship as a result. What is interesting about this private law reasoning is the way it evolves a differentiated approach to the regulation of surety arrangements, one which draws on ideas of pressure and misleading information developed in consumer protection regulation, and which is then applied to a slightly different context of family sureties for commercial transactions.

This example of family surety arrangements is merely indicative of how the dialogue with social and economic regulation begins to transform private law reasoning. Once private law embarks on this route of differentiation of contexts of contractual arrangements, it introduces much greater normative complexity into its reasoning processes. In particular, the striking feature of private law reasoning is that it becomes much more obviously concerned about the social and economic effects of its interventions. In order to determine whether or not its new differentiation achieves its purpose, the private law system has to observe the effects of its regulation, and then in the light of that information, it has to adjust its regulation. The effects of regulation are not necessarily either intended or expected effects. Businesses observe the regulation as a cost which needs to be minimized by cost-effective adjustments to their operations. In the example of the regulation of family surety arrangements, the effect of regulation is to cause banks to adjust their bureaucratic procedures with a view to minimizing the risk of invalidity of the security at the least cost. The main effect of regulation is the bank's revision of its formal procedures prior to granting a loan. Through observation of litigation coming before the courts, private law regulation can be adjusted in order to strike an

---

[22] *Barclays Bank plc v O'Brien* [1994] 1 AC 180, [1993] 4 All ER 417, HL; *CIBC Mortgages plc v Pitt* [1994] 1 AC 200, [1993] 4 All ER 433, HL.

efficient balance between imposing onerous duties on banks to comply with detailed bureaucratic procedures and the protection of vulnerable sureties. Private law reasoning, though conceptually framed in terms of the need to protect the consensual basis of transaction, develops its more precise regulation of secured transactions with wives by balancing the bureaucratic costs imposed on banks by more detailed and extensive requirements against the benefits to be achieved in terms of distributive outcomes of protecting wives' tenure in the matrimonial home. Within the normative complexity of private law reasoning, therefore, consequential or instrumental reasoning comes to dominate the other considerations of integrity and the political source of obligation.

These trends can be observed, for instance, in the leading English case concerning wives as sureties for their husband's business loans, *Barclays Bank plc v O'Brien*.[23] Lord Brown-Wilkinson presents a section entitled 'Policy considerations', which commences with acknowledging the source of his knowledge about the effects of private law regulation from the 'large number of cases of this type coming before the courts in recent years'. Having considered this evidence, he describes the regulatory policy in these terms:

It is easy to allow sympathy for the wife who is threatened with the loss of her home at the suit of a rich bank to obscure an important public interest, viz the need to ensure that the wealth currently tied up in the matrimonial home does not become economically sterile. If the rights secured to wives by the law render vulnerable loans granted on the security of matrimonial homes, institutions will be unwilling to accept such security, thereby reducing the flow of loan capital to business enterprises. It is therefore essential that a law designed to protect the vulnerable does not render the matrimonial home unacceptable as a security to financial institutions.

This statement of regulatory policy makes it clear that the objective of providing support to the construction of markets through the enforcement of security must prevail over distributive issues concerning occupation of the matrimonial home. The distributive task for regulation is reduced to the regulation of market practices, that is, a requirement is placed upon banks to disclose information about the nature of the contract, and to give a warning about the need to obtain independent advice. But the most striking feature of this speech, which is far from unusual, is the explicit statement of the instrumental objective of private law regulation. The validity or legitimacy of the judgment rests upon its success in defining the regulatory task and then manipulating private law doctrine to achieve that task efficiently.

Another way to describe what is happening in private law is to suggest

---

[23] [1994] 1 AC 180, [1993] 4 All ER 417, HL.

that the sharp distinction between private law reasoning and the reasoning linked with economic and social regulation becomes confused. Private law reasoning becomes less self-referential and closed as it seeks to grapple with the information about the effects of its regulation in different social contexts. The sharp limits on what was regarded as relevant information by the private law system become riddled with holes as private law reasoning seeks to ascertain the efficiency and efficacy of its regulation in particular contexts. We can speak of the relevance of former 'non-legal' reasons to the legal reasoning process. These 'non-legal' reasons are the empirical information about the impact of regulation, and how those subject to regulation, such as banks, have altered their conduct to adjust to regulation. These 'non-legal reasons' then provide the argument for fresh private law regulation by means of a reinterpretation of the principles of private law.

We should not conclude, however, that this instrumentalism in private law regulation reduces it to an exercise in economic or sociological reasoning. Legal doctrine retains both distinctive closure rules and procedural rules that restrict its acquisition and understanding of information. The insights available from other kinds of disciplines, such as political theory, economic analysis, empirical and sociological studies of market practices, will not easily be constructed as relevant facts for the doctrinal discourse. Legal doctrine must reconstruct its information about the effects of regulation by selecting the knowledge that can be translated into facts or principles which are relevant to the legal discourse. Economic arguments about efficiency, for instance, can normally be translated into legal discussions about whether consent to a transaction was given voluntarily on the basis of full information (the essential conditions for competitive markets and wealth enhancing transactions). Sociological observations about market conventions can be incorporated as implicit aspects of the agreement, known in legal discourse as implied terms or supplementary rules. General clauses in law, such as broad requirements of 'reasonableness' or 'good faith', can be used as gateways which permit social science perspectives to become relevant sources of information to legal doctrine. Contractual behaviour can be regarded as reasonable, if it contributes to a competitive market or conforms to an established market convention. Yet even with these methods available for private law reasoning, the discourse remains closed to much information about its impact. The information is often confined to the succession of factual instances that happen to be litigated before the courts. This information is in turn limited by the presentation of evidence that appears pertinent to the application of the legal regulation. Private law therefore remains a distinctive regulatory instrument with important structural weaknesses that impede its pursuit of instrumental objectives.

The Productive Disintegration of Private Law

In this chapter, we have been seeking to understand the dominant form of legal regulation of contracts, that is the private law of contract, as a type of discourse. Private law systems provide immensely sophisticated regulation due to the complexity of their normative orientation. But they can also provide gravely defective instruments for regulating contracts due to their self-referential character and closure rules. We noted in particular that the differentiation of the subsystem of contract law from other branches of private law, though serving to reduce complexity, impeded the possibility of productive learning across branches or classifications of private law regulation.

Yet my argument has been that private law is undergoing a transformation in its discourses. This change in the pattern of private law reasoning has resulted most immediately from an inevitable clash with the discourses of the economic and social regulation that were designed to address the inadequacies of private law as a form of distributive regulation caused by its lack of differentiation between the social contexts of contractual practices. The result of the collision between discourses has been the reconfiguration of private law reasoning, so that instrumental or policy concerns within its normative orientation become the dominant force of its evolutionary trajectory. Private law reasoning loses much of its special character as it seeks to incorporate social and economic reasoning within its normative orientation. Private law reasoning approximates much more to policy analysis and implementation.

Although I suggest that this transformation of private law reasoning is occurring in all advanced legal systems, it is interesting to observe some special factors that apply to Member States in the European Union. Here the project of harmonization of laws in order to create a Single Market has led to social and economic regulation of contractual practices at European level. This general regulation then has to be translated into more concrete rules that fit into the national private law and regulatory traditions. Since the European regulation may not be adequately implemented by national legislation, the national courts fall under an obligation to strive to achieve harmonization by the manipulation of all sources of national law, including private law. Reasoning in private law therefore has to be adjusted as far as possible to achieve harmonization with European regulatory goals. This internal logic of the constitutional arrangements of the European Union therefore poses two crucial challenges to the self-referential character of private law systems. In the first place, private law systems have to be adjusted so that they conform to the objectives of European social and economic regulation, which in turn requires the inclusion of consequentialist or instrumental reasoning as the dominant guide in private law. But since these objectives are often slightly opaque, national private law systems have to observe how these objectives are interpreted by other courts, that is the European Court of Justice and other national private law courts, in order to ensure harmonization of laws. The effect is that private law reasoning becomes in part an exercise in comparative law, in order to understand how the courts in different Member States have interpreted and implemented the objectives of European regulation.[24]

But I am not suggesting that private law can be reduced to some other discourse of economic or social regulation. The closure rules and self-referential concepts of private law remain the crucial elements in its construction of understanding of contractual practices for the purpose of regulation. In our example of family sureties, for instance, private law still thinks through its doctrinal categories such as the rule against undue influence or the rule against permitting family emotions to distort choices. What changes, however, is the extent to which this rule can be reinterpreted in the light of analogous policy and normative directions pursued in social and economic regulation. This search for reintegration of welfare regulation within private law reasoning compels private law to loosen its closure rules in order to ascertain the facts or events which permit an assessment of whether the effects of private law regulation achieve harmony with the objectives of social and economic regulation. Private law cannot remain oblivious to the demands of distributive policy and efficiency, but it has to harness them within its own discourse.

This account of the evolution of private law reasoning describes an uncertain outcome. The unresolved question is whether private law can integrate the discourses of social and economic regulation without collapsing into those discourses itself. Another way of presenting this question is to ask whether legal reasoning can avoid becoming just a branch of economic analysis or rational choice analysis. My view is that private law retains sufficient normative complexity to withstand such a reduction. It has the capacity to learn productively from the discourses of social and economic regulation, whilst at the same time preserving its other normative points of reference such as political conceptions of justice. In the context of private law, I do not favour the image of the law standing as neutral umpire above a host of competing discourses, which it seeks to regulate by developing rules of hierarchy, procedures for investigation and conflict resolution, and a search for internal legal coherence.[25] I prefer instead

---

[24] Collins, H., 'The Voice of the Community in Private Law', *European Law Journal* 3 (1997), 407–21; Joerges, C., 'The Impact of European Integration on Private Law: Reductionist Perceptions, True Conflicts and a New Constitutionalist Perspective', *European Law Journal* 3 (1997), 378.

[25] e.g. Habermas, J., *Between Facts and Norms* (Cambridge: Cambridge University Press, 1996), ch. 9.

the metaphor of harness: the private law system harnesses the reasoning of economic and social regulation and redirects it within its own operations. To this extent, I agree with Teubner's analysis in terms of systems theory:

Legal operations, by their very operative closure and, as a matter of principle, cannot reach out into the domains of non-law. As a result, law can only reconstruct its environment internally through closed self-referential operations. This internal reconstruction of the external world is never identical with the events as they happen in the external world. Even if their substance appears to be identical, they are different because they are recontextualized. For instance, at the very moment that law reconstructs moral arguments internally, they lose their relation to the criterion of universality and to the moral code. They are now subjected to the mechanics of equal/unequal treatment, pressed into the programmes of law (rules, principles, doctrines) and ultimately linked to the binary legal code of legal/illegal. Calculations of costs and calculations of power, policy arguments and scientific constructs, they are all treated by the law in the same way. They all become strange hybrids which are now, however, the sole responsibility of the legal discourse.[26]

The problem with this formulation is to understand the qualities of these hybrid forms of legal discourse.

Our answer has been that in the context of private law regulation of contracts, the hybrids have not been so dissimilar to the traditional private law style of reasoning that we described in terms of self-reference and closure. The integration of economic and social regulation into private law discourse forces greater differentiation between the private law regulation of the variety of contractual practices. Private law has to reinvent itself in a more contextual way, so that it can differentiate its approach according to new categories such as consumer transactions and more significant old categories such as employment. At the same time private law incorporates the kinds of consequentialist considerations that lead to the creation of these categories in economic and social regulation, such as the protection of consumers against sharp trade practices and the protection of employees against abuse of managerial power. The former general **rules** of private law therefore begin to disintegrate and are replaced by more local regulation informed by a more purposive approach to regulation. Yet these developments enrich the legal discourse. They enable it to become more refined in its differentiation and normative orientation. Furthermore, private law in its application learns from its environment about the effects of its rules on the subjects of regulation. This observation then permits the recursive process of further refinement of the legal rules in order to modify their effects (as they are understood by the law). This new style of private law may indeed be described as its productive disintegration.

---

[26] Teubner, G., 'Altera pars Audiatur: Law in the Collision of Discourses', in R. Rawlings (ed.), *Law, Society and Economy* (Oxford: Clarendon Press, 1997), 149, 166.

4

The Capacity of Private Law

How efficient and effective is the private law of contract as a technique for regulating markets and contracts? To pose this question at all compels us to make two controversial assumptions. In the first place, we assume that private law constitutes a regulatory technique, equivalent to other techniques of social and economic regulation of business, though it differs in its form, attributes, and capacities. Our second assumption is that private law pursues instrumental purposes like other types of legal regulation of markets, so that the comparative efficacy of private law in achieving its purposes can be measured, and the costs of this type of regulation can be compared to other techniques. These assumptions seem to conflict with the traditional understanding of private law as a mechanism for supporting the private ordering of civil society without seeking to organize or steer it.

In this chapter, we explore the implications of analysing private law as a regulatory technique. The special strength of private law regulation of contracts compared to other styles of regulation is analysed in terms of its 'reflexive' capacity. We then proceed to examine the structural weakness of private law as a regulatory instrument. Our special interest lies in detecting how these weaknesses in the capacity of private law can be overcome, and how private law itself is evolving mechanisms that enable it to address these weaknesses.

Private Law as Regulation

However private law regards itself within its own internal discourses, it can also be examined from an external point of view as one mechanism by which the state seeks to regulate markets. Private law certainly has similar effects in steering market behaviour to other types of social and economic regulation of business activity. Participants in markets may alter their behaviour in order to comply with private law rules. If the participants seek to make a legally binding contract, then they may put their contract into writing in order to comply with a legal requirement of formality, or they may create a token exchange such as a peppercorn in order to comply with the common law doctrine of consideration. My central question addresses the issue of how private law performs in terms of its effectiveness and cost compared to other forms of business regulation.[1] It is consistent with this approach to concede that private law may contain other objectives, such as providing an articulate justification for the recognition of fundamental obligations owed between citizens in civil society. In so far as private law possesses instrumental purposes, however, it is fair to ask whether it proves a satisfactory technique for achieving those purposes. Furthermore, if my argument in the previous chapter that instrumental purposes increasingly steer private law discourses is accepted, then it becomes more pressing to assess the efficacy and efficiency of private law in meeting those objectives.

Even so, some lawyers may still remain dissatisfied with my approach. It may run against the grain of their understanding of private law as a pre-political system of support for private ordering in civil society. This traditional interpretation of private law imagines a separation of the realm of the state from civil society. Inside the latter, individuals arrange their affairs often by engaging in commitments towards others. These private agreements comprise the private ordering of society. The role of the state is merely to support this private ordering, at least to the extent that it is compatible with general conventional moral standards. This function is achieved primarily by granting legal enforcement to most of these private arrangements and to protect property rights. The purpose of legal enforcement of contracts is not to steer private ordering, but rather to encourage it by constructing the possibility of making binding commitments with the force of law. As part of this function, however, legal rules may be devised to protect private ordering from abusive practices such as fraud and violence.[2] The purpose of such rules is believed to be one of safeguarding private ordering against abuse, rather than one of the imposition of policy objectives upon the participants.

This traditional interpretation of private law fits closely into a liberal, or even a libertarian, conception of the role of the state and the requirements of justice. It emphasizes the importance of choice and freedom of private individuals. The role of the state is the minimal one of holding the parties to their private arrangements, without seeking to impose upon civil society a particular conception of what is good or right. The values of private law are merely the elementary moral ideals of holding people to promises which have been made seriously, or the protection of legitimate expectations raised by private undertakings.

To examine private law as a form of regulation therefore appears to misunderstand its nature, and, perhaps even worse, to pose a challenge

---

[1] See generally: Daintith, T., 'Law as a Policy Instrument: A Comparative Perspective', in T. Daintith (ed.), *Law as an Instrument of Economic Policy: Comparative and Critical Approaches* (Berlin/New York: Walter de Gruyter, 1988) 3.
[2] Raz, J., 'Promises in Morality and Law', *Harvard Law Review*, 95 (1982) 916.

to its liberal or libertarian premises. I can admit that this book as a whole contests traditional understandings of the private law of contract. It regards private law as an instrument of the state for controlling and shaping private ordering according to a variety of competing policy objectives. The book also assumes that it is impossible for the law to adopt a position of neutrality with respect to the distributive outcomes of private ordering. Yet in this context, the crux of the issue does not turn on these general perceptions of the nature of private law. The crucial point is rather whether private law contains the normative complexity that I described in the previous chapter. Once it is admitted that one strand in the normative discourses of private law concerns instrumental policy objectives, then it becomes fair to assess private law as an instrument or regulatory technique.

It is only possible to exclude such questions about private law as a regulatory technique, if it is denied absolutely that private law is influenced by policy objectives. There may be some legal scholars who remain attached to an idea of private law as a sealed, self-referential discourse linked only to basic moral ideals such as the idea that promises ought to be kept. For them, the observation of the social effects of private law must be a matter of sublime indifference; consequentialist considerations in the formulation of private law doctrines must be an anathema. Yet I do not believe that such legal scholars really exist. Even the most traditional accounts of the private law of contract introduce references to instrumental considerations in their pages, though they remain crudely formulated and empirically unverified. The pages are in fact peppered with such considerations as the need for 'certainty' in the law, so that businessmen can plan their affairs. Of course, hidden in this appeal to certainty (which is not the same as doctrinal integrity, for a clear rule can be inconsistent with the values of the doctrinal system), there is an implicit rejection of some other standard or policy such as fairness by which to measure the effects of private law. These breaches of the seal of self-reference in order to admit consequentialist considerations indicate that even in the most traditional accounts of private law, instrumental considerations are not excluded entirely.

At the same time as the assumptions behind my question about the effectiveness of private law as an instrument of regulation raise the hackles of traditional private lawyers, they also present a puzzle to a modern breed of lawyers who use economics in the study of business regulation. These lawyers understand that it is appropriate to ask whether business regulation is efficacious and cost-effective. But they have a difficulty in appreciating that the same question should be asked of private law.

One reason for this difficulty seems to be an assumption that private law permits more or less unbridled freedom of contract. This assumption appears frequently in the contrast drawn by economics between the market guided by the invisible hand of competition and the controlled zone of conduct guided by business regulation. This contrast between markets and regulation often appears in economics, without the appreciation that the category of markets is in fact also a regulated arena, though it is a field which is regulated primarily by private law. Given the false assumption that markets in their pure state are virtually unregulated, however, it becomes possible to draw a sharp contrast between private law and other forms of social and economic regulation. It is assumed that only the latter types of regulation have as their objective the placing of restraints upon freedom in the market place by increasing the costs of undesired activities. My contention is that, on the contrary, private law and business regulation may differ in the degree to which they control market activity, but that it is wrong to suppose that private law does not also seek to regulate business. Private law is the index finger of the invisible hand that guides market economies.

Private law rules can be presented as addressing the same kinds of issues as those dealt with by regulation. If some of the purposes of business regulation include the correction of market failures or the redistribution of wealth, we can point to private law rules which serve similar functions. For example, private law rules about the bargaining process such as misrepresentation, duress, and undue influence can be analysed as correcting market failure,[3] or redistributing wealth.[4] Moreover, this parallel in functions between private law and business regulation emerges clearly when we examine the sources of regulation of a particular market activity. In the case of misleading advertising, for instance, we discover a common pattern in most jurisdictions that the sources of regulation combine private law rules with specialized regulatory techniques.[5] The two sources of regulation operate in tandem.

Where private law regulation differs from other kinds of business regulation is simply in the generality of rules, which only become specific when applied by private ordering and adjudication. Daintith reaches a similar conclusion with respect to the private law of property:

there seems to be no reason why we should not treat the security of enjoyment of land as an integral element of state management of the economy, distinguished from other policies by the degree of its generality, its importance and its antiquity rather than by any difference in kind.[6]

---

[3] Trebilcock, M. J., *The Limits of Freedom of Contract* (Cambridge, Mass.: Harvard University Press, 1993).

[4] Kronman, A. T., 'Contract Law and Distributive Justice', *Yale Law Journal* 89 (1980), 472.

[5] Trebilcock, M. J., 'Private Law Remedies for Misleading Advertising', *University of Toronto Law Journal* 22 (1972) 1.

[6] Daintith, T., 'Regulation', *International Encyclopedia of Comparative Law*, xvii (1995) ch. 10, 35.

The contrast drawn between private law and business regulation is also sustained by other false assumptions. The difference in kind between the two types of law is often thought to rest on the different sources of law. In Common Law jurisdictions, a frequent assumption is to equate the basic facilitative rules of private law ordering with judge-made law, and interventionist regulation with legislation. This contrast obviously breaks down in Civil Law jurisdictions where their private law Codes are the product of legislation.[7] But even in the context of the common law, this formal contrast collapses when we observe how legislation becomes integrated into the doctrinal fabric of the common law over the course of time. An example is the Statute of Frauds 1677, which began life as a regulatory measure, but over the centuries became the bedrock for the elaboration of the private law rules governing formalities in the formation of contracts. In the common law much legislation is also an attempt to codify and clarify the existing common law, as in the case of the Sale of Goods Act 1893 and the Bills of Exchange Act 1882. This legislation is interpreted as fitting into the doctrinal fabric of the common law, as creating and facilitating basic property rights and forms of transaction, with the effect that no distinction can be drawn between private law and business regulation.

The conventional contrast between private law and business regulation is also informed by an implicit contrast between, on the one hand, private law as an instrument that permits the promotion of private interests through contracts, and on the other, public law regulation as the embodiment of public interests. Here private law is separated from business regulation by describing the latter as having its source in public law, a formal distinction, which is then linked in an obscure way to a contrast between private and public interests. This view amounts to little more than a restatement of the unsupportable contention that private law lacks the normative complexity of including instrumental concerns for public policy. It also shares a rather naïve view of the content and operations of business regulation. Any close inspection of the practice of business regulation reveals that the regulatory standards applied are the product of bargaining between public officials and the regulated commercial interests, with little guarantee that the ill-defined public interest will prevail.[8]

A final misleading assumption that prises private law apart from business regulation focuses attention on the form of the regulation. As a matter of legal technique, private law differs substantially from those practices which lawyers normally describe as regulation of business and markets. Unlike modern forms of business regulation that employ specialized agencies and

---

[7] Daintith, T., 'Regulation', *International Encyclopedia of Comparative Law*, xvii (1995) ch. 10, 9.

[8] Stigler, G. 'The Economic Theory of Regulation', *Bell Journal of Economics and Management Science* 2 (1971) 1.

mandatory codes of practice, the law of contract forms part of the general law which is enforced by the ordinary courts. Unlike those modern forms of regulation, the law of contract lacks the power to promulgate detailed administrative rules and to police behaviour, but rather awaits a claim by a plaintiff and then applies the general rules of contract in order to settle the dispute. Lawyers therefore conventionally draw a contrast between, on the one hand, specialized mandatory regulation of particular business sectors such as utilities, and on the other hand, the general rules of private law that facilitate transactions and that form the backdrop against which instrumental regulation takes place.

But it is precisely this contrast in technique that interests me here. Instead of the contrast making comparison impossible, the differences in technique become the subject of inquiry. The question is whether private law viewed as a technique of business regulation has special advantages and disadvantages compared to other regulatory techniques. The major differences in the method of regulation pose a challenge for the analysis, but should not obstruct it altogether.

This examination of private law as an instrument of regulation has been attempted before. During the 1970s the work of consumer lawyers, particularly that of Leff and Cranston, presented a sustained attack on private law as an instrument of consumer protection on the ground that it was inefficient and ineffective.[9] For example, Leff observed in connection with private law regulation of 'unconscionable' clauses in standard form contracts:

What is the function of an unconscionability concept or clause? Briefly, it appears to be one technique for controlling the quality of a transaction when free market control is considered ineffective. It is one method for substituting government regulation for regulation by the parties.[10]

The conclusion drawn by these critics of private law in a consumer context was that public regulation was required for any effective consumer protection measures. The conclusion could be generalized: private law has negligible social effects.[11] This critique of private law was countered by a Chicago style of law and economics pioneered by Richard Posner,[12] which contended that in fact private law achieved a more efficient form and content of regulation than public regulation. It was also challenged

---

[9] Leff, A. A., 'Unconscionability and the Crowd—Consumers and the Common Law Tradition', *University of Pittsburgh Law Review* 31 (1970), 349; id., 'Injury, Ignorance and Spite—The Dynamics of Coercive Collection', *Yale Law Journal* 80 (1970), 1; Cranston, R., *Consumers and the Law*, 2nd edn. (London: Weidenfeld and Nicholson, 1984).

[10] Leff, A. A., 'Unconscionability and the Crowd', n. 9 above, 350.

[11] Epstein, R. 'The Social Consequences of Common Law Rules', *Harvard Law Review* 95 (1982) 1717.

[12] Posner, R., *Economic Analysis of Law*, 4th edn. (Boston: Little Brown, 1992).

implicitly in the work of legal historians such as Morton Horwitz, who contended that the distributive effects of private law rules were profound.[13] Here it will be argued that both positions were exaggerated. Private law possesses some considerable advantages as a regulatory instrument over public law regulation by virtue of its efficiency and reflexivity, but, in any particular instance such as consumer protection, the optimal regulatory solution in terms of efficiency and efficacy will usually be discovered in a combination of regulatory forms.

Reflexive Regulation

Our first task is to establish an analytical framework for a comparison between private law and other forms of economic and social regulation. A simple model describes three principal ingredients of any regulatory system. We shall need to refine this model further, but it suffices at this stage to permit a comparison between regulatory techniques. In addition, the simple model enables us to understand a key feature of private law regulation, which I shall describe as reflexive regulation.

The core element of the simple model consists of rules or standards that define the conduct required or proscribed. These rules may be created by a variety of processes ranging from parliamentary determination to self-regulation by the participants in the market. The second element consists of an agency charged with the task of monitoring compliance with the standards and to detect breaches. The final element consists of an enforcement mechanism, which is empowered to impose sanctions against deviance from the standards. Often a court will be charged with this responsibility for determining whether a sanction is deserved, but other agencies may be awarded similar powers such as the jurisdiction to withdraw a licence to trade.

This model of the three elements of regulation fits easily onto modern institutional arrangements for the regulation of particular business sectors such as utilities. In these contexts, a democratic legislature sets the general standards and policy goals, and then an administrative agency or regulator provides detailed guidance in the form of rules, performance targets, and prohibitions. Usually the same agency is charged with monitoring compliance with these standards, for which purpose it conducts investigations and inspections. Any breach of the standards revealed by monitoring can be challenged by the agency. Compliance with the rules can normally be achieved by education and negotiation with the perpetrator, using the

[13] Horwitz, M. *The Transformation of American Law, 1780–1860* (Cambridge, Mass.: Harvard University Press, 1977).

bargaining weapon of the threat of instituting legal proceedings for the imposition of a punishment. This threat usually provides a sufficient incentive to negotiate practices compatible with the regulation, provided that the threatened fine for breach of regulations is set at a sufficient level of gravity and is routinely enforced, for then rational economic choice will cause businesses to desist from that practice. Business regulation often employs the ordinary courts for the purpose of imposing these sanctions, but it is also possible to create specialized tribunals which possess the expertise for understanding technical information and the complexities of the regulatory framework of rules.

The same headings of standards, monitoring, and sanctions can also be employed as the tools for analysing the institutions and practices of the private law of contract.

Standards

The standards set by private law comprise both mandatory standards and 'self-regulation'.

Mandatory standards are usually discovered in the Civil Code or the equivalent precedents in the common law, supplemented in some instances by legislation. These mandatory standards include the rules governing the validity of contracts, compulsory terms, and the rules governing the procedures through which enforceable contracts can be made. The principal function of these mandatory standards is to set basic conditions for the valid exercise of the power of making legally enforceable contracts. These conditions contain both substantive and procedural elements. With respect to substance, mandatory rules place limits on the types of subject matter of transactions, as in the examples of the invalidity of contracts of slavery, the sale of endangered species, and the sale of parts of the human body. The procedural element contains some rules regarding formalities, such as a requirement of written documents or special oaths, together with rules governing unfair practices during negotiations such as the use of fraud and violence.

Most of the detailed standards governing a particular transaction are set by the parties themselves, as a type of 'self-regulation'. These standards are described as the terms of the contract. In some instances these standards will be the result of negotiation, but more typically they will be set by one of the parties and contained in a standard form contract. The use of the term 'self-regulation' may appear strange in this context. In studies of business regulation, the concept of self-regulation is used to describe the practice of members of an industrial sector agreeing to comply with a particular set of standards, such as a Code of Practice or a particular standard form contract. This self-regulation may then receive endorsement by a regulator as the appropriate standard, which can be enforced by the regulator. This type of self-regulation is a collective mechanism for the setting of standards across an industrial sector. In contrast, private law supports individualized negotiation of standards that apply solely to an isolated transaction between the parties. Apart from this particularized feature of the standards negotiated as terms of a contract, the practice endorsed by private law has the same quality of binding self-regulation as the collective model in business regulation.

As a supplement to self-regulation, private law often provides a model set of rules to govern a particular type of transaction such as a sale of goods. This model set of rules provides the detail of the regulation in the absence of express self-regulation. These rules serve the purpose of reducing transaction costs, because they can save the parties the expense of devising their own regulatory regime. Examples of such rules include the implied terms regarding quality and title in sales of goods, the articles of association for a limited company, and the allocation of the risk of negligent damage on to the supplier of a service. The supply of these 'default rules' by private law distinguishes this system of self-regulation from the practice of collective self-regulation by an industrial sector.

Monitoring

Monitoring compliance with these regulatory standards of private law is delegated to the parties themselves. They have the discretion whether or not to enforce the rules or to negotiate a revision of the standards. There is no policing and enforcement agency, but rather the parties to the contract have the discretionary power to enforce the standards through an ordinary court procedure. At most, private law may require one party to notify the other that it has committed a breach of the standards prior to taking steps to enforce the standards.

Sanctions

The sanctions available in the ordinary courts for breach of standards vary according to the type of rule which has been broken. For some of the mandatory rules, such as the requirements for the formation of a valid contract, the sanction is the declaration of the invalidity or unenforceability of the contract. In other words, the legal system declines to recognize the transaction as having created any binding commitments, so that the self-regulation contained in the agreement is ineffective. In respect of the other mandatory rules and self-regulation, the sanction is usually a liability rule that requires the payment of compensation to the injured party. In respect of the breach of some rules, such as the prohibition on fraud, both types of sanction will be available, so that the contract induced by fraud will be declared invalid and in addition the fraudulent party will be required to pay compensation for losses incurred under a liability rule. Unlike specialized tribunals often used by public regulatory systems for imposing sanctions, the private law system of regulation employs the ordinary courts. These courts possess considerable expertise in their knowledge of the rules of private law, but usually lack any specialized knowledge of the particular market which is being regulated.

Reflexivity

In scholarly examinations of regulatory techniques, a contrast is frequently drawn between 'command and control' styles of regulation and 'responsive' (or reflexive) regulation.[14] The former style of regulation approximates to criminal law. The rules are imposed by the regulator (or parliament); inspectors monitor compliance; and courts or specialist tribunals impose deterrent sanctions against breach of regulations. In contrast, responsive regulation seeks to achieve the collaboration and co-operation of those subject to regulation. In setting the standards, it favours the use of self-regulation, so that within a broad requirement fixed by legislation the participants can settle through negotiation the detailed rules to govern transactions. The advantages of seeking collaboration are expected to be that the participants will have better knowledge about the technical problems of regulating a particular market, that they will be in a better position than a regulator to tailor the rules precisely to this market sector, and that they will have a surer sense of what standards will prove practicable. With respect to monitoring and enforcement as well, responsive regulation promotes a strategy of securing co-operation from the participants in markets. Co-operation may be expected to achieve higher levels of compliance in general at the expense of strict enforcement of the rules in those few instances where monitoring detects a breach. Devices to secure co-operation are expected to reduce the costs of monitoring and enforcement, and to conserve the resources of the regulatory agency for the pursuit of particularly egregious cases. Although no single regulatory system probably corresponds to either of these paradigms, the policy

[14] Ayres, I., and Braithwaite, J., *Responsive Regulation: Transcending the Deregulation Debate* (New York: Oxford University Press, 1992). The term 'reflexive' is used within systems theory with a more technical meaning: Teubner, G., 'Substantive and Reflexive Elements in Modern Law', *Law and Society Review* 17 (1983), 239. I prefer the terminology of reflexivity, because it recognizes that the fundamental problem for regulation consists in the interaction between the operationally closed systems of legal regulation and contractual agreements. As a result, the theory of reflexive law is sensitive to the problem of the 'regulatory trilemma' discussed below. However, little turns on the distinction in terminology for my argument.

prescription is for an increase in the style of responsive regulation as a more efficient and effective way of achieving regulatory objectives.

The striking feature of private law as a system of regulation of markets is the extent to which it fits this model of responsive regulation. It achieves this approach to regulation both in the standard setting process and in the monitoring and enforcement mechanisms.

In the setting of standards, private law usually refrains from fixing in detail the obligations of the parties, but rather leaves these to be settled by negotiation and agreement through the express terms of the contract. There are some mandatory rules applicable to all legally enforceable transactions, and some further mandatory rules that govern particular types of transaction such as sales. Beyond these requirements, private law usually employs only default rules, which comprise regulations that apply only in the event of incomplete self-regulation by the parties. The principal advantage of this extensive power of self-regulation is that the parties can adjust the regulation to their particular business needs in the light of their information about the market. By use of this information, the regulation is better tailored to the particular circumstances of the transaction than general rules issued by a state agency, since the general rules will often prove under- or over-inclusive, and the agency may lack sufficient expertise to provide a practicable regulatory framework. The degree of self-regulation therefore permits adaptation to new kinds of business relations, which can be constructed by self-regulation. By subsequent agreement the parties can vary or modify the content of the rules as well, so that this regulatory technique provides considerable flexibility and potential for adaptation to changing circumstances. Another way of expressing this flexibility is to say that private law regulation confers alienable rights on the parties to the business transaction. This style of self-regulation is also likely to achieve an efficient level of regulation in the sense that the parties will only bargain for those rules which are vital to protect their interests. Due to the transaction costs involved, the parties to a contract will refrain from negotiation of every detail. The parties will rely in part on the assumption that the risk will not occur, and in part on the perception that the self-interest of the parties will lead them to further detailed negotiations in the event of the need to adjust the content of the rules in the light of changed circumstances.

The responsive quality of private law regulation is further enhanced by the devolution of the discretion to enforce the regulatory standards (both mandatory rules and self-regulation) to the parties themselves. This power can be used either to enforce the rules, or, more commonly, to provide the setting for the negotiation of an adaptation of the applicable standards in post-breach bargaining. The court only acts to enforce the agreement when one of the parties demands observance of the rules by the other. In this sense, the private law of contract uniquely among regulatory systems provides a species of self-enforced self-regulation. This constitutes an extreme example of responsive or reflexive regulation. It is this aspect of private law that is often used to draw the contrast with ordinary business regulation, for it is assumed that delegation of the discretion to enforce the standards to the parties themselves is inconsistent with regulation of markets in the public interest. But in fact the distinction cannot be drawn sharply, for economic and social regulation usually must rely upon reporting of breaches of standards by parties adversely affected such as consumers or workers. Without this supply of information, the regulatory agency usually lacks the capacity to monitor the effects of its regulation adequately. The decision to supply this information to the regulator is, however, a discretionary decision by the parties affected. The consumer may not bother to contact the relevant trading standards officer, and the worker may not wish to expose the unsafe working conditions for fear of reprisal or suffering economic loss. On closer inspection, therefore, the contrast between self-enforcement under the system of private law and public enforcement under business regulation is much less sharp than is commonly supposed.

The great strength of this private law regulation of contracts is plainly its responsive or reflexive quality. It devolves an extensive discretionary power of self-regulation to the parties. Subject to the requirement of a negotiated consensus, the rules produced will then be routinely enforced by the legal system through the agency of the ordinary courts. By conferring autonomy upon the parties to devise their own regulation, private law achieves considerable flexibility, which in turn achieves the advantage that the regulation permits experimentation with novel types of business transaction that might enhance productive efficiency. But the greatest potential advantage of reflexive law is the way in which it permits the subjects of regulation, in this instance the parties to a contract, to express their expectations of the relationship in their own language, so that their private regulation minimizes any distortion of communication that might be imposed by a regulatory framework.

This reflexive character of private law regulation works best when the parties negotiate the terms of the contract. The use of standard form contracts does not impede this process provided that the parties have the opportunity to negotiate variations from the model. When businesses impose standard form contracts upon consumers, however, the terms are likely to give expression solely to the expectations of the business. Adhesion contracts achieve only partial reflexivity. Consider, for instance, the following clause in a contract to supply a mobility aid to a consumer.

The company reserves the right at any time and without notice to vary or alter any of the design specification and packaging of equipment described in its sales literature.[15]

At first sight this term produces a one-sided contract, for the manufacturer appears to be entitled to substitute a different product for that promised under the contract. From the point of view of the manufacturer, however, in order to remain competitive, it must institute a process of continuous improvement in its products, and if this strategy is successful, the sales literature will inevitably lag behind. Since the variations in design are intended to benefit the consumer, the manufacturer does not foresee any unfairness arising. The contract term is reflexive because it represents the commercial situation accurately. The problem is that the clause is too broadly stated, for the consumer may be concerned that the new product design will be inferior or less suitable for her needs. The standard form failed to reflect these competing expectations, though no real conflict of interest was present. As a result of an intervention by the Unfair Contract Terms Unit of the Office of Fair Trading, a public regulatory agency in the UK, the clause was revised to achieve a fully reflexive character.

The company will use its best endeavours to supply the customer with the exact goods ordered but where this is not possible the company will notify the customer as soon as possible of any alterations to the design, specification and packaging of the equipment described in the sales literature and where the alteration is fundamental to the goods ordered the customer may terminate this contract and any deposit paid will be refunded.[16]

Partial reflexivity is a weakness of consumer adhesion contracts. The appropriate response is not a complete removal of the power to tailor contract terms to the precise market conditions of the transaction by the imposition of mandatory public standards on all sales contracts, but rather to renegotiate the clause so that it achieves a fully reflexive character that incorporates the expectations of consumers.

Private law thus addresses the problem of self-reference in its doctrinal discourse by seeking to maximize the opportunity for the parties to express the governing rules in their own terms. These terms of the contract still must be interpreted by the law, which reinserts the problem of self-reference, but the strategy of endorsing self-regulation tries to minimize the distortions of regulation. In other words, the private law of contract presents a distinctive approach to the problem of the 'regulatory trilemma'. As described by Teubner, this trilemma states that: either the legal rules may fail to have an impact on social practice, or they may subvert the

---

[15] Office of Fair Trading, *Unfair Contract Terms*, Issue No. 3, (London: March 1997), 72.
[16] Ibid.

desirable social practices by making impractical demands, or the law may lose the coherence of its own analytical framework by seeking to incorporate sociological and economic perspective in its reasoning.[17] Private law regulation minimizes the threat of the second limb of the trilemma by granting a wide scope for self-regulation. In so doing, however, it has to wrestle with the problem of retaining its own coherence (the third limb), and poses for itself major structural weaknesses in implementation (the first limb), to which we now turn our attention.

Standard Setting

It is well known that private law is a weak technique for implementing economic and social regulation. After all, it was the search for more effective regulatory techniques that led to the creation of modern styles of public regulation. The lesson was learned again in connection with measures of consumer protection, where it quickly became apparent that alterations in private law rights were insufficient to adjust market practices. Why exactly is private law an ineffective regulatory technique?

A simple answer points to the problem of access to justice: most people do not have the resources to vindicate their private law rights in the ordinary courts, so their rights remain unenforced and ignored. Although this answer contains an element of truth, in my view the problems for the efficacy and efficiency of private law as a regulatory technique run far deeper than this procedural obstacle of the expense of justice. The problem of access to justice is merely one aspect of the difficulties for private law in establishing an effective mechanism for the monitoring of compliance with standards and the enforcement of standards. Before we consider how that problem can be tackled by private law regulation, we need to consider the more complex problem of standard setting by private law. In the formulation of standards for guiding participants in markets, the private law of contract suffers from several structural weaknesses. These weaknesses include the difficulties of incorporating externalities in setting standards, the problems of setting standards with an adequate degree of specificity in order to provide effective guidance, and the lack of expertise in choosing between standards.

My interest in this discussion lies not so much in cataloguing this list of structural weaknesses in private law as a system of regulation, but rather to notice how private law is developing the capacity to remedy

[17] Teubner, G., 'After Legal Instrumentalism? Strategic Models of Post-Regulatory Law', in G. Teubner (ed.), *Dilemmas of Law in the Welfare State* (New York/Berlin: Walter de Gruyter, 1988) 299, 309.

these weaknesses. As private law undergoes the process of what was described in the previous chapter as productive disintegration, it evolves new capacities for redressing its own regulatory failures. It learns these capacities through its interaction or 'interference' with public regulation.

Externalities

A fundamental weakness of the private law regulation of contracts consists in the subordinate role played by third parties whose interests may be affected by the self-regulated transaction. Unlike a regulatory regime imposed by an agency that is required to consider the interests of all affected parties and other externalities, under the rules of private law the self-regulation represented by the contractual agreement denies the need to consider any spill-over effects. Private law lacks a clear mechanism for the interests to be voiced. Indeed, it is this weakness of the private law system of regulation which often provides the justification for much more interventionist styles of regulation that are designed to compel the parties to a transaction to internalize the costs of spill-over effects such as environmental damage and increased risks to the safety and health of other persons.

One of the important insights of advocates of consumer protection regulation is that the weakness of private law as a remedial system is the atomization of disputes. Private law treats each consumer's grievance about a product or a service as a separate event, isolated from similar complaints about the same product or service. Each decision about a breach of a consumer's contract handles the problem by examining the conflicting interests of the manufacturer or retailer and the individual consumer, without considering the impact of legal regulation upon other consumers in a similar position. In order to address this problem of incorporating third party effects into the formulation of regulation, advocates of consumer protection seek to 'reconceptualise little injustices as collective harms'.[18]

The blindness to externalities of the traditional private law of contract serves an important function in the constitution of markets. Markets can deliver an efficient satisfaction of personal preferences by empowering individuals to act solely in their self-interest when entering transactions. If participants in markets always had to consider the interests of others before entering transactions, then this remarkable mechanism for preference satisfaction would be impeded. When I purchase a washing machine, for instance, if I had to give priority to consideration of externalities such as the pollution of water by its effluent and the damage to the environment

---

[18] Nader, L., 'Disputing Without the Force of Law', *Yale Law Journal* 88 (1979) 998, 1021.

caused by its consumption of energy, then I might end up by deciding not to purchase the machine. If this behaviour became generalized, then the consideration of externalities would block the operation of the market for the satisfaction of preferences. By excluding the consideration of externalities from its regulation, the private law of contract therefore contributes to the construction of an efficient market.

Modern regulation of business insists, however, that we can have it both ways. We can preserve most of the efficiency of the market mechanism for the satisfaction of preferences, whilst at the same time using public regulation for the purpose of avoiding the worst undesirable externalities. This strategy proposes a division of functions between private law, which supports self-interested action, and public law, which compels participants in markets to take externalities into account. In the example of the washing machine, for instance, the private law of contract supplies the regulation for the enforcement of the contract to supply the machine, and some specific public regulation determines standards which reduce effluent discharge and energy consumption. But how accurate is this analysis of private law that claims it lacks the capacity to take into account externalities in its regulation of markets?

My contention is that private law is evolving the capacity to incorporate considerations of externalities in its formulation of regulatory standards and the application of its remedies. The courts usually resist any ostentatious embarkation upon the unruly horse of public policy and general regulation of contracts, preferring instead to confine the argument to the competing interests of the litigants and their original intentions. The interests of third parties can be taken into account, however, in the interstices of private law doctrine.[19] When determining the detailed content of these rules, the courts can take externalities into account by regarding the parties to the transaction as representative members of a group such as consumers, tenants, and employees. This strategy in private law reasoning has been learned from public law regulation, which characteristically sets the boundaries of its regulatory standards by reference to classes of participants in the market.

A court can devise rules designed to protect the interests of the group as a whole at the same time as disposing of the particular case. For example, by exercising the discretion to imply a default rule as an implied term in favour of a tenant in a particular contract for a lease, the court can in effect provide supplementary regulation of all leases of a similar type. We illustrated this process in the previous chapter in the discussion of the case

---

[19] These arguments are developed further in Collins, H., 'The Voice of the Community in Private Law', *European Law Journal* 3 (1997), 407–21.

Liverpool City Council v Irwin.[20] In that decision the court implied a term
into leases of apartments in high rise buildings that the landlord should
take reasonable care that the common areas of access should be kept in a
state of 'reasonable repair and useability'. We noted that the argument for
such a default rule based upon the joint intentions of the parties was weak
in the particular case, due to the evidence about the contrary intentions of
the landlord in devising the terms of the standard form contract. Nor could
the term be implied on the basis of 'business necessity', the legal test which
seeks to ascertain what would have been agreed explicitly by the parties in
the pursuit of their own self-interest. The self-interest of the landlords was
opposed to the proposed implied term, and it was not clear that any
particular tenant would prefer a higher rent combined with the implied
term to the actual agreement which was signed. The justification for the
default rule lies rather in a consideration of externalities, such as the
interests of tenants in high rise blocks in general, and the public interest
in improvements to the housing stock. In the private law reasoning in the
case, this concern for externalities is disguised by the adoption of a legal
test for the default rule of 'reasonable necessity'. This test looks simultaneously in both directions: it represents an endorsement of self-interested
action, whilst at the same time the qualifier of reasonableness permits the
court to insert a consideration of externalities into its reasoning process.
The test provides the private law of contract with the capacity to escape the
confines of supporting self-interested action exclusively.

The move from a consideration of the interests of the parties to the
litigation to the interests of a class which they represent has become a
standard technique in private law reasoning. This move then provides the
capacity for private law to incorporate a consideration of externalities into
its determining of standards and award of remedies. A typical example
learned from public regulation involves the classification of a litigant as a
'consumer'. The court sets a standard appropriate for all members of the
class, not simply the individual parties to the agreement. In *Smith v Eric S.
Bush,*[21] for instance, the issue concerned the power of surveyors to limit
their liability by contractual terms for negligent inspections of property
that failed to alert a potential purchaser to structural defects in a house.
The limitation of liability enabled the surveyors to provide a cheap service,
though it created a risk for purchasers that the property acquired would be
worth much less than the sale price. The Unfair Contract Terms Act 1977
empowered the court to determine the validity of the limitation clause on
the basis of whether it was 'fair and reasonable', which provided the
capacity for a consideration of externalities. In determining that the limita-

---

[20] [1977] AC 239, [1976] 2 All ER 39, HL.
[21] [1990] 1 AC 831, [1989] 2 All ER 514, HL.

tion clause was invalid, the court defines the class of contracts where such terms will be invalid by reference to the characteristics of the parties. On the one side is a professional with liability insurance, and on the other is a purchaser of modest means acquiring his or her most expensive asset. Lord Griffiths reveals the class of regulated contracts in his concluding remarks:

> It must, however, be remembered that this is a decision in respect of a dwelling house of modest value in which it is widely recognised by surveyors that purchasers are in fact relying on their care and skill. It will obviously be of general application in broadly similar circumstances. But I expressly reserve my position on valuations of quite different types of property for mortgage purposes, such as industrial property, large blocks of flats or very expensive houses.

This passage suggests that the private law regulation of terms purporting to limit the liability of surveyors will differentiate between classes of transactions according to the type of party receiving the advice and the property to be inspected. This differentiation by class is the hall-mark of the insertion of externalities into private law reasoning.

Once private law develops this capacity for considering externalities, then it poses many problems for assessment of the impact of regulation. One problem concerns the determination of the relevant class whose interests should guide the standards. The choice of class implicitly determines which externalities will be awarded priority in the legal reasoning. For example, the issue in *Co-operative Insurance Society Ltd v Argyll Stores (Holdings) Ltd*,[22] was whether the court should issue an injunction to require a supermarket in a shopping mall to remain open until other tenants could be found. The Court of Appeal issued the injunction in order to protect the interests of other tenants in the shopping mall, whose businesses would suffer if the supermarket closed for a period of time, and who had no possibility of redress for their reduction in income. But the House of Lords reversed this decision on the ground that the correct class to consider was the tenants of supermarkets, who would be reluctant to enter into these transactions, if they were compelled to keep their businesses open, even though they were trading at a loss. The selection of the relevant class determines the types of externalities that guide the legal reasoning. The Court of Appeal emphasized the interests of the business participants of the shopping mall as an interdependent business unit and sought to protect the operations of that market. The House of Lords, however, favoured the interests of supermarkets as a class of business entity, and therefore sought to protect the market for retail tenancies.

---

[22] [1996] Ch 286, [1996] 3 All ER 934, CA; revsd, [1997] 2 WLR 898, HL.

A more pervasive problem for the incorporation of externalities into private law reasoning consists in the lack of capacity of the ordinary courts to investigate the operation of markets and their inability to comprehend such information and transform it into practical regulation.[23] The court has no powers to conduct an empirical enquiry into the consequences of alternative rulings. This limitation is a consequence of the closure rules of private law reasoning. The court cannot know, for instance, whether an implied warranty of 'habitability' improves the position of tenants or has the undesirable effect of reducing the availability of rented accommodation, thereby driving up rents. Even if such information were available, it consists of statistical data, which has to be translated into the different discourse of private law regulation. Similarly, the court in *Smith v Eric S. Bush Ltd* could not be sure of the effects of its regulation of surveyors. Nevertheless, Lord Griffiths explained his assumption about the effect of regulation:

The result of denying a surveyor, in the circumstances of this case, the right to exclude liability will result in distributing the risk of his negligence among all house purchasers through an increase in his fees to cover insurance, rather than allowing the whole of the risk to fall on the one unfortunate purchaser.

This argument assumes that the increase in fees will not be so substantial as to discourage the use of surveyors by the class of purchasers receiving protection. Lord Griffiths dismisses this risk, even though there was some evidence before the court that the price charged for surveys with unlimited liability was greatly in excess of the standard fee. Reasoning in private law lacks the capacity to examine this evidence by the standards of an empirical and systematic economic analysis to discover where the new equilibrium will be set. Instead, private law regulation fixes the standard by reference to an economic hypothesis about the effects of regulation, and then awaits further information from subsequent litigation to determine the validity of the hypothesis. The source of information is, of course, haphazard and unreliable.

Some critics may conclude that private law should revert to its earlier stance of refusing to contemplate externalities in its reasoning. It should leave regulation for distributive purposes to agencies equipped with the capacity to carry out a systematic inquiry into the effects of regulation. But my view is that the evolution of this capacity of private law to consider externalities cannot now be reversed, and that its enhanced capacity for productive regulation of markets needs to be nurtured by the further loosening of its closure rules rather than aborted.

---

[23] Henderson, J. 'Judicial Review of Manufacturers Conscious Design Choices: The Limits of Adjudication', *Columbia Law Review* 73 (1973), 1531.

Public Goods

A guiding assumption of private law regulation provides that the objective of state sanctions should be to redress harm to an individual. Without some identifiable loss to a particular individual, then no damages may be awarded. This requirement may not apply to the remedy of declaring the invalidity of the transaction, though often evidence of harm is needed to provide support for allegations of breach of equitable standards such as undue influence. This emphasis upon harm to the individual no doubt fits closely into a liberal political philosophy where the principal role of the state is to deter actions which cause harm to the interests of others.

As a limitation upon the scope for regulation, however, this emphasis upon the need for harm precludes private law from tackling certain kinds of sharp practice in dealings.[24] Consider, for instance, a sign in a shop window proclaiming a 'sale' of goods. This implies reductions of price, and is plainly designed to draw customers into the shop. Once inside, they may agree to purchase 'bargains' and feel pleased with their purchases, though in fact they have paid the normal market price. Where is the harm in such an example? The shopper has acquired desired goods at the ordinary market price; this cannot be described as harm. If there is harm to anyone, it is the rival traders who may have lost sales as a result of the misleading advertising, but as third parties these competitors have no redress either.[25] Another example of the inability of private law to detect harm concerns consumer credit transactions. Where an individual is persuaded to enter a loan arrangement that in the long run he or she has no realistic prospect of being able to repay, private law can detect no harm unless the rate of interest is 'extortionate'. The loan represents an ordinary market transaction agreed under competitive conditions. The harm of driving the individual and dependants into bankruptcy, homelessness, and social exclusion cannot be recognized by private law regulation. Private law regulation is therefore disabled from regulating many sharp practices in the market, even though the prevalence of such practices either undermines its competitiveness or leads to social disintegration.

Many private law rules do in fact protect the institutional arrangements of the market and its competitive properties. Rules against fraud and misrepresentation, for instance, serve to deter lying and the supply of misleading information, practices which would undermine the competitiveness of the market and reduce trust. But these rules evolve in private law because the court can identify a particular individual who has suffered economic loss. What private law cannot achieve within its discourse is the

---

[24] Rice, D. A., 'Remedies, Enforcement Procedures and the Duality of Consumer Transaction Problems', *Boston University Law Review* 48 (1968) 559.
[25] Trebilcock, M. J., n. 5 above.

protection of abstract or collective interests unless those public goods coincide with private harms.

Insufficient Particularity

Another systematic problem for the efficacy and efficiency of private law regulation is caused by its traditional commitment to generality in respect of both procedure and substance. With respect to the procedural aspect, private law tends to apply uniform procedural and evidential rules to govern litigation across the whole range of contractual disputes. These rules were primarily devised in order to handle the most complex commercial disputes, since these cases occupied most of the business of the private law courts. These rules are then applied equally to the simple claim brought by a consumer for compensation for an unsatisfactory product. In the latter context, the elaborate rules governing the procedural contest, such as the disclosure of evidence requirements, seem to impose costs out of all proportion to the sum of compensation in dispute.

This problem of inefficiency can be partially solved by the differentiation of the ordinary courts into specialized branches, such as a commercial court, a small claims court, or courts with special expertise in particular types of transaction such as employment and landlord and tenant. Yet the commitment to generality in private law tends to undermine this type of differentiation. The general principles of civil procedure will be imposed in all these courts in the absence of specific statutory derogation, and a failure to apply these general rules will result in a successful appeal against the decision of an inferior tribunal. As a consequence, the cheaper and more efficient tribunals are frequently criticized for the unnecessary legal formality and the expense of their procedures.

This assault on the legalism of inferior tribunals seems to me to present an unattractive sweeping criticism. Part of the purpose of these rules of procedure is to ensure that both parties have a fair opportunity to state their arguments, and any weakening of these elements would deprive adjudication of one of its principal sources of legitimacy. Where the concern about legalism may represent a fair criticism of procedural rules is when these rules prevent tribunals from acquiring information about the particular transaction and the context in which it took place. But I doubt whether the general procedural rules have this effect to any great extent, for there are many ways around the artificial restrictions on the presentation of evidence.

With respect to the substantive aspects of private law, the tendency towards generality in rules again presents problems for the efficacy of regulation. The desirable level of particularity of any regulatory regime of rules always raises problems of balancing such concerns as transparency in formulation, their accessibility in the sense that the rules can easily be self-applied, and their congruence with policy objectives.[26] The clever solution to this problem produced by the private law of contract lies in the combination of general rules with extensive, particularistic self-regulation through agreement on the terms of the contract. Yet this strategy does not remove the difficulty for regulatory efficacy. In so far as regulatory objectives can only be achieved through general rules rather than self-regulation, then the commitment to generality in private law obstructs sufficient particularity in regulation.

We noticed this problem in the previous chapter in connection with exclusion clauses in standard form contracts. That problem of generality was that in commercial contexts exclusion clauses often represent an efficient exercise in self-regulation for the allocation of risk, but in consumer standard form contracts the practice of inserting exclusion clauses in the small print was interpreted rather as a sign of market failure. Private law reasoning was unable to produce legal reasoning that differentiated between these classes of contracts for the purpose of regulatory intervention. The general rule that favoured freedom of contract was applied to commercial transactions and standard form consumer contracts alike.

It is true that over a long period of time legal doctrine has developed specialized regulation for certain types of recurrent and familiar contracts such as the sale of goods. These nominate contracts often have special regulation, such as a standard set of default rules or implied terms or a particular style of remedy. But the list of nominate contracts remains short compared to the potential variety of business transactions. We therefore discover a wide range of modern commercial relationships such as franchises where no particularized regulation has yet developed. Another effect is that legal reasoning often seeks to classify these modern business relations within traditional categories in an inappropriate way, since the novel arrangements are hybrids and adaptations to new commercial objectives.

Modern legislation often introduces a decisive rupture with the traditional generality of the private law of contract by regulating for the discrete handling of particular types of contracts or contracts with parties with particular characteristics. In this vein, for instance, extensive regulation of the contract of employment distances it from traditional private law regulation. Similarly, consumer protection legislation introduces separate mandatory rules for consumer contracts. This legislation may be seen as responding to a regulatory failure of private law to differentiate its rules in

[26] Diver, C. S., 'The Optimal Precision of Administrative Rules', *Yale Law Journal* 93 (1983), 65; Baldwin, R., *Rules and Government* (Oxford: Clarendon Press, 1995) 175–85.

response to new policy objectives. Its effect is to narrow the sphere of transactions regulated principally by the private law of contract, and to subject the selected category to a heavily modified private law regime.

Modern private law responds to these challenges to its generality by developing the capacity to embrace greater differentiation in its regulation. This is part of the phenomenon we described as the productive disintegration of private law. We can now suggest that one reason why greater differentiation within private law rules governing contracts can be productive is that it facilitates more efficacious regulation of particular types of contract.

Although greater differentiation in the rules of private law permits more efficacious regulation of contracts, private law cannot proceed far down this road without presenting a crisis of legitimacy. Greater particularization of the rules renders the task of articulating the coherence of the legal doctrine much more formidable. If the rules differ according to the category of contract, then private law requires principles which can provide a rational explanation of the categorization and the reasons for differential regulation. The search for a coherent rationalization of private law doctrine also undermines the stability of rules that are presented as exceptions. We observed this problem before in connection with the principle of fairness in contracts. Once regulation permits the assessment of the fairness of terms in contracts in numerous particular instances such as consumer contracts, employment, and tenancies, then it becomes difficult to assert that the general principle of private law declines to assess the fairness of contracts. The question constantly arises whether some other category of contracts should also be subjected to a requirement of fairness. Yet if the private law principle is not a refusal to judge fairness, it is hard to say what it is. A particularistic, unprincipled private law regulation then can be attacked as lacking its basis of legitimacy in the rational articulation of fundamental principles of human association, that is the ideal of integrity in law. Private law regulation therefore puts up a stubborn resistance to the demand for increasing differentiation of its rules in order to preserve its own legitimacy. In other words, private law suppresses its potential regulatory efficacy in order to avoid the problem of the third aspect of the 'regulatory trilemma'.

This problem of insufficient specificity for the purposes of regulatory efficacy can be tackled most fruitfully by the development of default rules to supplement self-regulation. These supplementary rules or implied terms avoid the problem of generality by their presentation as default rules for a particular agreement. Yet at the same time, the rules can be developed to apply to a whole class of contracts, as we have noted, for instance, in the context of tenancies in high rise apartment buildings.

As supplementary rules, however, this regulation runs the risk of being ineffective due to the systematic use of express contractual exclusions in standard form contracts. The solution at this point for private law is to develop the idea that some supplementary rules cannot be waived at all, or cannot be excluded without express and conscious agreement. The former idea of compulsory terms encounters a different problem of doctrinal integrity, namely that default regulation should in principle always give way to express self-regulation. In England, such compulsory terms have required legislative intervention so far in order to provide a justification for their exceptional treatment. In the United States, some default rules, such as the implied warranty of habitability in residential leases, have been declared to be non-waivable on the ground of public policy, namely the public interest in health and safety in housing.[27] A second method of placing procedural obstacles in the way of exclusion of default rules can be developed by private law without significant revision of doctrine. The requirement of taking reasonable steps to notify the other party of any 'unusual and onerous' terms in a standard form contract has been interpreted as part of the ordinary doctrinal requirements for establishing the content of the terms of a contract.[28] In the American Restatement of Contracts 2d, the rule is presented as a method for determining the applicability of terms contained in a standard form document to the content of the agreement.[29] The stronger the procedural requirement, that is, the more steps required before reasonable notification has been given, the harder it will be to exclude the default regulation.

Guidance

One objection to regarding private law as a system of regulation is provoked by the comparative absence of explicit policy justifications. In public regulation, the legislation usually states its objectives either as a preamble or as a direction to a regulatory agency. But in private law doctrines, the formulation of principles describes a deontic order rather than a set of instrumental goals. Of course, one can attribute to particular private law rules a policy objective and then consider their effectiveness in achieving that objective. But the objection can always be made that this is not the correct policy objective to attribute to the rule, or indeed that to

---

[27] *Fair v Negley*, 257 Pa. Super 478, 390 A. 2d 240 (1978).

[28] *Interfoto Picture Library Ltd v Stiletto Visual Programmes Ltd* [1989] QB 433, [1988] 1 All ER 348, CA; in the USA, the term will not be binding if not brought to the buyer's attention and he was not made understandingly aware of it: *Henningsen v Bloomfield Motors, Inc,* 32 N.J. 358, 161 A. 2d 69 (1960).

[29] s. 211(3) 'Where the other party has reason to believe that the party manifesting such assent would not do so if he knew that the writing contained a particular term, the term is not part of the agreement.'

attribute a policy objective would be to misconceive the discourse of private law.

This vagueness and ambiguity with respect to policy objectives is both a strength and a weakness of private law regulation. The strength comes from the potential this leaves for each generation to reinterpret the rules of private law in accordance with contemporary policy objectives. The weakness for private law is that it persistently evades criticism about its efficiency and efficacy as a regulatory system over markets.

The strength which private law draws from the indeterminacy of its policy objectives can be illustrated by showing how its abstract concepts can be manipulated in order to favour rival policy objectives. The law of contract usually contains a general test for the legal enforceability of contracts, such as the requirement of 'consideration' in the common law and 'causa' in systems based closely on Roman law. This requirement is stated in sufficiently abstract terms that in its interpretation it can embrace either policies which favour an unrestricted free market or policies which favour controls over the fairness or justice of transactions. In the case of the common law doctrine of consideration, it requires that the parties should have agreed to an exchange, so that each party is expected to give up something of value in return for the reciprocal undertaking. The ambiguity here lies in whether the law regards what is being given up as something of value 'in the eyes of the law'. A policy that favours freedom of contract can simply assume that whatever has been requested amounts to something of value for these purposes, so that even if the request is for handing over a trivial item such as a peppercorn, this satisfies the requirement of consideration. But the identical legal principle can also justify controls over unfairness, as where the court may declare that a promise to perform a pre-existing legal duty does not amount to any detriment at all, and that therefore the requirement of consideration has not been satisfied. The same legal requirement can therefore be used for rather different instrumental policy objectives. This feature of the abstract and general rules of private law enables them to persist over long periods of time without ostensible change even though in their interpretation and application the policy objectives may fluctuate.[30] Private law regulation in the form of abstract rules and principles has the strength that it does not require reformulation in order to adjust to shifts in policy with respect to regulation of markets.

At the same time, of course, this regulatory style creates the weaknesses that it renders it more difficult to determine in advance the requirements of the legal regulation, and that it prevents challenges to the law based on

---

[30] Renner, K., *The Institutions of Private Law and their Social Functions*, O. Kahn-Freund (ed.) (London: Routledge, 1949).

criticism of the lack of effectiveness of the regulation. No-one can be sure in advance whether or not a court might decide to use the doctrine of consideration to police the unfairness of a transaction. If it fails to do so, the decision cannot be criticized on this ground, for the legal regulation has never explicitly claimed that its purpose includes the regulation of fairness.

Furthermore, the self-perception of private law adjudication that it concerns the resolution of a dispute rather than the regulation of a market by setting a standard tends to result in the production of standards which cannot guide market behaviour. As soon as private law departs from its abstract principle in order to determine the outcome of a particular case, the standard set by adjudication will often be tied closely to the facts of a particular transaction, so that it is difficult to generalize its application to other contracts. 'The implications for systematic policy development are serious: the most we can expect from the common law courts is sporadic, *ex post, ad hocery.*'[31]

This emphasis upon dispute resolution in individual cases also leads to the incapacity of private law to publicize its standards. The detailed regulatory standards produced by private law can only be gleaned from the reports of courts' decisions, which are seldom complete. These decisions are then only disseminated by uncoordinated private publicity in the form of books and articles about the law. Consider, for instance, the problem of discovering the appropriate standard of quality for a car. The general law informs the parties to the transaction that the car must be of 'satisfactory quality', but any further detail is almost impossible to obtain despite the fact that the purchase of a car almost certainly produces the major source of litigation in the area of consumer claims for product quality.[32] The decisions of the courts in the UK that deal with these issues are not published unless the case goes to appeal, and even then it requires the expensive advice of an expert lawyer to gather any useful guide about the requirements of the standard. Effective standard setting plainly requires the dissemination of information about the requirements, for otherwise exact compliance tends to be fortuitous. But the private law system can rarely achieve adequate dissemination of its standards to the regulated industry or market.

If we take the view that the merits of any form of regulation must always depend upon its relative success in achieving policy goals compared to other techniques of regulation, the vagueness of the policy objectives of private law regulation tends to defeat any intelligible assessment of the

---

[31] Belobaba, E. P., 'The Resolution of Common Law Contract Doctrinal Problems Through Legislative and Administrative Intervention', in B. J. Reiter and J. Swan (eds.), *Studies in Contract Law* (Toronto: Butterworths, 1980) 423, 444.

[32] For discussion of this example, see Ramsay, I., *Consumer Protection: Text and Materials* (London: Weidenfeld and Nicholson, 1989) 430–8.

efficacy of regulation. The secrecy of private law in respect of its detailed standards also obstructs such an assessment and places substantial obstacles in the way of compliance and enforcement. Public regulatory techniques usually have the relative advantage that their policies are usually articulated and their detailed standards publicized, so that we can assess their merits as interventions and their success in achieving compliance.

Private law can develop this capacity for setting standards that can guide participants in markets when it adopts a particular pattern of reasoning. It has to forgo the flexibility of abstract principle in favour of a more explicit rationalization of the policy behind the law. The policy statement combined with general principle can then produce more determinate guidance, which can be generalized across a series of transactions. We saw an example of this style of reasoning in *Smith v Eric S. Bush*,[33] the case concerned with the negligent valuation of a house by a surveyor. By stating the policy objective behind the creation of liability in negligence and the inability to exclude such liability in terms of consumer protection for major investments combined with loss distribution through the system of liability insurance, the court was able to provide an effective regulatory standard. For the vast majority of ordinary house purchases, the court makes it clear that surveyors must be subject to a standard of reasonable care and must also take out liability insurance against costs of breach of that standard. The clarity of the regulatory standard supplied by this private law reasoning depends upon the explicit articulation of the policy objectives of the rule imposed by the decision.

Expertise

The ordinary courts are the crucial agency in setting private law standards. In the Common Law jurisdictions the courts created private law through the system of precedent. In Civil Law systems, the ordinary courts provide the concrete regulation derived from the general, abstract provisions of the Civil Codes. The courts possess unrivalled expertise in the details of private law. At the same time, they lack all the necessary dimensions of expertise and information for the task of setting standards for regulating markets. We have already encountered some of these problems. Private law seeks to regulate all markets, which presents enormous difficulties in acquiring information about the operation of those markets and how contracts function within them. Since any business relation, from a trivial consumer purchase to a complex long-term international business transaction, falls within this jurisdiction, the judges will be unlikely to understand the

---

[33] [1990] 1 AC 831, [1989] 2 All ER 514, HL.

particular context of the self-regulation across the whole range of disputes brought before the court. To compound the problem, the principal source of information available to a court will come from litigation proceedings, which provide a distorted and unrepresentative sample of market practice because of the incidence of the taste for litigation.[34] Compared to a regulatory agency charged with the task of regulating a particular market, with the power to acquire systematic information about the operation of that market, private law courts are plainly disabled in their formulation of satisfactory standards.

Despite this lack of expertise, the Chicago school of law and economics tends to assert that private law regulation of business transactions is superior in terms of economic efficiency and sometimes even economic policy implementation to other forms of regulation.[35] The first step in this argument insists that many types of regulation of business tend to impair economic efficiency, since the regulation, by restricting market activity, reduces the opportunities for wealth-enhancing transactions. The second step demonstrates that many regulatory interventions have the potential to back-fire by actually harming the group which they are designed to protect.[36] An example of this problem might be the control of interest rates in consumer credit, which discourages lenders from making loans to high-risk groups such as the poor, with the ultimate effect of preventing the poor from obtaining credit at all. A third step in the argument points to the risk that regulatory intervention will be distorted away from its ostensible objectives by the political process, even creating the risk that the large businesses that are supposed to be controlled by the regulation may achieve the position of dictating the content of the rules. Although sometimes exaggerated, these steps in the argument do provide grounds for being suspicious of business regulation. It is the final step in the argument, however, which interests us most here. This conclusion asserts that the private law of contract usually provides the regulation best designed to promote efficiency, and that minor adjustments of private law rights and obligations will usually prove the superior regulatory strategy for setting standards.

This faith in the expertise of the ordinary courts to devise satisfactory regulation of business transactions seems to depend upon a perception that for the most part the courts maximize self-regulation or freedom of contract. Private law therefore avoids the objection to regulation in the first step of the argument by restricting opportunities for wealth-enhancing transactions in only a few rare instances. Minimizing mandatory regulation of business transactions is certainly a relatively straightforward task for

---

[34] See below Ch. 14.   [35] Posner, R., n. 12 above.
[36] This argument is examined critically in Ch. 11 below.

ordinary courts, so it becomes plausible to suppose that they can carry it out as well as most regulatory agencies. Private law also meets the second step in the argument by rarely seeking to pursue an ostensible policy of protecting particular groups in markets or redistributing wealth. Its regulation therefore cannot back-fire, since it tends to support wealth maximization as the predominant policy objective. Indeed, where private law attempts to deviate from this path of freedom of contract, as for example in the control over exclusion clauses in sales to consumers, the Chicago law and economics school tends to criticize this private law regulation on precisely the same grounds that it tends both to impair efficiency in the sense of wealth-maximization and to back-fire by harming consumers. The final virtue of private law regulation from this perspective is that the ordinary courts are relatively immune from turbulent political pressures, so that powerful interest groups cannot obtain advantageous concessions. This perception of the autonomy of court processes from political influence is certainly unfounded, for pressure groups such as insurance companies plainly use litigation as a technique to obtain favourable regulation. Nevertheless, it is true that the ordinary courts are relatively immune from political pressures compared to the legislature and regulatory agencies.

The major objection to this presentation of the virtues of private law regulation is simply that the priority which it awards to wealth-maximization as a goal for regulation may not accord with the preferred policy objectives of the regulation of markets. As soon as one departs from wealth-maximization as the sole objective by introducing some other task for regulation such as consumer protection, then the problem of the lack of expertise of the ordinary courts becomes a structural weakness of private law regulation.

A second objection to the arguments of the Chicago school questions whether the task of determining the rules which maximize wealth through transactions is in fact so simple. As soon as it is observed that free markets are not always competitive, but contain various market failures such as those caused by lack of information and unreliable information, the task of regulation in order to reduce or eliminate market imperfections becomes complex. For example, how far should private law control misleading information? We might argue on the one hand that only false information as opposed to misleading information should lead to the sanction of invalidity in private law, since only when the information is false can we be sure that it distorted the market. On the other hand, we may consider that misleading information, such as advertising which suggests that products are being sold at a bargain price rather than their normal market price, does distort markets by discouraging price comparisons, so that it should provoke private law sanctions. The determination of where to fix the limits of regulation in order to remedy market failures cannot be reached by some simple private law reasoning process, but requires an investigation of the consequences of market distortions and the likely beneficial effects of regulation. In drawing such fine lines at the outer limits of regulation, even when the policy objective is merely one of wealth enhancement proves to be a task which goes beyond the expertise of ordinary courts.

This lack of expertise in the ordinary courts in regulating markets is the inevitable corollary of the self-referential quality of private law reasoning. As long as a sharp distinction is drawn between, on the one hand, legal reasoning, and, on the other, social and economic enquiry, then the courts will lack the capacity to integrate information about the effects of regulation into their reasoning process. The path of reducing the self-referential quality of legal reasoning by drawing economic and statistical information into the process of adjudication might relieve this problem, but only at the price of subverting the integrity of legal doctrine itself. This tension goes to the heart of the regulatory trilemma. As the courts venture towards the introduction and assessment of social and economic information in their reasoning processes, this move towards the 'materialization' of law comes under criticism for creating a problem of legitimacy for the authority of the courts.[37]

The process of regulation through adjudication also suffers from an acute shortage of information. An efficacious regulatory system requires a 'feedback' loop, through which it can observe the effects of its regulation and then respond through re-regulation to shortfalls in compliance. The ordinary courts possess only an unreliable feedback mechanism. This mechanism consists of the litigated cases coming before the courts. The courts can observe the effects of their private law regulation in cases where the parties seek to contest the content of the regulation. In the example of the sale of cars, the courts can observe the consequences of their regulation that requires new cars to be free from any defects, and then adjust that standard in the light of any difficulties which it presents to car dealers. The defect of this feedback mechanism is that it provides highly selective information. Objections to the effects of private law regulation will only be voiced by those participants in markets who have a taste for litigation. In the context of consumer transactions, for instance, the courts are only likely to receive objections from businesses, for consumers will normally lack the resources and incentive to raise a point of law, that is, to challenge the existing regulation. This feedback mechanism is therefore likely to provide the

---

[37] The debate about the crisis of legitimacy provoked by the 'materialization' of private law has been pre-eminent in Germany: Weber, M., *Economy and Society* (G. Roth and C. Wittich eds.), (Berkeley: University of California Press, 1978), ii, ch. 8; Habermas, J., *Between Facts and Norms* (Cambridge: Cambridge University Press, 1996) ch. 9; Teubner, G. (ed.), *Dilemmas*, n. 17 above.

courts with a distorted source of information about the effects of regulation. As a consequence, even when the courts introduce into the legal
reasoning a more contextual appreciation of the regulatory context, they
are starved of reliable information about that context.

One conclusion that might be drawn from this problem of lack of
expertise is that the courts should simply abandon any attempt to provide
instrumental regulation through private law. Hayek even argues that the
operations of the market are always too complex and unknown for regulation to become a precise science regardless of the expertise of the agency.[38]
At best, regulatory agencies engage in a practice of trial and error, in which
the regulation is constantly altered as it is observed to be ineffective or
counter-productive with respect to its policy objectives. Hayek then
contends that this constant process of change is in itself damaging to the
economy, for it discourages long-term planning and investment in private
transactions. It also creates the opportunity for the political process leading to regulation to be abused either by distortions by interest groups or
simply the arbitrary use of power. He concludes that regulation of business
should be discouraged because it threatens the rule of law, by which he
means a respect for the freedom of the individual by controlling state
power. Private law regulation of the economy, provided that it is stable,
general, and not subject to political pressures, is the only desirable form of
regulation on this view. Since no one has the requisite expertise to regulate
business effectively, the second-best solution is to prefer simple, stable
regulation of the kind provided by private law.

My disagreement with this view returns us to the point of commencement of this chapter. Although private law often presents itself as a type of
pre-political support for private ordering without regulatory objectives, my
contention has been that in the formulation of standards private law has
always responded to instrumental concerns. The general rules of private
law therefore contain implicit policy objectives that can be compared to the
instrumental goals of business regulation. The question we have been
considering here is whether the courts possess the expertise and information to devise general, stable regulations, which provide adequate support
for a flourishing market economy. What is so worrying about the private
law system is that it lacks the mechanisms to acquire information about the
effects of regulation and the reasoning processes needed to incorporate this
information within its discourses. Hayek is right to insist that the regulation of markets is an extremely complex task which stretches the capacity
of human institutions to the limits. It is then astonishing, however, that he
should seek to vest this task in the ordinary courts exclusively, when this

---

[38] Hayek, F., *The Constitution of Liberty* (London: Routledge, 1960).

institution has such deep flaws in its capacity to acquire and process information about its environment.

Yet private law can generate tools for the acquisition of expertise. The relevant information can be acquired in a more systematic way by permitting the parties to the litigation to present statistical information and other forms of expert evidence. This right to supply information could also be extended to interested pressure groups as 'amicus curiae', who might be permitted to submit written briefs to the court that address the problem of setting an effective standard. These practices of using a 'Brandeis brief' containing statistical information and admitting information from pressure groups have become widespread in the US in the context of litigation about constitutional rights and public law issues. My argument is that they should also be extended systematically to private law litigation in order to grant the ordinary courts the capacity to overcome their lack of expertise in setting standards.

Monitoring and Enforcement

The private law system leaves monitoring and enforcement of the self-regulation and the mandatory regulatory standards to the parties to the transaction. This mechanism fits into the strategy of maximizing the flexibility or reflexivity of the regulation by conceiving of the rules as conferring alienable rights. The question which concerns us here is whether by relying on the use of resources by participants in the market rather than supplying public support, the private law system provides inadequate resources for monitoring and enforcement of standards. The absence of public financial resources to support regulatory compliance tends to limit the ability to enforce the rules to those with considerable wealth. The costs of litigation will often deter the enforcement of standards where the damage caused by the violation imposes only a minor cost on the plaintiff. When consumers experience minor problems with goods or services, for instance, it is most unlikely that they will turn to private law mechanisms of enforcement, even to the extent of contacting a lawyer. They will rather try to deal with the problem by making a complaint and seeking redress by informal means.[39] But more litigation about private law rights is not necessarily an advantage, for it imposes costs on the participants in markets. How can we describe and achieve an optimum level of monitoring and enforcement?

---

[39] National Consumer Council, *Seeking Civil Justice — A Survey of People's Needs and Experiences* (London: National Consumer Council, 1995).

Efficient Level of Enforcement

The appropriate level of enforcement may be described by a cost and benefit analysis. The costs of enforcement should be weighed against the benefits achieved by increasing the levels of regulatory compliance. The problem of the lack of resources of private litigants can then be described as a failure to achieve an optimum level of compliance due to insufficient enforcement proceedings. In the case of consumer contracts, this argument suggests that the private law enforcement procedure of a law suit to claim compensation for shoddy goods and services fails to achieve an optimum level of compliance, because in individual cases the costs of litigation exceed the benefits to be achieved, even though at an aggregate level the benefits of compliance with the regulatory standard of satisfactory goods exceed the total cost of litigation required in order to provide a sufficient degree of incentive for manufacturers and retailers to comply with the standard. This analysis therefore describes a collective action problem at the heart of the regulation of consumer contracts by private law.

To resolve this problem for private law regulation, a public or a collective group (such as a consumer organization) is required in order to pool resources. Such a consumer organization with the power to initiate litigation can achieve an optimum level of enforcement by commencing a sufficient number of test cases to provide the correct incentives for regulatory compliance. Consumer groups enjoy such powers in some jurisdictions of the Member States of the European Union, such as Germany and Italy. The power seems likely to be extended throughout the Community in order to harmonize the levels of regulatory compliance with European Directives aimed at consumer protection.[40]

We must be careful, however, not to make the mistake of assuming that the lack of resources for the enforcement of private law regulation necessarily leads to a failure to achieve an optimum level of enforcement. This mistake occurs when we forget that the major incentives for regulatory compliance do not depend upon legal sanctions, but rather upon other kinds of non-legal sanctions such as damage to the business reputation of a trader. The enforcement mechanism provided by the law is usually a minor

---

[40] Commission Green Paper, 'Access of consumers to justice and the settlement of consumer disputes in the single market', Com (93) 576, concerning the proposed Directive on Injunctions for the Protection of Consumers' Interests, OJ C389, 22.12.97, p. 51. Under the proposed Directive, which is expected to be adopted by the end of 1998, Member States will be able to designate as 'qualified entities' one or more independent public consumer bodies as well as private consumer bodies which will be able to seek injunctions in the courts of other Member States to stop traders contravening consumer rights under nine EU consumer policy Directives, including that on unfair terms. Department Of Trade and Industry, *Widening the Scope for Action under the Unfair Contract Terms Regulations: A Consultation Paper* (London: DTI, January 1998). The Lord Chancellor has also announced plans to consider the possibility of allowing representative actions more widely throughout public and private law.

consideration in the incentives for regulatory compliance. Retailers of goods, for instance, will generally comply with the standard of providing goods of satisfactory quality for the sake of establishing a good business reputation so that consumers return to the shop. Thus the question of the optimum level of resources to be spent on the enforcement mechanism must be assessed in the light of information regarding actual levels of compliance with standards in the absence of legal enforcement. When compliance appears to fall below an optimum level, and the enforcement mechanism appears to provide weak additional incentives, then we need to address the problem of the lack of resources inherent in the design of the private law self-enforcement mechanism.

Detection

The resources provided for an enforcement mechanism also must be adjusted in order to cope with the difficulty of proving that a violation of a regulatory standard has occurred.[41] In many instances of breach of contractual regulation, the failure to comply may be easy to establish. If the goods are damaged or do not function properly, then this defect can be established by casual observation. Nevertheless, problems of proof do occur frequently in contractual contexts. When the issue is compliance with a negligence standard, that is, whether the provider of services took reasonable care, the matter may only be resolved after lengthy consideration of past conduct which is not directly observable. Similarly, when the dispute concerns the loyalty of an agent, the evidence of corruption or failure to put the best interests of the principal first may be ambiguous.

One solution to this problem of detection is to provide public resources to supplement private litigants. Some regulatory standards are simultaneously criminal offences, as in the case of fraud and deceptive trade practices, so that the state's resources are used to detect breaches of standards and to enforce compliance. But criminal enforcement mechanisms only apply to a small segment of those contractual disputes where the breach of standards is hard to detect and to prove.

Another solution to the problem of detection is to transfer the burden of proving compliance onto the alleged violator. This reversal of the burden of proof is common in public regulation, where the business can defend itself against a criminal prosecution by arguing that the default occurred despite the exercise of due diligence. The trader has to reveal its operational and management methods in order to prove this defence of due diligence, which in turn creates the opportunity for a court to discern

---

[41] Landes, W. M., and Posner, R. A., 'The Private Enforcement of Law', *Journal of Legal Studies* 4 (1975) 1.

failure to comply with the regulatory standard. Private law regulation has the capacity to achieve similar methods of detection, though it is hampered by a principle that requires those who allege fault to produce the initial evidence. But if the courts regard proof of an unsatisfactory product or an inadequate service as sufficient evidence of breach of the regulatory standard, then the legal process can imitate public regulation by in effect requiring the trader to demonstrate the absence of fault. In a case such as *Smith v Eric S. Bush*, for instance, once the purchaser has demonstrated that the survey and valuation was plainly wrong, then the court can switch the burden of proof onto the surveyor to demonstrate that the defects in the property were not discoverable even on careful inspection. The capacity of private law to detect failures of regulatory compliance turns crucially on such techniques for the reversal of the burden of proof.

Poverty of Sanctions

Another major weakness of the private law system of regulation consists in its impoverishment with respect to penalties for violations of the rules. In relation to contracts, the penalties for breach of private law regulation are usually confined either to a declaration of the invalidity of the transaction combined with restitutionary remedies, or to the award of compensatory damages for breach of the self-regulation represented by the terms of the contract and the default rules. This range of remedies compares unfavourably with alternatives provided by public regulation and non-legal sanctions. For instance, both of these latter systems of penalties have the potential to exclude a trader from a market. Public regulation also has the potential to impose compulsory standardized terms in market sectors, or to provide pre-contractual clearance of standard forms in a sector so that objectionable terms are never used.[42]

The private law remedy of invalidity of a contract is weak in securing policy objectives. The declaration of invalidity only applies to a particular transaction, so, unlike a sanction of the removal of a licence or exclusion from a market, the penalty provides little incentive to refrain from the conduct in breach of the mandatory rules. The force of the incentive is further diluted by the presence of effective non-legal sanctions. For example, an illegal transaction in drugs may be deterred by legal invalidity, since the supplier will be reluctant to deliver the goods without payment in advance, but equally the purchaser will be reluctant to hand over the money until the drugs are in his possession. As many criminals discover,

---

[42] Cranston, R., *Consumers and the Law*, 2nd edn. (London: Weidenfeld and Nicholson, 1984), 80–1.

however, the way around the problem is to create effective non-legal sanctions, such as credible threats of violence, in order to ensure contract compliance. Legal invalidity in this instance therefore plays an insignificant role in deterring these types of market transaction.

The other principal remedy consists of a liability to pay damages in order to compensate for losses caused by breach of mandatory rules and self-regulation. A liability rule imposes a cost on businesses for breach of the rules, and therefore provides an incentive for compliance. The strength of the incentive depends, of course, upon the measure of liability. Under the traditional perspective of private law, the measure of damages has almost invariably been restricted to one of restoration or compensation for provable losses. This corrective justice measure regards the purpose of the remedy as one of restoring the balance of the wealth of the parties, either as considered prior to the formation of the contract, or as it would have been after proper performance of the contract. This narrow policy objective excludes the possibility of setting the measure of liability at a level designed to achieve an optimum level of compliance with the regulatory standards.

The idea of an optimum level of compliance recognizes that at some point the costs of performance in order to achieve compliance will exceed any benefits from performance which might accrue to the other party or society as a whole. The objective of a liability rule might be to provide an incentive to perform up to the point when the additional costs of compliance are higher than the benefits of performance. The strength of the incentive represented by the liability rule would also have to take into account the probability of a successful claim for liability being brought. As private law is largely self-enforced, the risk of liability to a sanction can be quite small in some circumstances such as consumer transactions. In order to counteract this weakening of the incentive toward compliance, the measure of liability would have to be augmented in those cases where successful actions are brought in order to achieve the appropriate level of incentive across a series of transactions. This use of deterrent or 'punitive' damages, as these measures are sometimes called, in order to distinguish them from the compensatory purpose of corrective justice, is, however, generally eschewed in private law systems. Private law lacks a mechanism for the escalation of sanctions that is designed to provide a credible threat against systematic or persistent deviation from its standards.[43] Again this represents a substantial structural weakness in the remedies available in private law to provide incentive for regulatory compliance.

The poverty of legal sanctions forces injured parties back onto non-legal

[43] Ayres, I., and Braithwaite, J., n. 14 above.

sanctions. The best recourse is to refuse to pay for a service or goods, or to reject the defective goods and to demand one's money back. Private law regards these non-legal sanctions with suspicion, however, for this tactic can obviously be used opportunistically in order to evade contractual obligations and to become unjustly enriched at another's expense. As a general principle, the law will not permit this self-help remedy unless the breach of contract has been substantial, so that usually the injured party remains liable to pay for the goods or services. By withdrawing the non-legal sanction for minor defects, the injured party is left with the expensive and ineffective course of seeking compensation. As Reynolds observes, 'The difficulty in English law is then that if the goods are not bad enough to be rejected there is no remedy at all (unless special contract terms provide it).'[44]

These weaknesses in the sanctions offered by private law for breach of its regulations are defended on the ground that an essential feature of private law should be that it focuses entirely on the dispute between the parties to the litigation and not consider broader issues such as those we called earlier externalities and public goods. To the extent that private law is developing the capacity to incorporate such considerations into its standard setting, then the argument in favour of restricting its remedies in traditional ways is undermined. The question becomes rather whether the remedy provides sufficient incentives to comply with the regulatory standard so that the objective of the regulation may be achieved. If the liability to pay compensation for loss fails to supply this incentive, perhaps because the plaintiff cannot point to any harm suffered or because the profits from breach of standard exceed the risk of liability, then private law needs to adjust its levels of compensation. In some instances the courts have introduced suitable variations, such as a remedy for the partial disgorgement of profits in order to combat the problem of profitable breaches of standards.[45] Although private law has this capacity to alter its remedial sanctions, English courts have been reluctant to depart from the tradition of compensatory damages.[46] This reluctance derives in part from tradition, in part from the conception of private law as a system of principles of corrective justice rather than one of regulation, but also in part from a more justifiable concern that damages in excess of compensation might deter participants in markets from entering into contracts.[47] We

---

[44] Reynolds, F., 'The Applicability of General Rules of Private Law to Consumer Disputes', in S. Anderman *et al.* (eds.), *Law and the Weaker Party* (London: Professional Books, 1982), ii, 93, 100.

[45] *Wrotham Park Estate Co v Parkside Homes Ltd* [1974] 1 WLR 798, [1974] 2 All ER 321; *LAC Minerals Ltd v International Corona Resources Ltd* [1989] SCR 574, 61 DLR (4th) 14.

[46] *Surrey County Council v Bredero Homes Ltd* [1993] 1 WLR 1361, [1993] 3 All ER 705, CA.

[47] Smith, L., 'Disgorgement of the Profits of Breach of Contract: Property, Contract and "Efficient Breach"', *Canadian Business Law Journal*, 24 (1994–5) 121.

examine the validity of this concern in the next chapter, where it will be argued that it is invariably over-stated.

Conclusion

The preceding catalogue of the structural weaknesses of private law as a system for the efficient and efficacious regulation of markets provides ample room for doubts about its merits compared to other styles of regulation. No doubt we could add further to this list of weaknesses if we extended the enquiry beyond the criteria of efficiency and efficacy. For instance, the lack of democratic procedures in the formulation of private law standards could be a ground for questioning the legitimacy of the regulatory system. But at the same time, we should not lose sight of the great strength of private law regulation that we identified as its reflexive properties. Furthermore, it is wrong to suppose that other forms of regulation, such as public rules administered by a regulatory agency, are free from defects or do not contain their own structural weaknesses.

My argument has been that the private law of contract has the capacity to overcome or diminish many of these structural weaknesses in its system of regulation. This capacity can be realized by the evolution of many of the contemporary tendencies that were described earlier as the productive disintegration of private law. The development of some of these capacities require procedural adjustments, such as permitting *amicus curiae*, granting standing to collective groups, the admission of statistical evidence, and using the burden of proof for the purpose of detection of violations of regulatory standards. Other capacities of private law require the evolution of reasoning to incorporate references to externalities, public goods, and the articulation of policy objectives for the regulation. These developments can be engineered without diminishing the crucial advantage of private law regulation over public regulation that we have described as its reflexivity with respect to regulation of markets and contracts.

My argument should not be taken to suggest that public regulation of markets is unnecessary. In stressing the structural weaknesses of private law regulation of contracts, we have noted frequently how public regulation can overcome these difficulties with respect to setting standards, monitoring, and enforcement. My conclusion is rather that private law regulation is more sophisticated and has greater potential than is commonly thought by advocates of public regulation.

Part 3

Regulation in the
Construction of Markets

5

The Construction of Markets

How does social behaviour move from taking to trading? In order to get what we want, we can either grab it even though someone may already possess it, or we can seek to exchange some item in our possession for the desired object. Taking something merely requires the ability to use force or deception. The reluctance to use these abilities depends upon respect for a normative system of property rights. No doubt the law plays a significant role in establishing and policing this system through criminal regulation, such as the laws of theft and fraud, and the private law which allocates property entitlements. But the establishment of these conditions regarding ownership is not sufficient for the construction of trading relations. An exchange of goods or services requires a complex social interaction. The exchange or contractual relation relies for its success upon communication, co-operation, and shared normative standards or expectations.

As a consequence, contractual relations inevitably carry a risk of disappointment or of betrayal. In an exchange, each party is always vulnerable to the decision of the other to mislead expectations or to fail to fulfil them. In a simple purchase of an item, the buyer may be disappointed by the quality of the product, or may be misled by advertising into believing that the product has qualities that it does not possess, or suffer the betrayal of never receiving possession of the goods. The seller may equally experience the betrayal of default in payment. In a long-term contract, such as an employment relation, the expectation of the employer for a productive employee may be dashed, or the employee may find the job less satisfactory than expected.

What convinces people to take the risks of trading? How do they select a particular contracting partner? How do they determine when the risks of disappointment and betrayal have been overcome sufficiently to warrant entry into an exchange relation? In the language of game theory, how do people overcome the problems of co-ordination and first mover? More broadly, how do exchange transactions become commonplace, so that we are able to describe their prevalence and frequency as the formation of a market?

These broad questions deserve no doubt a book in themselves. Our particular focus concerns the role of law in assisting the social relation of exchange. Is law necessary for the evolution of routine patterns of exchanges that amount to a market, or can markets exist without a state? Even if law is not essential, does a system of legal rules, sanctions, and courts supply a valuable ingredient in the construction of markets? If so, what kinds of legal regulation best contribute to the construction of successful markets. A development of answers to these questions occupies the chapters of Part 3 of this book.

Trust and Sanctions

The risk of loss from disappointment and betrayal can never be entirely eliminated. Disappointment arises when the reasonable expectations that describe the expected benefit from the transaction are not fulfilled. Betrayal occurs when the reciprocal performance is not forthcoming at all. These risks may be low in transactions performed simultaneously and instantaneously, as in the case of a purchase of goods in a shop, but even then the goods may lack the expected quality and therefore cause disappointment. The risks will be high in the case of a sale of goods between geographically remote parties on the basis of deferred payment or credit, which is the common situation in international trade. Every exchange therefore represents the taking of a calculated risk that the likelihood of potential gains from exchange exceeds the probability of losses occurring due to disappointment or betrayal.

This calculation of risk provides the axis for the decision to enter a contract. The calculation involves both sides of an equation. On the one side is the estimation of the expected benefits from the transaction, that is, the profit to be made or the satisfaction of wants. On the other side lies the fear of betrayal or disappointment. In making the calculation, one crucial variable will always be the value attached to the expected benefit. Where dazzling profits beckon or urgent needs such as hunger must be satisfied, then greater risks of loss can be countenanced. In addition to this variable of the value attached to the expected benefit, two other significant variables determine the outcome of this calculation. We will call these variables 'trust' and 'sanctions'. By the term 'trust', I mean a situation where each party places faith in the other to perform the transaction and to avoid or minimize disappointment. By the term 'sanctions', I mean the situation where each party can make a credible threat of punishing the other, usually by causing economic loss in the event of betrayal or disappointment. Although both trust and sanctions alter the calculation of risk by tending to favour entry into contracts, they differ in the way in which they affect the balance of the equation.

Trust operates on both sides of the equation of risks of loss and expected benefits, whereas sanctions merely suppress the risk of betrayal or loss. In a relation of trust, both parties wish to avoid disappointment by ensuring that the expected gains to both are realized. In the case of sanctions, however, the threat of punishment in the event of betrayal merely reduces the risk of loss. In the example of an employment relation, if trust exists between employer and employee, both parties seek to avoid betrayal by failure to perform work or make the payment due, but also they try to avoid disappointment by such actions as the employee making sure that the work is performed carefully and the employer eliminating unnecessary dangers from the workplace. Where sanctions alone sustain the transaction, then the implicit threat of 'no work, no pay' is likely to ensure that the work is performed by the employee, but the incentive does not extend to encouraging performance of the job to the highest standards possible. Due to the way in which trust bears on both sides of the equation in the calculation of risk, it is likely to provide superior foundations for the construction of markets. Yet trust is much harder to establish and sustain in market relations than sanctions, so that in practice sanctions provide the second best, though more prevalent, solution to the problem of the risk of betrayal or disappointment.

The core idea of trust is that each party places faith in the other to perform the transaction and to avoid or minimize disappointment. The source of this faith in the other party does not derive from general conventional moral standards, such as the idea that promises ought to be kept, but rather is always personal to the relationship between the parties. Trust involves placing reliance upon one's knowledge of the character of the other party. This knowledge derives either from intimacy established through past dealings and social interaction or from certain attributes of a person's identity.

From a knowledge of the past, one can infer that, at least in dealings with oneself, the other party will be concerned to avoid betrayal and minimize any disappointment regarding the exchange. This past experience may comprise previous transactions that proved satisfactory. The inference of trustworthiness may equally be drawn from other types of social interaction, such as gifts, co-operative work, or respectful behaviour.

From a knowledge of a person's identity, one can discover attributes that again permit the inference that, at least in dealings with oneself, the other person will be concerned to avoid betrayal and minimize disappointment. The crucial attributes concern membership of a group or association to which the other party to the transaction is also a member, or where membership confers a reputation for trustworthiness. Joint membership of a kinship group or a trade association signals to both parties the presence of an attribute that encourages them to put their faith in the other. Membership by one party of a professional group that regulates standards of conduct, such as an architect or an accountant, also supplies an attribute which supports trust. Membership of the group only confers this attribute, of course, if the group itself has established the reputation for trustworthiness, and where continuing membership is important to the self-esteem and prosperity of its members.

As between these two sources of trust, past dealings and personal attributes, Lorenz observes correctly no doubt 'that reputation is import-ant but no substitute for experience'.[1]

Where trust is available as the basis for an intended transaction, it has three main effects. First, it guides the selection of the other contracting party. There is usually a strong preference to enter transactions with persons with whom one has enjoyed previous positive experiences and to prefer them over strangers. It is wrong to think of markets as comprised of large numbers of transactions between strangers. A deeper analysis reveals that markets are comprised of a constellation of repeated patterns of transactions between familiar parties.

The second effect of trust is to overcome the problem of the vulnerability of the first mover. The vulnerability to betrayal remains, but the presence of trust encourages the parties to discount this risk as one of low probability and therefore enter the contract and commence performance. Luhmann describes the way in which trust operates as the reduction of the complexity of the available information. By extrapolating from existing information about the other party, participants in markets who share trust reduce the complexity of the information to be considered with respect to a trans-action by deciding that the actions of the other with respect to performance of the undertaking are to a considerable degree predictable.[2] In other words, when making the decision to enter a transaction and commence perform-ance, the presence of trust permits the exclusion of concerns about the risk of betrayal or disappointment, thereby enabling the parties to concen-trate their attention on the projected economic benefits of the contract.

The final effect of trust between the parties is that it reduces the need to guard against disappointment by specifying in detail the precise content of the reciprocal undertakings and then monitoring performance closely. In the presence of trust, it will be assumed that the intention to minimize disappointment will lead the other to fulfil reasonable expectations without the need to supply particulars of every aspect of those expectations and then check upon compliance with the terms of the contract. In other words, the transactions costs of contractual specificity and monitoring can be reduced by the presence of trust, which lowers the height of this potential barrier to

---

[1] Lorenz, E. H., 'Neither Friends nor Strangers: Informal Networks of Subcontracting in French Industry, in D. Gambetta, (ed.), *Trust: Making and Breaking of Cooperative Relations* (Oxford: Blackwell, 1989) 194.
[2] Luhmann, N., *Trust and Power* (Chichester: Wiley, 1979).

entry into transactions. In short, trust functions as an antidote to transaction costs.

Whereas trust serves to reduce the complexity of the information to be considered about a transaction, sanctions tend to augment complexity by requiring the construction of a credible threat of punishment with which to deter betrayal or disappointment. An effective sanction must alter the incentives in such a way that the option of breach of contract by betrayal or causing disappointment always remains unattractive compared to supplying the expected performance. Yet the potential sanction must not be so great that fear of it deters entry into the contract altogether. One does not enter a contract willingly where the threatened sanction for causing disappointment is death or financial ruin. Making oneself vulnerable to a sanction represents a calculated risk in which the chance of causing disappointment and incurring the sanction appears small compared to the chance of reaping the expected benefits from the transaction. The ability to punish default encourages each party to enter the transaction, since the risk of betrayal or disappointment has been substantially reduced. But the price of this incentive structure is the new risk of incurring an additional sanction oneself.

We can distinguish three forms of sanction. A legal sanction comprises a process concluding in an order by a court either to perform the contract backed by a threat of punishment for disobedience or to pay compensation for breach of contract backed by a threat to seize property to the value of the compensation due. The effectiveness of a legal sanction to deter betrayal or disappointment depends on many factors including the expense of invoking the legal process, the predictability of the imposition of the sanction by a court, and the cost of the sanction to the party in breach of obligation. Where the legal process proves expensive, unpredictable, and leads only to small sanctions, then the legal sanction will not serve the function of encouraging entry into transactions.

A second form of sanction may be described as a non-legal sanction, for it may be imposed without invoking the legal process. Non-legal sanctions seek to impose economic costs (and in some cases psychological costs such as distress) without invoking a legal procedure. Perhaps the most pervasive and effective non-legal sanction comprises a refusal to deal with the other party in the future. This sanction does not punish betrayal when it occurs, but rather removes the possibility of deriving any benefits in the future from subsequent transactions between the parties. The effectiveness of this sanction depends upon the possibility of excluding future transactions without incurring greater loss than by continuing to enter contracts with the risk of further betrayal. Another powerful non-legal sanction is the ability to damage the business reputation of the party in default by spreading this adverse news among participants in the market. This sanction aims to discourage others from taking the risk of betrayal or disappointment, thereby preventing the party in breach of contract from obtaining benefits in the future from a wide range of potential transactions. In effect, the sanction of damage to business reputation functions as the opposite of trust by serving as a signal that the risk of betrayal or disappointment should be regarded as sufficiently grave as to exclude consideration of the potential benefits of the transaction.

It is useful to delineate a third form of sanction that has great importance in commercial transactions. The sanction is constructed by using legal rules, but it can be imposed either without incurring the costs and the uncertainties of the legal process or by using a perfunctory, reliable, and inexpensive legal process. An example is a transaction with a pawnbroker. The borrower may obtain a loan of money by giving possession of a valuable item such as a ring to the pawnbroker. If the borrower fails to repay the loan, the pawnbroker may sell the ring and keep the proceeds up to the amount of the debt. Legal rules serve to construct this sanction, for the pawnbroker will be regarded as entitled under the law of property to sell the ring without becoming liable for legal sanction for theft or conversion. Yet the sanction of selling the ring occurs without the need to invoke an uncertain and costly legal process. As in the example of the pawnbroker, the principal form of this third type of sanction comprises a 'hostage', that is, a valuable asset that the betrayer will lose to the injured party by breaking the contract. We may describe this third form of sanction as one that is constituted by legal rules but applied without invoking a legal process by means of self-help as security.

All three types of sanction, legal, non-legal, and security, may be present in a particular instance and serve the function of providing an incentive to perform the contract according to expectation. In business relations where a high degree of trust sustains the practice of entering contracts, various sanctions may be available and serve as a kind of insurance or long stop against betrayal without any serious expectation that the sanctions will need to be invoked. By means of this combination of trust and sanctions, the risks of betrayal or disappointment can be countered to an extent sufficient to provide the necessary conditions for entry into contracts with others. In the absence of trust or sanctions, however, it is unlikely that voluntary transactions will occur unless the expected benefits are so great in value that caution is thrown to the winds. The presence of trust or effective sanctions (or a combination of both) provide the necessary conditions for the constitution of markets.

Markets Without a State

It is often the conceit of lawyers that legal sanctions supply the crucial bulwark against disappointment and betrayal in contractual undertakings.

This view of law as the instrument of state power which guarantees the order of civil society has also comprised a core assumption of Western political thought. A famous passage in Hobbes' *Leviathan* exemplifies this reasoning:

. . . he that performeth first, has no assurance the other will perform after; because the bonds of words are too weak to bridle men's ambition, avarice, anger, and other Passions, without the fear of some coercive power; which in the condition of her Nature, where all men are equal, and judges of the justness of their own fears cannot possibly be supposed.[3]

The vital 'coercive power' must be provided by an external force or agency such as the state through its laws. We also discover this theme in modern jurisprudence, as in H. L. A. Hart's description of the 'minimum content of natural law', where he describes the basic legal institutions which are necessary to hold a society together. In addition to the institution of ownership of property,

the division of labour, which all but the smallest groups must develop to obtain adequate supplies, brings with it the need for rules which are *dynamic* in the sense that they enable individuals to create obligations and to vary their incidence. Among these are rules enabling men to transfer, exchange, or sell their products; for these transactions involve the capacity to alter the incidence of those initial rights and obligations which define the simplest form of property. The same inescapable division of labour, and perennial need for co-operation, are also factors which make other forms of dynamic or obligation-creating rule necessary in social life. These secure the recognition of promises as a source of obligation. By this device individuals are enabled by words, spoken or written, to make themselves liable to blame or punishment for failure to act in certain stipulated ways. Where altruism is not unlimited, a standing procedure providing such self-binding operations is required in order to create a minimum form of confidence in the future behaviour of others, and to ensure the predictability necessary for co-operation. This is most obviously needed where what is to be exchanged or jointly planned are mutual services, or wherever goods which are to be exchanged or sold are not simultaneously or immediately available.[4]

In this passage, Hart argues for the necessity of a 'standing procedure' to enforce contracts based upon the natural fact of the division of labour. This procedure has to be an external coercive power because the altruism of individuals is limited. The conclusion reached is that legal or law-like enforcement of contracts is a necessary feature of any social order.

The thesis that legal enforcement of contracts is necessary for markets and the division of labour also infuses many of the classics of sociological

---

[3] Hobbes, T., *Leviathan* (Oxford: Oxford University Press, 1955) (first published 1651), 89–90.
[4] Hart, H. L. A., *The Concept of Law*, 2nd edn. (Oxford: Clarendon Press, 1994), 196–7.

thought. Durkheim's analysis of modern society as united principally by 'organic solidarity', as opposed to previous social orders bound together by 'mechanical solidarity', is described by reference to different types of law. He contrasts, on the one hand, 'penal law' that enforces mechanical solidarity by reinforcing the 'conscience collective', with on the other hand, 'co-operative' and 'restitutive' law that supports the modern form of 'organic solidarity'. The central example of this co-operative law is the law of contract: 'the contract is, par excellence, the juridicial expression of co-operation'.[5] Durkheim appears to infer from the fact that the law of contract occupies a prominent position in modern legal codes that this legal phenomenon reflects the significance of 'organic solidarity' in binding modern societies with their market economies together.

On closer inspection, however, these assumptions about the significance of law in the constitution of market economies do not appear warranted. When we examine closely the way in which people decide to enter transactions the role of law appears at best peripheral and in many instances wholly irrelevant. In order to overcome the risks of betrayal and disappointment, trust and sanctions are vital, but within these mechanisms the legal sanction available for breach of contract appears to occupy only a marginal role. Other devices designed to construct trust and non-legal sanctions play a more prominent part in enabling the parties to overcome the problem of first mover or co-operation.

We can observe this relative lack of importance of legal sanctions most clearly in markets unsupported by state power in the form of law. In traditional societies social anthropologists have observed sophisticated patterns of exchange developed without any institutions resembling state law. During his enforced sojourn in the idyllic Trobriand islands of the South Pacific at the beginning of this century, the social anthopologist Malinowski described extensive patterns of trade in fish, yams and other basic commodities occurring without courts, rules of contract law, and legal sanctions.[6] The exchanges relied primarily upon trust, and each gift in anticipation of exchange serves to reinforce that trust. In the modern world, we can discover markets without a state in the shanty towns of the third world poor, where the dispossessed and displaced people of the world create their own local economic order without the assistance of state power.

Keith Hart's study in 1965–8 of trade in the shanty town on the edges of Accra between the 'Dickensian mob, of water carriers, bread sellers, shit shovellers, taxi drivers, pickpockets, and prostitutes' is interesting because

[5] Durkheim, E., *The Division of Labor in Society* (New York: Free Press, 1933) (originally published 1893), 123.
[6] Malinowski, B., *Crime and Custom in Savage Society* (London: Routledge & Kegan Paul, 1926).

neither the ties of kinship of traditional societies nor legal sanctions are available to the traders.[7] In seeking the means of subsistence the slum dwellers 'lacked effective sanctions; the state's presence in the slum was intermittent and punitive (occasional police raids)'.[8] The market economy in this context works rather on the basis of personal relations described by Hart as a kind of friendship, though plainly the claims of friendship and familiarity were routinely exaggerated by the participants in order to promote transactions and to gain access to markets. For a similar reason transactions were routinely facilitated by gifts and bribery, that were designed to establish signals of friendship and confidence. The pretensions of friendship established trade between the parties by encouraging trust. Here is a revealing example of the role of trust in the absence of legal or non-legal sanctions:

Atia had been hawking a camera around with intermittent success: the problem was that it was 35 mm and his customers were often unwilling to wait until the film was used up. His breakthrough came when he went to a girls' secondary school with 600 pupils and persuaded the principal to allow him to take the girls' photographs at weekends. Many others had tried and failed; but, as he put it, his sweet approach worked. He spent over £10 on chickens, eggs, and gifts of money before she agreed and gave him exclusive photographic rights in the school.

Trade was brisk; every weekend he got through two or three films 'cutting' the girls . . . He used to try to get an advance where possible, usually half. Those who gave him an advance were asked to write their names in a book, although he was himself illiterate. This was to stop any false claims; but in general he worked on a degree of mutual trust. If no advance had been paid and he made two copies which were refused, he couldn't force them to pay. If he had tried force, he said, maybe they would have ganged up against him and stopped buying his pictures altogether. So he relied on goodwill. Some girls would pay for a bad photo and later tear it up. If he heard of this, he would do them a new set free. Sometimes he 'fell down' when he spoiled the whole negative and had to refund all the advances.[9]

The interesting point about this story is that trade proceeded briskly without the possibility of either party imposing sanctions for breach of trust.

The parties to transactions in the shanty town of Accra were often bound together, however, by credit. In the absence of regular sources of income, the purchase of daily items such as food was impossible without a high level of credit. Breach of contract therefore risked the dissolution of the credit relation on which the debtor relied for access to basic goods and services. Preservation of the credit relation, which entails close fidelity to contractual arrangements, provides the incentive of non-legal sanction to deter betrayal by failure to pay for goods received. Within this credit

[7] Hart, K., 'Kinship, Contract, Trust: The Economic Organization of Migrants in an African City Slum', in D. Gambetta (ed.), n. 1 above, 176, 177.   [8] Ibid.
[9] Ibid. 181.

relation, we discover a long-term business relation, which as it survives becomes the basis for genuine trust and confidence. The research reveals stable patterns of trading relations without legal support, though the business relations are constantly vulnerable to deception, opportunism, and external shocks to the market. A fragile combination of trust and non-legal sanctions keeps this economic order lurching along.

Hart concludes the study by asking 'the question of what takes the place of law as the major source of sanction in economic relations?'[10] He found that systemic use of violence was rare. 'Reputation, name, honour, the macho complex offered much more scope for creditors and rentiers hoping to shame their clients into payment.'[11]

Above all, economic life depended on the discovery of complementary or shared interest which might make commercial agreements self-reinforcing in the short and medium term.

Nevertheless, a significant part of all this wheeler-dealing hinged on friendship, on the trust generated by shared experience, mutual knowledge and the affection that comes from having entered a relationship freely, by choice rather than status obligation. Whenever my landlord introduced me to one of his 'good friends', I knew that he was almost certainly a crook, probably from another ethnic group, a member of a criminal fraternity stretching back decades with a common background of gambling dens, police raids, gaols, diamond smuggling, drug rings, and all the rest. These were the men he turned to when he needed to trust someone, not his family or his fellow tribesmen.[12]

This passage illustrates the earlier contention that, when the chips are down, trust based upon experience is more reliable than trust based on membership of an association.

The contrast between this unreliable market economy and the markets of Western economies with strong state power is not in fact as great as might be assumed. There are fascinating parallels in the way credit binds parties together into more or less trusting relations in Greenberg's study of the market for consumer goods in a poor neighbourhood in the United States.[13] He examines the operations of Walker-Thomas Furniture Co., an 'easy credit' retailer selling items such as furniture and electrical goods through door-to-door sales representatives. The store has about 20,000 credit accounts with customers drawn almost exclusively from the poor and unemployed who cannot obtain credit from other retail stores. In fact credit is the only method of payment for most items, which permits far

---

[10] Hart, K., 'Kinship, Contract, Trust: The Economic Organization of Migrants in an African City Slum', 185.   [11] Ibid., 185.
[12] Ibid., 185.
[13] Greenberg, D. I., 'Easy Terms, Hard Times: Complaint Handling in the Ghetto', in L. Nader (ed.), *No Access to Law: Alternatives to the American Judicial System* (New York: Academic Press, 1980) 379.

higher prices to be charged than those demanded in ordinary retail stores. The sales representative can transform the customer's standard of living by supplying goods on credit, thereby establishing a bond of friendship, augmented by small gifts for regular paying customers and a speedy repair service, and then this relationship is invoked in order to obtain priority in payment over other creditors. The sales representative ensures this advantage by cashing the government benefits check and deducting the repayment at source. The credit relation then establishes a relation of dependency. The sales representative can permit flexibility in payments, such as a temporary abatement, which reinforces the perception of customers that they have to rely upon and trust the representative. The sales representative also uses the payment record to determine whether complaints about the products will be rectified. Once repayments have been made to cover costs, however, the flexibility disappears:

> That customers perceive the merchant—not the law—as arbiter emerges most clearly in situations in which they have 'lost', that is, failed to convince the salesperson to extend payments. At that point, Walker Thomas initiates all sorts of harassing activity: threatening letters, scaled on a continuum of increasing nastiness; early-morning and late-evening phone calls from the collection manager demanding immediate payment and vowing to send out the truck that very day; attempts to force payment through contacting customers' friends and relatives (whose names are conveniently provided on the 'Buyer's Financial Statement,' which all customers fill out before making any purchase); and repossession of goods from the customers' homes when they are absent . . . After the customers revealed these tactics to me, I asked them whether the tactics were illegal. They all replied, to the last one—no matter how angry or upset they may have been—'Oh, no, I missed my payments.'[14]

In this retail market, therefore, the initial contractual relation is established and sustained by trust, but when it turns sour, non-legal, or rather illegal sanctions are routinely employed. Great efforts are expended in excluding the legal system, so that if a customer threatens to take a complaint to an outside consumer protection agency, the salesperson may offer to pay for the repair himself.[15] In this way, the salesperson both restores trust and reputation in the market, and avoids legal scrutiny of unlawful practices such as excessive interest rates and breach of warranty. No doubt the cost of the repair is already included in the price, though the consumer perceives the repair as a favour. Although this retail market is untypical in western economies, it reveals how a market may be constituted outside the law, indeed in contravention of the law, on the basis of trust and non-legal sanctions.

[14] Ibid., 385–6.   [15] Ibid., 388.

This evidence of markets without a state or operating outwith the state suggests that the assumption that law plays a crucial role as an external enforcer in the construction of markets is misplaced. The key elements which encourage transactions are the presence of trust and sanctions, but those sanctions certainly do not have to be provided by a legal system. The availability of a legal sanction is rarely the key determinant in encouraging the parties to enter a legal transaction, and nor is the legal sanction the principal way in which the parties seek to protect themselves against the risk of disappointment. When we examine the reasons given by parties for entering transactions with particular persons, the reasons tend to emphasize foremost the importance of trust, and then secondly, the practical economic considerations, which we have called non-legal sanctions, as the effective discipline. The available legal sanctions are viewed at best as a last resort, to be employed, if ever, when the performance of the contract and possibility of future business relations between the parties seems improbable. In addition, when we examine the incidence of litigation about contracts in Chapter 14, we shall discover that resort to the legal process is a luxury item beyond the purse of most participants in markets.

Further support for this insight about the marginal significance of legal sanctions may be discovered in instances of common transactions in developed economies normally supported by reliable state power, but which are of doubtful legal validity. Although a legal sanction may not be available, the presence of trust, non-legal sanctions, or a combination of both, ensures that disappointments prove rare. In a path-finding survey of contractual behaviour in the United States in the 1950s, Macaulay gives several examples of unenforceable contracts that were routinely employed to govern contractual relations:

Moreover, it is likely that businessmen are least concerned about planning their transactions so that they are legally enforceable contracts. For example, in Wisconsin requirements contracts—contracts to supply a firm's requirements of an item rather than a definite quantity—probably are not legally enforceable. Seven people interviewed reported that their firms regularly used requirements contracts in dealings in Wisconsin. None thought that the lack of legal sanction made any difference. Three of these people were house counsel who knew the Wisconsin law before being interviewed. Another example of a lack of desire for legal sanctions is found in the relationship between automobile manufacturers and their suppliers of parts. The manufacturers draft a carefully planned agreement, but one which is so designed that the supplier will have only minimal, if any, legal rights against the manufacturers. The standard contract used by manufacturers of paper to sell to magazine publishers has a pricing clause which is probably sufficiently vague to make the contract legally unenforceable. The house counsel of one of the largest paper producers said that everyone in the industry is aware of this because of a leading New York case concerning the contract, but that no one cares.[16]

In these examples of commercial relations, the long-term economic interests of both parties bind them together regardless of any potential legal sanction. Another example of frequent contractual relations without legal sanctions concerns 'quotations' for commercial work; a court would probably not regard these estimates as amounting even to a formal offer, let alone a binding contract, but a business will often regard itself as bound by its quotation in order to protect its reputation.[17] These phenomena are hardly new: the Statute of Frauds 1677 required sales of goods worth more than £10 to be recorded in writing and signed, but this requirement was certainly not observed in specialized markets and exchanges during the nineteenth century.[18]

These examples of markets unsupported by state sanctions for breach of contract can also be extended to consumer transactions. Although a publican could not sue a consumer for debts,[19] the English pub thrived on the simple principle of cash on the spot. Similarly, betting shops proliferate in every high street in England despite the unenforceability of the transactions. The consumer guarantee issued by a manufacturer in the box containing its product may also not be legally binding on the manufacturer unless the consumer can demonstrate that the existence of the guarantee was a reason for purchasing the particular product from a retailer. Nevertheless, manufacturers will invariably comply with their guarantee, albeit strictly construed against the consumer, for failure to do so will result in damage to their business reputations.

International trade, that is, trade between citizens of two different states across the border, has always presented the participants with the problem of creating a market without the reliable support of state power. The risk of disappointment or betrayal is accentuated because there is a danger that the state will not impose sanctions for breach of contract when one of its own nationals is sued by a foreigner. Merchants engaged in international commerce overcame these difficulties by developing extensive international networks of trust based upon kinship and personal knowledge. Building on these relations, the merchants developed legal

---

[16] Macaulay, S., 'Non-Contractual Relations in Business', *American Sociological Review* 28 (1963) 45, 60.

[17] Macaulay, S., 'The Use and Non-use of Contracts in the Manufacturing Industry', *Practical Lawyer* 9(7) (1963) 13, 17.

[18] Ferguson, R. B., 'Commercial Expectations and the Guarantee of the Law: Sales Transactions in Mid-Nineteenth Century England', in G. R. Rubin and D. Sugerman (eds.), *Law and Economy: Essays in the History of English Law 1700–1920* (London: Professional Books, 1984), 192, 201. See also Comment, 'The Statute of Frauds and the Business Community: A Re-Appraisal in Light of Prevailing Practices', *Yale Law Journal* 66 (1957), 1038.

[19] Under the 'Tippling Act', 24 Geo. 2, c.40, (1750).

devices of credit, such as the medieval 'tratta' or letters of payment which evolved into the modern Bill of Exchange. These documents were negotiable (or could be alienated), so that when debts came to be settled, the debtor and the creditor were within the same legal jurisdiction and many legal and non-legal sanctions (such as damage to reputation) would be available to the creditor.[20] Ordinary state courts often lagged behind in recognition of the effectiveness of documentary credit arrangements, but the merchants' own courts would enforce them.[21]

A remarkable feature of contemporary international trade in the context of the globalization of the economy is the extent to which the contracts seek to establish their own non-state systems of adjudication and normative standards through commercial arbitration clauses.[22] The terms of the contract enable the parties to select their judges (arbitrators) and the rules applicable to their transaction which can be the laws of any state or even a set of rules which are not part of any state legal system, the so-called 'lex mercatoria'.[23] It is only when the debtor chooses to ignore the award of the arbitrator, and run the risk of damage to reputation which would effectively exclude them from international trade, that the creditor may seek recourse to state law to enforce the award of the arbitrator.

These observations throw considerable light on the general issue of the role of the law in the constitution of markets. They suggest that markets can flourish where there is trust without the need for sanctions. But such a level of trust is only likely to exist in a small closed community. More commonly, the market will deter disappointment and betrayal by a combination of trust and non-legal sanctions. We can therefore discover flourishing markets where no effective state power exists to impose legal obligations. Even where a powerful modern state is present, the legal sanctions are likely to play only a minor role in deterring behaviour which causes disappointment.

The Construction of Trust

It is important to notice that trust is constructed through social interaction. The most fruitful source of trust comes from prior dealings or

---

[20] Braudel, F., *Civilization and Capitalism*, ii, *The Wheels of Commerce*, trans. S. Reynolds (London: 1982), 142; Trakman, L. E., *The Law Merchant: The Evolution of Commercial Law* (Colorado: Rothman, 1983), 109 (samples of medieval bills of exchange *etc.*)

[21] Postan, M. M., *Medieval Trade and Finance* (Cambridge: Cambridge University Press, 1973), 49–54.

[22] Teubner, G., 'Global Bukovina: Legal Pluralism in the World Society', in G. Teubner (ed.), *Global Law Without a State* (Aldershot: Gower, 1997) 3.

[23] Mertens, L., 'Lex Mercatoria: A Self-applying System beyond National Law?', in G. Teubner (ed.), n. 22 above, 31; Trakman, L. E., n. 20 above; Dezalay, Y., and Garth, B. G., *Dealing In Virtue: International Commercial Arbitration and the Construction of a Transnational Legal Order* (Chicago: University of Chicago Press, 1996), 85–91.

experience. Trust is also likely to be present where the transactions occur within kinship groups or within an ethnic group which has an identifiable membership within a broader society.[24] There are many careful studies of the way ethnic groups create bonds of trust, such as the Jewish diamond merchants of New York,[25] and the Chinese ethnic community involved in marketing smallholders' rubber in Singapore and West Malaysia.[26] Membership of the kinship or ethnic group serves as a signal of trustworthiness, an indication of a reputation for reliability, provided of course the transaction occurs between two members of the same group. In economic terms, by limiting transactions to the kinship or ethnic group, the parties eliminate the costs of finding out about the other's reliability, though at the price of foregoing some potentially worthwhile transactions with strangers. Members of the group will conform to these expectations not only because of the social obligations of kinship but also because the implicit threat of exclusion from the group for disappointing expectations will entail both exclusion from the market and from a social community.

In addition, it is possible for participants in markets to augment levels of trust by initiating deliberate patterns of social interaction.[27] They can devise institutions such as trade associations, codes of practice for industrial sectors, 'umbrella contracts', or framework agreements that describe the expected course of the business relation. A particularly elaborate form of the institutional creation of trust occurs in exchanges or 'bourses', membership of which can only be achieved and maintained by demonstrating the practice of trustworthy behaviour. These 'club markets', such as Stock Exchanges, futures markets, the Baltic Exchange for shipping in London, the Liverpool cotton market in the nineteenth century,[28] and the diamond merchants of New York,[29] comprise formal codes of conduct, private arbitration and mediation systems for the resolution of disputes, and the power to exclude from membership and to impose punitive sanctions for deviant behaviour. The advantage to the members is not only the facilitation of trade which the trust engenders, but also a reduction of transaction costs because deals can be struck informally. Another device for augmenting trust consists in the establishment of industrial sector

---

[24] Winn, J. K., 'Relational Practices and the Marginalization of Law: Informal Financial Practices of Small Businesses in Taiwan', *Law & Society Review* 28 (1994) 193.

[25] Bernstein, L., 'Opting Out of the Legal System: Extralegal Contractual Relations in the Diamond Industry', *Journal of Legal Studies* 21 (1992) 115.

[26] Landa, J. T., 'A Theory of the Ethnically Homogeneous Middleman Group: An Institutional Alternative to Contract Law', *Journal of Legal Studies* 10 (1981) 349.

[27] Zucker, L. G., 'Production of Trust: Institutional Sources of Economic Structure, 1840–1920', *Research in Organizational Behavior* 8 (1986) 53.

[28] Simpson, A.W.B., 'The Origin of Futures Trading in the Liverpool Cotton Market', in P. Cane and J. Stapleton (eds.), *Essays for Patrick Atiyah* (Oxford: Clarendon Press, 1991), Chapter 8. [29] Bernstein, L., n. 25 above.

standards of quality and safety for products, to which all participants in the market agree to conform.

In advanced industrial societies, the presence of institutions which establish or augment trust may provide a competitive advantage.[30] The competitive advantage derives in part from the reduction of the costs of making contracts, the transaction costs. Where there is trust, it is likely that the parties will dispense with elaborate contracts, will refrain from detailed monitoring of performance, and will not need to create economic incentives and sanctions such as security interests against default. Perhaps more importantly, in a relation of trust the parties may expect each other to co-operate in the performance of the contract by, for example, providing useful information or suggestions for innovation.[31] This co-operation should increase the profitability of the transaction for both parties. A comparative study of German, Italian, and United Kingdom transactions in the same market sectors reveals the important contribution to the formation of trust provided by trade associations, quality assurance organizations, and industry standards for quality and safety of products.[32] These institutional arrangements, which are stronger in Germany and Italy than the United Kingdom, may reduce price competitiveness, but they appear to promote co-operation and the capacity to adapt to a changing environment.[33] They permit the business partners to enter into long-term contractual commitments with less wariness about the allocation of risks and the protection of investments.

One problem confronting businesses and individuals is how to create a signal to others in the market that indeed they are trustworthy in this sense. In the absence of past intimate knowledge or common membership in a trade association, trust in the required sense cannot be convincingly established. Nevertheless, almost equivalent benefits may be obtained by constructing a good business reputation for fair dealing. This requires an economic investment which will be wasted if the reputation is subsequently damaged by publicized default on contracts.[34] One common technique for businesses consists in establishing and advertising heavily a brand name for

[30] Deakin, S., *et al.*, 'Contract Law, Trust Relations, and Incentives for Co-operation: A Comparative Study', in S. Deakin, and J. Michie, (eds.), *Contracts, Co-operation, and Competition* (Oxford: Oxford University Press, 1997) 105.

[31] Collins, H., 'Quality Assurance in Subcontracting', in S. Deakin, and J. Michie, (eds.), n. 30 above, 285.

[32] Lane, C., and Bachmann, R., 'The Social Construction of Trust: Supplier Relations in Britain and Germany', *Organisation Studies* 17 (1996) 365; Lane, C., 'The Social Regulation of Inter-Firm Relations in Britain and Germany: Market Rules, Legal Norms, and Technical Standards', *Cambridge Journal of Economics* 21 (1997) 214.

[33] Arrighetti, A., *et al.*, 'Contract Law, Social Norms and Inter-Firm Co-operation', *Cambridge Journal of Economics* 21 (1997) 182.

[34] Klein, B., and Leffler, K. B., 'The Role of Market Forces in Assuring Contractual Performance', *Journal of Political Economy* 89 (1981) 615.

a product. This investment will be wasted if the product is exposed as unreliable or of poor quality, so there is a strong economic incentive to live up to the reputation for trustworthiness. For individuals, they can invest in obtaining a good credit rating by regularly paying their bills and by working hard to obtain satisfactory references from previous employers and landlords. Another common technique for signalling one's trustworthiness is simply to charge a relatively high price. Manufacturers of products have also sought to signal their trustworthiness and the quality of their product by issuing consumer guarantees about the product, but this technique has not proved successful, since poor quality producers can easily imitate the guarantee without the intention of fulfilling its requirements.[35] Retailers build a reputation for trustworthiness as well by their handling of complaints and returns of goods. The overriding goal of shops seeking to establish their trustworthiness is to maintain good public relations, which leads to the practice of accepting returns of goods without question.[36]

The willingness to take the risk of disappointment by performing one's side of the transaction first also provides a clear signal of trustworthiness. In effect, the first mover offers a gift, like the slum dwellers of Accra, which simultaneously presents a sign of trustworthiness and also places the recipient under a diffuse social obligation to reciprocate.[37] Similarly, in a large commercial transaction, a contractor may commence performance and make irretrievable investments in plant and machinery specific to the expected contract even before formal enforceable contracts have been exchanged. Paley gives the example of a two million dollar investment based upon a combination of personal trust within a history of dealings and the expectation of the continuation of a long-term business relation, without any formal enforceable contractual rights as a protection against the waste of the investment.[38] In response, the second mover can merely perform the promised undertaking, or, in order to signal that the trust should be reciprocated, the second mover can acknowledge a greater

---

[35] Good quality manufacturers may also weaken their guarantees to deal with the problem of 'moral hazard', that is, consumers may not be careful of products and present fraudulent claims: see Lutz, N. A., 'Warranties as Signals Under Consumer Moral Hazard', *Rand Journal of Economics* 20 (Summer 1989) 239; Arrow, K. J., 'The Economics of Moral Hazard: Further Comment', *American Economic Review* 58 (1968) 537.

[36] Kamkas, A., and Rosenwasser, R., 'Department Store Complaint Management', in L. Nader (ed.), n. 13 above, 283.

[37] Blau, P. M., *Exchange and Power in Social Life* (New York: Wiley, 1964); Rose, C., 'Giving, Trading, Thieving, and Trusting: How and Why Gifts Become Exchanges, and (More Importantly) Vice Versa', *Florida Law Review* 44 (1992) 295; Posner, E., 'Altruism, Status and Trust in the Law of Gifts and Gratuitous Promises', *Wisconsin Law Review* (1997) 567.

[38] Palay, T. M., 'Comparative Institutional Economics: The Governance of Rail Freight Contracting, *Journal of Legal Studies* 13 (1984) 265, 277.

obligation, by for example proving co-operative and flexible in the performance of the contract. Similarly, the risk of loss of sunk or irretrievable investments may provide a signal of trustworthiness. One reason why franchisors demand an irretrievable capital investment from franchisees may be to help to select or screen applicants,[39] for those willing to make the investment thereby signal their trustworthiness. The pursuit of trust therefore provides the parties with an incentive to give priority to the business relation rather than to confine their attention to the precise contractual undertakings.

The Construction of Non-legal Sanctions

The effectiveness of non-legal sanctions depends upon their potential to impose economic loss on a party to a contract who causes disappointment or betrayal. The sanction of a refusal to do business with a person in breach of contract in the future will be very powerful, for instance, where the deceiver derives much of its business or income from the other contractor. Equally in consumer contracts, as the customers of Walker-Thomas Furniture Co. well appreciated, a customer who fails to pay bills runs the risk of being excluded from vital goods and services in the future. Perhaps the key incentive to perform contracts faithfully, particularly with regard to quality, derives from the greater benefits to be achieved from the income from a stream of future sales rather than one-off benefits from defaults. The publican resists the temptation to water down the beer for fear of losing regular customers.

Another important non-legal sanction comprises damage to business reputation, with the consequent loss of confidence and trust. The sanction of damaging the other's business reputation will be augmented where the information about default can be disseminated rapidly to other participants in the market.[40] This power to disseminate damaging news about reputation combined with the threat of the non-legal sanction of expulsion from the market are the key ingredients of the success of 'club markets'. These trade associations combine to monitor actions and then to impose sanctions such as exclusion from the market. In the New York Diamond Dealers Club, which regulates about 80 per cent of the rough diamonds transactions in the United States, a system of arbitration polices fair trade practices and provides a monitoring system of the reputations of dealers.[41]

---

[39] Dnes, A. W., '"Unfair" Contractual Practices and Hostages in Franchise Contracts', *Journal of Institutional and Theoretical Economics* 148 (1992) 484, 496.

[40] Klein, B., and Leffler, K. B., 'The Role of Market Forces in Assuring Contractual Performance', *Journal of Political Economy* 89 (1981) 615.

[41] Bernstein, L., n. 25 above.

But such an association is not essential to establish a mechanism for exposing cheaters. An informal 'coalition' between traders also suffices to establish a mechanism for disseminating information about cheating.[42] On this interpretation, the core ingredient of a coalition comprises an implicit and long-term agreement to share information about the reputation of agents. This exchange of information is then used as the basis for declining to trade with other parties with poor reputations. An example developed by Grief of such a coalition concerns Jewish traders operating throughout the Middle East in the eleventh century without any effective state sanctions to protect their elaborate and risky merchant ventures conducted through agents at a distance:

The Maghribis employed each other as agents, and all retaliated against any agent who had cheated a coalition member. Their social and commercial network provided the information required to detect and announce cheating, and the multilateral punishment was self-enforcing, since the value of future relations with all the Maghribis kept an agent honest.[43]

In contrast, a club market has institutions for implementing formal sanctions against members who develop poor reputations.

The parties to a contract can, however, devise powerful non-legal sanctions without much assistance from third parties.[44] They can arrange, for example, that one or both parties should incur considerable expense in advance, which would be wasted if performance of the contract is not completed satisfactorily. We have already noted this use of 'sunk investments' in franchise contracts; the franchisee, who wants to be licensed to use a particular trading name and business format, will be required to make substantial investments in plant and machinery that would be wasted if the franchise relation fails to prosper and the right to use the trading name is withdrawn.

We observed above that in commercial dealings a common technique for establishing sanctions uses 'security' or proprietary rights to create the capacity to punish a defaulter. This sanction employs the rules of the legal system with respect to the allocation of ownership of property, but does not invoke the legal process in order to impose the penalty. In order to borrow money, for instance, often a person will be required to give conditional title to some item of valuable property such as a mortgage of a house to the bank, or the pledge of a valuable ring to the pawnbroker. In the event of

---

[42] Clay, K., 'Trade Without Law: Private-Order Institutions in Mexican California', *Journal of Law, Economics and Organization* 13 (1997) 202.

[43] Grief, A., 'Institutions and International Trade: Lessons from the Commercial Revolution', *American Economic Review, Papers and Proceedings* 82 (1992) 128, 130.

[44] Kronman, A. T., 'Contract Law and the State of Nature', *Journal of Law, Economics and Organisation 1* (1985) 5.

failure to repay the loan, the lender may then sell the asset and recover its money. Similarly, the advance payment of a deposit for a service will be forfeited if the balance is not paid on time. The hostage may either comprise 'an ugly princess', that is something only of value to the debtor, or may have general market value equivalent to the amount of indebtedness. This use of security is a non-legal sanction in the sense that the lender is not required to follow a legal process in order to recover compensation, but may simply recover and sell the property in the market. (This traditional legal position is now generally altered for consumer credit transactions, so that a legal process must be pursued prior to the realization of a security interest, though we observed that these procedures were not followed in the Walker-Thomas Furniture Co. example.) The giving of a security right enables the borrower to provide a credible commitment to the creditor not only by providing an assurance of performance, but also by limiting the borrower's power to obtain additional excessive borrowing, which would reduce the likelihood of compliance with the contract.[45]

These examples illustrate how an important dimension of the discrete communication system of a contract involves the construction of effective non-legal sanctions. The objective of the parties is to render the contract 'self-enforcing' in the sense that the economic incentives favour diligent performance heavily over default and betrayal.[46] The legal system may play a peripheral role in channelling the construction of these non-legal sanctions by, for example, recognizing the validity of proprietary claims contained in security interests. The law of contract can also provide a formal ceremony, such as the Roman practice of 'stipulatio', which contributes to the publicity of reciprocal promises and therefore ensures greater damage to reputation in the event of default. The legal system may also confirm the results of the application of a non-legal sanction if it is employed. In a contract of employment, for instance, the most powerful sanction available to an employer is simply to refuse to pay wages if the employee fails to perform the assigned work. The legal system can confirm this action by endorsing the principle of 'no work, no pay', so that the employee is denied any legal sanction to counter the employer's use of economic power. In the common law, the method used to support this type of sanction is the construction of the contract in order to discover 'conditions' that provide the order of performance of the parties. These interpretations of the contract appear to track closely the relative credit risks presented by the parties, so that the party who presents the higher risk of default, such as the employee, is required to

---

[45] Mann, R. J., 'Explaining the Pattern of Secured Credit', *Harvard Law Review* 110 (1997) 625.

[46] Klein, B., 'Self-Enforcing Contracts', *Journal of Institutional and Theoretical Economics* 141 (1985) 594.

perform first as a condition of the contract.[47] Breach of this condition entitles the other to withhold performance and terminate the contract. Similarly, in the law of sales, the law supports the non-legal sanction of rejection of the goods for inadequate quantity or quality by granting the buyer a defence to a claim for the price. This self-help remedy of rejection is so powerful, however, that the defence to a claim for compensation may be lost easily, as where a shortfall is so slight that a court regards rejection as unreasonable,[48] or where the buyer fails to reject the goods within a reasonable time after having had the opportunity to inspect them for defects.[49]

These observations concerning the importance of non-legal sanctions in providing the incentive to keep bargains suggest that the legal system only plays a minor role in establishing markets. It is true that many legally enforceable contracts are made in markets, but the sanctions for breach of contract do not appear to be crucial in ensuring that contracts are performed. These contracts often serve another purpose, however, which is to construct the mixture of incentives and penalties which comprise effective non-legal sanctions and security. It can be said with only a little exaggeration that the principal purpose of making contracts is to avoid the need to rely upon the law of contract.

The Significance of Legal Sanctions

These conclusions about the importance of trust and non-legal sanctions in enabling markets to be constituted leave the law playing a minor role. In determining whether the parties will take the risk of entering into a contract, the presence of trust supported by the availability of non-legal sanctions appears much more significant. We should ask therefore what significance, if any, should be attributed to the legal system and the sanctions available in the courts for breach of contract in the constitution of markets?

The role played by legal sanctions depends in part upon their strength. The normal remedy in private law for a breach of a contractual relation consists in damages designed to compensate a party for economic losses caused by the breach. In common law systems, these losses will be calculated as the 'net loss', that is, after offsetting any benefits obtained by making an alternative transaction with another party.[50] Where there is a

---

[47] Patterson, E., 'Constructive Conditions in Contracts', *Columbia Law Review* 42 (1942) 903.

[48] Sale of Goods Act 1979, s. 30(2A), as amended by Sale and Supply of Goods Act 1994, s. 4.

[49] Sale of Goods Act, 1979, s. 35 as amended by Sale and Supply of Goods Act 1991, s. 2.

[50] Harris, D., 'Incentives to Perform, or Break Contracts', *Current Legal Problems* 45(2) (1992) 29, 34.

competitive market for goods and services, these net losses are likely to prove minimal, since an alternative contract at a similar price can be obtained. In general, the law will not award any punitive damages for breach of contract which exceed the net loss, and nor will it permit the parties to the contract to agree to a measure of compensation which is likely to exceed the net loss. These sanctions are therefore rather weak, and it will only be in exceptional cases, as where no market alternative was available, that damages may prove substantial. This weakness of private law sanctions for breach of contract suggests that they provide little incentive to perform contracts, though equally and perhaps more significantly, the possibility of legal sanctions does little to deter entry into legally enforceable contracts either. The popular image of the law as a fierce enforcer of contracts is therefore misleading. As Macaulay once observed, 'Contract law in action is a defective product, promising far more than it can deliver.'[51]

In some jurisdictions, penal regulation, particularly in relation to consumer contracts, provides a more substantial deterrent against misleading trade practices. Similarly, some jurisdictions employ administrative agencies to monitor and deter unfair contractual practices committed against consumers or other protected classes such as employees and tenants. These types of measures seem to be effective on the whole in deterring the kinds of abuses at which they are directed, no doubt because they address the twin problems of access to justice and the weakness of sanctions. They control behaviour in the market to a degree which the ordinary private law compensatory measure of damages awarded by a court cannot. These regulatory measures operate only at the fringes of markets, deterring egregious abuses, but they must contribute to some extent to the willingness particularly of consumers to enter into transactions.

Despite this insight that legal sanctions play a minor role in the construction of markets, some economic analysis of contract law, sometimes described as the Chicago School and associated most closely with the writings of Richard Posner, often adopts legal sanctions as its central focus. This perspective begins by viewing the entry into transactions from a cost/benefit analysis. The benefit comprises the expected gain from performance of the transaction, and the cost comprises the risk of incurring a legal sanction for breach of contract. This formula differs from my earlier analysis where the benefits were similar but the costs were described as the risk of betrayal or disappointment. In this economic analysis, the legal sanction is regarded as the principal incentive to perform contracts. This

---

[51] Macaulay, S., 'Long-Term Continuing Relations: The American Experience Regulating Dealerships and Franchises', in C. Joerges (ed.), *Franchising and the Law*, (Baden Baden: Nomos, 1991) 179, 189.

potential cost is treated as the full measure of the cost of betrayal or disappointment. In effect, the legal sanction is regarded as a reliable proxy for the potential costs of entering contracts. The precise measure of the legal sanction then becomes the main focus of enquiry, for the aim is to achieve a legal sanction that secures an efficient level of performance of contracts, by which is understood a pattern of benefits exceeding costs. This economic analysis generates two powerful insights.

The first insight is that the general wealth of the community will be increased if 'efficient breach' of contract is permitted. Although in general full performance of contracts according to expectations will produce the most benefit for the parties at the least cost, in some instances the legal system must tolerate default as the most wealth enhancing outcome. An efficient breach of contract (by the Pareto standard) occurs where default leaves neither party worse off once compensation has been paid, and leaves at least one party better off than would have occurred as a consequence of performance of the contract. From this analysis it can be inferred that according to the regulatory policy of efficiency the law should not seek to compel performance of contracts where a party decides to breach and pay compensation after a suitable cost/benefit calculation. This conclusion rules out the possibility of remedies of compulsory performance, such as injunctions and orders of specific performance, and also indicates that punitive damages should not generally be permitted.[52]

The second insight generated by this economic analysis suggests that the purpose of the legal sanction should be to ensure that neither party is worse off as a result of the breach of contract, so that the remedy should match that loss exactly. This criterion produces a complex (and controversial) formulation for the measurement of compensatory damages including wasted expenditure, the cost of irretrievable investments, opportunity costs, and so forth. This formula rules out the possibility of other kinds of considerations being employed to augment or reduce damages, such as a concern for the redistribution of wealth, the furthering of regulatory objectives of deterring sharp practices, or the protection of vulnerable or socially excluded groups in society. In short, efficient levels of sanctions, judged by reference to the net wealth of the parties to the transaction and ignoring all other considerations (by dubbing them as externalities) favour the private law compensatory remedy.

What importance should be attached to this economic analysis? It is interesting that it conforms quite closely to the conclusions reached by legal doctrine, though the occasional discordance such as orders for

---

[52] Posner, R., *Economic Analysis of Law*, 4th edn. (Boston: Little Brown, 1992) 131; criticized in Atiyah, P., *Essays on Contract* (Oxford: Clarendon Press, 1990) 131; Friedman, D., 'The Efficient Breach Fallacy', *Journal of Legal Studies* 18 (1989) 1.

specific performance and awards of punitive damages, which are the obses-
sion of economic analysis,[53] provide interesting clues as to the greater
sophistication and complexity of legal reasoning than the simple economic
models. But if the hypothetical cost/benefit analysis about legal sanctions
only rarely occurs in practice, so that what guides the behaviour of the
parties is more likely to be the norms of trust in a business relation and
consideration of potential non-legal sanctions, then surely the economic
analysis sends us down a blind alley. The legal sanction cannot be regarded
as an accurate proxy for the costs of entering transactions, that is, the costs
of betrayal or disappointment, since the most important sanctions will be
contained in the non-legal remedies and the realization of security. In the
case of requirements contracts, for instance, it did not matter that there
was no legal sanction at all, and therefore no legal costs at risk in entering
contracts, for the important sanctions were the non-legal sanctions of a
refusal to trade in the future combined with damage to business reputation.
The businesses were uninterested in the legal position because they had to
hand the more powerful sanction of the capacity to wreck the other's
business.

It is possible to rescue this style of economic analysis in part by broaden-
ing its hypothetical cost/benefit analysis to include non-legal sanctions. If,
for example, the most powerful threat and the most substantial cost of
breach consists in the risk that the injured party will refuse to trade in the
future with this contracting partner, then it might be argued that the
parties have chosen to support their transaction by this economic incentive
rather than the possibility of any legal sanction, so that a court should
decline to impose a legal sanction. This analysis might justify, for instance,
a legal rule which declined to enforce requirements contracts, even though
they are routine business transactions, since the non-legal sanctions or
incentives are generally sufficient to ensure that the parties abide by their
arrangement. The economic analysis might also suggest that the legal
sanction should be employed where the expectation that non-legal sanctions would be effective to ensure performance of the contracts turns out to
be unfounded or the result of a miscalculation.[54] Here the role of legal
sanctions is to supply what the parties believed was already present in their
transaction, that is, adequate economic incentives to minimize the risk of
disappointment.

---

[53] Goetz, C., and Scott, R., 'Liquidated Damages, Penalties and the Just Compensation
Principle', *Columbia Law Review* 77 (1977) 55; Rea, S.,'Efficiency Implications of Penalties
and Liquidated Damages', *Journal of Legal Studies* 13 (1984) 147; Clarkson, K., *et al.*,
'Liquidated Damages v Penalties: Sense or Nonsense', *Wisconsin Law Review* (1978) 351;
Kronman, A.T., 'Specific Performance', *University of Chicago Law Review* 45 (1978) 351;
Schwartz, A., 'The Case for Specific Performance', *Yale Law Journal* 89 (1979) 271.
[54] Charney, D., Nonlegal Sanctions in Commercial Relationships', *Harvard Law Review* 104
(1990) 373.

Yet this style of economic analysis still seems to misunderstand how contractual relations are constructed. The model views legal and non-legal sanctions as the punishment to be applied in the event of default. But in the construction of market relations, the non-legal sanctions supply more than a threat of punishment. They serve as signals as to the credibility of the commitment, the trustworthiness of the parties. In the case of franchises, the cost of sunk investments for both parties establishes their good faith in the intention to co-operate to bring the business relation to fruition. Without such a signal, the parties would be unwilling to enter into the contract at all, even if adequate legal sanctions were available to compensate for any losses resulting from breach. The form of economic analysis which emphasizes the significance of such incentive structures, signals, and investments in the construction of markets is known as 'institutional economics'.[55]

Institutional economics grasps better the point that the incentive structures of contracts, the devices for establishing the credibility of commitments such as hostages and sunk investments, and the techniques for sustaining co-operation such as governance structures, should not be regarded as sources of potential sanctions, but rather the basis on which the parties achieve the necessary degree of trust for entry into contractual relations. The risks of disappointment or betrayal are not countered typically by the display of even more threatening sanctions, but rather the parties to the contract seek to minimize the perception of those risks in order to induce beneficial contractual relations.

That is not to say that the possibility of obtaining financial compensation for breach of contract will never assist in the construction of markets. But we should be cautious in assuming that it is the legal sanction or a payment equivalent to the measure of legal damages that supplies this incentive towards performance of undertakings. In studies of informal settlements of commercial disputes, we discover that it is rare that the compensation demanded or expected amounts to the legal entitlement. The informal settlement rather focuses upon such items as wasted expenditure in carrying out an order and rarely considers the dimension of loss of profits.[56] The preference is for a settlement under which no money changes hands, and in which compensation takes the form of credit on future transactions.[57] We should infer from this evidence that even where the

---

[55] For an overview: Wiggins, S. N., 'The Economics of the Firm and Contracts: A Selective Survey', *Journal of Institutional and Theoretical Economics* 147 (1991) 603; Goldberg, V. P., *Readings in the Economics of Contract Law* (Cambridge: Cambridge University Press, 1989).

[56] Comment, 'The Statute of Frauds and the Business Community: A Re-Appraisal in Light of Prevailing Practices', *Yale Law Journal* 66 (1957) 1038, 1061–2.

[57] Beale, H., and Dugdale, T., 'Contracts between Businessmen: Planning and the Use of Contractual Remedies', *British Journal of Law and Society* 2 (1975) 45.

potential imposition of a financial penalty helps to constitute the market relation, the legal sanction remains insignificant because it does not guide or determine expectations with respect to the amount or form of compensation payable. Thus the assumption of some economic analysis of contract law that the measure of the legal sanction determines the level of incentives for performance of contracts, as in the theory of efficient breach, seems to bear little relation to the actual practice of commercial parties, for whom the expected measure of compensation is often much lower.

We should therefore sustain our argument that legal sanctions play only a minor role in the constitution of markets. The insights provided by the Chicago school of economic analysis should be limited to their contribution to the design of a strategy for regulating markets. They reveal that private law remedies correspond closely to a particular policy of securing the efficiency of markets. We then have to weigh up this regulatory policy against other concerns, such as the exclusion of traders who routinely employ deceptive practices, which may suggest other kinds of deterrent remedies. But in the design of legal regulation of markets more generally, the more important objective must be to establish conditions, facilities, and legal institutions that permit the making of credible commitments and the construction of trust between the parties.

The place of legal sanction in that objective appears deeply ambiguous. Here we encounter the paradoxical relation between trust and legal sanctions. On the one hand, the presence of a readily accessible powerful system for imposing sanctions against contractual default can certainly contribute to the establishment of trust between parties. The depiction of a market without a state by Keith Hart, with its tactics of bullying, humiliation, and the experience of frequent disappointment, suggests that in contrast markets with state sanctions can contribute to an environment of trust. Within a market with an effective legal system, the possibility of binding oneself to legal sanctions will certainly assist new businesses without a trade reputation to encourage trust in their promises. On the other hand, it is apparent from studies by Macaulay,[58] and Beale and Dugdale,[59] amongst others, that the invocation of legal sanctions, the threat to sue for breach of contract, can rapidly displace norms of trust and co-operation and replace them with antagonistic self-interested assertions of rights. The vulnerability to the imposition of state sanctions for breach of contract assists in establishing the credibility of the commitment and constructs a source of trust, but once the legal process is invoked by either party, the reliance upon trust is fractured and displaced by contractual reasoning about rights to legal sanctions or the invocation of non-legal sanctions.

---

[58] Macaulay, S., n. 16 above, 45.   [59] Beale, H., and Dugdale, T., n. 57 above.

Once we recognize that the parties to a contract are unlikely to wish to pursue legal sanctions even in the event of breach of contract, then we can also appreciate that they will pay little attention to the question of whether the agreement is legally enforceable in the first place. What is far more important is whether or not the other party is perceived as trustworthy. If there is trust, then the parties will not wish to displace this by an insistence upon securing a legally enforceable transaction with its implicit threat of legal sanctions for disappointment. Legal enforceability will only become a matter of concern when trust is absent and there are no clear incentives (non-legal sanctions) for fulfilment of expectations. For example, in an American study of whether manufacturers in Connecticut complied with the requirement for contracts of sale to be in writing, the survey found that manufacturers only insisted upon written contracts or acknowledgements when either the customer was unknown from prior dealings, or the manufacturer 'lacked confidence in the customer's integrity'.[60] The legal sanction was plainly insignificant in this commercial context:

Since almost all the manufacturers never resort to litigation as a method of resolving their disputes, and since all but a handful usually either seek no compensation at all or are satisfied to settle for less than their legal right of recovery, the legal enforceability of the promises of the parties with whom they deal apparently means little to them.[61]

The Adjudication Process

Another common mistake of some types of economic analysis is to confine an examination of the role of law in markets to the application of legal sanctions. Although the application of a state sanction provides the occasional dramatic conclusion of the legal process, the more pervasive effect of the legal system in steering social behaviour derives from the dissemination of its legal reasoning into other communication systems. This impact concerns how the law thinks about issues, how it expresses its reasoning, and the place in which these ideas are propounded.

During the legal process regarding a contractual dispute, the legal system provides a system of reasoning which selects information about the events which have occurred. Legal reasoning, as we have discussed in Chapter 3, is closed in the sense that it gathers information selectively, regarding much as irrelevant and some points as crucial. The reasoning occurs ultimately in a court setting. The court provides an authoritative statement of what has happened. This statement is usually regarded by the community as reliable, as fact, as truth. Moreover, it is a public statement,

[60] Comment, n. 56 above, 1054.   [61] Ibid. 1062.

which can be heard and acted upon by all members of the trading community.

These features of the legal process become especially important when the constitution of a market depends heavily upon business reputation as a source of trust. A judicial determination that a person has broken a contract transforms the position from one of murky mutual recrimination and rumour to one of an authoritative declaration of untrustworthiness. Members of the community will then adopt the typical non-legal sanctions of refusal to trade with the merchant whose reputation has been so damaged. In this context, it is not the legal sanction which serves the purpose of providing incentives to fulfil undertakings, but the court's declaration of right and wrong. In other words, the court serves the function of collecting and disseminating what participants in the market regard as reliable information about trustworthiness.[62]

This function of the legal process need not be performed by an institution which possesses all the trappings and powers of a modern court. What is required is rather a body that is respected by the trading community as an impartial and reliable finder of fact or truth. This body could be a committee of a trading association, such as a medieval guild, an arbitrator, or an Ombudsman charged with the role of consumer watchdog. In particular, the body does not require the power to impose effective sanctions itself. Its influence upon contractual behaviour stems instead from the independent reactions of participants in the market to its authoritative judgements about business reputation. In game theory this institution is therefore described as a 'reputation mechanism', for in the case of repeated games (transactions) where the individual cannot enforce the contract, a reputation mechanism which observes behaviour and confers good and bad business reputations for compliance with contracts can be used to help to establish a credible commitment not to cheat on a particular transaction.[63] During medieval times, for instance, many international trade fairs held their own courts, such as the Champagne courts. The courts had no real power to impose a sanction against traders found to be in default, for the merchants came from all over Europe and might be only intermittent traders at the fairs. Nevertheless the courts were respected as arbiters of truth, so that a judgement against a trader either had to be met expeditiously and publicly, or that trader would be ostracized and excluded by the private actions of other merchants. The

---

[62] Bendor, J., and Mookherjee, D., 'Norms, Third-party Sanctions, and Co-operation', *Journal of Law, Economics & Organization* 6 (1990) 33.

[63] Clay, K., 'Trade Without Law: Private-Order Institutions in Mexican California', *Journal of Law, Economics and Organization* 13 (1997) 202.

court's pronouncement activated a multilateral reputation mechanism amongst all traders.[64]

The legal process, or equivalent types of umpires, can therefore play an important role in creating trust in markets and facilitating the application of non-legal sanctions, without ever invoking the power to impose legal sanctions. It is this adjudication mechanism that may be the most important contribution of the legal system to the construction of markets. Even so, it is not an indispensable mechanism, for alternatives to legal adjudication can provide an equivalent service. Furthermore, trading can take place without any such mechanism at all. We noticed in connection with Walker-Thomas Furniture Co. that the company took considerable steps to avoid customers resorting to any such authoritative mechanism so that it retained the power to insist upon its own version of when it had breached its obligations. As long as the customers retained trust in the sales representatives, they were prepared to accept these unilateral determinations of right.

Conclusion

This chapter has addressed the large question of the contribution of law to the construction of markets. We shall return to this theme several times. In the next chapter, we examine in closer detail the determinants of the behaviour of individuals in contractual relations, which throws further light on how the legal system interacts with the social practice of entering transactions. Later chapters include studies of the role of lawyers, the importance of markets constructed without the state in modern economies, and the optimal form of legal regulation. At this stage, however, we can reach some tentative conclusions.

Markets are comprised of patterns of entry into transactions by individuals. They choose to do so where the perceived benefits of the transaction outweigh the perceived risks of disappointment or betrayal. When transactions take place, the risks of disappointment or betrayal have not been eliminated, but they have been displaced, so that they no longer present a formidable obstacle to trade. Displacement occurs when the parties have a relation of trust based upon either a personal relation or a business reputation. Much activity in relation to contracts should be understood as creating the conditions under which this trust can be established. To make a commitment credible, a party may have to demonstrate that a valuable business reputation is at stake, or that investments will be lost.

---

[64] Milgrom, P. R., *et al.*, 'The Role of Institutions in the Revival of Trade: The Law Merchant, Private Judges, and the Champagne Fairs', *Economics and Politics* 2 (1990) 1.

Alternatively, the parties can construct non-legal sanctions or security, so that the evident risk of loss from betrayal or disappointment is heightened, the commitment becomes more tangible, and the contract becomes effectively self-enforcing.

Aside from the construction of the normative system of property rights that is presupposed in all trading activity, the legal system makes a marginal contribution to this construction of markets. Legal sanctions rarely make a significant contribution to the construction of trust, and the invocation of the legal process can often damage perceptions of trust-worthiness. Legal adjudication, on the other hand, like other systems of authoritative determinations of right, can contribute to the construction of trust by providing an ingredient in the enforcing of non-legal sanctions regarding business reputations. Contrary to many assumptions in political theory and classic sociological thought, the enforcement mechanism provided by the state seems to be a dispensable element in the construction of markets, as illustrated by the many examples of markets without a state.

6
Rationality of Contractual Behaviour

Contractual behaviour often appears puzzling to the external observer. A legally enforceable contract is broken, but the injured party fails to assert any legal rights. A contractor demands extra money for the performance of a contractual undertaking agreed at a fixed price, and the other party willingly agrees without protesting against this apparent extortion.[1] Two businesses agree a contract, which their legal advisors tell them is probably unenforceable, but they appear to be unconcerned.[2] Many contracts are performed even though one party incurs a financial loss.[3] Some businesses such as large retail stores provide a replacement for goods even though the goods originally supplied were not defective and complied precisely with the written contract.[4] A purchaser of raw materials asks for less than the contractually agreed quantity, and the supplier agrees to the reduction without objection or price variation.[5] These are all common observations of contractual behaviour, and, at first sight, they appear quite odd.

Although contractual undertakings are often regarded as quintessential forms of rational self-interested action, these observations of contractual behaviour appear to detect an opposite type of motivation, which might be described as altruistic or even irrational. Why do the parties not stick to their contractual undertakings? Why do they not pursue their immediate self-interest by demanding performance of the contract or insisting upon the limits of their express contractual undertakings? Why do they not threaten to enforce the contract in the event of breach? Contractual

---

[1] e.g. *Williams v Roffey Bros & Nicholls (Contractors) Ltd* [1991] 1 QB 1, [1990] 1 All ER 512, CA.

[2] Macaulay, S., 'Non-Contractual Relations in Business' *American Sociological Review* 28 (1963) 45 (on requirements contracts, discussed in the previous chapter); Palay, T. M., 'Comparative Institutional Economics: The Governance of Rail Freight Contracting', *Journal of Legal Studies* 13 (1984) 265.

[3] Schultz, F., 'The Firm Offer Puzzle: A Study of Business Practice in the Construction Industry', *University of Chicago Law Review* 19 (1952) 237.

[4] Kamkas, A., and Rosenwasser, R., 'Department Store Complaint Management', in L. Nader (ed.), *No Access to Law: Alternatives to the American Judicial System* (New York: Academic Press, 1980) 283.

[5] Daintith, T., 'Vital Fluids: Beer and Petroleum Distribution in English Law', in C. Joerges (ed.), *Franchising and the Law: Theoretical and Comparative Approaches in Europe and the United States* (Baden Baden: Nomos Verlagsgesellschaft, 1991) 143.

behaviour appears to be rife with actions that appear to run contrary to rational self-interested action.

My first objective in this chapter is to explain how this kind of behaviour can be interpreted as rational action. It is true that the behaviour may not always be in the immediate economic self-interest of a party to a contract, but this should not be the only measure of rational action. Following an analysis of the rationality of contractual behaviour in terms of a competition between communication systems, we then examine the significance of the phenomenon that participants in markets appear to attach little weight to formal contractual relations. My analysis is also compared to a different type of explanation based upon the observation of the phenomenon of relational contracts. The chapter concludes by considering the implications for legal regulation of the complicated picture of competing rational standards of contractual behaviour. As ever, the underlying purpose of the enquiry is to discover how legal regulation may better achieve its objective of supporting transactions and markets.

Three Frameworks of Contractual Behaviour

We can begin to discern the rationality of these aspects of contractual behaviour by distinguishing between frameworks or points of reference within which actions take place. Most human action is oriented towards a particular normative system. It obtains its meaning and purpose by being directed towards the satisfaction of particular standards. These standards fit together to provide a systematic orientation for particular actions. Conduct acquires its point and purpose by using these standards as a reference. The rules of soccer, for example, provide the action of kicking a ball into a net with standards of reference which give it meaning (a goal) and purpose (to win the game). Unlike the simple model of a game, however, the social interaction of making transactions often involves multiple frameworks of reference.

In connection with contractual behaviour, I suggest that we can distinguish usefully, though schematically, between three dimensions or normative systems governing action: the business relation, the economic deal, and the contract. These three points of reference for contractual behaviour provide standards which the parties use to guide their own behaviour and their evaluation of the other party's behaviour. The patterns of social interaction described by these normative systems produce a differentiation between the communications between the parties according to the dominant point of reference. In other words, the parties to a contract can think and converse about their relationship in three radically different ways.

Business Relation

The social and business relation between the parties both precedes the transaction and is expected to persist after performance. It consists of the trading relation between the parties, made up by numerous inter-actions, some of which may involve contracts, but often will consist of enquiries, discussions of plans, and sorting out problems which have arisen. Surrounding and sustaining the trading relation, we are also likely to discover informal social relations, such as business lunches, links through family or social networks of friendships, membership of clubs, and ethnic identity.

We have already observed that this business relation provides an important source of the trust which encourages parties to enter into transactions. The normative system of orientation for this dimension is principally concerned with the development and preservation of trust, though in the event of betrayal it may also guide actions of recrimination and punishment. An important ingredient of this normative context will be the customary standards of trade, for conformity with these standards and support for their institutional framework will have served to create trust between the parties.

Action oriented towards the business relation has as its predominant purpose the preservation and enhancement of trust. Actions will be understood within this framework as either demonstrations of trustworthiness, or the opposite, a sign of betrayal. Failure to keep a promise sealed by a handshake within a long-standing business relation may therefore be treated as a deliberate signal that the business relation should no longer be regarded as a source of trust. Equally, the keeping of a promise, even though both parties are aware that this will cause economic losses, represents an affirmation that the business relation will be awarded priority in dealings between the parties, so that trust will be enhanced. The communication system of the business relation examines contractual behaviour with regard to the degree to which actions sustain or subvert the bonds of trust between the parties.

Economic Deal

Next, there is the deal or agreement between the parties, which specifies the reciprocal obligations created by this discrete transaction, and which establishes the economic incentives and non-legal sanctions. Economic rationality provides the normative framework of reference for this dimension of contractual behaviour in market transactions. It suggests a calculus of both short-term and long-term economic interest by which to measure and assess contractual behaviour. The communication system between the parties examines behaviour by reference to rational self-interested action.

Within this frame of reference, actions are assessed solely by reference to economic self-interest. A breach of a contract in order to avoid loss represents a rational application of the criteria, despite the betrayal and loss of trust which the breach causes. The key measurement concerns the price or cost of performance in relation to the value placed upon the expected benefit. Rational conduct by this criterion requires contractual performance only when the benefits exceed costs of default combined with costs of making alternative transactions in the market.

The economic calculation within this framework has to integrate both long-term and short-term interest. It might be worth accepting short-term losses for the sake of long-term gains from contractual relations with a particular party. A useful model to describe this framework of both short-term and long-term interest is a repeated non-cooperative game.

In the model of a non-cooperative game, both parties pursue their economic self-interest, but are unable to control the actions of the other, and therefore cannot dictate outcomes. Their actions must be guided by predictions of the rational behaviour of the other, who also operates under the same conditions of uncertainty and lack of control over outcomes. Communication between the parties is always possible, but there is no guarantee that statements will be true or that any promises will be kept. This feature of the lack of reliability makes the game 'non-co-operative'. It is sometimes assumed in the economic theory of games that in the context of legally enforceable contracts we must be exploring the terrain of co-operative games. But our earlier insight with respect to the insignificance of legal sanctions in steering contractual behaviour reveals that such an assumption is false. The presence of a legally enforceable contract makes little difference to the credibility of commitments.

The parties' predictions of the other's future behaviour therefore place most weight on an analysis of the other's self-interest. The worker will perform the job because she needs her wages to survive; the employer will pay the promised wage as long as the required work has not been completed. Both parties count on this self-interest in order to predict the behaviour of the other. The creation of non-legal sanctions is a way of guiding how this self-interest will determine action, so that conduct becomes more predictable. This model of rational action emphasizes how self-interested action, such as defective but cheaper performance of a contract, must be assessed by reference to the costs incurred by the predictable response of the other party, such as the imposition of the non-legal sanction of a refusal to pay the agreed price in full.

This model derived from game theory has to become more elaborate in order to grasp the point that most transactions occur within a trading relation that persists over a period of time. The transaction of a consumer purchasing goods in a shop, for instance, is likely to be one of an indefinite series of transactions between the parties. The theory of repeated games suggests that such a series of transactions will always be inherently unstable. In the final transaction of the series, there is an incentive to cheat, as in the case of the shopkeeper providing defective goods, because the sanction of withdrawal from the trading relation is removed in the final transaction of the series.[6] Knowing this problem, the consumer will be reluctant to enter each transaction for fear that the shopkeeper will treat it as the final one in the series and therefore cheat. The solution to this problem lies in ensuring that for every transaction in the indefinite series the shopkeeper will benefit more from continuing the series than cheating on that particular transaction. In the case of retail sales, this condition is likely to be met, for the benefit of cheating on a particular transaction is usually likely to be far less valuable than the benefit to be obtained from the profit margins on the indefinite series. Under this model, therefore, long-term interest in the context of an indefinite series of transactions usually requires proper performance of contractual undertakings. The game of repeated transactions achieves stability or equilibrium, because long-term interest nearly always requires the sacrifice of the short-term interest to cheat. Under this model, therefore, uniquely self-interested, short-term benefits from contractual behaviour are unlikely to prove the determinative guide to conduct.

Contract

The third normative framework of contractual behaviour is constituted by the standards provided by the self-regulation contained in the contract. This frame of reference orients conduct to the identification of rights and obligations established by any formal documents, explicit agreements, and accepted customary standards. It guides the parties in making assertions of rights and correlative claims to obligations to perform or pay compensation. The self-regulation provides another frame of reference by which to judge whether the other party has defaulted or cheated.

Lawyers will often be employed to guide and to articulate the discourse generated by this contractual orientation, so that it may be described as legalistic. But this framework is not exactly the same as how the law thinks about the conduct of the parties. The contractual discourse is not confined to lawyers. The parties to a deal may decide that it would be prudent to iron out the details of a potentially divisive issue in a formal way, not because they expect ever to have a legal dispute, but for the purposes of clarifying the problem and determining the allocation of risks and liabilities in advance.

---

[6] Telser, L. G., 'A Theory of Self-enforcing Agreements', *Journal of Business* 53 (1980) 27.

This attention to the details of planning is not necessarily connected to the possibility of legal enforcement. For example, in Palay's study of rail freight contracting in the USA, most of the contracts which the parties negotiated were probably unenforceable due to regulations governing interstate commerce, but this lack of enforceability in no way discouraged the parties from committing some complex aspects of the transaction to a written agreement.[7] During performance of a contract as well, the parties may raise points in this legalistic mode. One party may argue that she never agreed to the contract, because she never signed the documents. Another party may point to the small print in the standard form contract in order to rely on an exception clause which absolves him from breach of contract. Indeed, lawyers may have a rather less legalistic approach to detailed points of interpretation than the layman, since they are aware that a court may adopt a rather looser, purposive, or 'common-sense' interpretation of the legal rules and the terms of the contract.[8] How the law thinks about the terms of a contract may therefore differ from the way the layman expounds this contractual framework, even though the layman may believe that he is tracking legal argumentation.

This third framework may be described more accurately therefore as how the contract thinks about the relation between the parties. It emphasizes the autonomous, unsituated obligations constituted by the formal agreement. The formation of the agreement creates a new system of communication between the parties, which is distinct from the communication systems established by the business relation and the economic deal. The way in which the contract thinks about disputes is a framework which isolates the transaction from its economic and social context. The communication system of contract treats the obligations undertaken as absolute undertakings, firm commitments, which cannot be revised except through the process of revising the contract itself by agreement. It is this third framework which describes the discrete communication system represented by the contractual relation.

Competing Norms of Contractual Behaviour

By distinguishing these three dimensions of economic transactions, we can understand many puzzling features of contractual behaviour. Each dimen-

---

[7] Palay, T. M., n. 2 above.

[8] e.g. Lord Hoffman, *Investors Compensation Scheme Ltd v West Bromwich Building Society* [1998] 1 WLR 898, HL; Lord Wilberforce, *Reardon Smith Ltd v Tngar Hansen Tangen (The Diana Prosperity)* [1976] 1 WLR 989, HL; Sir Robert Goff, 'Commercial Contracts and the Commercial Court', *Lloyds Maritime and Commercial Law Quarterly*, [1984], 382; Lord Steyn, 'Contract Law and the Reasonable Expectations of Honest Men', *Law Quarterly Review* 113 (1997) 433.

sion has its own normative standards by which the parties guide their behaviour. The dimensions can each be described as closed, self-referential communication systems, which have their distinct 'internal point of view' of the rules and standards which are appropriate to processing information and resolving conflict. Conduct can be rational with respect to one set of normative criteria, but irrational with regard to the others. The examples of contractual behaviour given at the beginning of this chapter reveal occasions when one framework has been regarded as determinative, even though it leads to action which is neither optimal nor rational under another criterion. In short, it does not make sense within the other communication systems.

The parties to a transaction are engaged in what appears to be a simple event, such as a sale of apples at the market stall. But their conduct will be guided to some extent by all three frameworks simultaneously. The parties have to steer a way through these competing systems of guidance. Their understanding of the meaning and significance of contractual behaviour differs according to the way in which they constitute a hierarchy between the competing or colliding communication systems.

Consider the simple example of a clear breach of a contractual expect-ation such as the delivery of goods. The business relation may encourage the disappointed party to ignore the breach of contract for the sake of preserving a harmonious business relation. Similarly, the business relation may encourage the party who has caused disappointment to make amends, even if there is not in fact any legal obligation to do so due to the presence of some exclusion clause in the written contract. In relation to the deal, considerations of economic interest predominate, so that short-term and long-term economic interests will have to be weighed when considering a response to disappointment. Often these calculations will suggest a compromise of interests, a settlement which protects the economic advan-tages to both parties of the transaction, albeit at a reduced level. When one party fails to deliver the goods on time, the response within the commu-nication system of the deal may be to accept late delivery or to reject the goods entirely according to the calculus of self-interest. The settlement of any dispute will be determined in a way which preserves the economic viability of the deal for both parties by means of a compromise of interests. The normative context of the contract provides the final dimension of the transaction, where the parties assert conflicting rights on the basis of the agreement. These rights do not admit compromise, but the winner takes all. The buyer asserts the right to reject the goods for late delivery, or insists on the right to full and prompt contractual performance. The seller points to the small print of the contract that contains an excuse or limitation of liability.

These distinctions between communication systems explain what is happening in common observations of contractual behaviour, for the actors may orient themselves towards one normative context to the exclusion of others. In Macaulay's study of business contracts in America, he describes what happened when a regular business customer cancelled an 'order'. The sales representative took no action, and, on inquiry, did not consider that a breach of contract had occurred.[9] Here the sales representative's conduct is oriented principally towards the long-term business relation. This strong orientation towards the preservation of trust excludes the contractual framework from conscious consideration altogether. In addition, there will be the calculation within the business relation that a threat of litigation over the breach of contract might damage the trust which sustains the business relation. The behaviour of the sales representative is also consistent with the repeated game model of the economic deal. Although it is plainly not in the short-term economic interest of the seller to accept a breach of contract without compensation, the prediction of the buyer's response to threats of litigation may be the non-legal sanction of withdrawal of business. With this prediction, it becomes rational for the seller to avoid a claim which might provoke such a response, and to wait until later when this concession may be taken into account in settling a future disagreement.

In another striking example, Beale and Dugdale report on the handling of complaints about defects in products supplied within a business relation. If the complaint is accepted as justified, there will be an offer of repair without charge, or a willingness to reduce prices in future transactions.[10] These responses maintain the value of the particular deal to both parties, and simultaneously seek to preserve the business relation for the future. There was almost certainly a breach of contract in such cases, for which a legal sanction of financial compensation could have been claimed. But this course of action does not seem to have occurred to the actors themselves. Indeed, no money changes hands. Their conduct studiously avoids the contractual orientation towards rights and correlative obligations, but rather awards priority to the business relation, and second place to the business deal.

In these studies also, the subjects observe that appeals to legal rights, or the written documents containing the legal contract, are likely to be regarded as a form of bad faith or betrayal. This interpretation of events occurs because such appeals to legal rights signify the transition to a rival normative context. The norms of the business relation and the calculus of economic interests of the deal are abandoned in favour of the conflictual

---

[9] Macaulay, S., n. 2 above.
[10] Beale, H., and Dugdale, T., 'Contracts between Businessmen: Planning and the Use of Contractual Remedies', *British Journal of Law and Society* 2 (1975) 45, 59.

assertion of an antipathy of interests and a demand for entitlements without compromise.

In an extended examination of these competing norms of contractual behaviour, Daintith describes the practice of long-term contracts in sales of iron ore to steel mills. This is an international market with few buyers and sellers, where the business relations were for the most part long-term. In the early 1970s the purchasing contracts for iron ore were for a fixed term (perhaps 10 years), a fixed quantity (or a minimum quantity), and a fixed price. But currency fluctuations and the collapse of the steel market rendered such arrangements unworkable. To respond to currency fluctuations, the parties initially agreed an adjustment of prices, and then modified the agreements to an annual negotiation of prices. To respond to the decline in demand, however, for a long time there was no alteration of the minimum quantity specified in the contract. Instead, the sellers merely permitted the buyers to order according to their requirements, though this position was sometimes reflected in a subsequent amendment to the contract to include a tonnage flexibility clause. Although the external crises forced many breaches of contract, there was no resort to litigation or arbitration. These problems were handled by co-operation and flexibility between the businesses. The strict legal entitlements contained in the self-regulation represented by the contract were of far less importance to the behaviour of the parties than the norms derived from the desire to preserve the business relation and the need to make the deal work for both parties. As Daintith observes:

In most cases, today, the parties are performing a relationship different from that written in the contract, in which non-contractual norms, like fairness in quantity reductions, may be more important than contractual ones.[11]

The vestigial adherence to the old formal contract, even though it did not in practice determine the conduct of the parties, can perhaps be explained by the symbolic importance of maintaining the express commitment to long-term business relations.

Within larger business organizations, we may observe that different departments of the firm may select rival normative contexts. Whereas the sales representative may regard the business relation as pre-eminent, the legal department may read the events within the contractual framework as a breach of contract against which legal action should be taken. The general manager may view the same event through an economic perspective, making a calculation of short- and long-term economic interest in determining the appropriate response to a breach of contract. The

---

[11] Daintith, T., 'The Design and Performance of Long-term Contracts', in T. Daintith and G. Teubner (eds.), *Contract and Organisation* (Berlin: Walter de Gruyter, 1986) 164, 186.

production division will focus on the technical specifications, the time-scale for delivery, and whether satisfactory performance was ever practicable. The presence of these rival perspectives within a collective actor such as a firm may explain sudden shifts in the dominant normative orientation during a dispute.[12]

As well as these studies of commercial contracts, we can point to the competing norms of contractual behaviour in the context of consumer purchases. When a consumer complains to a shop that recently purchased goods are faulty, the normative framework adopted by most retailers is directed towards the business relation and the deal. The legal rights of the parties are rarely introduced into the conversation. For example, in a questionnaire directed to retailers in Edmonton, Alberta, no retailers mentioned that legal rights and obligations were relevant to their approach to the handling of the complaint. The important factors were business reputation and the desire to preserve the long-term business relation through repeat purchases. Indeed, most of the returns of goods in some shops had no legal basis at all, as when the customer decided that she did not like the colour of the item, but that did not alter the retailer's policy of accepting the goods back.[13]

Apparently puzzling contractual behaviour therefore becomes comprehensible once we recognize that the parties may be orienting their action towards competing norms of contractual behaviour. Studies of business practice reveal that the frames of reference provided by the relation and the deal are likely to carry greater weight than the strict contractual point of view. The position becomes reversed, however, once the parties perceive that the business relation itself has broken down and that the deal cannot be retrieved by compromise of interests. A premature assertion of the contractual perspective by pointing to strict entitlements under the contract is regarded as a hostile act, for it conveys the message that the business relation is no longer valued, and that a compromise of interests is no longer possible.

The 'Non-Use' of Contracts

An interpretation that has been placed upon these empirical studies of contractual behaviour is that contracts are not used by businessmen, or that the contract is irrelevant in business dealings, or even that contracts actually impede business deals. This interpretation of the non-use of

---

[12] Macaulay, S., n. 2 above, 66.
[13] Ramsay, I., 'Consumer Redress Mechanisms for Poor-Quality and Defective Products', *University of Toronto Law Journal* 31 (1981) 117, 129.

contracts by businessmen has been presented most powerfully by Macaulay himself:

Most businessmen have an attitude towards contracts that can best be described as indifferent or even hostile . . . They remark 'contracts are a waste of time; we've never had any trouble because we know our customers and our suppliers; if we needed a contract with a man we wouldn't deal with him. Lawyers just get in the way.'[14]

This interpretation of the attitude of businessmen seems to me to be confusing and misleading.

One problem with this interpretation is the confusion between the contractual frame of reference and the use of the law in order to enforce rights. It is certainly true that the legal system is rarely employed to enforce self-regulation by contract, but this does not mean that the self-regulation contained in the contractual agreement is unimportant in guiding contractual behaviour. The reasons for the absence of litigation range broadly over such matters as cost, calculations of the risk of failure, and the damage to business reputation and long-term business relations. In many instances legal enforcement may simply not be viable because of the weak financial position of the debtor. It is quite possible, therefore, for the self-regulation established by the contract to comprise the key normative orientation for the parties, even though they rarely have any intention to use the legal system to enforce that regulation. They use the contract as a point of reference during negotiations towards a settlement of a dispute, even though they have no intention of resorting to law.

A more fundamental problem with the claim that the empirical studies reveal the non-use of contract lies in its failure to appreciate the presence of all three normative frameworks in all contractual contexts. The parties to the contract will be conducting their discourse within each system of thought, but in many instances one discourse will take priority over the others. The contractual framework does not disappear when the injured party prefers to ignore the breach of contract and to emphasize instead the norms derived from the business relation or economic interest. The contractual framework may be invoked at any time. It will be resuscitated if the parties perceive that the long-term relation is about to terminate or the considerations of economic self-interest now point in the direction of strict contractual enforcement of a discrete transaction. In the absence of these conditions, however, which will normally represent the situation in successful trading relations, we should expect the contractual framework to be

---

[14] Macaulay, S., 'The Use and Non-use of Contracts in the Manufacturing Industry', *Practical Lawyer* 9(7) (1963) 13, 14. The significance of this theme in the sociology of contractual behaviour is considered in Campbell, D. 'Socio-Legal Analysis of Contract', in P. A. Thomas (ed.), *Socio-Legal Studies* (Aldershot: Dartmouth, 1997) 239.

temporarily occluded. The important point to remember is that all three frameworks will normally be available as a discursive resource through which the parties may negotiate improvements to their position.

We can discover, however, good evidence in these surveys of business practice of calculated decisions to avoid the creation of a legally enforceable contract or at least a formal contractual document, so that it cannot provide the basis for an alternative discourse for negotiations and disputes. Here the 'non-use' of contract, at least in the sense of using detailed written contracts and orders, has the purpose of foreclosing arguments about entitlements. The record of an interview with the Vice President in Charge of Sales of a manufacturer of paper explains why the company has no written contracts with any of its customers despite the high values involved:

Practically, the contracts [used previously] were all one sided. They bound us but provided nothing in return. We could not make the publishers or printers eat the excess paper and take it when they could not use it. Moreover, when a publisher or printer cancels an order for paper, he has just lost a big order or his magazine is in trouble. He is a difficult man to hold for damages then. On the other hand, we do not need contracts with our big accounts—they will take the paper and pay for it. Thus a contract gives us nothing but reduces our flexibility in allocating paper to customers we want to favor.[15]

The final sentence reveals the determinative purpose of avoiding formal contractual documents: it permits flexibility in addressing the needs and interests of all customers, so that valued customers can be given preferential treatment and these business relations reinforced.

Another objection to the claim about the non-use of contracts is that the findings of the original studies in the context of American industry in the 1950s and 1960s cannot be generalized. Times have changed, the post-war boom is over, and so it is probable that under the pressure of global competition the behaviour of businesses towards contracts has altered. Such pressures might account for the apparent proliferation of lawyers in the USA, their heavy involvement in hammering out major deals, and indeed their invasion as a profession of all forms of regulation of business and dispute resolution.[16] Furthermore, it may be doubted whether the attitudes of American businessmen will be replicated in other cultures such as Germany or Japan. Do these studies only provide us with a partial view, perhaps emphasizing manufacturing industry at the expense of construction and service industries such as banking and professional

---

[15] Macaulay, S., *et al.*, *Contracts: Law in Action* (Michie Co., Charlottesville, 1995), 415.
[16] Dezalay, Y., 'Between the State, Law, and the Market: The Social and Professional Stakes in the Construction and Definition of a Regulatory Arena', in W. Bratton, *et al.*, *International Regulatory Competition and Coordination* (Oxford: Clarendon Press, 1996) 59, 64.

services, where the contracts may be the dominant normative framework for contractual behaviour? My own view is, however, that once Macaulay's thesis about the non-use of contracts is interpreted in the way I have suggested, then the evidence tends to support its generalization across markets and across time.

Later studies of business behaviour seem to me largely to confirm the earlier descriptions of the presence of competing normative frameworks. We still find that the vast majority of businesses across a broad range of industrial sectors are willing to accept substantial contract modifications on the basis of trade practice, long-term business relations, or in order to support a particular deal.[17] It is true that the questionnaires in the surveys are now completed by corporate counsel rather than a business manager, perhaps signifying the widespread insertion of lawyers into management systems, but these counsel seem to behave in the same way as their predecessors. They deny hotly the suggestion that they are more likely to focus on legal rights than other non-lawyer executives.[18] This finding seems plausible to me; lawyers are especially capable of performing a contractual discourse, but they have always been deal-makers and fixers, perfectly competent to grasp and deploy the alternative rationalities. To be a lawyer does not mean that you think like a lawyer all the time. Even a lawyer can shift between the competing norms of contractual behaviour.

There are suggestions of some variations in business cultures, but also the discovery of considerable similarity.[19] In Germany, there is evidence suggesting that the formal contractual undertakings are viewed more centrally in constituting the business deal, so that greater attention will be paid by businessmen to the documents.[20] On the other hand, the contractual document will not necessarily be regarded as limiting the commitments, so that flexibility in settlements and adjustment of undertakings can be expected in the light of the business relation and the working of the deal. In contrast, in Japan there is a concern expressed (often by foreign commentators) about a lack of 'contract consciousness', where the business relation and the deal are believed to eclipse the contractual norms. But surveys designed to test this suggestion appear to discover no significant difference, with perhaps only a slightly greater emphasis on business

---

[17] Weintraub, R. J, 'A Survey of Contract Practice and Policy', *Wisconsin Law Review* (1992), 1, 19.   [18] Ibid., 26.
[19] Blegvad, B., 'Commercial Relations, Contract, and Litigation in Denmark: A Discussion of Macaulay's Theories', *Law and Society Review* 24 (1990) 397; Macaulay, S., 'Elegant Models, Empirical Pictures, and the Complexities of Contract', *Law and Society Review* 11 (1977) 507.
[20] Arrighetti, A., *et al.*, 'Contract Law, Social Norms and Inter-Firm Co-operation', *Cambridge Journal of Economics* 21 (1997) 171.

considerations over contractual entitlements in Japan.[21] Perhaps the only real difference is the greater involvement of lawyers in the formation of contracts in common law countries compared to Japan, which in turn may reflect the greater complexity of private law regulation.[22] A better interpretation of contractual behaviour in Japan would emphasize the greater significance of non-legal sanctions, such as harm to reputation, which would then tend to displace the significance of contractual terms and legal sanctions. There is also evidence that the Japanese courts are more alert to these dimensions of the business relation, so that the legal process is more designed to reinforce normative standards based upon the continuation of the business relation than their Western counterparts.[23]

My interpretation of the alleged 'non-use' of contracts is therefore that the contractual frame of reference is used whenever it is rational to do so. In the series of repeated games that represents most trading relations, however, it is rarely rational to invoke the contractual discourse. By switching away from the construction of trust within the long-term business relation and from the desire to make the deal work for both parties, the contractual discourse normally threatens both immediate and long-term economic interests. The non-use of contracts is not fuelled by an irrational hatred of lawyers, nor a blinkered incompetence in business planning, but guided by good business sense.

Relational and Discrete Contracts

In an influential series of works, Ian Macneil has argued that classical legal doctrine understands contractual relations from a particular perspective, that of the discrete transaction. How the private law of contract thinks about action is to measure it against the precise express obligations contained in the contract. The classical law assumes that the terms of the contract (supplemented by implicit understandings between the parties) provide a comprehensive normative framework by which to guide and judge the conduct of the parties. Macneil suggests, however, that this classical law model has proved an unsatisfactory tool for the regulation of what he calls 'relational contracts'. These contracts have the features

---

[21] Nottage, L., 'Bargaining in the Shadow of the Law and the Law in the Light of Bargaining: Contract Planning and Renegotiation in the US, New Zealand and Japan,' in Feest, J., and Gessner, V. (eds.), *Interaction of Legal Cultures* (Onati: Onati International Institute of Sociology of Law, 1997).

[22] Kitagawa, Z., 'Use and Non-Use of Contracts in Japanese Business Relations: A Comparative Analysis', in H. Baum (ed.), *Japan: Economic Success and Legal System* (Berlin/New York: Walter de Gruyter,1997) 145, 148.

[23] Haley, J. O., 'Relational Contracting: Does Community Count?', in H. Baum (ed.), n. 22 above, 167, 169.

that performance persists over a period of time and that the contract provides an incomplete specification of the obligations. For these relational contracts, the assumption of the classical law that the contractual terms provide complete self-regulation (or as Macneil says 'presentation') is plainly untenable.[24]

Legal doctrine has in response sought to adapt its regulation to suit relational contracts. The principal requirement of this adaptation is to introduce a greater degree of regulation of the content of contract in order to address the problem of incomplete self-regulation. The content of this regulation also needs to be tailored to the long-term nature of the economic relation. We examine this problem of the legal response to incomplete planning in the next chapter. We also consider the extent to which these alterations in the approach to regulation of contracts represent a transformation of the classical law of contract in the subsequent chapter. Here we address the preliminary issue concerning the idea of a relational contract as an explanation of contractual behaviour.

The contrast between discrete and relational contracts presents a possible explanation of puzzling contractual behaviour. It suggests that in discrete contracts, that is, isolated, brief transactions, such as purchase of petrol from a service station, contractual behaviour will be governed by sharply defined commitments and entitlements. In contrast, in relational contracts, such as a long-term requirements contract or a major construction project, then contractual behaviour will be oriented towards the long-term business objectives of the parties, and it will recognize the need for co-operation and adjustment in order to achieve those objectives. This comparison between discrete and relational contracts does throw some light on differences in contractual behaviour. Yet it is implicit in my earlier analysis that the contrast between relational and discrete contracts tends unfortunately to obscure the most important distinctions in the analysis of contractual behaviour. The comparison elides the three frameworks of reference, and, by so doing, obstructs a complete explanation of the rationality of contractual behaviour, which in turn may lead to unsatisfactory regulatory conclusions. The contrast between discrete and relational contracts proves inadequate as a tool of analysis, because of its implication that these dimensions present oppositions.

My contention is rather that all three dimensions are always present in contractual relations, though contractual behaviour may attribute a dominant position to one or the other in any particular case. Consider, for

---

[24] Macneil, I, 'Contracts: Adjustment of Long-term Economic Relations under Classical, Neoclassical, and Relational Contract Law', *Northwestern University Law Review* 72 (1978), 854; Macneil, I. R., *The New Social Contract: An Inquiry Into Modern Contractual Relations* (New Haven: Yale University Press, 1980); Macneil, I., 'Values in Contract: Internal and External', *Northwestern University Law Review* 78 (1983) 340.

example, the weekly purchase of groceries from a supermarket. This transaction has the three dimensions or points of reference which orient contractual behaviour. As a business relation, the expectation and hope of the supermarket is that the consumer will return to the same store every week. It invests considerably in the business relation by trying to provide a pleasant atmosphere in which to shop, efficient and friendly customer service, loyalty cards for discounts, and a willingness to accept the return of goods by the consumer without the need to demonstrate any defects. The transaction also represents a deal, in which the customer seeks competitive prices, and the supermarket needs to secure a profit margin, not necessarily in a particular week, but over a series of contracts. There is also the contract, a sale of goods as a discrete transaction, in which each item is sold for a fixed price, and default rules supplement this self-regulation by standards of product quality. We can neither characterize this transaction as discrete nor relational, for both dimensions are present: the contractual form may be discrete, an isolated exchange, but probably the dominant orientation of the contractual behaviour of the supermarket is towards the relational aspect. For a dispute about the price of an item, probably the contractual framework will provide the dominant frame of reference, so that the parties will agree that the correct price is the price that was offered by a sign on the shelves or the goods themselves. For a dispute about quality, the supermarket is likely to orient its conduct towards the business relation in order to maintain trust, and towards the long-term profitability of a series of deals with that consumer. My analysis suggests, therefore, that all transactions have both discrete and relational dimensions, and that these classifications obscure the importance of variables along three different dimensions of normative orientation.

My analysis also suggests that the length of time during which performance of a contract is likely to occur should not be regarded as significant for the purpose of the analysis of contractual behaviour. A long-term contract may have the precise, complete self-regulation of a discrete contract in its contractual terms. The contract may specify, for example, exact quantities, quality, and prices of goods to be delivered over a number of years. The significance of this contractual dimension in orienting the conduct of the parties will depend on its relative dominance compared to the other dimensions of the deal and the long-term business relation. In Daintith's study of the long-term iron ore contracts, the original contracts conformed to the pattern of complete self-regulation, and so apart from the period of time over which deliveries were to be made, were similar to an isolated sale of goods. His study reveals, however, that the business deal aspect of the normative framework predominated when the parties had to adapt to a change in circumstances, so that the preservation of a profitable business relation for both sides to the transaction governed their conduct at the expense of the normative framework provided by the contract. Equally, in a short-term, isolated transaction, such as the purchase of petrol from a service station, although the law may supply a complete system of presentation through its regulation of sale of goods contracts, the contractual behaviour at least of the service station is likely to be oriented heavily towards the business relation and the benefits of a long-term sequence of contracts. The brand name and its business reputation will be important to secure trust, and the long-term repeated game dimension of the deal will encourage the service station to suppress thinking about the transaction as a precise set of entitlements and favour instead the relational dimension of good customer relations.

Insofar as the contrast between discrete and relational contracts purports to be a tool for the analysis of contractual behaviour, my contention is that it proves unhelpful. The source of the difficulty lies in its attempt to link patterns of contractual behaviour to real phenomena, that is, types of transaction. My approach links contractual behaviour rather to communication systems, that is to the normative points of reference that guide behaviour. The different communication systems steer behaviour in divergent directions in many instances. These divergences may be more intense in relational contracts, where the business relation system of communication may be thinking about behaviour in the opposite way to the direction indicated by the contractual frame of reference. But I have suggested that all three communication systems will always be present in contractual relations, and that all three will be required to provide an adequate explanation of the rationality of contractual behaviour in every instance.

Reasonable Expectations

Does this explanation of the rationality of contractual behaviour have any implications for the legal regulation of contracts? We have already observed that the way the law thinks about contractual relations is closely analogous to the contractual system of communication. The understanding of rights and entitlements presented by the contractual framework can be translated almost effortlessly by the law into its own self-referential discourse. The buyer's complaint that the goods supplied were defective becomes in law the similar allegation that the seller has broken the express or implied term of the contract to supply goods of satisfactory quality. Moreover, similar closure rules apply to the contractual framework and the legal analysis. The facts that are relevant to the contractual framework, such as the terms of the contract and the performance which has been supplied, will usually be the same facts as those examined in the legal enquiry. This coincidence is, of course, not accidental: the legal system observes contractual practices, and parties to contracts observe legal reasoning. There is cross-fertilization and mimicking of argumentative strategies and closure rules.

The principal effect of this coincidence is that legal reasoning tends to reinforce the contractual framework and at the same time subvert the other discourses of the business relation and the deal. Does this impact of the law on contractual behaviour matter? Does this analysis of the tension between legal regulation and the dimensions of contractual behaviour described as the business relation and the deal suggest that private law discourse is fundamentally misconceived in its approach to regulation of market practices? Should legal regulation be reoriented towards a capacity to understand the competing normative impulses in contractual behaviour? Armed with this capacity, legal regulation would then adjudicate on the collision between the discourses, in some instances favouring strict contractual entitlements, but in others favouring implicit obligations based upon the deal or the business relation. If legal regulation took on this task, then we would have to know how it should develop criteria for adjudication between the competing normative frameworks.

We can explore these rather abstract questions in the context of a particular case. In *Williams v Roffey Bros and Nicholls (Contractors) Ltd*,[25] the plaintiff carpenter agreed with the defendant building contractor to perform work on the refurbishment of twenty-seven flats in return for a fixed sum of £20,000. The plaintiff fell behind schedule in the work. This delay concerned the defendant because under the main contract for the building works a clause reduced payment for late completion of the refurbishment. The defendant promised to pay the plaintiff an extra amount of £10,300, at the rate of £575 per completed flat as an inducement to speed up the work. The defendant also realized that the original price had proved too low for the transaction to be commercially viable for the plaintiff. The plaintiff completed work on eight flats, but the defendant only paid £1,500 more. The plaintiff then sued for the balance due under the modified agreement.

The legal report of the case does not disclose the nature of the prior business relation between the parties. This information is irrelevant under the closure rules of the legal analysis. We may surmise, however, that participants in the construction business in a locality are likely to be familiar with each other. The empirical studies indicate that, despite the practice of competitive tendering, contracts are usually awarded only to those sub-contractors who have had prior dealings with the main

---

[25] [1991] 1 QB 1, [1990] 1 All ER 512, CA.

contractor.[26] We can infer, therefore, that an on-going business relation was likely to be influential in steering the behaviour of the parties. The principal effect of this consideration on the facts was to discourage the parties from rupturing the relation by breaking away from the contractual undertaking.

At the same time, it is apparent from the history of the events that the business deal was an important consideration in the minds of the parties. The reasons for the modification of the original fixed price contract were premised on the need to ensure that the transaction remained commercially viable for both parties. The main contractor needed to complete the transaction on time, in order to avoid the reduction of profits that was threatened by the penalty for delays. At the same time the sub-contractor needed to receive an adequate reward for its work, for otherwise it would be tempted to concentrate on other more profitable jobs. The solution was to agree a modification that restored the commercial viability of the deal for both parties.

This combination of the business relation and the deal steered the behaviour of the contracting parties up to the point when litigation commenced. Until that moment the original contractual arrangement for a fixed price had little practical significance. It did not affect the speed of the carpenter's work or the amount of payment that the main contractor expected to make in fact. Once the dispute over the extra payment entered the realm of legal reasoning, however, suddenly the contractual framework became paramount. The defendant insisted that the original agreement for a fixed price was binding, and that any subsequent modification was invalid on the technical ground of the absence of fresh consideration. There was allegedly no fresh consideration for the modification, because the sub-contractor had merely promised to do what it was already contractually bound to do for the defendant. In other words, this was an opportunistic price increase that a court should not enforce. The plaintiff countered that the modification was binding as a valid revision or variation of the contractual relation. The dispute therefore focused on two competing versions of the contractual framework, and the considerations of the deal and the business relation that formerly motivated the parties were forgotten or ignored.

One view of how the law ought to approach the regulation of such disputes insists that it is appropriate for legal discourse to concentrate exclusively on the contractual framework. Legal regulation should support the authority of the contract as normative framework to guide action. It would be a mistake on this view to deviate from this straight path. It is

---

[26] Eccles, R., 'The Quasifirm in the Construction Industry', *Journal of Economic Behaviour and Organization* 2 (1981) 335.

better that the parties themselves should by mutual agreement decide to shift their normative orientation in the light of how they view the circumstances. If they decide that preservation of the relation or the deal is more important to them than an insistence upon the contractual framework of the terms of the contract, we should assume that this is rational self-interested action and leave them to do so by accepting the legal validity of any compromises or adjustments. It would be dangerous, however, for the law to substitute its own judgement for when the contractual framework should be modified by reference to the other normative frameworks, for this move runs a high degree of risk of error in making assessments of what is in the best interests of the parties. A court may feel, for instance, that one party should not insist upon its strict contractual rights in the light of the change of circumstances or fresh information. Yet the court should not be tempted to substitute its own judgement for that of the parties, since it may thereby force on at least one of the parties, and possibly both, a less than optimal outcome. In other words, legal regulation should forge exclusive links between the contractual framework and its own self-referential reasoning and closure rules. The law should not seek to achieve direct understanding of the other communication systems present in the social relation of the transaction.

The opposite view criticizes this decontextualization of legal discourse. It objects to the exclusive reference to the contractual framework. It is the business relation and the deal that do most to constitute and sustain business relations. To use self-referential discourses and closure rules that deliberately exclude all this information about the environment of a business dispute is a recipe for poor regulation. The law will inevitably obstruct rational contractual behaviour whenever that rationality is based upon the normative frameworks of the business relation and the deal. On this view, the law needs to become more sophisticated in its examination of contractual practices. It should not remain fixated on the information about the contractual framework, but should revise its closure rules in order to incorporate into its reasoning an assessment of the need for support for rational contractual behaviour based upon the business relation or the deal. This revision can be achieved by inserting into the legal discourse a broader or open-textured standard for gathering information about normative expectations.

Such a broader standard might be described as 'reasonable expectations'. Instead of the legal discourse determining entitlements by reference solely to the contractual framework contained in documents and express agreements, the standard of 'reasonable expectation' is calculated to expand the range of information that will describe the standards governing the contractual arrangement. It may be a reasonable expectation, for instance, that despite the presence of a fixed price contract, the parties will anticipate a price adjustment in the event of either mistaken assumptions about costs or unforeseen contingencies. If the legal system is to be supportive of markets in order to overcome problems of distrust, then it should, on this second view, try to be responsive to the alternative normative orientations that represent the whole range of the expectations of the parties. A legal system which fails to support those reasonable expectations will inevitably undermine its contribution to the constitution of markets.

If this second strategy were adopted by legal regulation, it would be hard for legal regulation to understand the communications between the parties concerning the establishment of trust in the business relation and economic self-interest in the deal. These sources of expectations would have to be inserted into the discourse of legal regulation by techniques such as open-ended standards which inevitably reduce the predictability of legal outcomes. For example, the law might adjust its regulation to require performance of contracts, not according to the letter of the contract, but according to a standard of good faith or co-operation. This adjustment would then permit a court to assess whether the expectations of the parties to the contract included the standard that a change of circumstances would require alterations such as additional obligations in the expected performance.

Compared to the stark evidence of the written contract, however, the court will encounter difficulty in abstracting from the conduct of the parties the content of their normative standards based upon the deal or the business relation. The best evidence is likely to be found in past conduct, such as previous dealings or deviations from the contractual self-regulation in practice. But even this evidence is always open to different interpretations. The fact that one party did not insist upon payment on the exact date specified but rather accepted late payment on one occasion provides ambiguous indications of the content of the normative standards. It might be argued that this waiver of breach should be interpreted as an isolated event without implications for future expectations, or that it signalled an agreed revision of the standards applicable to the transaction based upon the business relation or the economic self-interest of the deal.

These two views define the terms of a central debate among contract lawyers. On the one side, those who favour certainty and predictability in legal regulation insist that legal regulation should track the contractual framework as closely as possible, whilst of course leaving the contracting parties free through their discretion of self-enforcement to release each other from the legal obligations. On the other side are those who favour a contextualized approach to legal reasoning, which incorporates into legal reasoning information about all three normative standards that guide rational contractual behaviour. The task of legal reasoning on this latter view is to determine the hierarchy of normative contexts in relation to each particular contractual dispute.

In my view, however, this debate hinges on what appears to be on closer inspection a false dilemma. If we look again at *Williams v Roffey Bros*, both parties were compelled by the traditional legal discourse to present their argument in terms of the contractual framework. The dispute centred on two different versions of the contractual framework, the original fixed price contract, and the informal modification at a higher price with incentives. Legal disputes invariably take this form because the self-referential discourse of the law requires this style of presentation. The assertions of the parties always have to be couched in the language of contractual entitlement, based upon narrow closure rules about the content of the agreement. The interesting question is how the court resolves these conflicts. Unless the court reaches the conclusion that one version of the contractual framework is without foundation in the evidence, then it has to select between them on some other criterion. In this case the Court of Appeal decided that the modified contract contained the definitive statement of the contractual entitlements. It favoured the revised contract on the ground that the defendant had secured commercial benefits (and therefore, dubiously, fresh consideration) from agreeing to the price increase. These benefits included changing work practices, so that at least some of the flats were completed on time in order to avoid the penalty, and the avoidance of the cost of having to make alternative contractual relations. These considerations plainly bring aspects of the normative framework of the deal into the legal discourse in order to resolve the conflict between the competing versions of the contractual framework.

In my view, therefore, the private law system is inevitably drawn into a broader examination of the normative frameworks that guide rational contractual behaviour. The courts cannot resolve disputes solely by reference to the contractual framework unless one version of the contract has no evidential foundation. It is true that the discourses of private law regulation are reluctant to acknowledge the need to drop their tight closure rules by adopting open-ended standards that ostentatiously incorporate other normative frameworks. An assessment of the advantages and disadvantages of a more explicit expansion of normative reference points by the reformulation of legal doctrine into open-ended standards such as 'reasonable expectations' requires more detailed examination in relation to particular regulatory issues. In the next chapter, we examine one problem for the traditional approach, which is the priority it tends to attach to written statements of the contractual framework. In the subsequent chapter, we tackle the most divisive issue of whether considerations of economic efficiency support the traditional exclusive emphasis in legal discourse upon the contractual framework.

7
Planning and Co-operation

What do contract lawyers do? They are employed principally for two tasks: first, to help to plan a transaction, and second, to participate in dispute settlement. The planning role forms the larger proportion of their work. In this chapter we consider first the significance of this planning role to the practice of creating and performing contracts. The limited role of planning in contractual practices suggests methods by which the law should observe and regulate planning. We then examine the difficulties encountered by lawyers in devising appropriate plans for business relations. The major difficulty concerns the inevitable incompleteness of contractual planning. For the purpose of legal regulation of contracts, the important issue becomes how the legal system should understand and respond to incomplete self-regulation. In addition, legal regulation needs to help to overcome the inherent defects of contracts as planning instruments for long-term, sustained co-operation. The underlying meaning of contractual relations always refers to their impermanence, subject always to 'the ever-present threat of dissolution',[1] and therefore the finite scope of the commitment. When confronted by an economic relation intended to be of indefinite duration and left deliberately incomplete in its description of obligations, the legal system can only provide appropriate regulatory support by transforming the ordinary meaning of contract in legal discourse.

Lawyers as Engineers

Contract lawyers seek to translate the economic deal into a legally enforceable written agreement. In so doing, lawyers assist in the construction of the deal, because they can draw on their experience of previous similar transactions in order to suggest model terms or obligations which express the economic interests of the parties. In this age of the word-processor and computer networks, the lawyer typically relies on the firm's data bank of precedent contracts, and then customizes the package in the light of any

---

[1] Selznick, P., *Law, Society and Industrial Justice* (New York: Russell Sage Foundation, 1969) 59.

idiosyncrasies of the transaction. For complex or unfamiliar transactions these precedents can be described as a kind of 'engineering' for a business relation, because they suggest to the parties a particular channel through which their economic objectives can be realized with the least transaction costs.[2] Drawing on this experience of previous transactions, the lawyer can also alert the parties to possible contingencies which may arise and which may not have occurred to the parties, and then suggest ways in which these contingencies can be handled efficiently through contractual provisions. No doubt the negotiations between lawyers about the details of the transaction also uncover ambiguities and disagreements in the substance of the deal, which it may be advisable for the parties to address before entering the transaction rather than awaiting an acrimonious dispute to arise.

Given the significance of this planning role for practising lawyers, it is not surprising that many of the leading empirical studies of contractual behaviour have examined the extent to which businessmen plan their transactions. These surveys, such as those by Macaulay,[3] and Beale and Dugdale,[4] are designed to elicit information on the question whether businessmen use contracts as an instrument of planning. This is the lawyer's perspective on why contracts are needed: to plan for contingencies. The general conclusion of these studies is perhaps unsurprising, though none the less shocking to lawyers. Businessmen focus their attention on the economic deal, not the contract. They are interested in the core exchange of goods and services, and do not pay much attention to the task of planning for contingencies. From the perspective of the parties, the crucial elements are price, the goods (quality and quantity), timing, and trustworthiness. The task of planning for contingencies is left to the legal department of the firm, or outside lawyers, who will supply usually a standard form contract to be signed without detailed consideration by the businessmen. For the businessmen interviewed, the principal utility of the written contract is to help to clarify the content of the economic deal.

If you get the intent spelled out, you won't have any trouble. People perform commitments they understand.[5]

The remaining issues that are typically included in the written contract by the lawyers will usually, though not invariably, receive scant attention from the parties to the transaction.

[2] Bernstein, L., 'The Silicon Valley Lawyer as Transaction Cost Engineer?', *Oregon Law Review* 74 (1995) 239.

[3] Macaulay, S., 'Non-Contractual Relations in Business', *American Sociological Review* 28 (1963) 45.

[4] Beale, H., and Dugdale, T., 'Contracts between Businessmen: Planning and the Use of Contractual Remedies', *British Journal of Law and Society* 2 (1975) 45.

[5] Macaulay, S., 'The Use and Non-use of Contracts in the Manufacturing Industry', *Practical Lawyer* 9(7) (1963) 13, 14.

The task of planning performed by contract lawyers involves a number of distinguishable issues. First, lawyers may help to resolve any ambiguities in the stipulated performance by suggesting express terms for the contract which provide greater detail for the economic deal. Second, lawyers seek to allocate risks of foreseeable and unforeseeable contingencies between the parties. Risk allocation can be achieved by many contractual devices including disclaimer and exclusion clauses, which in effect absolve one party from being held to be in breach of contract, if the failure to perform results from the contingencies described in the clause. It is possible to devise such a broad term that in effect performance becomes almost optional in law, though not of course within the context of the business relation. Third, lawyers use the contract to construct non-legal sanctions or self-enforcing legal sanctions such as security interests. Fourth, lawyers give detailed attention to the manner in which any disputes should be resolved and the types of remedy available to either party. In this list, the first element is the one carefully scrutinized by the parties to the transaction, but the other three elements will typically constitute the bulk of the document.

How useful and important is this planning function performed by lawyers? Since businesses frequently use lawyers for this planning role despite the cost of their services, we must infer that they consider that the benefits outweigh the costs, at least over a series of transactions. What are the benefits? The greater precision in the description of the reciprocal obligations combined with mechanisms for resolving subsequent minor disputes may remove some obstacles to the completion of the transaction, thereby permitting both the business relation and the deal to be protected despite difficulties and disputes between the parties. The clarity of the documents in allocating entitlements may also assist the process of reaching a settlement in the event of a dispute, for there will be less room for specious arguments about exceptions and qualifications. There is some comparative evidence that the German business practice of always using formal contractual documents and institutionalized trading standards to determine expectations achieves greater confidence in predictions of probable legal outcomes, which in turn reduces litigation in favour of settlements.[6] The empirical studies of business practice invariably observe, however, that normally the parties will prefer not to invoke the legal documents for fear of souring the business relation and creating an additional obstruction to the completion of the deal, so this careful planning may not be referred to at all when the businesses are seeking a solution to their dispute. The allocation of risks in advance can also be beneficial

---

[6] Arrighetti, A., *et al.*, 'Contract Law, Social Norms and Inter-Firm Co-operation', 21 *Cambridge Journal of Economics* (1997) 171, 187–8.

because the parties can insure with third parties against contingencies for which they bear the risk, which achieves an efficient level of insurance cover. The planning of non-legal and partially legal sanctions may prove the most valuable attribute of a formal contract, though often, as we have seen, the most powerful non-legal sanctions will be available without a formal contract at all.

Finally, of course, lawyers provide what should be a legally enforceable agreement, though any informal agreement between the parties is also likely to be legally enforceable, subject to any legal requirements for formalities such as a written document or registration. The value of achieving a legally enforceable contract depends crucially upon whether there are effective non-legal sanctions, for if the non-legal sanctions can be relied upon to deter breach then the addition of a legal sanction provides a negligible benefit. It follows that in many instances, the best advice a lawyer might give is to tell the parties to adopt a non-binding agreement.[7]

That advice may not often be given, but it can be discovered in such commercial examples as 'letters of intent', 'letters of comfort', and in framework agreements. A letter of intent represents a preliminary indication of a willingness to proceed with entry into a business transaction, though subject to detailed negotiations leading to a formal binding contract. A letter of comfort is typically given by a parent company to a creditor containing a promise to support the liquidity of its subsidiary that is seeking to raise capital from the creditor, without the letter or assurance itself amounting to a legally enforceable guarantee of the debt. In a framework agreement, the parties to a commercial transaction describe their intentions with respect to the conduct of future business without entering into a binding commitment. Legally enforceable undertakings will only be created subsequently by separate contracts. Such a framework agreement was the subject of litigation in *Rose & Frank Co v JR Crompton Bros*:[8]

This arrangement is not entered into, nor is this memorandum written, as a formal or legal agreement, and shall not be subject to legal jurisdiction in the law courts either of the United States or England, but it is only a definite expression and record of the purpose and intention of the three parties concerned, to which they each honourably pledge themselves with the fullest confidence—based on past business with each other—that it will be carried through by each of the three parties with mutual loyalty and friendly co-operation.

The courts usually hold that these 'gentlemen's agreements' are not legally enforceable, arguing that the intention was plainly to rely on each other's good faith and honour, or, as we might say, trust based upon the experience

---

[7] Bernstein, E. A., 'Law and Economics and the Structure of Value Adding Contracts: A Contract Lawyer's View of the Law and Economics Literature', *Oregon Law Review* 74 (1995) 189.   [8] [1925] AC 445, HL.

of past dealings combined with the non-legal sanction of termination of the potentially lucrative long-term business relation. The courts therefore recognize the possibility of the rationality of the exclusion of legal sanctions as a possible remedy where alternative non-legal sanctions are available or the risks of betrayal and disappointment are discounted on the basis of trust. Lawyers can plan transactions so that the timing of entry into binding legal commitments occurs only when the additional legal sanction is necessary in order to establish the credibility of the commitments.

Informality in Business Dealings

Despite the potential utility of the lawyer's planning role for business, there is a tension between the formality of planning and the informality that often characterizes the creation of the business deal. The business parties concentrate their attention on hammering out the economic deal and regard its main elements as their contract. The legal system observes this oral or informal agreement, but is typically more impressed by the subsequent documentary evidence of the transaction contained in the planning documents. The formal agreement in writing contains the seductive attraction that it provides a more comprehensive scheme of self-regulation that may indeed provide a precise answer to the dispute which is the subject of litigation. Yet to place such emphasis upon the written documents often does not correspond to the intentions and expectations of the business parties themselves. They may not have read or considered these documents, or they may have assumed wrongly that their own standard terms of business would govern the transaction. Their deal was established by the oral agreement about the central elements of price and technical specifications; as one businessman is reported to have observed, 'we like to have agreements, not contracts'.[9] The legal system regards the documents as central to the contractual framework, whereas the parties themselves regard this documentation as insignificant: the standard business conditions on the back 'don't mean a thing'.[10] The agreement on the deal is important, for that communicates precise expectations of performance, but the contractual documents which regulate what will happen when things go wrong is best left unsaid for fear of damaging trust or discouraging the deal.

The legal system commits itself to the enforcement of the self-regulation

[9] Deakin, S., *et al.*, 'Contract Law, Trust Relations, and Incentives for Co-operation: A Comparative Study', in Deakin, S., and Michie, J. (eds.), *Contracts, Co-operation, and Competition* (Oxford: Oxford University Press, 1997) 105, 122–3.
[10] Lyons, B., and Mehta, J., 'Private Sector Business Contracts: The Text Between the Lines', in S. Deakin and J. Mitchie (eds.), n. 9 above, 43, 58, quoting a business contractor.

of the contract, but the tension between the informality of business agreements and the use of planning documents presents the legal system with the problem of determining which agreement represents the contract. We can distinguish three instances of this tension between informality in agreements and the formality of planning documents. The first issue concerns the management of the conflict between the temporal priority of the oral agreement and the subsequent more complete self-regulation of the planning documents. The second problem is provoked by a surplus of planning documents that contradict each other. The final issue is the potential conflict between the informal agreement and the content of an agreed planning document.

Sequential Agreements

The timing of the use of the lawyer's contribution presents an enormous difficulty. During the negotiations for a transaction, businesses are likely to discuss the deal aspect of the transaction, but leave the 'paperwork' till later. The deal may well be completed in the minds of the parties by a handshake or an order placed by a telephone call. The deal having been struck, the paperwork follows, and there may be signatures placed on the written documents. Macaulay reports:

Seven lawyers from law firms with business practices were interviewed. Five thought that businessmen often entered contracts with only a minimal degree of advance planning. They complained that businessmen desire to 'keep it simple and avoid red tape' even where large amounts of money and significant risks are involved . . . Another said that businessmen when bargaining often talk only in pleasant generalities, they think they have a contract, but fail to reach agreement on any of the hard, unpleasant questions until forced to do so by a lawyer . . . It is likely that businessmen pay more attention to describing the performances in an exchange than to planning for contingencies or defective performances or to obtaining legal enforceability for their contracts.[11]

The legal system observes this behaviour within its own terms of analysis. Private law is likely to reach the conclusion that the informal deal represented a legally enforceable contract. It satisfies the normal requirements of 'offer' and 'acceptance'. The problem then arises as to the relevance of the subsequent documents and signatures. Should these be regarded as part of the binding contract?

To the extent that the written documents vary from the oral agreement by supplementing the obligations or even contradicting them in some respects, it might be argued that the documents do not represent part of the contract, but rather constitute a unilateral attempt to vary the terms of

---

[11] Macaulay, S., n. 3 above.

the contract without the consent of the other party, an attempt which the law will invalidate. The strange consequence of this legal reasoning is that a great deal of planning provided by lawyers might be regarded by the law as having no legal relevance in the event of litigation. But the alternative line of reasoning is equally unattractive. To permit the oral agreement to be overridden by the documents would discourage reliance upon informal agreements, with a consequent increase in transaction costs.

The underlying problem is that the parties have in a sense made two contracts: the oral deal containing the business details of the trans-action, and the written document constituting the planning elements. The former has temporal priority, and greater significance in shaping the expectations of the parties. The latter is more complete and specific, so that it can be regarded as a better articulation of the self-regulation, and if the document has been signed, it may be regarded as having greater importance due to the significance customarily attached to the performance of this ritual. When a dispute arises, however, the court may have to choose between these two contracts in the event of inconsistency.

In a commercial context, the common law resolves this problem by reference to rules that seek to investigate the parameters of trust between the parties. In other words, the conflict over the contractual framework is resolved by reference to the other normative frameworks in which the transaction was situated. One rule examines the business relation prior to the disputed contract in order to determine whether the written docu-ment had been regarded in the past as forming part of the transactions. Under this principle, if it can be shown from the prior course of dealing that the written documents were regarded as relevant and constitutive of the contractual relation, then the court will regard them as having been included in the agreement at dispute by implication. For example, in *Henry Kendall & Sons v William Lillico & Sons Ltd*,[12] the seller of animal feed received three or four orders a month from the buyer on the telephone. The seller would send a written contract note to the buyer shortly after the phone conversation. The seller's standard terms of business placed the risk of latent defects in the product on the buyer. The court held that the written contract note became part of the oral agreement by implication due to the course of dealing between the parties. Under this reasoning, the basis of trust in the business relation is used by the court to justify the incorporation of the subsequent paperwork into the legal analysis of the contract. The argument tends to prove less successful, however, in the context of consumer, where in the spirit of consumer protection, the

---

[12] [1969] 2 AC 31, HL.

court usually requires the presentation of the documents prior to the formation of the contract.[13]

Another technique for determining the relevance of the planning documents to the contractual relation is to regard those documents as representative of the customs of the trade. Under this legal reasoning, the court assumes that in commercial contracts, an informal agreement between businesses in the same trade will contain by implication the customs of that trade, since these customs represent the presuppositions of the parties when entering an informal transaction. Once it becomes established practice that these customs are contained in a written document, the standard terms of business used by participants in the market, then the court can insert the paperwork by implication into the oral deal. In a case involving the hiring of a crane between two companies in that line of business, the document was sent after the telephone agreement about the price, and the document became part of the contract. The evidence was that all the businesses in that trade used standard terms, and that these terms were the same apart from minor variants, because they were based on 'the Contractors' Plant Association form'. The court concluded that the standard business conditions were inserted into the contract by implication.[14] Under this reasoning, indeed, it perhaps does not even matter that the written documents were never presented or sent, for the argument invoking trade convention as the basis of trust should be successful even if by some oversight the document was never transmitted.

These illustrations indicate that the courts can be adept at reinserting the planning documents into the contractual relation when they have been omitted from the business deal. The legal reasoning becomes rather forced, since the court has to overcome the temporal problem that the documents were only delivered well after the deal had been struck. But the merit of these doctrines is that they permit the parties to commercial transactions to take advantage of the benefits of planning documents without the need for the expense of inserting them ostentatiously into the informal, low transaction cost, business deal.

The advantage of such informal dealing to the parties is also connected to the construction of trust between them. The willingness to act on the basis of the handshake or telephone conversation, even though written documents will be subsequently issued, provides a strong signal of trustworthy behaviour. An insistence upon the stance that no binding commitments have been made until the written contracts have been agreed

---

[13] *Hollier v Rambler Motors (AMC) Ltd* [1972] 2 QB 71, [1972] 1 All ER 399, CA; *Parker v South Eastern Rly Co* (1877) 2 CPD 416, CA; *Chapleton v Barry UDC* [1940] 1 KB 532, CA; *Thornton v Shoe Lane Parking Ltd* [1971] 2 QB 163, [1971] 1 All ER 686, CA.
[14] *British Crane Hire Corporation Ltd v Ipswich Plant Hire Ltd* [1975] QB 303, [1974] 1 All ER 1059, CA.

and signed would indicate on the contrary grounds for distrust that might discourage the transaction. The consequent reluctance to insist upon the completion of the formal agreement before the deal becomes binding presents the courts with the occasional instance when negotiations for the written contract finally break down, even though in the mean time the parties have been acting in reliance on the deal. The question for a court is whether or not it should find that a binding contract existed on the evidence of the informal undertakings, even though both parties made it clear that the planning documents needed to be agreed prior to the creation of a legally enforceable contract. If the court decides that the existence of continuing negotiations over the planning documents leads inevitably to the conclusion that the parties had not reached an agreement, then it must hold that the contract never existed, even though the expected obligations or deal may have been performed. The court can provide some protection for the reliance upon the informal agreement by requiring the buyer to pay a reasonable sum for benefits received under the private law of unjust enrichment.[15] The objection to this restitutionary relief is that it ignores the likely solution that would have been produced by the planning documents themselves. But the merit of this doctrine is that it provides legal support for the first mover, and therefore supplies some limited insurance for parties who signal their trustworthiness by commencing performance prior to the completion of the formal contract.

Surplus of Planning Documents

A celebrated problem that arises from the insertion of planning documents into transactions after the informal agreement on the deal concerns 'the battle of forms'. In these cases, both parties try to insert their contradictory planning documents into the contractual framework. The problem for legal reasoning lies in the choice between the two documents when neither party has agreed explicitly to abide by the other's standard terms of business.

In a typical case, after oral discussions and possibly agreement on the economic deal between the parties, the purchaser sends an 'order form', which on its face specifies the technical requirements for the product and on the back contains standard business conditions. The supplier then confirms the order by sending a document which confirms the price and technical requirements, but which on its back contains a different and contradictory set of business conditions. This correspondence may be extended, but in the mean time performance of the agreement will commence and the goods will be delivered. If at that point a dispute arises, a typical legal analysis will look for an agreement between the parties. The

---

[15] *British Steel Corp v Cleveland Bridge and Engineering Co Ltd* [1984] 1 All ER 604.

legal reasoning looks for an offer which is matched exactly by an acceptance. If the document containing an apparent acceptance in fact proposes different terms, then the legal analysis insists that the document represents a fresh offer or 'counter-offer'. If the negotiations continue no further, then a court will have discovered from the relevant facts that the parties never agreed on whose standard business conditions should govern the relation. Thus either the court will be driven to the legal conclusion that, in the absence of an offer and an acceptance of the same terms, the parties never made a legally enforceable contract; or, more commonly, it will attempt to determine that one set of terms prevailed by agreement inferred from conduct.

These decisions often appear arbitrary, because the court cannot obtain guidance about which version of the contractual framework should govern the relation from further evidence about the deal or the business relation. This evidence is typically unhelpful, because parties did not regard the 'paperwork' of the standard form as significant. The consequence of this informality combined with a surplus of standard form planning documents is that, as Macaulay once wryly observed, 'A great deal of business is done on an offer and counter-offer'.[16]

The legal reasoning appears to be aware that it focuses on matters which the parties themselves do not regard as significant, for it is reluctant to follow its own logic that, since the standard business conditions did not coincide, there cannot have been a legally enforceable contract. Nevertheless, the legal reasoning remains mesmerized by the documentary evidence of agreement, so that in order to achieve concordance with the market expectation that indeed a deal had been struck, the court has to manipulate the documentary evidence in order to fit its requirements for a legally enforceable contract. Perhaps a more cogent solution would be for courts to determine the content of the contract by reference solely to the oral or informal agreement. Planning documents could be incorporated into this agreement insofar as they are consistent with each other and the oral agreement. This approach would certainly correspond more closely to the intentions and expectations of the parties, given their typical lack of interest in the paperwork.

Conflicts between Informal and Formal Agreements

Such an approach to the battle of forms raises the final problem of the resolution of conflicts between the informal agreement and the formal documents. Although commercial parties may sign a written document, perhaps without reading it in full, this event may occur in the context of

---

[16] Macaulay, S., n. 5 above, 17.

various oral assurances which qualify or even contradict the written document drawn up by the lawyers.

In order to prevent these oral assurances from becoming binding and disrupting the planning documents, it is common for lawyers to include an 'entire agreement' clause under which the written agreement proclaims that it constitutes the complete contract between the parties and that any oral promises should not be regarded as binding. This statement probably contradicts the expectations of the parties, who will have concentrated their attention on the oral assurances that defined the economic deal rather than the small print of the document. This attempt to arrogate to the planning role the function of constituting the business deal should be regarded by the courts with suspicion when called upon to determine whether oral assurances are binding. It is tempting for a court to regard the tangible, formal documents as superior evidence of the terms of the transaction, but this would be to misunderstand the limited role of these documents in commercial transactions as planning for contingencies rather than constituting the deal.

The practice of awarding priority to the planning documents is known in the common law as the 'parol evidence rule'. This rule tends to exclude evidence from oral statements and informal documents such as letters designed to vary or contradict the terms of a deed or other written instruments signed by the parties. The rule is not an absolute bar to extrinsic evidence, but it raises a strong presumption that the signed document constitutes the entirety of the contract. This presumption can be rebutted, however, where convincing evidence can be introduced of the existence of a collateral oral contract that introduces a qualification,[17] or where it is successfully argued that oral or informal documents were also intended to constitute a part of the contract.[18]

In concluding that there is no need to reform the parol evidence rule, the English Law Commission argued that the presumption is so weak that it causes no injustice.[19] Although this conclusion may be correct, it fails to appreciate that a better approach would be to recognize different priorities between the informal deal and the planning document. With respect to the principal aspects of the deal, such as the price and the goods to be delivered, then, given that the parties to the transaction will have concentrated their attention on these points in the oral or informal negotiations, it

---

[17] *De Lassalle v Guildford* [1901] 2 KB 215; *City and Westminster Properties (1934) Ltd v Mudd* [1959] Ch 129.

[18] *Evans (J) & Son (Portsmouth) Ltd v Andrea Merzario Ltd* [1976] 2 All ER 930, [1976] 1 WLR 1078, CA; *Amalgamated Investment & Property Co Ltd v Texas Commerce International Bank Ltd* [1981] 3 All ER 577, CA.

[19] Law Commission, *Law of Contract: The Parol Evidence Rule*, Report No. 154, Cmnd. 9700 (1986).

would conform better to the objective of enforcing the self-regulation of the parties to award priority to the informal agreement over the written document. If the dispute concerns the details of the planning for risk or other aspects of remote contingencies inserted by the lawyers, given the improbability that the parties considered these terms at all, it makes sense to award priority to the written documents in the form of a presumption against extrinsic evidence.

Incompleteness in Planning Documents

Contracts are invariably incomplete. Although lawyers plan for contingencies through the terms of the contract, the planning can never be complete. We should distinguish, however, between three radically different conceptions of incompleteness in contracts.

The first conception of incompleteness fastens on the limitations of human foresight and observes that not all eventualities will be foreseen. Unexpected or improbable events may occur that destroy the factual assumptions on which the transaction was based. In the legal analysis, the question is which party bears the risk of the contingency. The answer usually turns on the meaning or construction of the planning documents or written contract. These documents often allocate all risks, no matter how unexpected the contingency, by using general phrases, such as 'the seller will not be liable for delays in delivery howsoever caused'. But these general clauses may not be regarded as determinative of the issue, if it is believed that the unlikely event that has occurred was outside the intended scope of the planning documents. The argument becomes that the planning document, when properly interpreted, is incomplete, because either it has a gap in dealing with a particular contingency or its coverage does not extend to the events which have occurred.

A second conception of incompleteness considers the problem of dealing with foreseen events which cannot be predicted precisely in advance. The parties to the contract will be aware, for instance, that inflation will push up the costs of production of goods destined for a long-term supply contract, but the exact measure of inflation can only be estimated. The contract will be incomplete in coping with this problem of inflation to the extent that its provisions cannot provide an exact adjustment of the price in order to compensate for the change in costs of production: the provisions are too coarse in their classification of future states.[20] There is no gap in the planning document here. The problem is rather that the planning

---

[20] Schwartz, A., 'Relational Contracts in the Courts: An Analysis of Incomplete Agreements and Judicial Strategies', *Journal of Legal Studies* 21 (1992) 271.

documents do not correspond exactly to the business intentions of at least one of the parties. The argument is that there is a lack of correspondence between the 'deal' and the written contract.

A third conception of incompleteness in contracts can be described as incompleteness by design. Where the parties realize that they will wish to modify the arrangement over time in the light of changing market conditions and technologies, then the contract will eschew tight, fixed commitments, and rather emphasize the need for flexibility and the exercise of discretion. In a construction project, for instance, modifications may be authorized by the architect, and in the employment contract the employer retains a managerial discretion to require alterations in production methods and to redirect labour. Here the contract leaves important details to be settled by either further negotiation, a governance mechanism of some kind, or unilateral self-regulation. The parties achieve flexibility in their arrangement, but at the price of indeterminacy in the specification of the obligations. The regulatory problem that arises is that subsequent performance by one party may not correspond to the business expectations of the other party. Contracts that are incomplete by design often provide no guidance on how to resolve such disputes.

Risk

The first type of incompleteness presents a problem of the allocation of risk. In the absence of a detailed and explicit term governing the contingency which has arisen, it can be argued that the risk of loss caused by the event which has occurred has not been deliberately allocated by the planning function of the contract. Yet it can usually be argued in flat contradiction that the general terms of the contract have in fact allocated the risk onto one party. For example, a 'fixed price' contract implies that the price should not be altered no matter what contingency occurs. To deal with this problem of the allocation risks, the legal system faces an unpalatable choice. Either it can adopt the fiction that the risks have been deliberately though perhaps implicitly allocated by the contractual agreement, or it can empower the courts to allocate the risks retrospectively.

Under the former route, legal reasoning presumes that all risks have been fully 'presentiated' in the contractual agreement,[21] so that the terms should be interpreted as having implicitly allocated the risk onto one party. In a fixed price contract, for instance, a court will typically infer that by

---

[21] Macneil, I., 'Contracts: Adjustment of Long-term Economic Relations under Classical, Neoclassical, and Relational Contract Law', *Northwestern University Law Review* 72 (1978) 854.

implication the seller has assumed the risk of increases in production costs.[22] It is argued that this conclusion must accord with the intentions of the parties, since they could always have inserted into the contract an express provision to reverse that allocation of risk. In the absence of planning documents that can be construed as providing a comprehensive allocation of risk, the devices of implied terms and supplementary laws permit legal reasoning to develop default rules for the allocation of risk in standard types of transactions, such as the principle that the risk of destruction of the goods passes with title to the goods.[23] The parties are presumed to have intended this allocation of risk in the absence of a contrary express term. These default rules have the potential advantage over strict or literal interpretations of the planning documents of incorporating any applicable market conventions which may conform more closely to the expectations of the parties.

The second route of the retrospective allocation of risks occurs at two stages of the legal process. When the courts assess the measure of compensation, they can determine the allocation of risks. Some losses will be held to be too remote to be recovered on the ground that they were unexpected risks at the time of the formation of the contract. By denying the plaintiff's claim for damages, these rules about the measure of compensation allocate the risk onto the plaintiff.[24] These rules denying recovery for remote types of loss provide for an exception where the plaintiff has notified an unusual risk to the defendant prior to the formation of the contract. Although such notification may be rare,[25] it can enable the courts to permit the oral discussions between the parties regarding the business deal to shape the award of remedies for unexpected risks.

A more blatant form of retrospective allocation of risks consists in judicial revision of the terms of the contract in the light of the change in circumstances. The doctrine of *force majeure* in civil law systems prevents the recovery of damages for breach of the terms of the contract. The doctrine of frustration in Common Law systems terminates the contract automatically and prevents the recovery of damages. Some courts in the US have gone further and revised the terms of the contract with the objective of restoring the viability of the 'deal' to both parties to the contract. Judicial revision of contractual terms is usually criticized by contract lawyers. The practice overrides the ostensible intentions of the parties with regard to the allocation of the risk in the planning documents. It

---

[22] *Davis Contractors Ltd v Fareham UDC* [1956] AC 696, [1956] 2 All ER 145, HL.

[23] Sale of Goods Act 1979, s. 20.

[24] Shavell, S., 'The Design of Contracts and Remedies for Breach', *Quarterly Journal of Economics* 99 (1984) 121.

[25] Danzig, R., 'Hadley v. Baxendale: A Study in the Industrialization of the Law', *Journal of Legal Studies* 4 (1975) 249, 282.

runs the risk, therefore, of reversing the actual intentions of the parties with respect to risk allocation. Furthermore, this judicial interference may be objectionable because the agreed allocation of risk would have influenced the outcome of the negotiations with respect to the price. It is argued that a court should not alter the allocation of risks without simultaneously making a price adjustment in order to restore the balance of the bargain.

In the light of the empirical studies regarding the importance attached to the planning documents by the parties to the contract, however, it seems more plausible to suppose that instead of fully presentiating the risks in their contract, the parties refrained from deliberate allocation of risks for many unlikely events. This reluctance to address problems of remote risk in the business deal stems in part from the transaction costs of negotiation, but more importantly this abstention is due to the expectation arising from the business relation and market convention that in the event of serious external shocks the parties would renegotiate the terms of the transaction. By proposing a judicial revision of the terms of the contract, a court may therefore be upholding the implicit understandings of the parties, which will then compel the defendant to renegotiate in accordance with the original business expectations.

The courts usually, though not invariably, favour a literal interpretation of the express terms of the contract over devices for the reallocation of risks, thereby displaying a reluctance to contextualize contractual relations. This legal doctrine then creates an incentive for the parties to use lawyers to plan for every contingency through contractual terms. Businessmen may not pay much attention to the contractual paperwork, but that does not mean that they refrain from investing in the expensive kind of insurance against risk provided by detailed contractual planning for contingencies.[26] We can therefore observe the phenomenon of contracts as long as a book, in which elaborate provisions seek to cope with every possible future state of affairs. The clauses in these contracts often seek through their generality and abstraction to exclude liability for as wide as possible a range of future contingencies that might prevent or increase the costs of performance. A typical example is the *force majeure* clause,[27] which purports to exclude liability for any events outside the control of the party under the obligation:

[The supplier of a ship for carriage of goods] has the right to cancel its performance under this Contract whether the loading has been completed or not, in the event of force majeur, Acts of God, perils or danger and accidents of the sea, acts of war,

[26] Weintraub, R. J., 'A Survey of Contract Practice and Policy', *Wisconsin Law Review* (1992) 1, 17.
[27] In a 1988 survey of large American businesses, in the long-term contracts about 40% reported the use of *force majeure* clauses: ibid.

warlike-operations, acts of public enemies, restraint of princes, rules or people or seizure under legal process, quarantine restrictions, civil commotions, blockade, strikes, lockout, closure of the Suez or Panama Canal, congestion of harbours or any other circumstances whatsoever, causing extra-ordinary periods of delay and similar events and/or circumstances, abnormal increases in prices and wages, scarcity of fuel and similar events, which reasonably may impede, prevent or delay the performance of this contract.[28]

Legal regulation provokes these transaction costs, which might otherwise be avoided by either a contextual interpretation or the development of a power of judicial revision.

The argument in favour of judicial revision based upon the empirical studies of business behaviour is that the planning documents which purport to provide a comprehensive allocation of risk should be regarded as a separate discourse from the construction of the original business deal. The deal is likely to be situated in a context of commercial convention where neither party expects the transaction to proceed on the same terms if some event radically changes the likely benefits to each party. We can glimpse this alternative way of analysing the events in the decisions of arbitrators, that is, specialist adjudicators selected by the parties, precisely because of the arbitrators' knowledge of these conventions.

In one of the leading English cases, *Davis Contractors v Fareham UDC*,[29] the arbitrator accepted the builder's argument that the fixed price contract to build 78 houses for the Council had become unprofitable due to shortage in raw materials and skilled labour, and that it was implicit in this context of a construction deal that some additional payment was expected for these increases in costs. The courts roundly reversed the arbitrator's decision: they inferred from the planning documents, which made no mention of possible variations of the fixed price, that the risk of cost increases had been allocated by the contract onto the builder. In other cases, however, the courts may defer to

a commercial arbitrator's findings as to mercantile usage and the understanding of mercantile men about the significance of the commercial differences between what was promised and what in the changed circumstances would now fall to be performed.[30]

These arbitrators seem to be less entranced by the circumlocutions of the planning documents drafted by the lawyers and more sensitive to the expectations of the parties with respect to the business deal than the ordinary courts.

---

[28] The *force majeure* clause subject to litigation in *J Lauritzewn A S v Wijsmuller B V, The Super Servant II* [1990] 1 Lloyd's Rep 1, CA.   [29] [1956] 2 All ER 145, HL.
[30] Lord Diplock, *Pioneer Shipping Ltd v BTP Tioxide Ltd, The Nema* [1981] 2 All ER 1030, 1036.

At bottom the question posed in these cases of the allocation of risks is whether priority should be accorded to the planning documents that comprise the formal contract or whether greater emphasis should be placed on the business deal and its context. The interventions of judicial revision under the doctrines of *force majeure*, frustration, or 'commercial impracticability' are often justified by the need to achieve justice between the parties. Yet this principle fails to provide a guide for a selection between the standards set by the different frameworks of the business deal and the planning documents. The formal documents usually appear to gain the advantage in the courts, no doubt because they are expressed in a legalistic discourse that links itself directly to legal reasoning, whereas the vague expectations of the business deal cannot be expressed so easily in a language of entitlements. Yet, if the courts wish to do justice between the parties rather than referee the quality of the lawyers in devising comprehensive risk allocation, they should not attach such weight to the paperwork, but concentrate their energies on an investigation of the context, the market conventions, and the assumptions of the parties in framing their core deal. Such an investigation may lead to the conclusion that the planning documents devised by the lawyers failed to grasp the way the parties expected to allocate risks in the event of improbable contingencies. From this conclusion, the court should then not hesitate to engage in suitable measures of judicial revision of the planning documents.

Insufficient Specificity in Self-regulation

The second type of incompleteness occurs where the mechanism for allocating risks fails to conform to the business expectations of the parties by proving too coarse a description of contingencies. For example, long-term contracts commonly insert a price-indexing clause in order to cope with inflation,[31] but the index can only provide a rough proxy to the supplier's rise in costs. The supplier's real costs may deviate considerably from the general index, if the supplier's factors of production are subject to exceptional price increases. This problem of price indexing occurred in the ALCOA case.[32] Under a sixteen-year contract with an option to renew for an additional five years, ALCOA agreed to convert alumina supplied by Essex into molten aluminium. The contract contained detailed provisions designed to raise the price with the wholesale price index, but this index failed to account for the sharp rise in the cost of

---

[31] In a 1988 survey of large American businesses, in the long-term contracts which were used, 72% reported the presence of price indexing clauses: Weintraub, R. J., n. 26 above, 17.
[32] *Aluminium Co of America v Essex Group,* 499 F Supp 53 (WD Pa 1980).

energy to ALCOA, so the contract ceased to be profitable and losses began to mount up.

It might be supposed that a pricing mechanism which reflects real costs could avoid this problem of insufficient precision in self-regulation. But contract prices determined by a 'costs plus' formula also present their pitfalls, as illustrated by a dispute between General Motors and Fisher Body in the 1920s.[33] Fisher Body supplied a particular kind of closed auto body to General Motors. The contract provided Fisher Body with an exclusive supplier deal in order to protect its substantial investment in production machinery. To guard General Motors against opportunistic price increases from its exclusive supplier, the contract fixed the price on a cost plus 17.6 per cent basis (where cost did not include interest on invested capital). General Motors became dissatisfied with this pricing mechanism after its demand for the closed auto body parts increased dramatically. General Motors complained that Fisher Body now benefited from a substantial increase in body part output per unit of capital invested, but this economy of scale was not reflected in the price charged. Due to this lack of specificity in the pricing mechanism, General Motors eventually forced a merger of the two businesses, so that it could obtain the savings in costs from mass production.

This second form of incompleteness presents the legal system with especially difficult issues for regulation. On its face the contract has made elaborate arrangements for the determination of the contract price or some other detail. This form of incompleteness again presents the legal system with the choice of either strictly enforcing the express provisions in the planning documents or revising them in the light of the informal understandings of the parties. The formal style of interpretation which predominates in the courts fixes the rights of the parties by reference to the planning documents rather than by reference to business expectations. The ALCOA case was exceptional, because the court set aside the contract and imposed a new pricing formula. Although such judicial revision of a contract is much criticized for failing to uphold the allocation of risks agreed by the parties, thereby undermining the utility of contracts as a planning tool, the decision might be defended by a more contextual analysis of the parties' expectations with respect to risk. In this long-term supply contract, the parties are probably bound together by ties of economic integration, so that neither has incentives to destroy the contract. The parties know that the deal must remain profitable for both sides over a period of years, for otherwise the disadvantaged party will seek to extract itself from the contract. The purpose of the indexing of the price was part

[33] Klein, B., *et al.*, 'Vertical Integration, Appropriable Rents, and the Competitive Contracting Process', *Journal of Law and Economics* 21 (1978) 297, 308–10.

of the solution to this problem supplied by the planning documents. But the solution failed, the planning was incomplete, so the court reverted to the underlying economic objectives of the parties in order to provide criteria for judicial revision of the terms.

The parties can seek to provide self-regulation to deal with contingencies which render the planning documents too crude (despite their detail) to express the business expectations fully. A common kind of clause in Germany is a hardship clause. This term of the contract requires the parties to renegotiate in the event of an unforeseen contingency which renders the contract unprofitable for one party. This clause is rarely used by lawyers in Britain, the United States, or Italy.[34] One reason for this reluctance may be the sense that the term is too vague to be enforceable in a court. This judgement may be a correct prediction of judicial behaviour, but this behaviour is itself the result of the judicial reluctance to look behind the planning documents in order to supplement them by reference to the business expectations of the parties.

The more elaborate and detailed the planning documents become, the less likely it seems that a court will intervene to alter this product of self-regulation. My argument criticizes this stance on the ground that the elaborate plans provide detailed insight into the business expectations of the parties, from which it can be inferred that the planning document was incomplete in its solution to the anticipated problem. In the ALCOA case the court realized that the plan was to protect the company against price rises in its supplies, so that it could reform the detailed plan in order to make it correspond to this intention or expectation.

Flexibility

It is the third conception of incompleteness, that is, incompleteness by design in order to achieve flexibility, which presents the most intractable problems for the legal system. A tension exists between the lawyer's performance of the planning role and the advantages of flexibility to the parties. Flexibility in defining the required performances can be advantageous in order to exploit new market opportunities, to take advantage of innovations in design and technology, and to permit the deal to continue despite external shocks which render the original bargain economically unsatisfactory for one or both parties. This flexibility can be blocked by a contract which specifies the content of the obligations exhaustively. The parties can address this problem by leaving crucial aspects of the terms of

---

[34] Arrighetti, A., *et al.*, 'Contract Law, Social Norms and Inter-Firm Co-operation', *Cambridge Journal of Economics* 21 (1997) 171, 187.

the contract, such as price and quantity, incomplete, or by devising triggers requiring renegotiation of the terms. But such moves tend to undercut any tangible, measurable commitment between the parties, so that a court might decide that the agreement was not legally enforceable for lack of certainty or the absence of an essential term such as price. Flexibility is then achieved only at the risk of removing the availability of legal sanctions.

The seriousness of this risk of unenforceability from the defect of vagueness or uncertainty depends crucially upon whether a court can find evidence from previous dealings or customs of the trade from which to infer the necessary implied terms in order to render the agreement sufficiently certain to be enforced. The decision in *Hillas & Co Ltd v Arcos Ltd*[35] is instructive. The buyer purchased an option which merely stated:

Buyers shall also have the option of entering into a contract with sellers for the purchase of 100,000 standards for delivery in 1931. Such contract to stipulate that whatever the conditions are, buyers shall obtain the goods on conditions and prices which show to them a reduction of 5% on the f.o.b. value of the official price list at any time ruling during 1931.

On its face this option is extremely uncertain: the nature, quantity, and specification of the goods is obscure, the price vague, and the remaining terms left up in the air. The option had to be left imprecise, however, because it was a 'forward' contract for timber in the next season, so that the parties could not know exactly what might be available, and in what quality it would be produced, and what prices would govern. The Court of Appeal refused to enforce the option; it was merely an 'agreement to agree a contract at a later date'. But the House of Lords enforced the option by filling in the remaining terms by referring to previous dealings between the parties in Russian timber and 'the course of the trade'. In the absence of such a framework of market convention in which the contract is embedded, however, a vague agreement will be regarded as legally unenforceable.

The risk of unenforceability becomes greater when the contemplated transaction involves a joint business venture which will persist over a period of time. Here the courts will be confronted with more than the task of filling in the gaps in a discrete transaction, for they will be required to assess whether contractual behaviour either amounts to an acceptable exercise of discretion within the framework of the transaction, or an instance of opportunism that subverts that framework. As Hadfield observes in the context of franchise contracts:

To the extent that courts cannot distinguish between the derogation of a commitment in an incomplete contract and an exercise of the flexibility which is a part of

---

[35] *The Times*, July 29, 1931, CA; (1932) 147 LT 503, HL.

that commitment, incomplete contracts cannot fully function in their role as anchor for many complex transactions.[36]

This challenge for lawyers of planning flexibility can be addressed though not resolved entirely. One method is for the parties to agree upon a governance structure for their relation, which is empowered to supplement or modify the written contract in the light of changing circumstances. A neutral third party might be awarded the power to render some of the obligations more specific at a future date and to determine how any dispute should be resolved. It is common, for instance, for the price of rental business property to be raised periodically, and in the event of the parties being unable to agree the new rent, for it to be fixed by a neutral professional valuation. Where such a governance structure provides a method for resolving all aspects of incompleteness in the contract, then in a sense the contract is no longer incomplete at all. In a construction project, for instance, if the architect is empowered to modify the details of the project and to determine what amounts of payment are due, then virtually all problems of incompleteness will have been addressed:

> The powers of the architect or arbitrator, whatever they may be, are conferred by the contract. It seems to me more accurate to say that the parties have agreed their contractual obligations are to be whatever the architect or arbitrator interprets them to be. In such a case, the opinion of the court or anyone else as to what the contract requires is simply irrelevant.[37]

There remains, however, some residual incompleteness with respect to the issue of how the neutral third party should exercise the discretion conferred by the contract.

This issue of the indeterminacy of the criteria for the exercise of discretion becomes especially significant when the governance structure awards the discretionary power to one of the parties to the contract. In a contract of employment, for instance, the discretionary power conferred on management to direct labour towards its most productive use resolves the problem of incompleteness in the definition of the worker's performance obligations. But this governance structure creates a power relation that creates considerable scope for opportunism on the part of management. The discretionary power can be exercised to require workers to perform tasks which were beyond their expectations under the contract, though on a simple construction of the terms conferring the discretionary power on management these unexpected obligations might be regarded as falling within the contractual power to modify and supplement the

---

[36] Hadfield, G. K., 'Problematic Relations: Franchising and the Law of Incomplete Contracts', *Stanford Law Review* 42 (1990) 927, 928.

[37] Lord Hoffmann, *Beaufort Ltd v Gilbert-Ash Ltd* [1998] 2 All ER 778, 783, HL.

obligations of the worker. The contract in these instances is therefore not so much incomplete as one-sided, for it confers a unilateral power of self-regulation. We consider this problem of regulating the power created by governance structures in Chapter 10.

Another method for addressing the problem of flexibility through contracts is for the parties to agree to terms which express the obligations in outline terms only, together with terms expressing their willingness to co-operate, to perform in good faith, and to avoid the imposition of hardship or unfairness on either party to the deal. Such a 'framework' contract expresses clearly the expectations arising from the business relation, and describes the nature of the deal that the parties envisage. In the absence of more specific provisions, however, a court may not be able to point to any specific undertakings which have been broken and which deserve a legal sanction. The problem of creating flexibility without some form of governance structure is that on paper the contract is likely to undercut any tangible commitment between the parties. The parties will be expecting, however, that future negotiations will render the transaction more complete and specific. It may often be advisable to avoid detailed planning for contingencies at the outset lest the specificity of rights and obligations provides the capacity for opportunism during these subsequent negotiations.[38] The kind of opportunism that might occur would be a refusal to waive a contractual right without compensation that amounted to an attempt to gain a disproportionate benefit from the transaction (rent-seeking).

It is plain that in practice the formal contractual requirements will normally be ignored by the parties in the determination of whether or not to accede to a request for modification of the deal. The evidence drawn from surveys confirms that most businesses would agree to a modification of the price in a long-term contract or an adjustment of future contractual obligations provided that the request appeared reasonable under trade practice.[39] We observed the same type of flexible behaviour in the long-term supply contracts for iron ore discussed by Daintith, where the willingness to accept orders for less than the contractual minimum operated outside the terms of the contract.

One buyer, indeed, went so far as to say in interview that it as an unwritten rule that the buyer can only be asked to lift the tonnage he can reasonably be expected to consume, whatever his contractual commitments may be.[40]

---

[38] Hviid, M., 'Relational Contracts, Repeated Interaction and Contract Modification', *European Journal of Law and Economics* 5 (1998) 179.
[39] Weintraub, R. J., n. 26 above, 19.
[40] Daintith, T., 'The Design and Performance of Long-term Contracts', in T. Daintith and G. Teubner (eds.), *Contract and Organisation*, (Berlin: Walter de Gruyter, 1986) 164, 184–5.

Similarly, we can find many illustrations of one party incurring additional costs, not required as part of performance of the contract, but regarded as an important contribution to the strengthening of the long-term business relation.[41]

If a court has to interpret a contract where the parties did intend flexibility in their relation, then there is plainly a danger that the court will not give sufficient weight to this intention when construing the contract. The dispute between the parties might concern, for instance, the quantity of supplies which had been ordered; the terms of the contract might state no fixed minimum amount, but merely suggest that the buyer should determine its requirements in good faith in the light of the continuing relation between the parties. When the supplier complains to the court that the buyer has ignored the business relation, has placed orders with other suppliers, and has effectively stopped ordering from the plaintiff, the court can point to the flexibility of the terms of the contract which do in fact permit this behaviour, unless some special meaning can be given to the commitment to place orders in good faith in the light of the continuing business relation. Within the framework of a legal doctrine which assumes that all risks are fully presentiated, that all entitlements and obligations have been specified in advance, then the interpretation placed on the clause is likely to defeat the expectations of the supplier. As Campbell and Harris suggest:

Just as the static and purportedly fixed allocations of risk under presentation turn on competitive bargaining between rational utility-maximizing individuals, so the plausibility of writing contracts in an open-ended fashion turns on assuming a co-operative attitude to the resolution at the appropriate time of the problems initially left open-ended. Without such a shift in attitude, formal provision for flexibility is fruitless, for one cannot create a co-operative attitude by writing down that such an attitude will be taken to contingencies as they arise. One needs the attitude to make the writing have any meaning.[42]

In short, the traditional approach to the interpretation of contracts based upon presentation and the complete allocation of risk, tends to undermine any possibility of constructing a legally enforceable agreement with flexibility at its core. A better style of interpretation would require the courts to consider the possibility that the parties' expectations included a commitment towards co-operation and flexibility. If that expectation appears central to the dynamics of the deal, as it might in many kinds of long-term business relations such as franchising,[43] then the duty to co-operate

---

[41] e.g., Palay, T. M., 'Comparative Institutional Economics: The Governance of Rail Freight Contracting', *Journal of Legal Studies* 13 (1984) 265, 277.
[42] Campbell, D., and Harris, D., 'Flexibility in Long-term Contractual Relationships', *Journal of Law and Society* 20 (1993) 166, 173. [43] Hadfield, G. K., n. 36 above, 927.

should supplement and even override express terms of the contract, in order to provide legal support for wealth-maximizing potential for this type of transaction.

A connected problem for legal regulation consists in how to assess the validity of additional self-regulation. In the spirit of co-operation and flexibility the parties may agree informal modifications to their earlier formal agreement. These modifications may be mutually advantageous, in which case legal regulation usually has little difficulty in interpreting them as variations of the original agreement. But equally the modifications may impose additional burdens on one party without any commensurate increase in benefits. An employee may be asked to take on additional duties, or a franchisee to comply with burdensome alterations in the business format, without any increase in payment. These modifications could be interpreted as contributing to the objective of the flexible contractual relation or, on the contrary, they could be interpreted as opportunistic 'rent-seeking' or 'hold ups' by a party in a stronger bargaining position.

In Common Law systems of private law, the assessment of the validity of such modifications is given to the doctrines of consideration and economic duress. The doctrine of consideration is incapable of performing the task, because it always demands 'fresh consideration', that is a reciprocal commercial benefit. This doctrine rules out the possibility of valid disadvantageous modifications. The doctrine of economic duress is more suited to the task, because it examines the question of opportunism directly. The problem lies rather in the formulation of an adequate test which is capable of distinguishing between opportunism and the type of flexibility needed in contracts left incomplete by design. The policy objective in determining such a test should be the encouragement of self-regulation by the parties in order to provide further specificity to their undertakings as they acquire new information and experience. This objective suggests that the question of economic duress should be guided by a contextual enquiry into the origins of the proposed modification. If the modification represents an adaptation to fresh information, changes in technology, or market conditions, then in contracts left incomplete by design it should be regarded as a valid instrument of self-regulation by modification.

Conclusion

Our examination of the contribution of lawyers to the construction of markets and transactions has focused on their primary role of formulating the planning documents which allocate risks. The central difficulty for legal regulation concerns how the law should regard these planning documents in the determination of legal rights. Legal reasoning is attracted to this precise expression of entitlements contained in the persuasive evidence of formal documents signed by the parties, but I have argued that this is a dangerous attraction, because the planning documents do not express adequately the business expectations of the parties to the contract. In other words, the priority accorded to the planning documents gives preference to the framework of the contract, whereas the parties are much more likely to have attached greater significance to expectations grounded in the business relation and the business deal. Legal reasoning achieves some degree of sensitivity to this problem by recontextualizing contractual agreements. It is ironical, but not surprising, that the courts prove most adept at this task when the job requires the incorporation of standard forms containing the relevant market conventions into informal agreements. Where the task requires the revision of the planning documents or the interpretation of broad clauses designed to achieve flexibility and adjustments in performances, however, the courts normally fail to grasp the point that, in order to give effect to the business expectations based upon the long-term relation and the balance of the deal, they should be less mesmerized by the words of the planning documents.

8
Formalism and Efficiency

What kind of legal regulation of contracts is good for business? My argument has been progressing gradually towards this fundamental question. If we assume that the principal purpose of legal regulation is to support the construction of markets, thus leaving aside distributive issues for the time being, what conclusions might be drawn from our previous observations about the role of law?

The starting-point is my first argument that legal regulation is rarely significant in the construction of markets. In particular, the law plays a peripheral role in the construction of trust between the parties, though it can make some contribution by devices such as the creation of security rights and other types of credible commitments. Legal sanctions for breach of contract are also rarely as important as other informal sanctions such as damage to reputation, though again the legal process, as an organized reputation mechanism, may contribute to the imposition of this informal sanction. My second argument was that an examination of business behaviour in relation to contracts revealed the presence of three distinct rationalities or normative frameworks guiding action. Within these rationalities, the parties emphasized the priority attached to the business relation or the embedded social relation. A secondary, though important consideration, was the success of the business deal for both parties. Rational business behaviour accorded low priority to the contractual frame of reference, that is, the specification of entitlements. We discovered that an emphasis upon contractual entitlements could easily be interpreted by the other party as a betrayal of trust, which would damage trade and the construction of markets: 'any attempt to shelter behind contractual provision or even frequent citation of contractual terms would destroy the firm's reputation very quickly'.[1] This tension between the contractual framework and the rival business relation and deal became more pronounced in our

---

[1] Beale, H. and Dugdale, T., 'Contracts between Businessmen: Planning and the Use of Contractual Remedies', *British Journal of Law and Society* 2 (1975) 45, 47; 'If you have to have resort to the precise wording of a contract, the relationship is beyond the point of no return (British mining machinery supplier)', Deakin, S., *et al.*, 'Contract Law, Trust Relations, and Incentives for Co-operation: A Comparative Study', in S. Deakin and J. Michie, (eds.), *Contracts, Co-operation, and Competition* (Oxford: Oxford University Press, 1997) 105, 123. Cf. Macaulay, S. 'Organic Transactions: Contract, Frank Lloyd Wright and the Johnson Building', *Wisconsin Law Review* (1996) 75, 114.

exploration of the planning documents supplied by the lawyers. We observed how the legal system tended to accord priority to these planning documents in the interpretation of the events, whereas these documents were the least significant dimension of the expectations of the parties. Recall that dismissive remark: the contract 'don't mean a thing'.[2]

During our discussion of the tension between the objective of supporting the expectations of the parties and the distracting planning documents, we observed how the courts were sometimes able to refine their approach to the contract in order to give greater weight to expectations founded on the business relation and the business deal. That observation paves the way to the central thesis of this chapter that the kind of legal regulation of contract which best suits the interests of business is one which supports the expectations of business in entering transactions. This thesis only becomes controversial when it is understood to suggest that legal regulation should follow the parties' own rational ordering of the normative frameworks for their expectations. In other words, legal regulation should seek to give priority to the business relation, with secondary attention to the business deal, and relegate the contract to a peripheral role.

To understand why this thesis will raise the hackles of many lawyers, we need to appreciate the paramount importance which they attach to the value of certainty in the regulation of contracts. In the minds of most lawyers, certainty is the chief virtue of good contract law. Clear rules, it is frequently repeated, let the parties know where they stand, enable precise planning documents to be written, and permit settlements of disputes to be reached expeditiously. Businessmen, it is commonly believed, want minimal regulation, so that they can exploit all available market opportunities without the expense of regulatory compliance. They also want on this view the maximum certainty of legal entitlements, so that it should be clear when a binding contract has been made, and what precise obligations have been incurred. The anathema to business from this perspective would be a detailed set of regulatory requirements combined with judicial discretion to revise or reinterpret the contractual undertakings. Behind this assumption about the kind of law that is good for business lurks a vision of the social constitution of markets. This vision imagines businesses to be constantly entering into transactions with a variety of new parties, with each transaction being negotiated to achieve a market clearing price in return for the specified undertakings, so that the businesses in the informed pursuit of their conflicting interests are likely both to maximize their own wealth and the total wealth of society. This picture embraces the familiar economic analysis of impersonal markets comprised of individuals seeking to

---

[2] Lyons, B., and Mehta, J., 'Private Sector Business Contracts: The Text Between the Lines' in S. Deakin and J. Mitchie (eds.), n. 1 above 43, 58, quoting a business contractor.

maximize their self-interest through trade. Presupposing this analysis of market transactions, it then becomes common sense to perceive the interests of business to lie in a law of contract which permits freedom of contract in all its aspects, so that each transaction can adjust precisely to the forces of supply and demand, combined with the certainty provided by clear legal rules, so that once a deal has been struck, it affords the parties with guarantees of the legal enforceability of the precise entitlements described in their agreement.

This attachment to formal law has been challenged by others, especially Kennedy, because it tends to skew the law away from the pursuit of distributive goals.[3] We shall see in later chapters that it is true that the efficient and efficacious implementation of regulation against unfairness and unjust power relations in contracts tends to require more open-ended standards. But my argument presents a more insidious threat to lawyer's conventional fidelity to the virtue of certainty through clear rules.

My contention is that the type of law that best contributes to the construction of markets and a vibrant economy would be one that avoids clear-cut entitlements based upon the contractual framework in favour of a more contextual examination of business expectations based upon the business relation and the business deal. In order to achieve this style of legal reasoning, it is necessary to reduce its formalism, and to point the courts towards an investigation of the relations and expectations in which the contract is embedded. In this chapter, my argument is developed in greater detail and evidence to support it is presented from several sources, especially the example of commercial arbitration. Finally, we consider the question whether private law has been adjusting its methods of reasoning away from formal rules in order to accord better with the interests of business as they have been identified in this chapter.

The Form of Legal Doctrine

The conventional view that urges the necessity of certainty through formal rules contains important insights. When businesses develop innovative types of economic relations, they expect that the law will be capable of adapting its rules to encompass novel forms of transaction in the realm of legal enforceability. In order to fulfil this need, the legal system has to evolve from enforcing standard model transactions such as the sale of goods to reach a high degree of abstraction in its rules. The generality of the rules escapes the confines of particular types of agreement, in order to regulate

---

[3] Kennedy, D., 'Form and Substance in Private Law Adjudication', *Harvard Law Review* 89 (1976) 1685.

any kind of idiosyncratic transaction that the parties devise to further their business interests. Perhaps the first formal, authoritative statement of this abstract generality in private law was announced in Article 1108 of the French Code Civil in 1804:

There are four essential conditions for the validity of a contract.
  (1) consent of the parties to the obligations.
  (2) capacity to make contracts.
  (3) a certain subject matter for the transaction.
  (4) a lawful cause.

Although the Code proceeds to provide more detailed rules for particular types of transactions, this brief, abstract statement, embraces the ideal of generality, for it merely requires the parties to reach a clear agreement about their deal (subject to restrictions about unlawful objectives and the incapacity of children) in order to achieve an enforceable contract. Generality does not require a uniform set of rules for all types of contracts, but it does require a high degree of abstraction of general principle that permits novel types of transaction to be supported by law. This type of generality is an important ingredient in the idea of freedom of contract.

The conventional view also suggests that the legal system should provide mechanisms for the inexpensive, routine enforcement of contracts. This requires the legal system to keep formalities to a minimum and to provide ready access to the courts and enforcement procedures at reasonable cost. These features were the main attraction to businesses of the local merchants' courts, which proliferated in medieval Europe.[4] It is also possible for the legal system to achieve the same result by supporting and enforcing the outcomes of private adjudication and enforcement procedures such as arbitration. This emphasis upon reliable legal sanctions for breach of contract is usually exaggerated, because, as we have observed, other kinds of sanctions will usually amount to stronger incentives to perform an undertaking. Nevertheless, in so far as entry into a legally enforceable contract can assist in the creation of a credible commitment, which may be especially important in the absence of a history of prior dealings on which trust has been built up,[5] it is clearly necessary for the legal system to provide routine, inexpensive enforceability in order to give that commitment much substance.

The conventional view is also correct to insist that the legal system should endeavour to reduce the transaction costs to the parties whenever they enter into a contract. For this purpose the law should enforce informal

---

[4] Trakman, L. E., *The Law Merchant: The Evolution of Commercial Law* (Colorado: Rothman, 1983), ch. 1.
[5] Weintraub, R. J, 'A Survey of Contract Practice and Policy', *Wisconsin Law Review* (1992), 1, 24.

agreements and minimize the need for legal services. This objective can also be assisted by the development of 'default rules' for standard types of transactions, so that, unless the parties expressly agree to the contrary, the default rules will determine the obligations owed in law. Provided that the implied obligations correspond to the terms which the parties would have chosen if they had engaged in the expense of setting out all the details of the agreement, the law will have saved that type of transaction cost.

These attributes of generality, routine enforceability, and minimizing transaction costs serve as important guides to the type of law of contract which serves the interests of business. Max Weber combined the first two attributes into a measure of the 'calculability' of legal entitlements. He argued that calculability could best be achieved by a legal system comprising fixed entitlements determined by a precise set of rules. As part of his general sociology of the evolution of capitalism, he argued that one reason why market economies had flourished in Western Europe was that they could draw on the intellectual resource of the rules and principles of Roman law and a formalist legal tradition in order to create a legal system of contract law which maximized calculability.[6]

To those who had interests in the commodity market, the rationalization and systematization of the law in general and, with certain reservations to be stated later, the increasing calculability of the functioning of the legal process in particular, constituted one of the most important conditions for the existence of economic enterprise intended to function with stability and, especially, of capitalistic enterprise, which cannot do without legal security.[7]

Max Weber described this form of contract law which maximized the calculability of legal entitlements as formal logical legal rationality. He contrasted the predictability that could be achieved by a systematic body of rules with the uncertainty produced by the exercise of substantive rationality in law. When a court decided a case according to substantive rationality, it would take into account all pertinent normative considerations, including legal doctrine, but extending to morality, economic interest, public policy, and practical matters. In the language of systems theory, Weber suggested that a closed, self-referential legal discourse of contract best achieved a calculable regulatory discourse. This seems plausible, because substantive legal rationality implies that the courts should have a discretion to weigh a large variety of factors in each case, and then determine the balance of the merits of the dispute through this opaque process. In contrast, if the role of the courts is confined to the application

---

[6] Trubeck, D. M., 'Max Weber on Law and the Rise of Capitalism', *Wisconsin Law Review* (1972) 720.
[7] Weber, M., *Economy and Society* (G. Roth and C. Wittich, eds.), (Berkeley: University of California Press, 1978) ii. 883.

of a system of rules promulgated in advance according to a distinctive mode of legal reasoning, this kind of rationality should produce much more predictable outcomes. In confirmation of this hypothesis, Weber discerned a political history behind the emergence of formal logical private law systems such as the German Civil Code, in which business interests pressed for this type of law. Although many interest groups combined in an alliance to promote formal legal rationality,

Most prominent among these were the bourgeois interests, which had to demand an unambiguous and clear legal system, that would be free of irrational administrative arbitrariness as well as of irrational disturbance by concrete privileges, that would also offer firm guaranties of the legally binding character of contracts, and that, in consequence of these features, would function in a calculable way.[8]

The link between formal logical legal reasoning and business interests was also attractive to Weber because he wanted to establish a homology between the dominant type of legal reasoning exemplified by the German Civil Code and his general theme of 'rationalization' as a characteristic of modern societies.

Weber then addressed the difficulty for his thesis presented by the Common Law style of reasoning used in the advanced capitalist societies of England and the United States.[9] The Common Law, unlike Codified systems based on Roman law, appeared not to conform to the paradigm of formal logical rationality, but rather through its process of drawing analogies with previous decisions on similar facts seemed to embrace large elements of substantive rationality. In his inconclusive discussion of the problem, he explored not only the possibility that the Common Law did embrace a variant of formal logical rationality, but also the contrary hypothesis that the Common Law had harnessed substantive legal rationality to be predictable by routinely favouring the interests of business. As the argument twists and turns, it becomes evident that the sharp conceptual distinction between formal and substantive rationality begins to collapse, since all systems of contract law present in their interstices a substantive ideology which shapes the form and content of the law.[10]

Despite these ambiguities in his position, Weber provides sustained support for the lawyer's intuition that formal rules governing entitlements serve the interests of business best. In entering markets, businesses require calculability in their commitments. This calculability is best achieved, according to Weber, by a distinctive style of legal reasoning. This reasoning uses clear general rules, which are applied to the facts of disputes without any intervening substantive discretion. On this view, in order to support a

---

[8] Ibid. 847.   [9] Ibid. 889–92.
[10] Cotterell, R., 'The Development of Capitalism and the Formalisation of Contract Law', in B. Fryer *et al.*, (eds.), *Law, State and Society* (London: Croom Helm, 1981) 54.

vibrant market economy, the law of contract must comprise clear general rules applied according to their ordinary meaning.

Closure and Expectations

According to my argument, however, Weber was correct to point to the importance of calculability in business, but misunderstood the nature of the calculability sought by the parties to commercial contracts. They want the law to support their expectations from the transaction, but as we have seen in our discussion of the competing normative frameworks surrounding contractual discourse, these expectations comprise a complex bundle of standards. As well as expectations based upon the express commitments contained in the contractual undertakings (the contractual framework), the parties also form expectations with respect to both the norms of the 'business deal' and the 'business relation'. The expectations from the business relation derive from the two dimensions of the embeddedness of economic transactions described above, that is, the context of particular market conventions acknowledged by the parties, and the personal relations between the parties. My argument is that calculability requires the protection of expectations in business transactions, and that these expectations are built simultaneously upon the three competing normative frameworks of contractual discourse.

The task for legal regulation of commercial transactions then becomes one of being sensitive to all three competing normative frameworks, and to seek to reconcile their claims of reasonable expectations through an evaluative discourse. The law needs to give due weight to the precise undertakings formed in the contractual discourse, whilst at the same time recognizing the force of expectations based upon the economic deal and the parties' history of dealings. Formal logical legal rationality may have a strong capacity to understand and regulate the contractual normative framework successfully, for it can translate the express undertakings into self-regulation supported by fixed legal entitlements. The abstract principles of formal logical legal rationality can rigorously enforce the self-regulation of the parties within a clearly defined space left to self-regulation (the rules for the formation of valid contracts). What the process of the application of general rules to contracts cannot achieve is the more complex task of an evaluation of the competing normative frameworks on which expectations are based. This task requires such moves as bringing into the picture the presuppositions of the parties based upon a history of prior dealings or a particular market context, in order to qualify or extend the expectations based upon the express contractual undertakings. Legal regulation that fulfils business expectations therefore shuns an exclusive focus upon the discrete contractual discourse.

Lord Devlin tells a story which reveals sharply this contrast between enforcement of entitlements through formal law and the protection of the expectations of business:

I have had business men in my chambers, when at the bar, who, when a particular point of difference arose, have said how it would be solved according to the customary practices in the trade. 'But', I have interjected, 'that is not what the contract says'. 'Oh, the contract, let me see it', and when his attention is directed to the document which he has signed, and which he is probably considering in any detail for the first time, he is apt to say: 'Well I cannot help that; I told you the way things are always done.'[11]

In this encounter we notice the businessman using trade custom as the normative framework, whereas the lawyer trained in the reasoning of the law treats the contract as the exclusive source of rights and obligations. To enforce the written contract according to a system of formal entitlements will defeat the expectations of business when the contract does not incorporate the norms of the business relation in which it is embedded.

In order to achieve a concordance between the legal outcome and business expectation, legal reasoning has to avoid the kind of hermetic closure of legal discourse that Weber idealized in his paradigm of formal logical rationality. Legal reasoning must instead permit the facts of the convention or the pattern of prior dealings to be regarded as relevant to the determination of the dispute. This might be achieved, for instance, by insisting that custom can supplement and qualify the interpretation of contractual entitlements. Similarly, by using open-textured standards such as 'good faith' or 'reasonableness', the legal enquiry can be directed towards an exploration and specification of the conventions and expectations within the business relation. As a part of this strategy for permitting the informal standards of the relation to become determinative in legal reasoning, the law of contract has to resist the universalizing tendency of formal logical rationality to apply the same rules to every type of transaction, because a single rule may fail to make the kinds of differentiation between types of transactions and business relations which the parties expect. These arguments suggest that the type of law of contract favoured by business would not comprise a rigid, systematic body of rules. The most appropriate form of legal regulation would temper its formalism with a sensitivity to the particular facts of the case, especially the history of prior dealings, and an understanding of the informal conventions (and formal trading standards where available)[12] governing the business relation.

---

[11] Devlin, P., 'The Relation between Commercial Law and Commercial Practice', *Modern Law Review* 14 (1951) 249, 266.

[12] Formal standards promulgated by trade associations may be available in some countries such as Germany: Arrighetti, A., *et al.*, 'Contract Law, Social Norms and Inter-Firm Co-operation', *Cambridge Journal of Economics* 21 (1997) 171, 188.

The key feature of this legal regulation that best serves the interests of business must be the production of the capacity to protect business expectation (or calculability) by creating a legal discourse that can evaluate simultaneously the competitive normative frameworks of the business relation, the deal, and the contract. This capacity requires the contextualization of contractual disputes, an ability to differentiate between contexts in the light of custom and usage and the economic interests of the parties, and the power to reformulate regulation in the light of revisions of normative standards in the market.

What evidence might be used to support this hypothesis? How may we undermine Weber's persuasive story of how bourgeois interests promoted Codification and formal logical legal reasoning? The strongest evidence is surely to be found in the selection of a forum for dispute settlement. If we find that businessmen are pleased to submit their disputes to the ordinary courts which deploy formal logical rationality, then we might surmise that the narrow sense of calculability favoured by Weber is indeed the dominant preference of business with respect to the form of legal regulation. If, on the other hand, we discover that merchants use every device possible in order to avoid those courts, not only because of their expense and delays, but also because they defeat business expectations by using formal logical legal reasoning, then we have a convincing riposte. Further evidence to support the hypothesis may be discovered in the competition between legal jurisdictions. If formal logical legal rationality is the preference of merchants, then we should expect that those legal systems that approximate the closest to its ideals would be the choice of law in international business transactions. If, however, businessmen seek legal regulation of a broader range of expectations, then we might expect them to prefer legal systems which can avoid this type of closure in favour of a flexible brand of substantive legal reasoning.

Commercial Arbitration

The choice of forum represents a selection of a regulatory authority. Given that the parties to a contract can never achieve completeness in their self-regulation contained in the express terms of the contract, they require a mechanism to resolve disputes arising from incompleteness. By selecting a forum for adjudication, the parties also select the system of regulation to be applied. If the parties choose a court, then they will submit to the ordinary private law of contract. If, however, they choose another forum that differs in its expertise and regulatory standards, then implicitly they have rejected ordinary private law reasoning for another source.

Arbitration comprises the selection by the parties of their own adjudicator to resolve the dispute according to procedures and standards agreed by the parties. In practice, the parties will not set out all these procedures and standards, but merely refer the dispute to an established body of arbitrators. In particular trades or industrial sectors, the merchants will select the arbitration system created by their own association, often established as a committee of the association. In the example of the New York diamond traders' arbitration system:

Arbitrators explain that they decide complex cases on the basis of trade custom and usage, a little common sense, some Jewish law, and, last, common-law legal principles.[13]

In shipping disputes and international trade, it is more common for the parties each to select an arbitrator of their own choice, drawn often from an established self-validating institute of expert arbitrators, and these arbitrators may themselves select a third 'umpire'. Whatever the method for selection of an arbitrator, the key point is that the selection also involves the choice of the expertise, procedures, and normative standards to be applied to the dispute.

It is difficult to discover reliable evidence about the choice of forum by businesses. We can discover court statistics that provide a rough indication of the extent to which businesses choose a court in order to vindicate contractual rights. Unfortunately, precise comparable figures about the rival fora for dispute settlement cannot be obtained, in part due to their variety and number, and in part due to their privacy. The available evidence in London suggests, however, that some form of arbitration is the dominant forum for the resolution of disputes about commercial contracts except where the dispute consists merely in a claim for debt or money owed. This is the informed opinion of many commercial lawyers.[14] Similar observations have been made with respect to the USA:

The American Arbitration Association now handles close to 10,000 of these disputes [i.e. commercial contract disputes] each year. In addition, an untold number are handled similarly under private industry agreements.[15]

The view that arbitration is the dominant forum for adjudication of commercial disputes is further supported by observation of the almost invariable insertion of an arbitration clause in commercial contracts, though of course the parties may decide by agreement not to submit

---

[13] Bernstein, L., 'Opting Out of the Legal System: Extralegal Contractual Relations in the Diamond Industry', *Journal of Legal Studies* 21 (1992) 115, 127.

[14] Devlin, P., 'The Relation between Commercial Law and Commercial Practice', *Modern Law Review* 14 (1951) 249, 258: 'Many commercial disputes are dealt with in the first instance by arbitration.'

[15] Sander, F. E. A., 'Alternative Methods of Dispute Resolution: An Overview', *University of Florida Law Review* 37 (1985) 1, 5.

ultimately to arbitration. Perhaps the most convincing evidence comes from the absence of work for the higher courts in major contractual disputes. In respect of cases involving a contractual dispute resolved by a trial in the United Kingdom, the higher courts (including the Commercial Court[16] and Official Referee's Court) only process about 300 cases a year.[17]

The Official Referee's Court itself is something of a hybrid between court and arbitration, so its business can be presented as a partial rejection of ordinary private law regulation. The Official Referees were created in the nineteenth century to avoid jury trials in cases that involved prolonged examination of documents including accounts, scientific investigation, or site inspections.[18] As in arbitration, the jurisdiction of the Official Referees depended upon the consent of both parties (though now the plaintiff selects the jurisdiction and the defendant is entitled to object on numerous grounds), and appeals on matters of fact were restricted except in cases involving professional negligence or fraud. Unlike arbitration, however, the proceedings share the formalities of a courtroom. The main bulk of the business of this court concerns disputes connected to the construction industry, which often involve quantities of documents and many experts giving evidence. With the number of cases channelled towards this forum running at 1500 a year, and 86 cases disposed of by trial,[19] it is clear that for construction litigation this specialist forum is regarded by litigants as having a significant advantage over ordinary courts, though the advantage lies not in terms of cost but rather in the expertise of the adjudicator. Unless businesses manage to avoid the escalation of disputes into the stage of adjudication almost entirely, therefore, then we must infer that most disputes arising from commercial contracts are resolved outside the traditional court system.

This situation is far from new. Ferguson describes how arbitration of commercial disputes was employed heavily in particular market sectors in the nineteenth century, and is now the dominant system of dispute

---

[16] The Commercial Court is really part of the ordinary court system, but contains judges who specialize in disputes related to ships, insurance, carriage of goods, international transactions, banking and finance, the purchase and sale of commodities, and legal supervision of arbitration: Lord Chancellor's Department, *Judicial Statistics 1996* Cm 3716 (London: HMSO, 1997) 33.

[17] Ibid. 32, 33, 41. The picture is different if one examines the initiation of litigation, for a very high proportion of disputes in the higher courts are resolved by settlement. About 9000 writs involving contractual disputes might be issued by the higher courts in a year.

[18] Judicature Act 1873, s. 83, revised by Arbitration Act 1889, s.14. Administrative changes under the Courts Act 1971 s. 25 and Supreme Court Act 1981 s. 68 now mean that specially appointed circuit judges are given the particular tasks of official referees' business. Fay, E., *Official Referees' Business* (London: Sweet and Maxwell, 1983).

[19] Lord Chancellor's Department, n. 16 above.

resolution by adjudication for substantial commercial contracts.[20] He argues that considerations of cost and speed give arbitration a relative advantage over litigation, but more important considerations drive business away from courts towards arbitration:

But its decisive virtue is that arbitrators are chosen for their personal knowledge and experience of the trade in which the dispute has arisen so that they have the requisite technical expertise and a detailed grasp of commercial practice.[21]

We can understand this reference to expertise and practice as signifying that the arbitrator can bring other normative contexts into adjudication as well as the formal contractual entitlements of ordinary private law.

Arbitrators can recontextualize the agreement, by linking the discrete communication of the contract into the network of relations and multiple standards in which the agreement was embedded. In other words, an arbitrator is likely to fulfil the business expectations of the parties, which depend in part upon observance of norms drawn from market conventions and business relations, even when these norms run contrary to formal legal entitlements. As Sugerman and Rubin observe of modern English legal history,

Commerce and industry might value certainty and calculability. But often they also preferred their own adjudicators (thus, the wide use of arbitration or the demand for special 'commercial' juries); and they valued the ability to formulate their own private or 'home-made' legislation, as opposed to that laid down by Parliament or the courts.[22]

The reason for this preference for private self-regulation lies surely in its quality of substantive reasoning. The panel of arbitrators does not engage in unrestrained substantive reasoning. It limits it normative framework to the contract and the rules and expectations of the trade. But within this analysis, it does not give priority to the discrete contractual communication, but holds itself open to the competing normative points of reference drawn from the community. These arbitrators protect the broader sense of business expectation rather than enforce the precise commitments undertaken.

This objective becomes clear in the standard form of contractual planning documents that confer powers on arbitrators:

. . . the Arbitrator shall, without prejudice to the generality of his powers, have power to rectify the contract so that it accurately reflects the true agreement made

---

[20] Ferguson, R. B., 'The Adjudication of Commercial Disputes and the Legal System in Modern England', *British Journal of Law and Society* 7 (1980) 141.   [21] Ibid. 145.
[22] Sugerman, D., and Rubin, G. R., 'Towards a New History of Law and Material Society in England, 1750–1914', in G. R. Rubin and David Sugerman (eds.), *Law, Economy and Society: Essays in the History of English Law 1750–1914* (London: Professional Books, 1984) 1, 9.

by the Employer and the Contract, to direct such measurements and/or valuations as may in his opinion be desirable in order to determine the rights of the parties and to ascertain and award any sum which ought to have been the subject of or included in any certificate and to open up, review and revise any certificate, opinion, decision . . . requirement or notice and to determine all matters in dispute which shall be submitted to him in the same manner as if no such certificate, opinion, decision, requirement or notice had been given.[23]

The ordinary common law itself resisted this pluralism in the regulation of commercial agreements. It sought to eliminate competition and to subject private arbitration to the formal logical rationality of the ordinary private law. The issue was presented not in terms of competition for work but rather a matter of constitutional principle. For example, Lord Devlin insisted that the integrity of the legal system needed to be protected against the centrifugal tendencies of commercial arbitration through judicial review of arbitrators' decisions in order to ensure their conformity to private law regulation:

If each trade or each market made its own laws there would be no uniformity and might be no publicity. It might be cheaper for the litigants in a particular case, but it would be bad for the community as a whole, for no citizen can arrange his affairs, commercial or otherwise, in accordance with the law, unless its principles are fixed and ascertainable, and departure from them to suit individual cases is forbidden.[24]

Notice that the argument for certainty based upon formalism is now married with arguments invoking the ideal of the Rule of Law: that law should be public, ascertainable, and fixed. Formalism in the law of contract becomes not only essential for business, but also part of the liberal constitutional order.

Yet market forces have tended to trounce this alleged constitutional principle. The desire of businesses to select their own default regulatory system and to select one other than the formal rationality of the private law system has proved an inexorable force. The legal profession has always sought to capture the work of arbitration. Legislation designed to subordinate its practices and rules to the ordinary law of contract was always one of their goals. In recent years, however, there has been a succession of legislative reforms of arbitration in England designed to restrict judicial review.[25] These

---

[23] The JCT Standard Form of Building Contract (1980 edition) Private without Quantities, clause 41.4.

[24] Devlin, P., 'The Relation between Commercial Law and Commercial Practice', *Modern Law Review* 14 (1951) 249, 260.

[25] Arbitration Act 1996. S. 9 (4), for instance, requires a court at the request of one of the parties to stay legal proceedings before a court if the contract contains an arbitration clause, the only exceptions being when the arbitration agreement itself is void, inoperative, or incapable of being performed. (But the courts may be granted a broader discretion in domestic (as opposed to international) commercial agreements under s. 86.)

measures render arbitration even more flexible in respect of the normative standards that it can apply to business disputes. The pressure behind these reforms derives from international regulatory competition.[26] Different centres for arbitration compete for the lucrative business of major commercial contract dispute settlement by adjudication. Each arbitration centre in effect creates a club market for justice. These club markets compete on the basis of flexibility in procedures and normative standards combined with expertise in commercial matters. The response of lawyers must now be to colonize most commercial arbitration systems rather than to integrate them into the ordinary court system.[27]

This interpretation of the reasons for the prevalence of arbitration for the resolution of commercial disputes suggests that businesses have over the centuries demonstrated a clear dislike for the standard setting regulation provided by the ordinary courts. Although this dislike derives in part from the expense and delays of the ordinary courts, a deeper problem concerns the sources of the normative standards themselves. Private law reasoning is relatively closed to the competing normative considerations governing contractual behaviour outside the discrete communication system provided by the formal contract itself. As a result, it cannot translate the expectations grounded in business relations and conventions of dealing easily into its default standards for regulation. Commercial arbitration appears to be favoured precisely because it can provide a more complex process of reasoning which marries adjudicated outcome with business expectations more closely. Yet the form of reasoning employed by arbitrators does not detract from the predictability or calculability of outcomes. On the contrary, there is evidence to suggest that decisions of arbitrators are more predictable than those of judges using the formalism of private law, due largely to the way in which arbitrators seek to ensure that their decisions conform above all else to established custom and usage of the trade.[28]

Common Law Reasoning

In drawing the contrast between commercial arbitration and ordinary courts, we have assumed that all private law systems display a high degree

---

[26] Dezalay, Y., 'Between the State, Law, and the Market: The Social and Professional Stakes in the Construction and Definition of a Regulatory Arena', in W. Bratton *et al.*, *International Regulatory Competition and Coordination* (Oxford: Clarendon Press, 1996) 59, 85.

[27] Flood, J., and Caiger, A., 'Lawyers and Arbitration: The Juridification of Construction Disputes', *Modern Law Review* 56 (1993) 412.

[28] Bonn, R. L., 'The Predictability of Nonlegalistic Adjudication', *Law and Society Review* 6 (1972) 563, 571–2 (interviews with lawyers involved in commercial arbitration in the US textile trade; the author, however, rejects the argument in the text, stressing instead the importance of the choice of the individual arbitrator as the main source of predictability).

of closure in their formal logical rationality. On this assumption, they are equally likely to defeat business expectations by regarding their sources of norms and expectations in custom and business relations as irrelevant to the task of standard setting. As a generalization this view may serve well enough, but I want to consider the possibility that the difference in styles of legal reasoning between Codified systems and the Common Law reveals a potential in the latter to reduce its degree of closure. Can Common Law reasoning be presented as relatively adept at achieving a concordance between legal outcome and business expectation?

The reasoning of the Common Law undoubtedly shares a degree of closure with other modern legal systems. The history of commercial law reveals a tension between the courts seeking to preserve the integrity of their own private law doctrinal system and the need to respond to customs of the merchant community. There is considerable historical evidence that in the competition between legal jurisdictions merchants avoided the ordinary courts like the plague. In medieval and early modern England, merchants preferred to use local courts that adhered to the customs of the trade rather than the King's or centralized state courts.[29] The main attraction of medieval merchants' courts was that they were familiar with and would enforce the local customs of the trade.[30] Until the nineteenth century, the ordinary courts competed usually unsuccessfully for business with local merchants' courts.

This position was partially reversed during the nineteenth century as a result of a subtle revision of the private law dispensed by the ordinary courts. The doctrinal solution for which Lord Mansfield is famous was to claim that the 'mercantile laws', that is, the customs of the merchants, had been incorporated as a type of special law into the common law. This move enabled the courts to insert customs and trade standards into the normative expectations protected by ordinary private law. This solution to the problem was incomplete, however, for the mercantile laws were reformulated as formal rational laws. The customs and rules of the trade fixed the new legal standards, so that when custom changed, as with the invention of new kinds of negotiable instruments, the common law rejected their validity:[31]

We must by no means be understood as saying that mercantile usage, however extensive, should be allowed to prevail if contrary to positive law, including in the latter such usages as, having been made the subject of legal decision, and having

[29] Arthurs, H. W., 'Special Courts, Special Law: Legal Pluralism in Nineteenth Century England', in G. R. Rubin and D. Sugerman (eds.), n. 22 above, 380.
[30] Trakman, L. E., n. 4 above.
[31] Chorley, R. S. T., 'The Conflict of Law and Commerce', *Law Quarterly Review* CLXXXIX (1932) 51.

been sanctioned and adopted by the Courts, have become by such adoption part of the common law.[32]

The history of the development of most financial instruments can be told as one of the persistent failure of the courts to recognize the commercial utility of these devices, their failure to grant them legal recognition because they did not fit into the default categories of the formal rational system of private law, and then the ultimate need for the legislature to intervene in order to restore some harmony between law and commercial expectation.[33] As a result, the mercantile courts were promptly replaced by the proliferation of private arbitration. In view of this history, the Common Law system does not appear to be a strong candidate for the type of openness to competing normative frameworks that would fulfil business expectations.

Yet we need to consider more carefully the capacity of Common Law reasoning for contextualization of contractual disputes. Those features of Common Law reasoning that Weber regarded as demonstrating some puzzling features of substantive reasoning do possess a special potential for loosening its closure. The relative absence of formal statements of rules compared to a Codified system, and the need to formulate rules through an inductive process after an examination of analogous precedents, creates the continuous opportunity to revise the formulation of the rules themselves. The relative weakness of the Common Law's system of classification permits what we called earlier the 'productive learning' from the clash of doctrinal subsystems, particularly the law of contract and tort. But most deeply, the inseparability of law and fact in the Common Law system, the way in which rules can only ever be stated in their context, frustrates the aspirations of legal scholars to develop the doctrinal abstraction necessary for formal logical rationality to achieve a high degree of closure. These features suggest that the Common Law is comparatively open to what Karl Llewellyn called 'situation sense',[34] a confusing concept,[35] which we might interpret as an examination of the facts of a case in the light of the conventions which regulated the expectations of the parties to the transaction.[36] This method of reasoning can employ open-textured or indeterminate rules in order to render these conventions relevant to the legal enquiry, and it can differentiate between market contexts by emphasizing

[32] *Goodwin v Roberts* (1875) LR 10 Ex 337, 357.
[33] Chorley, R. S. T., n. 31 above. This story is examined in greater detail in the next chapter.
[34] Llewellyn, K., *The Common Law Tradition: Deciding Appeals* (1960), 60.
[35] Twining, W., *Karl Llewellyn and the Realist Movement* (London: Weidenfeld & Nicholson, 1973) 216–27; Feinman, J. M., 'Promissory Estoppel and Judicial Method', *Harvard Law Review* 97 (1984) 678, 698–705.
[36] For an elaboration of the idea in the context of implied terms: Rakoff, T. D., 'The Implied Terms of Contracts: Of "Default Rules" and "Situation-Sense"', in J. Beatson and D. Friedmann (eds.), *Good Faith and Fault in Contract Law* (Oxford: Clarendon Press, 1995) 191.

the particular factual matrix of each case. Can we find evidence that the Common Law system is more open in its operations to the complex expectations of businessmen, the laws of the merchants?

It is worth recalling the decision in *Hillas & Co Ltd v Arcos Ltd*.[37] In that case, the House of Lords enforced an option to purchase goods which lacked a clear object and a fixed price. Such a result flies in the face of formal legal rationality, where the basic conditions for the enforceability of contracts invariably require certainty and clarity on these vital issues. The Court of Appeal followed this logic by insisting that the parties had failed to enter a legally enforceable contract. But the House of Lords relied upon the 'course of trade', that is the history of the business relation between the parties, in order to protect the expectations of the buyer. In other words, the Common Law court was able to invoke the competing normative frameworks of the business relation and the business deal in order to describe and enforce the expectations of the parties to this commercial contract. Viewed solely through the techniques of formal legal reasoning, the Court of Appeal examined the contractual discourse in isolation, and finding it opaque and incomplete, declined to find an enforceable agreement at all. After all, the agreement purported to comprise a sale of goods, but it lacked an 'object' and a price. But the House of Lords balanced the formal doctrinal requirements of certainty that emphasized the contractual documents against the expectations generated by the context of the transaction, thereby giving effect to the necessarily incomplete but economically rational forward contract for timber.

A study by Lewis of the law and business conventions governing the sub-contracting of work in the construction industry is also instructive in revealing how legal reasoning in the Common Law can accommodate business expectations in its determinations.[38] The issue confronting law reformers was whether a sub-contractor should be legally bound by its fixed price bid for a particular construction task once the general contractor had used that bid successfully in winning the whole job. In the United States, the courts had held the sub-contractor to be bound to this firm offer by manipulating the vague legal doctrine of promissory estoppel. But in Britain the legal position appeared to remain that the sub-contractor's bid could be withdrawn, even if relied upon by the general contractor, until a formal contract for the work had been established by acceptance of an offer. It was proposed to alter English law to follow the American rule (with modifications), because this was perceived by legal scholars to be just and fair. But Lewis's study reveals that the American business convention

---

[37] *The Times*, July 29, 1931, CA; (1932) 147 LT 503, HL; see above, p. 168.

[38] Lewis, R., 'Contracts between Businessmen: Reform of the Law of Firm Offers and an Empirical Study of Tendering Practices in the Building Industry', *British Journal of Law and Society* 9 (1982) 153.

differed from English practice. The American courts were responding to the convention of the industry, discovered by the courts,[39] and confirmed by survey evidence,[40] that bids could not be withdrawn except for good reasons established by convention, and the application of the doctrine of promissory estoppel provided the type of open-textured standard which enabled the courts to support that convention. In contrast, the survey evidence in the British study revealed no such convention that bids were binding, so the courts had refrained from developing legal doctrine to render the bid enforceable. The law reform proposals were eventually dropped.

These studies reveal how closely the reasoning of the Common Law can track business convention and expectation thanks to its relative willingness to contextualize a dispute. The doctrinal argument suggested that a rational legal system should protect the expectation of the main contractor by holding the subcontractor to its bid. The American courts demonstrated how this was consistent with the equitable principle known as promissory estoppel. But this doctrinal argument was only successful in America because the private law rule fitted precisely the business conventions and expectations in this field where business relations provide a crucial normative context.[41] In England, however, the doctrinal argument was rejected, not because of its incoherence, but because it would have conflicted with different business expectations and conventions. Two Common Law systems therefore reach opposite legal outcomes in the same business context due to the different business expectations.

The closeness by which the Common Law doctrine tracks business convention can be further illustrated by an examination of how the American private law regulation has developed. By exploiting the open-textured standard of 'reasonable reliance' contained in the private law regulation, the courts can match their decisions precisely to business expectations. An intrinsic feature of the bidding system is that the subcontractor may be successful in too many bids, so that it will not be able to cope with the volume of demand. Since the bidding system is itself selected

---

[39] e.g. 'in accordance with the custom prevailing in the building trade in New Orleans an offer by a subcontractor to a general contractor to do work is irrevocable after the contractor has used the estimate as a basis for his offer to the owner and the owner has accepted the general contractor's bid', *Harris v Lillis*, 24 So. 2d 689, 691 (La.App., 1946).

[40] Schultz, F., 'The Firm Offer Puzzle: A Study of Business Practice in the Construction Industry', *University of Chicago Law Review* 19 (1952) 237, 260 (a study in Indiana); Note, 'Another Look at Construction Building and Contracts at Formation', *Virginia Law Review* 53 (1967) 1720, 1740 (a study in Virginia). The degree of reliance upon 'firm offers' appears to be greater in other sectors of industry, reaching 95% of firms expecting such offers to be relied upon in a survey of legal counsel employed by large businesses in the United States: Weintraub, R. J, n. 5 above, 28.

[41] Eccles, R., 'The Quasifirm in the Construction Industry', *Journal of Economic Behaviour and Organization* 2 (1981) 335.

by main contractors as their way of doing business, there seems to be a recognition that they should bear the risk of over-demand for a sub-contractor, so that if a subcontractor pulls out for this reason without undue delay, it is not regarded as a breach of the conventional standards of business practice and therefore will cause no damage to reputation. In legal terms, a court will have to conclude that the reliance was not reasonable in the circumstances. Similarly, there is evidence to suggest that although the subcontractor will be bound by the bid under the conventional standards of the trade despite having made a minor mistake in calculating the price,[42] if the mistake is substantial so that the general contractor must have realized that there had been error, probably the subcontractor will not be bound by the bid under the convention.[43] This result will have to be justified again in the legal terminology of the absence of reasonable reliance. On the other hand, under the conventions of the business, the subcontractor will normally feel bound to complete the bid if there is an unexpected rise in the price of materials.[44] So we do not find a legal exception grafted onto the doctrine of promissory estoppel to provide an excuse in the event of changed circumstances. Another aspect of the con-vention insists that the general contractor can no longer rely upon the bid if the general contractor begins to engage in bid shopping.[45] As one subcontractor observed, 'If the contractor has acted in good faith, we will do the job'.[46] To engage in bid shopping, that is soliciting lower bids from other subcontractors having used the original bid for the purpose of constructing the main bid for the work, is perceived to amount to a repudiation of implicit reciprocal reliance on which the bidding process functions, so that this disqualifies the general contractor from then promoting an opportunistic claim based upon reliance.

In order to achieve the protection of business expectations, the system of reasoning must display this degree of sensitivity to the subtleties of normative context. The market conventions have to be incorporated into the formulation of the regulatory standards. The system of reasoning must be capable of resisting abstraction in favour of diversity of rules or a plurality of standards. For example, a tendering system for awarding

---

[42] In the Virginia study of 53 subcontractors, 100% of subcontractors regarded themselves as bound despite the error, Note, n. 40 above, 1734.

[43] In *Albert v RP Farnsworth & Co*, 176 F. 2d 198 (C.A.5th circ., 1949), the general contractor realized that a mistake had been made and gave the subcontractor the opportunity to raise the bid prior to tendering for the main contract; discussed in Schultz, F., n. 40 above, 245, n. 25, and 253. In *Williams v Roffey Bros & Nicholls (Contractors) Ltd* [1991] 1 QB 1, [1990] 1 All ER 512, CA, the general contractor realized that a mistake had been made and subsequently agreed to a price adjustment; the litigation arose from an attempt to renege on part of the price rise.   [44] Schultz, F., n. 40 above, 267.

[45] *Preload Technology, Inc. v A.B. & J. Constr. Co.* 696 F. 2d 1080 (5th Cir. 1983).

[46] Schultz, F., n. 40 above, 267.

contracts is commonplace in many business and government contexts. A formal doctrinal reasoning system always presses for these tendering systems to be subjected to the same rules and principles. It tends to insist, for instance, that a tender can never be binding whatever the context, for it represents an offer of a contract, not an acceptance. A legal system that successfully resists this degree of closure would recognize that the context can reveal contrary business expectations that should be protected by the legal system. The conventions may differ significantly in the context of tendering for public projects, for instance, for there may be an expectation of good faith and fairness from the public authority,[47] or the public authority may indicate that it will conform to specific fair procedures.[48]

The Common Law method of reasoning can achieve this task of grasping the facts of conventions in order to realize the expectations of the parties particularly well by virtue of its attributes of resisting the reduction of legal discourse to a systematic, highly self-referential set of rules combined with its emphasis on the factual matrix of each particular case. In this sense, the Common Law method of reasoning is peculiarly well adapted to achieving the broader sense of calculability or protection of expectations, which I have argued is probably the better meaning for the concept if we are asking what kind of law of contract is good for business. Of course, other, more formally rational legal systems, can achieve a similar adaptation. They can qualify the rigour of the doctrinal system by the development of open-textured rules or general clauses, such as the requirement of 'good faith' in German law. In addition, in the development of exceptions or qualifications to the generality of the rules, the exceptions can bring in explicit references to the importance of achieving concordance with the customs of business. In French law, for instance, the exception that an offer must be kept open for a 'delai raisonable' or a 'delai morale', brings with it an express recognition that the market conventions about how transitory an offer should be regarded are crucial in determining the length of time in which the offer must be kept open.[49] These examples illustrate how all legal systems need to respond to the broader sense of calculability or the protection of expectations. My suggestion is merely that the Common Law mode of reasoning has demonstrated an unusually strong capacity in many instances to achieve this blending between the competing normative frameworks that make up the expectations of business arising from contractual undertakings.

---

[47] *Heyer Products Co. v United States*, 140 F. Supp. 409 (Ct.Cl. 1956).

[48] *Blackpool and Fylde Aero Club Ltd v Blackpool Borough Council* [1990] 1 WLR 1195, [1990] 3 All ER 25 (CA).

[49] Cass.req.27.6.1894, S.1898.1.434; for a discussion, see Ghestin, J., *Traité de Droit Civil II Les Obligations: Le Contrat* (Paris: L.G.D.J., 1980) 167.

The Virus of Formalism

Although I have suggested that the Common Law style of reasoning may be relatively open to the task of weighing competing normative considerations due to the imbrication of law and fact in its reasoning processes, the differences between legal systems are not so marked as to convey a measurable advantage to one or other in the competition to provide dispute settlement systems for international business transactions. London may be a world centre for commercial dispute settlement, but it is clear that this does not result primarily from the virtues of the Common Law, but rather from the flexibility of the arbitration systems which establish pluralism in standard setting. The Common Law may be the most popular choice of law for commercial agreements, but this result may be explained simply by the preference of lawyers for familiar law combined with economic dominance in international trade of first England and then the United States. The weaknesses of Codified systems in respect of their reasoning processes, if they exist, have also been tackled by further differentiation between sub-systems within the legal system, so that a Commercial Code, a Banking Code, and so forth are created to permit adjustment of private law regulation to business convention.

We should also notice that the contrast in the degree of formal legal rationality observed by legal systems may no longer be as great as when Weber puzzled over the link between formalism and capitalism. In Germany, for instance, whereas the legal scholars in private law still provide a dazzling display of abstract formal logical reasoning as every issue is subjected to rigorous classification and solution under the Code, it has to be observed that the German courts display a much greater sensitivity to context and business convention, exploiting the opportunities presented by general clauses to expand the relevant normative contexts for the legal determination. The most notable example is the famous article 242 of the Civil Code: 'The obligor is bound to carry out his performance in the manner required by good faith with due regard to prevailing usage.' This provision enables the court to insert standards drawn from other normative contexts than those set by the contract and the entitlements of private law. At the same time, however, the Common Law reveals much stronger tendencies towards legal formalism.

Once the centralized Royal courts in England began to assume jurisdiction over ordinary contractual disputes in place of local merchants courts, and a differentiated occupational group of lawyers achieved monopoly control over the processing of such disputes, the conditions for the elaboration of a formally rational law of contract were in place. The Common Law of contract received a succession of transplants from Civil Law systems, such as the idea of agreement comprised of offer and acceptance.[50] The real significance of these transplants lies not so much in the substance of the legal doctrine, but rather in the method of reasoning which the concepts required. The imported doctrines enabled self-referential systems of reasoning to evolve, which forced a closure upon the relevance of the facts of the dispute. In other words, the transplants contained a virus that discovered a conducive host body in the dispute process of the Common Law courts. The virus was the formal rational mode of reasoning which spread like a fever throughout the process of contract adjudication.

The ministrations of legal scholars committed to the scientific elaboration of the law only served to raise the temperature, to heighten the degree of self-referentiality.[51] The much admired text on the English law of contract by Sir Gunther Treitel,[52] for instance, certainly presents the law with as much rigour, detailed classification, and other attributes of formal logical rationality as any German text. Every case, though grounded in its facts, can be slotted into a rich classificatory apparatus, so that the formal rules can be presented as providing solutions to every problem. The relevance of mistake in the formation of a contract, for instance, is divided into four principal categories, each of which is then subdivided into numerous classes with their own distinctive rules, perhaps as much as eighteen in all. The point that the doctrine of mistake has hardly ever been applied by the courts is of course sublimely irrelevant to this elaboration of the logic of the doctrine.

Businesses responded to this developing autonomy of law strategically. Where a discourse of strict entitlements based upon a system of rules seemed advantageous, then the courts would be selected as the forum for adjudication of disputes. The courts became full of small businesses claiming debts from consumers or other small businesses.[53] Where, however, the business expectation could only be fulfilled by a contextual consideration of the dispute, taking into account market convention and the implicit understandings of the business relation, the strategy was to seek an alternative forum usually in the form of private arbitration.[54] Disputes between

---

[50] Simpson, A. W. B., 'Innovation in Nineteenth Century Contract Law', *Law Quarterly Review* 91 (1975) 247; Nicholas, B., 'Rules and Terms—Civil Law and Common Law', *Tulane Law Review* 48 (1974) 946.

[51] Sugerman, D., 'Legal Theory, the Common Law Mind and the Making of the Textbook Tradition', in W. Twining (ed.), *Legal Theory and Common Law* (Oxford: Blackwell, 1986) 26.

[52] Treitel, G. H., *The Law of Contract*, 9th edn. (London: Sweet & Maxwell,1995).

[53] Rubin, G. R., 'The County Courts and the Tally Trade, 1846–1914', in G. R. Rubin and D. Sugerman (eds.), n. 22 above, 321. Vincent-Jones, P., 'Contract Litigation in England and Wales 1975–1991: Transformation of Business Disputing?', *Civil Justice Quarterly* 12 (1993) 337. See Chapter 14, below.

[54] Ferguson, R. B., 'The Adjudication of Commercial Disputes and the Legal System in Modern England', *British Journal of Law and Society* 7 (1980) 141; Arthurs, H. W., 'Special Courts, Special Law: Legal Pluralism in Nineteenth Century England', in G. R. Rubin and D. Sugerman (eds.), n. 22 above, 380.

contractors with regular trading relations and those involving elaborate long-term contractual commitments were diverted into arbitration systems provided by the trade or selected by the parties. The objective was to find adjudicators familiar with the conventions of the market, who could take into account the full context of the business dispute.

Modern legal systems have a tension buried in their laws of contract. The tension emerges in the remark by the eminent judge Lord Steyn: 'A theme that runs through our law of contract is that the reasonable expectations of honest men must be protected. It is not a rule or principle of law. It is the objective which has been and still is the principal moulding force of our law of contract.'[55] The law consists of rules and principles, but unfortunately the objective of supporting reasonable expectations of merchants cannot be reduced to a systematic legal discourse. The drive for doctrinal coherence and the separation of legal reasoning from moral, political, and economic thought pushes the legal system towards the closure of formal legal reasoning. Yet, if the law of contract is to achieve the purpose favoured by business of supporting expectations arising from transactions and their surrounding context, the legal system must eschew closed reasoning in favour of doctrines which render the facts of these expectations central to its determinations. This purpose can only be achieved by open-textured rules, the supplementation and qualification of contractual entitlements by custom and expectation,[56] and the interpretation of events and terms in the light of those expectations.

A Transformation in Legal Doctrine?

This tension at the heart of legal reasoning in the law of contract produces in lawyers a permanent but unstable vacillation between rigorous formalism and contextual substantive reasoning. But it can be argued that changes in the type of productive and distributive economic relations have favoured the development of the latter in advanced industrial societies. The predictable legal outcomes of legal entitlements produced by formal legal reasoning may be more important for the calculability suitable for discrete transactions than for the calculability of the expectations of flexibility and co-operation that we have observed in certain types of long-term contract. In a loan agreement, perhaps, the business interest lies squarely

---

[55] Steyn LJ, *First Energy (UK) Ltd v Hungarian International Bank Ltd* [1993] 2 Lloyd's Rep 194, CA.

[56] Cornish, W. R. and Clark, G. de N., *Law and Society in England 1750–1950* (London: Sweet & Maxwell, 1989) 206: 'The implied term accordingly stands as the common law's chief device for a cautious and circumspect alignment of individual contracts with general expectations.'

in the calculability that the borrower will be required to repay capital and interest exactly as stated in the terms of the contract. In a franchise agreement, however, or any kind of principal and agent relation, an insistence upon strict entitlements may well obstruct advantageous modifications, so that the calculability of entitlements may not be so important as a stress on the expectation of co-operation during performance of the contract. As these intermediate or hybrid economic relations lying between discrete contracts and organizations proliferate in the economy, then it may be suggested that legal doctrine can only accommodate them appropriately in the light of the business expectations by making a decisive shift in the form of legal reasoning towards contextual substantive reasoning based upon open-textured rules.

This stress on the importance of co-operation in long-term contracts requires closer inspection. Campbell and Harris explain the idea of co-operation as a long-term utility maximizing strategy within a business relation where both parties know that the other has an interest in preserving and developing the long-term business relation.[57] This interest in preserving the relation derives from the reason for the development of a long-term business contract in the first place: to protect idiosyncratic investments, that is, expenditure incurred in developing the business relation which would be wasted or considerably reduced in value if it could not be put to use in that particular relation. Examples of such 'sunk investments' might include either the building of machinery to create products suitable for that particular customer, or the acquisition of knowledge and skills (human capital) necessary to perform a particular task for an employer which could not be used readily in other employment, or the search costs involved in finding a suitable business partner. In order to have an assurance that these investments will not be wasted, the investor will secure a long-term contractual commitment, such as a long-term supply contract for components, or a 'career track' employment relation, which provides legal protection against the loss of sunk investments. Yet a long-term contract cannot usually state with precision the mutual expectations of the parties, since contingencies will arise which necessitate adaptation in the terms of the relation. Furthermore, if maximum benefit is to be reaped from the sunk investments, the parties must be willing to develop their relation in the light of new market opportunities, new technology, and advantages accruing from the sharing of information. These considerations indicate that it is in the long-term economic interest of both parties to adopt a co-operative attitude towards their business relation. To insist upon a strict interpretation of the original agreement is likely in the long

---

[57] Campbell, D., and Harris, D., 'Flexibility in Long-term Contractual Relationships', *Journal of Law and Society* 20 (1993) 166.

run to reduce the potential wealth for both parties accruing from the relation. Provided both parties have risked 'sunk investments', then they can be confident that this long-term co-operative relation can be maintained despite the temptations of short term opportunism. A manufacturer, for example, may spot an opportunity for forcing down the price of a component from a supplier, and perhaps this is permitted under the terms of the contract, but this will jeopardize the potential advantages of staying with a single supplier in sharing the costs of research and development, in developing innovative designs, or finding new technologies to reduce the costs of production even further, since the supplier may withdraw this vital form of co-operation in response to what it perceives as a breach of trust.

The paradigm example of such co-operative long-term contractual relations occurs in what have been described as 'supplier partnerships'.[58] Here the supplier of a component enters into a long-term contractual relation with an assembler of a product. This is described with the metaphor of partnership because each party expects the other to be flexible in the development of the relation rather than confining performance to the letter of the contract. Lorenz describes the business relation:

in exchange for improved performance by the subcontractor on quality and delivery, the client firm will make every effort to guarantee a level of work; furthermore, any adaptations to price, quantity and delivery are to be made in a non-opportunistic way by both sides, with full disclosure of the relevant information. In particular, this implies that the subcontractor will not be unconditionally dropped if a differential in terms of price or quality emerges with respect to competitors. Rather, clients stated that they operate a system of advance warnings; a reasonable period is allowed to their partner to match the competition. It also implies that clients will not pull back work in-house each time product demand falls. A number of firms observed explicit sharing rules to resolve problems associated with uncontrollable fluctations in demand.[59]

If this analysis of the co-operative nature of long-term contractual relations is correct, then it suggests that a legal analysis of such contracts which restricts the obligations to the precisely stated entitlements under the rules of law may in an important sense frustrate the potential for the agreement to maximize the joint wealth of the parties. The conventional legal and economic view of contracts as establishing entitlements that give incentives for performance may misconceive the central feature of these transactions which is to establish procedures and a context for adapting the

---

[58] Collins, H., 'Quality Assurance in Subcontracting', in S. Deakin and J. Mitchie (eds.), *Contracts, Co-operation, and Competition* (Oxford: Oxford University Press, 1997) 285.
[59] Lorenz, E. H., 'Neither Friends nor Strangers: Informal Networks of Subcontracting in French Industry, in Gambetta, D. (ed.), *Trust: Making and Breaking of Cooperative Relations* (Oxford: Blackell, 1989) 194.

exchange relation to changing conditions.[60] The implicit co-operative dynamic may require the law to recognize that certain kinds of diffuse expectations should be permitted to override the express terms of the agreement, or that at least the express terms should be supplemented by broader co-operative standards. In an employment relation, for example, an employee who wishes to withdraw co-operation can choose to 'work-to-rule', that is perform the contract according to its express terms. A 'work-to-rule' is an effective strategy in industrial conflict precisely because it frustrates the potential advantages to the employer of co-operative relations, such as the employee's willingness to be flexible in order to overcome unexpected problems of production. The legal response in favour of supporting co-operative relations might be to assert that there exists an implied obligation to perform in 'good faith', or at least not to act in a way calculated to frustrate the employer's business interests.[61]

Building on this insight into the dynamic of long-term contracts, it can be suggested that the law of contract has been slowly evolving the form of its legal doctrines in order to respond to alterations in types of relations of production.[62] The classical law of contract, which predominated in the nineteenth century, strove to achieve through formal legal rationality using a clear set of rules and doctrines a fixed set of contractual entitlements. This legal formalism was suitable for supporting business expectations in the kinds of economic relations found in the developing market economy, where small businesses entered into many discrete contracts with suppliers and customers. In the twentieth century, however, long-term supply contracts, distribution systems based upon franchises, and employment relations in a career hierarchy, require the law to evolve mechanisms for recognizing and supporting expectations of flexibility and co-operation. The legal response to these new economic institutional arrangements can be found in part in specialized statutory interventions, such as the regulation of the employment relation, but also in shifts towards the use of more open-ended general clauses for regulating the content of contractual obligations, and the toleration of a higher degree of informality in the creation and modification of contractual duties. Many of these themes of modern contract law such as the duty to perform in good faith find explicit statement in the American Uniform Commercial Code and in the Restatement of Contracts 2nd.[63]

---

[60] Crocker, K. S., and Masten, S. E., 'Pretia Ex Machina? Prices and Process in Long-Term Contracts', *Journal of Law and Economics* 34 (1991) 69.

[61] *British Telecommunications plc v Ticehurst* [1992] ICR 383, CA.

[62] Esser, J. P., 'Institutionalizing Industry: The Changing Forms of Contract', *Law and Social Inquiry* 21 (1996) 593.

[63] This was partly the result of Karl Llewellyn's deliberate attempt to harmonize the rules of the UCC with business convention: Wiseman, Z. B., 'The Limits of Vision: Karl Llewellyn and the Merchant Rules', *Harvard Law Review* 100 (1987) 465.

Does this legal response to alterations in productive and distributive relations amount to a transformation in the law of contract? In a body of influential writings, Macneil distinguishes 'classical contract law', which was the embodiment of formal legal rationality, an intermediate 'post-classical contract law', which contained some modifications of the strict rules and entitlements in order to cope with long-term contractual relations satisfactorily, and finally 'relational contract law', which has evolved, more recently and hesitantly, as the legal doctrines seek to broaden their perspective on the co-operative nature of economic transactions by recognizing their embeddedness in prior business relations.[64] Although this is an interesting and powerful suggestion, which has been taken up fruit-fully in economic theory,[65] it seems to provide too radical a description of the evolutionary trajectory. The argument for change based upon alter-ations in productive and distributive economic relations suggests rather a pressure for greater differentiation in the law of contract and a rejection of inappropriate legal formalism in the context of flexible and co-operative business relations. In any case, we should not expect a simple economic functionalism to account for the evolution of legal doctrine, for we have already noted how the law of contract is shaped as well by other factors including political theory and public policy. The normative complexity of legal doctrine involves a broad-ranging ideological dispute conducted for the most part by an intellectual élite, which responds only indirectly to the changing currents and social forces in society. A better understanding of any transformation in the law of contract would have to analyse how alterations in economic institutions, variations in political theory, new emphases of public policy, and fresh rationalizations of the coherence of legal doctrine all combine to create a new character for the legal regulation of transactions.[66]

Nevertheless, in our earlier examination of the construction and inter-pretation of planning documents, and this discussion of the form of law that best protects the expectations of business from contractual under-takings, we can detect significant pressures for legal reasoning to drop its

[64] Macneil, I., *The New Social Contract: An Inquiry Into Modern Contractual Relations* (New Haven: Yale University Press, 1980); id., 'Contracts: Adjustment of Long-term Economic Relations under Classical, Neoclassical, and Relational Contract Law', *Northwestern University Law Review* 72 (1978) 854; id., 'Values in Contract: Internal and External', *Northwestern University Law Review* 78 (1983) 340; Gordon, R., 'Macaulay, Macneil, and the Discovery of Solidarity and Power in Contract Law', *Wisconsin Law Review* (1985) 565. In Macneil's work the evolutionary story of contract law adapting to new types of economic relations is suggested, but he also indicates the importance of other factors in the evolution of legal doctrine.

[65] Williamson, O. E., 'Transaction Cost Economics: The Governance of Contractual Relations', *Journal of Law and Economics* 22 (1979) 233.

[66] In another book, I seek to develop this possibility: Collins, H., *The Law of Contract,* 3rd edn. (London: Butterworths,1997), ch. 2.

legal formalism in favour of a more differentiated approach to regulating contracts. The extent to which formal legal regulation of entitlements can assist the construction of trading relations must vary across the spectrum of possible contractual relations. In demonstrating a willingness to complete contracts left incomplete by design by drawing upon market conventions and the history of the business relations, private law systems of regulation can provide assistance to the construction of markets, or at least not obstruct the creation of trust by providing occasions for legally endorsed opportunism.

Conclusion

The question of what kind of contract law is good for business does not admit of a simple answer. Businesses require calculability, but the expectations which determine the content of the calculation vary in the depth to which they are embedded in business relations and market conventions. The differentiation in degrees of embeddedness between these expectations tracks to some extent the different types of contracts found in production and distribution relations. Businesses therefore require pluralism in the normative orientation of adjudication systems, which to a considerable extent they have created for themselves by the institution of private arbitration.

The Common Law method of reasoning, by engaging in a less tightly self-referential doctrinal system with its case method always undermining perceived closure rules regarding evidence of expectation, may enjoy a relative advantage over Codified systems of law in achieving this differentiation in normative orientation. But the virus of legal formalism, so often mistakenly advocated on the ground of its contribution to certainty or calculability, always threatens to incapacitate the subtle balance achieved by the common law between closure and embeddedness, between the contractual discourse and the expectations based upon the business relation and the business deal.

9
Contract as Thing

As an elaboration upon one of our core themes, the constitution of markets, we turn now to consider the role of law in the construction of certain types of financial transaction. We shall focus on two types of financial instrument: negotiable instruments and futures contracts. These transactions have considerable importance in commerce, but they present almost intractable problems both in their creation and in their legal regulation. These problems are so intense that it will be argued that private law has proved incapable of providing any productive assistance in the construction or regulation of these transactions, and that the legal system as a whole is almost irrelevant to these trading relations. Far from law providing the necessary external coercive power to encourage traders to avoid betrayal or default, in these cases of financial instruments the law is impotent.

Money

The distinctive qualities of these contractual arrangements can be introduced by considering the familiar example of money. In the purchase of goods in a shop, the normal method of payment consists in the delivery of bank notes and coins. These bits of paper and metallic tokens have little intrinsic worth. Their value lies rather in their potential use for payment in other transactions. Money circulates in the economy by being accepted continuously as a valid payment of debts. In its origin, money in the form of notes represents a contract. It contains a promise of payment by a bank or a similar holder of funds. The contract exists between the bank and the 'bearer', that is any person who possesses the note and presents it to the bank for payment. In the sale of goods in a shop, therefore, in return for the goods the shopkeeper demands and receives a document that represents a contract between strangers, a bank and the original 'bearer' of the note.

From the perspective of our previous discussions about the importance of trust and non-legal sanctions in the construction of markets, the acceptance of payment by money appears quite remarkable. It involves the possibility of making credible commitments of trustworthiness based upon remote, impersonal promises. The shopkeeper accepts as payment from a customer a contract made between strangers, the bank and the original bearer of the note, which contains nothing more substantial than a promise to pay. We have understood that transactions rest upon the credibility of the commitments contained in them, and that this credibility depends upon a mixture of the trust established between the parties based upon historical interaction and reputation, and the availability of powerful non-legal sanctions to deter betrayal and disappointment. None of these sources of credibility are present in the case of money except reliance on the reputation of the bank for honouring its commitments. Money and other financial instruments were undoubtedly crucial to the rapid expansion of market economies, yet they presented almost insuperable problems for the construction of trust and sanctions. Our special interest here lies in the question of what role the law played in serving to constitute this aspect of markets.

A second feature of payment by money is in many ways even more puzzling. A legally enforceable contract usually creates a binding set of obligations owed between the parties to the contract. The law thinks of this relation as private, as a personal bond between the parties, and this isolated and discrete form of association is central to the meaning of contract. In the case of money and many other financial instruments, however, this personal obligation is transformed into an item of property. The promise by the bank to pay becomes a thing in itself, a thing that can be sold, divided, used as security, and given away, just like a can of beans. As a thing, the promise becomes capital, not merely an item for consumption. This metamorphosis of a personal obligation owed between two people into an item of property, a chattel, a fluid capital asset, in short—cash— required the legal system to develop a new differentiation in its system of classification. As well as the traditional division between personal obligations created by contract and the law of property governing ownership of chattels such as livestock and furniture, the legal system was asked to recognize a hybrid: a contract in the form of a financial instrument which should be treated in many respects as a chattel, as a thing in itself.

The example of money highlights these twin problems presented by the construction of markets with financial instruments. The problem of establishing a credible commitment based upon a mere promise to pay by a stranger required elaborate institutional arrangements for the construction of trust and non-legal sanctions. When called upon to provide assistance in the construction of this aspect of the market, the legal system encountered the fundamental blockage that its system of classification of events denied the possibility that contracts could be things. Although this blockage was eventually removed by further conceptual differentiation with respect to some financial instruments such as money, cheques, bills of exchange, and promissory notes, in some fields of commercial practice such as futures contracts, the legal system has never been able to supply productive regulation of the transactions at all. These specialized markets have therefore created for themselves their own extra-legal institutional and regulatory structures, which we have called 'club markets'.

Money represents a special case for regulation of markets in financial instruments, since the state (or institutions backed by the state) has assumed the role of guarantor of its validity and fungibility. Leaving aside this special instance of regulation using public power, we can examine the construction of markets in other analogous types of financial instruments that possess the similar quality of contracts being regarded as a thing. The most common form of document is usually described as a negotiable instrument.

A negotiable instrument payable to bearer consists of a document containing a promise to pay a sum of money to the person in possession of the document. Two features mark out this type of financial instrument. First, the right to claim the sum of money can be transferred very simply by handing over possession. The second feature is that the promise can be enforced by the bearer of the document regardless of any problems regarding the validity or enforceability of the instrument when it was originally created or transferred, subject only to a requirement of good faith (bona fide purchaser for value). The cumulative effect of these features is to transform the contract containing the promise to pay into a thing itself, which can be sold or otherwise disposed of like a chattel.

By the last quarter of the nineteenth century, the Common Law courts fully accepted the legal possibility of contracts as things in the form of negotiable instruments. But the mercantile practice of using negotiable instruments had been prevalent at least since the fifteenth century. The Common Law courts had viewed these contracts with suspicion and had only hesitantly accorded the legal effects intended and expected by merchants.

Formality

In our observations of contractual practice, we have noted that as part of the planning function many contracts will be reduced to written documents. Lawyers tend to insist on written documents, in part as a device to clarify the content of the undertakings, and in part to provide evidence in any subsequent dispute about the existence and scope of the contractual obligations. But in the case of negotiable instruments, we encounter a different use of formality. These contracts have no legal validity, and indeed no existence at all, unless they are contained in a written document. The document or instrument is not simply an evidentiary requirement, but is constitutive of the transaction. This use of formality in agreements to constitute a thing marks a sharp break with the traditional purposes of regulatory requirements of formalities.

For the purpose of giving effect to the general regulatory objective of supporting transactions and markets, there is little reason to impose a requirement of formality in order to obtain legal enforceability. The creation of a document that records the undertakings of the parties to a contract does not itself directly contribute to the establishment of trust or the construction of non-legal sanctions. A signature on a document does not reduce the risk of betrayal or disappointment. Nor does it add to the power of the disappointed party to inflict economic loss on the defaulter. The documentary evidence of the undertaking does assist, however, in the application of some non-economic sanctions such as damage to business reputation by providing evidential support for the allegation of betrayal. The use of documents to record contracts is therefore less likely where relations of trust have displaced the fear of risk of betrayal. An oral agreement sealed by a handshake will be regarded as an adequate expression of a solemn undertaking, and indeed an insistence upon written documentation may be interpreted as a sign of distrust and suspicion. It is perhaps for this reason that businessmen so often prefer to conclude transactions orally, and then leave the paperwork to the lawyers. Orality signifies trust, not an unwillingness to be bound.

The legal system, however, observed these contractual practices that accorded equal validity to oral agreements with suspicion. For the purpose of invoking the king's power to enforce an obligation, more conclusive proof of the contractual undertaking was required. The medieval forms of action were linked inextricably to methods of establishing proof in order to determine which contracts might be enforceable. The principal forms included a 'covenant', that is a written, sealed, document, and an action in debt for recovery of money or fungibles owed to the plaintiff established by 'wager of law' (a method of proof using numerous witnesses under oath). Contractual disputes outside these forms of proof could not be resolved by the courts, so that for instance executory contracts and claims on oral contracts for defective performance were unenforceable in those courts.[1] At this stage, formality was not a requirement for a valid contract, though without a covenant it would be difficult to enforce most types of contractual claim in the courts.

For the purposes of the legal determination of disputes, however, it was always tempting to use written records as conclusive evidence of the past, and to doubt the probity of assertions of contractual rights without

---

[1] Baker, J. H., *An Introduction to English Legal History*, 2nd edn., (London: Butterworths, 1979) 271.

supporting documentary evidence. The parol evidence rule prevented litigants from questioning the document as an accurate record of the reciprocal undertakings. Breaches of oral agreements without performance by one party leading to the creation of a debt were therefore denied enforcement in the king's courts, and reason seems to have been connected to the problems of proving the obligation and its breach. Although the ordinary courts began to enforce oral agreements in the sixteenth century by accepting new forms of action linked to proof before a jury, the suspicion of informality persisted and resulted in the Statute of Frauds. This regulation of the legal process was designed to prevent the admission of false evidence about the existence of transactions by requiring certain contracts such as those dealing in interests in land to be evidenced in writing.

In the evolution of legal doctrine, therefore, the forms of action, the rules of evidence, and the methods of proof were all designed to protect the integrity and efficiency of the legal process itself, rather than to help to construct and regulate markets. For this reason, the rules invariably become diluted and attenuated, for convincing non-documentary evidence of serious though informal undertakings based upon trust will inevitably occur and induce a court to abandon its requirement of formality for the sake of protecting the genuine expectations of the parties. By the nineteenth century, examples of this tension between the formality requirements of the integrity of the legal process and the need for the legal system to support the business practice of informal dealing can be found in the battles over the parol evidence rule and the exceptions to the Statute of Frauds. These cases represent the exceptions to the parol evidence rule, or the occasions when the court refused to permit the Statute of Frauds to be used as an instrument of fraud itself.

A similar approach towards formality was evident in the early history of financial instruments. A deed or document under seal, known as a bond, could be used as conclusive proof of a debt, for it provided a formal acknowledgement that a sum of money was owed. If a bond or covenant under seal recited that a debt was owed, then this record was regarded in legal proceedings as conclusive of the truth. Even if the money had in fact been repaid, the document trumped this evidence, so the court required fresh payment in full in return for surrender of the bond. But the covenant it contained remained a personal obligation between the parties, which could only be altered by the agreement of the parties. Yet this perception of evidentiary value of formality did not accord with the practice of merchants to regard the document as constitutive of the contract, of the thing to be exchanged in markets.

The legal system needed to understand the practice of merchants in using negotiable instruments within its own conceptual structures in such a way that the absence of formality rendered the transaction void, of no existence within the legal observation of events, rather than being merely unreliable evidence of the transaction. The tension can only be reconciled by the creation within the legal discourse of a separate classification for negotiable instruments, outside the normal principles of the law of contract, in which formality is constitutive rather than merely evidentiary.[2]

Legal Pluralism

If the legal system experienced a problem in treating formality as going to the existence of contracts, the further step of recognizing that the document was regarded by merchants as a thing itself that could be traded presented an almost insuperable difficulty. What was required was a private law doctrine which acknowledged that the passing of possession of the document could transfer the ownership and the enforceability of the right that it recorded to the new bearer. The common law courts resisted this transformation of contract into property until the late nineteenth century.

The idea that contractual promises could become a species of property that could be bought and sold contradicted the legal analysis that contracts created personal obligations limited to the parties to the agreement. For example, statutory reform was required in the late nineteenth century to create the position that promises to pay money would be in general assignable to others in law,[3] so that debts could be sold like an item of property. In the case of simple promissory notes, in 1702 Lord Holt gave a notorious judgment denying any legal recognition to the mercantile practice of treating them as negotiable instruments:

That the maintaining of these actions upon such notes were innovations upon the rules of the common law; and that it amounted to the setting up a new sort of specialty, unknown to the common law, and invented in Lombard Street, which attempted in these matters of bills of exchange to give laws to Westminster Hall.[4]

---

[2] A similar view of formality has recently been introduced in England for transactions involving interests in land, so that the absence of formality apparently renders the contract void: Law of Property (Miscellaneous Provisions) Act 1989, s. 2. But this reform can only operate successfully, if transactions in real property become sharply differentiated from ordinary principles of contract law. The legislation implicitly recognizes that this differentiation is not possible by promptly acknowledging in a paradoxical way that the informal void promise may nevertheless become enforceable in equity under the doctrine of proprietary estoppel. [3] Supreme Court of Judicature Act 1873, s. 25(6).

[4] *Clerke v Martin* (1702) 2 Ld Raym 757; The decision, though perhaps sound on the basis of legal precedent (Holden, J. M., *The History of Negotiable Instruments in English Law* (London: University of London, Athlone Press, 1955) 79–84) was quickly reversed by statute: Promissory Notes Act 1704; Chorley, R. S. T., 'The Conflict of Law and Commerce' *Law Quarterly Review*, CLXXXIX (1932), 51, 52–3.

In other words, Holt was objecting to the creation of a new form of property (specialty) out of a contract merely on the basis of the practice of bankers and brokers (the inhabitants of Lombard Street) without the approval of parliamentary legislation (the occupants of Westminster Hall).

On a superficial view, therefore, the practice of treating financial instruments as negotiable was often unsupported by the law. It appears as a market without a state. Yet this interpretation would be to disregard the legal pluralism of the early modern period. The merchant community could turn to their own courts to recognize the effectiveness of financial instruments to create property. In the medieval period these courts had been prepared to enforce oral agreements to the extent that they satisfied the conventions of the trade, thereby obtaining much of the business of commercial contracts. Their standards of proof and evidence within a smaller business community did not require the intricacies of the forms of action of the king's courts. Similarly, the merchant courts began to accept the possibility of financial instruments by the fifteenth century in order to accede to the needs of the business community. For example, by the fifteenth century the 'debentures' in the form prescribed by the Staple Court, which comprised a declaration that a sum of money was owed, could be passed between merchants almost as currency.[5] The men of Lombard Street therefore not only created their own specialty, but also created their own courts to enforce these rights according to the expectations of the parties. The power of these courts rested, as we have noted, not in their ability to invoke the king's coercive sanctions but rather as a reputation mechanism within the mercantile community.

But these financial instruments seem to have proliferated even without any kind of enforcement by merchant courts, relying instead upon trust and non-legal sanctions within the trading community.[6] It was the goldsmiths and other moneylenders who issued bills of exchange and treated them as negotiable in the sense of regarding the bearer as entitled to the face value of the note regardless of possible defects in the title of prior holders or parties to the original contract. These documents became effective simply upon the basis of business reputation. In Amsterdam at the beginning of the seventeenth century, an Exchange Bank was formed to print bills of exchange which could be cashed at the bank.[7] These documents earned the reputation for being as reliable as gold, so that they could be used around the world for purchasing any goods. Using these bills of exchange, for instance, in the 1620s Dutch businessmen entered a forward contract with English fishermen for all the cod from the waters of

---

[5] Postan, M. M., *Medieval Trade and Finance* (Cambridge: Cambridge University Press, 1973) 49.   [6] Ibid., 54.
[7] Barbour, V., *Capitalism in Amsterdam in the Seventeenth Century* (Baltimore: John Hopkins Press, 1950) 43.

Newfoundland even before the fishing season had opened. In England at about the same time, members of the Goldsmiths guild acted as deposit takers and issued promissory notes payable to the bearer in exchange, thereby creating a form of paper currency long before a banking system with statutory support developed.[8]

Legal pluralism was eventually harnessed in the late nineteenth century by the common law of the king's courts establishing its hegemony. The solution was to regard mercantile custom or law as a type of implied term of these contracts, the 'unwritten law' of the transaction, so that in enforcing rights under negotiable instruments the courts could explain that they were merely upholding the express and implicit agreement of the parties.

> The law merchant thus spoken of with reference to bills of exchange and other negotiable securities, though forming part of the general body of the lex mercatoria, is of comparatively recent origin. It is neither more nor less than the usages of merchants and traders in the different departments of trade, ratified by the decision of Courts of Law, which, upon such usages being proved before them, have adopted them as settled law with a view to the interests of trade and the public convenience, the Court proceeding herein on the well-known principle of law that, with reference to transactions in the different departments of trade, Courts of Law, in giving effect to the contracts and dealings of the parties, will assume that the latter have dealt with one another on the footing of any custom or usage prevailing generally in the particular department. By this process, what before was usage only, unsanctioned by legal decision, has become engrafted upon, or incorporated into, the common law, and may thus be said to form part of it.[9]

The history of the development of negotiable instruments reveals the constitution of a particular market without the support or endorsement of state law. Trust and non-legal sanctions were sufficient to establish the viability of such transactions, but the business community that needed this form of credit arrangement also created an external power in the form of merchants courts to supervise and channel the practice, and then to act as a collective reputation mechanism for the purpose of enhancing the impact of non-legal sanctions. It was only centuries later that the state courts found ways of accommodating this market within its doctrinal system, and then took over the supervisory and regulatory role.

Futures Contracts

Contracts for the sale of goods usually contemplate the situation of the goods being in existence and identifiable. A *forward* contract, however,

---

[8] Holden, J. M., *The History of Negotiable Instruments in English Law* (London: University of London, Athlone Press, 1955) 72–3.

[9] *Per* Cockburn CJ, *Goodwin v Robarts* (1875) LR 10 Exch 337, Exchequer Chamber.

consists of a sale of a commodity at a future date, and at the time of the formation of the contract the commodity such as a crop or a fisherman's catch need not be in existence. This technique for 'hedging' against price variations is common in the mercantile community. The Common Law judges, perhaps drawing upon a Roman law line of reasoning, viewed the possibility of a sale of a non-existent item with deep suspicion.[10] This attitude is revealed in *Couturier v Hastie*.[11] Under the contract subject to dispute, a seller of a cargo of corn in a ship was seeking to obtain payment. The corn had never been delivered, because the captain of the ship had unloaded the goods and sold them to prevent them from being damaged prior to the formation of the contract. The seller claimed that payment was due, however, on the ground that, under the terms of the contract, he had not promised to supply the corn, but merely to supply the appropriate shipping documents that would entitle the buyer to possession of the corn on arrival in port. Although the vendor's argument was probably correct on the basis of the planning documents (the scheme being one of passing the risk of loss onto the buyer once the goods had been loaded), the court insisted that 'the basis of the contract in this case was the sale and purchase of goods'. It followed on the ordinary principles governing sales of goods that the failure to supply the goods defeated the claim for their price. The court seems to have been unable or unwilling to grasp the point that this transaction involved a sale of documents not a sale of goods.

A *futures* contract differs from a forward contract by creating an even more abstract entitlement. These contracts can be traded as objects in themselves. Each contract contains a right which can be measured precisely against the value of other futures contracts in the same commodity. For example, a contract for a hundred bushels of grade 'A' wheat due at a particular maturity date can be traded as a thing of identical value to a contract with the same content and maturity date. In the perceptive analysis by Telser,

A futures contract is a financial instrument traded on an organised futures market such that all contracts of the same maturity date are perfect substitutes for each other. All forward contracts of the same maturity date are not perfect substitutes for each other because the identities of the parties to the contract are pertinent and may differ from one contract to another. The validity of a futures contract is independent of the identity of the buyer and seller. A futures contract is highly fungible (liquid).[12]

Private law had a fundamental problem in treating such future sales as transferable or negotiable, for it insisted upon its basic principle that

---

[10] Sale of Goods Act 1979, s. 6.   [11] (1856) 5 HL Cas 673.
[12] Telser, L. G., 'Why There are Organized Futures Markets', *Journal of Law and Economics* 24 (1981) 1.

ownership could only be passed by a vendor with good title (*nemo dat quod non habet*—roughly, 'you can't sell what you don't own'), so that any defects in the title of the original vendor undermined the validity of subsequent transfers. By analysing the futures contract as a variant upon an ordinary sale of goods, the common law could not grasp the idea that this type of contract was regarded by merchants as analogous to a negotiable instrument that could be traded free from any defects in title.

Why are there futures contracts (or derivatives)[13] in many commodities? Traders who require a regular supply of a commodity, such as a mill owner who needs supplies of raw cotton, have to be able to assure themselves of a regular supply. It is possible to enter into long-term contracts with commodity producers, as we have seen in connection with iron ore contracts.[14] But these personal undertakings rely heavily on the trustworthiness of the parties and are vulnerable to opportunism. A forward contract provides the manufacturer with the right to obtain a certain quantity of a commodity long in advance of requirements. It permits the manufacturer to hedge against fluctuations in price and to avoid economic dependence upon a small number of suppliers.[15] But forward contracts cannot easily be disposed of when they provide an excess to requirements. Once futures contracts have been created, they can then be sold and resold, thereby ensuring that a competitive market price is available for participants in the market. These participants consist of those seeking to hedge against price movements, for which privilege they must pay a small premium, together with speculators who are prepared to gamble against movements in prices.[16] The contract thus becomes a 'thing', a fungible item, the object of the sale itself.

The striking feature of futures contracts from our point of view is the inability of the legal system to constitute a market in which they can subsist. Trading in futures only occurs within organized markets, which function largely outside the legal system. In principle, of course, a contract for the sale of a commodity comprises exactly the type of transaction which a legal system enforces routinely in the ordinary courts. What the state's legal system cannot apparently achieve is the provision of the facility to

[13] Futures contracts in commodities are a type of derivative, for derivatives consist of any type of investment where the pay-offs depend upon the (future) prices of other well-defined assets or commodities. The term derivative is usually employed in connection with futures contracts involving financial instruments including currencies. For these financial derivatives, club markets are unnecessary, because the commodity is already defined either by the state in the case of currency or by an existing club market such as an Exchange in the case of shares. It is therefore possible to have simple trading relations (over the counter) in financial derivatives.

[14] Daintith, T., 'The Design and Performance of Long-term Contracts', in T. Daintith and G. Teubner (eds.), *Contract and Organisation*, (Berlin: Walter de Gruyter, 1986) 164.

[15] Telser L. G., and Higginbottom, H. N., 'Organised Futures Markets: Costs and Benefits', *Journal of Political Economy* 85 (1977) 969.

[16] Weller, P., *The Theory of Futures Markets* (Oxford: Blackwell, 1992) 2–3.

trade in these futures contracts as if they constituted a commodity themselves. For this transformation of contracts into things, the participants in the market need to create an organization, often called an 'Exchange' or 'Bourse', which we have described as a club market.

Club Markets

A club market is created by a group of traders for their mutual protection and to obtain efficiency gains through savings on transaction costs. If a group of people are regularly doing business with each other, then they will rely predominantly upon trust and non-legal sanctions in order to make credible commitments. The advantage of a club market is that it permits the expansion of membership of the trusted group and at the same time increases the potential severity of non-legal sanctions. The rudimentary form of a club market is that the members agree to be bound by the rules of the association. These rules contain as the central ingredient an undertaking to honour any undertakings made between members of the group. The sanction for non-compliance with this rule will be exclusion from the group, and therefore deprivation of access to the market. This threat is equivalent to the sanction of withdrawal of a licence to trade, and is therefore far more powerful than unorganized reputation mechanisms which employ the normal threat of a personal refusal to do business with the defaulter in the future. In addition, the club can extract financial compensation from members, and the availability of this sanction is usually protected (unlike private law regulation) by limiting membership to individuals rather than limited liability corporate entities.[17]

Within a club market, the traders can also profit from other dimensions. The contracts may be made with utmost informality, a handshake or an order registered on a computer record. The informality is possible in part because of the high levels of trust, and in part because the rules of the association usually specify a specially tailored set of default rules appropriate to this type of market transaction. This informality then reduces transaction costs. Similarly, the market usually has institutional arrangements for reckoning and balancing accounts between its members at periodic intervals, so that the transactions costs of making payments are greatly reduced. By minimizing transaction costs, the opportunity is then created for speculation in contracts with much smaller differences in prices.

The value of the rules of the association can be enhanced by the

---

[17] Pirrong, S. C., 'The Efficient Scope of Private Transactions-Cost-Reducing Institutions: The Success and Failures of Commodity Exchanges', *Journal of Legal Studies* 24 (1995) 229, 234.

provision of a domestic arbitration system administered by members of the trade itself. The arbitration system usually provides a cheap way of resolving disputes about such difficult matters as quality, but perhaps more importantly its relative expertise compared to ordinary courts enables it to govern the market by adjudication through efficient rules.

A final benefit created by a club market for its members is that it can constitute a separate legal entity, an unincorporated association or a company, which can own the market and its assets. These assets consist of trading reputation, expertise, and knowledge about the market. The association can defend these assets against third parties, thereby protecting their value for its members. One example is the way club markets may be reluctant to provide information about current prices without payment of a fee on the ground that the exchange's efficient pricing mechanism is one of the key benefits to its members.[18]

Club markets were not created initially for the purpose of transforming contracts into things. The savings on transactions costs and the enhancement of the reputation mechanism of non-legal sanctions supply a major incentive for a large market to form such an association. In share dealings, for instance, where the object being bought and sold is a contractual right to an uncertain income from a share in the equity of a company, stock exchanges provide a regulatory framework over their members to minimize the risk that the bits of paper (or these days electronic records) may turn out to be non-existent or valueless. Similarly, in the clearing house arrangements between banks for meeting cheques and promissory notes, we can discover a self-regulatory system that both enhances the reputation of banks in providing the service of cheques and simultaneously creates a reputation mechanism for punishing defaulters. All Japanese banks, for instance, conform to a rule prohibiting dealing in any manner with clients that dishonour cheques twice during a period of six months. As a result, few businesses can survive dishonouring a cheque, and this non-legal sanction enhances the credibility of these financial instruments.[19]

Yet a club market, once created, offers this potential of the constitution of a futures market. The club market can supply three essential ingredients for a futures market: first, a standardized, mandatory style of commodity description; secondly, a standardized mandatory contractual package of terms or entitlements; and third, a mechanism for creating an irrevocable and unimpeachable obligation.

The first requirement, the mandatory style of commodity description,

---

[18] Mulherin, J. H., *et al.*, 'Prices are Property: The Organization of Financial Exchanges from a Transaction Cost Perspective', *Journal of Law and Economics* 34 (1991) 591.

[19] Haley, J. O., 'Relational Contracting: Does Community Count?', in H. Baum (ed.), *Japan: Economic Success and Legal System* (Berlin/New York: Walter de Gruyter, 1997) 167, 181.

removes an obstacle to fungibility. Unless there is a convention by which the qualities of the commodity can be described with precision, a forward contract must always face the problem of incompleteness in its description. Private law, with its emphasis upon self-regulation, permits the parties to create their own definition of standards, but this remains a private agreement that has to be renegotiated for every transaction. Market-wide conventions can be set by statute, as in the case of weights (pounds, kilos) and measures (feet, metres), but parliament probably lacks the time and expertise to provide detailed conventions for every sector of trade. It concentrates its regulation of standards upon essential consumer transactions, such as the purity of bread and ale.[20] A club can provide a rich conventional classification system for the abstract things to be sold, such as types of cotton or interests in a company. This classification system defines precisely the attributes of the property right, like a description of a particular grade of cotton or a classification of gold bullion, but in a mandatory standardized form, so that the contract can be sold in the confidence that this abstract property does represent a future right to a certain thing which is exactly equivalent to another contract containing the same quantity of the commodity. Simpson's historical study of the evolution of a futures market in cotton at Liverpool reveals how cotton as a commodity could be described in a huge variety of grades and qualities.[21] It is only in this context that the terms of the contract litigated in *Raffles v Wichelhaus*[22] can make sense. The contract was for the sale of 125 bales of Surat cotton, *guaranteed middling fair merchant's Dhollorah*, to arrive on the ship Peerless from Bombay. The phrase in italics only makes sense within the context of a conventional system of classification of cotton. The formation of an exchange enabled the participants to agree upon a mandatory system of classification, which then enabled them to enter into precise forward contracts.

The second important ingredient supplied by club markets, which enables the transformation from forward contracts to futures contracts, is the requirement of standardization of contracts. The document recording the contractual right takes on a uniform standard form, so that secondary purchasers know precisely what is being purchased.[23] The contract for the sale of the commodity must contain a standard set of conditions, so that quantities can be compared in price without the need to examine the details of the terms. The standardized package must also

---

[20] Assize of Bread and Ale, 1266.
[21] Simpson, A. W. B., 'The Origin of Futures Trading in the Liverpool Cotton Market', in P. Cane and J. Stapleton (eds.), *Essays for Patrick Atiyah* (Oxford: Clarendon Press, 1991) 179.
[22] (1864) 2 H & C 906, 159 ER 375, Exchequer.
[23] Greeley, H. T., 'Contracts as Commodities: The Influence of Secondary Purchasers on the Form of Contracts', *Vanderbilt Law Review* 42 (1989) 133.

conform precisely to established trade practices in the spot market, so that the futures contracts provide a reliable route for hedgers against price variation:[24]

The exchange defines the terms of a contract such that all contracts of a given class are perfect substitutes and such that the validity of a transaction in that contract does not depend on the identity of the principals.[25]

In particular, the standard contracts for futures specify a limited number of delivery dates, perhaps monthly, so that sales and purchases for each accounting period can be matched up in the traders' 'positions'. Once this step has been taken, then the standardized contract can itself be traded as a commodity. Trading in this fixed commodity is motivated by hedging and speculating about price volatility.[26]

The third element of futures contracts supplied by a club market was to turn the contract into a thing both by preventing the original parties from cancelling the contract, and by preventing any subsequent challenge to the validity of the transaction. Unlike ordinary contracts that create personal obligations between the parties which can be modified or rescinded by agreement, the futures contract, once created, will circulate in the market between traders by further sales or assignments, and so, for the contract to preserve its value as a commodity, it must not be possible for the original parties to the transaction to destroy it or modify it. In his study of the construction of the futures market in cotton, Simpson discovers the appropriate change in the rules of the Liverpool association in about 1873 to the bald declaration that 'No contract shall be cancelled on any ground'.[27] As futures markets have evolved, they have developed more effective techniques for ensuring the irreversible nature of the contractual obligations. One standard method has been to interpose the club market as a party to every contract, so that for each transaction the exchange becomes the buyer from one trader and the seller to the other. This addition to the contractual relations enhances trust by putting the resources of the whole market behind each transaction, and at the same time it greatly reduces transaction costs by permitting a daily settlement through offsetting all sales and purchases through a clearing house.[28]

---

[24] Powers, M. J., 'Effects of Contract Provisions on the Success of a Futures Contract', *Journal of Farm Economics* 49 (1967) 833.
[25] Telser L. G. and Higginbottom, H. N., n. 15 above, 973.
[26] Veljanovski, C. G., 'An Institutional Analysis of Futures Contracting', in B. A. Goss (ed.), *Futures Markets: Their Establishment and Performance* (London and Sydney, Croom Helm, 1986) 13, 20–21. [27] Simpson, A. W. B., n. 21 above, 179, 203.
[28] The development of clearing houses from informal rings of traders at the close of the nineteenth century in the USA is described in Williams, J., *The Economic Function of Futures Markets* (Cambridge: Cambridge University Press, 1986) 4–10. The clearing houses also overcame the legal problem that traders were acting originally as agents, so that in off-setting contracts in rings, they were arguably acting without the principal's authority. Members of the exchange became principals to the contracts with the clearing house.

Another method devised for enhancing trust is for clearing houses to demand 'margins' from traders. The margin represents in effect a variable deposit (or security) against default on transactions, which can be calculated on the average difference between buying and selling prices together with the quantity of exposure to price variations (that is, the difference between the amount of purchases and sales).[29]

The private law system of contract was unable to achieve these three conditions. It could not supply the conventions for rich classification of the commodity. It could only determine the content of the obligation by reference to the contractual description chosen by the parties. The courts could fill in elementary implicit understandings, such as that the intention to trade in tow did not include an intention to enter into a contract for the purchase of a commodity containing tow and hemp.[30] But it could not provide a detailed classification of the types of cotton and use it to fulfil the expectations of the parties. This could only be supplied by mandatory rules of the association, established conventions in the business, and expert arbitrators familiar with the rules and conventions to adjudicate any disputes. Nor could private law regulation take the second step of imposing a mandatory standard form contract on the parties. The central regulatory tool used by private law of permitting extensive self-regulation could not be reversed to exclude the possibility of variations in standard forms. But of course, as soon as variations are permitted, then it becomes far more difficult to trade in contracts as a commodity since contracts cease to be perfect substitutes for each other. 'Contract heterogeneity raises transaction costs by reducing market liquidity.'[31] Nor could private law regulation ensure that the contracts could not be cancelled or avoided. These contracts for the sale of generic goods were not specifically enforceable in the courts, and nor could private law ignore consensual modifications to the contract by the original parties to the contract without contradicting the basis premise of its regulation that contractual obligations are personal and consensual. The solutions to these problems had to be created by a club market, which provided its own regulatory system that operated outside of, and to some extent in opposition to, the private law regulation of contracts.

As well as these defects of private law regulation, club markets also address another pervasive structural weakness of private law regulation that we described earlier as 'self-enforcement'. In order to enhance the reflexive character of private law regulation, the power to enforce its standards is routinely delegated to the parties to the transaction them-

---

[29] The collection of margins and interposing the exchange as party to the contract developed in the USA in the 1920s: Williams, J., ibid. 14.
[30] *Scriven Bros & Co v Hindley & Co* [1913] 3 KB 564.
[31] Veljanovski, C. G., n. 26 above, 32.

selves. This delegation of enforcement enhances the capacity of the regulatory system for adjustment and modification of standards. Yet it also creates the structural weakness of a risk that routine failure to enforce the mandatory regulatory standards of private law, such as the rules against fraud, will inevitably reduce the level of trust in markets. In the language of game theory, there is no punishment of actors who fail to enforce the regulatory standards of private law, so the potential advantage in the construction of markets of establishing patterns of conformity to those standards may be lost.[32] Club markets appear to function as a solution to this problem by establishing a monitoring system, which punishes not only those who breach the trading standards, but also those who fail to take steps to enforce those trading standards. In other words, the committee of the club market will not only punish members who breach its trading rules, but will also punish those who cover up breaches by others. Club markets therefore replace the self-enforcement mechanism of private law by a type of public enforcement mechanism analogous to criminal regulation. In markets that trade in such intangible interests as futures contracts, which depend for their existence upon high levels of trust and integrity between traders, it seems that the self-enforcement mechanism of private law regulation lacks the capacity to assist in the construction of the market.

A similar story about the origins of the insurance market can also be told with reference to the institution of club markets. In the case of marine insurance, for instance, the Dutch established a Chamber of Assurance in 1598. The function of this Chamber was to develop printed standard form contracts of insurance, to provide a place to 'register' policies, thereby providing reliable evidence of their existence and content, and then to adjudicate between merchants over any disputes arising. The Lloyds market for insurance in London also works as a club market with its rules of association and requirements of membership. At Lloyds, the assumption of risk described in an insurance policy is subdivided into smaller parcels of risk that are then sold in the closed market to trustworthy dealers or 'names'. In many sectors of the economy, therefore, the role of the legal system and legal sanctions appears to have been minimal in constituting markets.

Club markets are not always essential for treating contracts as things. It is possible, for instance, to replicate these features by a framework agreement or umbrella agreement between two or more parties, so that in effect they create a local private club market. Trading in futures can also take place off the exchange, but the pricing and determination of the nature of

---

[32] Axelrod, R. M., *The Complexity of Cooperation*, (Princeton: Princeton University Press, 1997) 40–42.

the contract as a product depends upon the existence of the exchange. To achieve complete confidence in paper representing the right to property in the future, however, club markets appear to have served commercial interests well. These markets can function in complete isolation from the legal system. Ferguson describes, for instance, how legislation in England prohibited options and speculative time bargains in public or joint stock and other public securities, that is, a futures market in shares. Despite this threat of criminal sanctions and the legal unenforceability of these transactions, it appears that the public regulation had no effect on the behaviour of members of the Stock Exchange.[33] On the contrary, any member who might default upon such criminal and void transactions would be excluded from the Exchange, and the rules of the Exchange prohibited recourse to the courts (a rule which itself was unlawful). The club market achieved the routine enforceability of those transactions which it regarded as commercially desirable wholly without the law.

Self-Regulatory Associations

The story of futures contracts differs from that of negotiable instruments in the following respect. We find a repeated pattern in the history of commercial law that a new kind of transaction, usually involving credit arrangements and financial instruments, is created within the mercantile community. At its inception, its credibility rests upon the possibility of non-legal sanctions, particularly damage to reputation. The law plays no part in this imaginative construction of new forms of commercial relations. When the transaction is first litigated before the courts, indeed, it is usually declared invalid, because it fails to conform to a recognized pattern of transaction, and, as a result, the transaction breaches some basic private law principle for the creation of contractual obligations, such as consideration in the case of bankers commercial credits or the doctrine of privity in the case of negotiable instruments.[34] These determinations by the courts do not appear to have any effect on the use of these new types of commercial transaction, however, since their force rested in any case upon non-legal sanctions. After a period of time, the legal system adjusts its requirements by differentiating the legal rules in order to be able to create a new form of regulation suitable for the new financial instrument. In the case of negotiable instruments, for instance, legal reasoning distinguishes them from ordinary contracts as a special category to which the normal private law of contract rules do not apply.

[33] Ferguson, R. B., 'Commercial Expectations and the Guarantee of the Law: Sales Transactions in Mid-Nineteenth Century England', in G. R. Rubin and D. Sugerman (eds.), *Law, Economy and Society: Essays in the History of English Law 1750–1920* (London: Professional Books, 1984) 192.   [34] Chorley, R. S. T., n. 4 above, 51.

Where the story about futures markets differs from this historical cycle is that the legal system as a system of private law regulation is unable to contribute to the construction and support of this type of commercial contract. Private law is systematically incapable providing the web of mandatory rules needed for such a market transaction that turns a contract into a thing. Merchants have to create their own equivalent to a regulatory system: the club market. In this context of futures markets, therefore, the private law system of regulation is not merely marginal to their creation, but it is fundamentally incompetent in its design and basic principles to assist in the construction of markets.

The club market is itself a form of association created by contract. Members join the association through a contract of membership in order to participate in the market. The rules of the association regulate the operation of the market. But this self-regulation is not merely designed to prevent abuses, for the rules constitute the market itself. The rules enable the construction of a contract as a thing, a commodity which can be traded.

The final question to be considered is how best to regulate the contract which creates the club market. Should the rules of the association be regarded as simply a species of contract subject to the principles of private law, or should a distinctive method of regulation be designed?

In some instances, it has been argued that public law principles should be applied to club markets. These public law principles are normally applied to agencies of the state in order to ensure that they conform to their limited powers and follow fair procedures. In order to apply these principles to club markets, it is suggested that club markets operate a form of devolved regulatory power analogous to state agencies. In relation to these markets, the state has permitted the club to perform functions which otherwise would be awarded to state agencies. Given this role as deputy regulator, then it can be suggested that in the exercise of these quasi-governmental powers the club market should be held to the standards of public law.[35] On the other hand, it has been argued that associations based upon contract should never be subject to public law principles, but should instead be regulated by the ordinary private law of contract.[36] The basis in contract, that is private ordering, excludes the requirement to conform to the public standards established for the state's exercise of power.

There are many types of self-regulating associations, such as trade unions, social clubs, and financial services regulatory bodies. The source of their power varies from contract, to statutory authorization, to market

---

[35] *R v Panel on Takeovers and Mergers, ex p Datafin plc* [1987] 1 All ER 564, CA.

[36] *R v Lloyd's, ex p Briggs* [1993] Lloyd's LR 176; *R v Disciplinary Committee of the Jockey Club, ex p Aga Khan* [1993] 2 All ER 853, CA.

convention. A general approach to the regulation of these bodies needs to be sensitive to the differences in their tasks and the varied source of their authority.[37] In the narrow context of club markets, however, my argument suggests that their principal function is to establish a system of trust and sanctions for the constitution of a particular type of market. In order to achieve this function, club markets have to deviate from the rules of private law in order to create the commodity to be traded (contracts) and to establish the requisite level of trust and sanctions. The club market serves a governmental function in the sense that it provides an alternative to private law as a system of sanctions to support transactions and an alternative to the courts for its enforcement and collective reputation mechanism. This analysis of its functions suggests that neither private law nor public law standards may be appropriate for the regulation of a club market.

This conclusion suggests further that the regulation of club markets should commence with a high degree of respect for their autonomous institutions. These markets devise their own structures for the formulation of rules and their enforcement. In the Liverpool cotton market, for instance, Simpson's study describes procedures for private arbitration, and then appeals to a superior committee which developed its own 'case-law' by observing precedents.[38] It is hard to imagine circumstances when it would be justifiable for the state through its courts to upset such decisions, for any rival standards of adjudication would threaten the tight system of trust and sanctions which sustains these precarious markets. It is not sufficient, for instance, for a court to allege that the committee of the club market has misinterpreted its own rules, for this interpretation, no matter how perverse an interpretation of the published rules, is likely to have been adopted in order to restore trust in the market. Perhaps the only type of regulation which would be compatible with the necessary respect for the autonomy of club markets might be the application of rules designed to protect trust in its self-governing organizations. For example, a rule of natural justice or procedural due process that requires a hearing before a member can be excluded might be justified as a measure designed to protect the club from an abuse of power which might damage its credibility among its own members. The objective of such a rule would not be the imposition of public law standards on these self-regulating associations, but rather to deter conduct which might lead to their self-destruction.

Although such standards as due process and natural justice are usually associated with public law, it might be a better regulatory strategy to perceive these standards as implied terms or default rules within the

---

[37] Black, J., 'Constitutionalising Self-regulation', *Modern Law Review* 59 (1996) 24.
[38] Simpson, A. W. B., n. 21 above, 179.

contract of membership. If these rules have their source in public law, then they may be regarded as mandatory rules, which cannot easily be adapted to the particular circumstances of the regulatory mechanism established by the club market. In contrast, if these standards represent default rules concerning the internal governance of the club market established by the rules of the association, then by means of express rules the association can tailor the principles to its own particular conditions of existence and success. It may appear strange to suggest that private law can produce default rules that mimic ideas in public law such as natural justice or procedural due process, but this capacity of private law has been demonstrated in several instances such as the rules of trade unions,[39] trade associations,[40] and some organizations established by statute.[41]

This respect for the autonomy of club markets should be diminished to the extent that the state deliberately allocates regulatory powers to these associations. In the context of UK financial regulation, for instance, some associations have been allocated roles designed to protect investors which would otherwise have been exercised by public regulatory bodies.[42] When the association exercises such powers, then the default standards of regulation can be drawn more appropriately from public law.[43] But it should not be assumed that club markets function as quasi-governmental bodies. On the contrary, the presumption should be that these self-regulatory associations only serve to protect the public interest in the sense that they provide an indispensable mechanism for the constitution of markets in which contracts are treated as things.

---

[39] e.g. *Radford v National Society of Operative Printers, Graphical and Media Personnel* [1972] ICR 484, Ch.D (implied term of natural justice).

[40] *Lee v Showmen's Guild of Great Britain* [1952] 2 QB 329, CA (no evidence to support the finding of the committee); *Nagle v Feilden* [1966] 2 QB 633, CA (discriminatory exclusion from membership); *McInnes v Onslow-Fane* [1978] 3 All ER 211 (natural justice and duty to act fairly); see generally: Frase, A. R. G., 'The Role of the Exchange', in Parry, H., *et al.*, *Futures Trading: Law and Regulation* (London: Longman, 1993) 73, 84–6.

[41] *Malloch v Aberdeen Corporation* [1971] 1 WLR 1578, HL (schoolteacher employed by local authority entitled to natural justice); *R. v BBC ex p Lavelle* [1983] ICR 99 QB (implied contractual right to be heard); *Stevenson v United Transport Workers Union* [1977] ICR 893, CA (implied jurisdictional limits on power of committee). For a more general discussion, see: Oliver, D., 'Common Values in Public and Private Law and the Public/Private Divide', *Public Law* (1997) 630.

[42] The Financial Services Act 1986 in the UK does provide a loose regulatory framework over the London Clearing House (s. 39, and Sched. 4) and of futures trading (Chapter 1 of part 1 and Sched. 1, para. 8. through the Security and Futures Authority), where the purpose of the rules is mostly that of investor protection.

[43] e.g. *R v Stock Exchange, ex p Else* [1993] 1 All ER 420.

Conclusion

This study of regulation for the purposes of supporting transactions involving financial markets concludes this part of the book. It provides a striking illustration of our main theme, which has been to insist upon the peripheral role played by legal sanctions for breach of contract in the construction of markets and transactions. But this observation does not lead to the conclusion that regulation is unnecessary for flourishing markets. On the contrary, this chapter has insisted on the vital importance of regulation in markets for financial instruments. The regulation has to be supplied, however, either by adjudicators who have the capacity to contextualize contracts and avoid the closure of private law doctrine (the merchant courts), or more drastically by an alternative, private system of regulation, operating outwith the law, which can propound the appropriate contextual standards and supply the necessary ingredients for the construction of trust and sanctions (the club market).

Our attention now turns to the other main purpose of regulating contracts: to reverse the distributive results of transactions. In a market economy, contracts provide the principal mechanism for altering initial endowments. Recall the story of Tom Sawyer, who first sold the right to whitewash the fence for assorted items such as marbles and candy, and then traded those items for Sunday School tickets of achievement, finally trading those tickets for the glorious prize of a Bible. By sharp dealing, Tom moves from the position of drudge to the most envied boy in the community. In the fourth part of the book, we consider the question of what regulation may be required to control this kind of sharp reversal of fortunes facilitated by markets.

Part 4
Distributive Tasks of Regulation

10
Power and Governance

How does a free agreement between equal citizens lead to the creation of relations of power and domination? This question introduces a central controversy in the analysis of contractual practices. Whereas some theorists perceive this dimension of power in contractual relations as an adjunct of disparities of wealth and market position, others present this aspect of contractual relations as a benign technique for overcoming practical problems of transactions costs and incompleteness in contracts. Both accounts contain important insights, though neither is complete on its own.

The former strand in the explanation of how contracts create power relations emphasizes the way in which contracts can be used to take advantage of existing disparities in wealth. In this vein, Max Weber observed:

The great variety of permitted contractual schemata and the formal empowerment to set the content of contracts in accordance with one's desires and independently of all official form patterns, in and of itself by no means makes sure that these formal possibilities will in fact be available to all and everyone. Such availability is prevented above all by the difference in the distribution of property as guaranteed by law. The formal right of a worker to enter into any contract whatsoever with any employer whatsoever does not in practice represent for the employment seeker even the slightest freedom in the determination of his own conditions of work, and it does not guarantee him any influence on this process. It rather means, at least primarily, that the more powerful party in the market, i.e., normally the employer, has the possibility to set the terms, to offer the job 'take it or leave it', and, given the normally more pressing economic need of the worker, to impose his terms upon him. The result of contractual freedom, then, is in the first place the opening of the opportunity to use, by the clever utilization of property ownership in the market, these resources without legal restraints as a means for the achievement of power over others.[1]

Although this explanation of the source of power relations in contract as a reflection of disparities in wealth may sometimes provide a sufficient account, the existence of power relations established through contract,

---

[1] Weber, M., *Economy and Society* (G. Roth and C. Wittich, eds.), (Berkeley: University of California Press, 1978) ii. 730.

especially in commercial contracts, appears to be more widespread than might be indicated by the presence of inequality of bargaining power.

The alternative explanation for the presence of hierarchy presented by transaction cost economics insists that the power relation or 'governance structure' is an efficient response to problems of creating efficient contractual arrangements.[2] In many instances the parties to a transaction will not be in a position to agree to every detail regarding expected performance in advance. The precise product required from a supplier may not be established until the supplier has carried out the necessary research and development work. Similarly, the parties may be uncertain about the likely costs of performance, due to the presence of unknown factors such as geology, war, market demand, and weather, so they may wish to make adjustments to the plans during the course of performance in the light of further information about costs. Even if it were possible to agree terms to handle such contingencies, a possibility which often seems unlikely, the costs of constructing such an agreement might prove considerable. An efficient strategy which keeps transaction costs to a minimum is for the parties to create a governance structure for their relation, so that a body is given discretionary power to resolve these issues when the relevant information is available.[3] This body might be a relatively neutral third party,[4] as in the case of architects and surveyors giving instructions to contractors during the performance of construction contracts, or might be one of the parties themselves, as is routinely the case in employment relations and automobile manufacturers' relations with distributors.[5] These governance structures provide an economical method for coping with uncertainty by minimizing transaction costs.

As well as the problem of uncertainty, transaction cost economics (which is perhaps better described as the new institutional economics) stresses the importance of 'sunk' or 'idiosyncratic' investments. These comprise costs incurred by the parties during the performance of the contract which are specific to that transaction and cannot be recovered either in full or in part in the event of termination of the contract. In a franchise contract, for instance, the franchisee often incurs considerable costs in starting up the

---

[2] Williamson, O. E., 'Transaction Cost Economics: The Governance of Contractual Relations', *Journal of Law and Economics* 22 (1979) 233; id., *The Economic Institutions of Capitalism* (New York: Free Press, 1985).

[3] Stinchcombe, A. L., 'Contracts as Hierarchical Documents', in A. L. Stinchcombe and C. A. Heimer (eds.), *Organization Theory and Project Management: Administering Uncertainty in Norwegian Offshore Oil* (Oslo: Norwegian University Press, 1985) ch. 2, 121.

[4] Maher, M. E., 'Transaction Cost Economics and Contractual Relations', *Cambridge Journal of Economics* 21 (1997) 147, 157.

[5] Beale, H., *et al.*, 'The Distribution of Cars: A Complex Contractual Technique', in D. Harris and D. Tallon (eds.), *Contract Law Today: Anglo-French Comparisons* (Oxford: Oxford University Press, 1989).

business such as investment in premises and machinery and learning the skills required to operate the franchise; at the same time the franchisor invests the accumulated reputation of the franchise name in the franchisee's business, which may be significantly damaged by the franchisee failing to maintain the quality required. The contract will incorporate many devices to protect these investments. A lengthy duration of the contract will go some way to the protection of investments.[6] The contract uses incentives to encourage both parties to protect each other's investments, as for example determining income by commissions on sales or in franchises by profit sharing. The contract will contain 'hostages' such as security interests or payments in advance or in the case of franchises a high initial fee to obtain the franchise. In addition, the parties may agree to governance structures designed to protect their investments. The franchisor typically insists upon the power to issue detailed instructions about how the franchisee should run the operation, which is backed up by the power to terminate the contract peremptorily in order to protect the investment of its reputation. Similarly, employers use disciplinary procedures to ensure that employees make the most productive use of the capital investments in plant and machinery. Employees may bargain with employers for grievance and arbitration systems in order to protect their investments in firm-specific skills against unjustified disciplinary action and termination of employment.[7] On this view, therefore, many governance structures established by contracts may be explained as an efficient response to the problem of achieving adequate protection of sunk investments rather than a brute display of economic power by the rich and the privileged.

Having made this broad contrast between explanations of hierarchies established by contracts, we will consider a number of types of power relations established through contracts, in order to assess the strengths and insights of the rival accounts. The purpose of evaluating these rival explanations is to consider their implications for legal regulation. Under the former explanation of power in contractual relations, the case for regulation relies upon the ambition to prevent disparities in wealth and resources from being used to create oppressive power relations in civil society. The objective of regulation would be either to reduce the disparities of wealth and resources or to invalidate and replace the terms which express oppressive power relations. Under the latter explanation of power relations in terms of efficiency, the case for regulation becomes much weakened. If the power relation is necessary for the parties to achieve the enhancement of wealth envisioned by their contractual relation, then

---

[6] Joskow, P. L., 'Contract Duration and Relationship Specific Investments: Empirical Evidence from Coal Markets', *American Economic Review* 77 (1987) 168.

[7] Williamson, O. E., *Economic Institutions*, n. 2 above, 243.

any intervention by the law might frustrate that objective and harm the economic interests of both parties. The purpose of regulation on this latter analysis should be confined to measures designed to enhance the efficiency of the governance structure of the contract by means of inserting additional default rules or compulsory terms. The discussion of these rival analyses and prescriptions for regulation is organized around three paradigms where contracts often establish power relations: mass adhesion contracts, principal and agent relations, and unincorporated associations and analogous hybrids.

Mass Contracts

Standard form contracts, in which a business effectively dictates the terms of the contract to another by insisting on the use of its standard terms of business, became a commonplace practice in consumer transactions in the twentieth century. Legal doctrinal writers wondered whether these standard forms could amount to the terms of a contract, since it was hard to maintain that the consumer had genuinely consented to the terms. The consumer rarely read the printed terms and so was unaware of their content. Even if the consumer had attempted to do so, the terms were hard to read and understand, since they were printed in small typeface and couched in legal jargon. Furthermore, it was clear that most standard forms were issued on a take it or leave it basis, with no opportunity for negotiation, so they were often described as 'adhesion contracts'. Nevertheless, the courts did regard the standard form as part of the contract, provided that it had been issued or was referred to at the time of the formation of the agreement.

Functions of Mass Contracts

An adhesion contract creates a power relation between the business and consumer, but this is not always apparent from the documents. On their face they merely recite a transaction, such as a sale of goods, and determine the respective obligations of the parties. The power relation created by this contract derives from three of its common features. First, unlike a negotiated contract, the standard form economic transaction is not the product of joint self-regulation, but rather it is the product of unilateral regulation by one party exclusively. Secondly, close inspection of the terms usually reveals a pattern in which the risks are allocated routinely onto the consumer by extensive use of disclaimers and exclusion clauses. The effect of such clauses is that the business retains a discretion to perform the contract and to determine how it should be performed, whereas the consumer is bound to make payment, except perhaps in the event of complete failure of performance by the business.

The third dimension of the power relation arises in the event of a dispute about performance of the contract. By the combination of exclusion clauses and restrictions on possible avenues for legal redress, the standard form purports to grant the business strong bargaining power in post-breach negotiations. When the consumer makes a complaint, the business can point to clauses that exculpate or greatly diminish the responsibility of the business for default, which serve to discourage the pursuit of the complaint. On the other hand, the standard form often contains many devices enabling self-enforcement by the business against the debtor, so that there is no need for negotiation at all. The message to the consumer is to pay up or the goods will be repossessed, and any defects in the goods are not the responsibility of the business.

Striking evidence of this third dimension of the power relation in adhesion contracts is revealed by a study conducted by Yates in 1974–6 in the United Kingdom, prior to the introduction of most of the consumer protection legislation. In a survey of businesses designed to study their use of exclusion clauses in contracts, most standard form agreements issued to consumers contained extensive exclusions of liability. Even under the weaker protection for consumers at the time, many of these clauses were void and possibly even minor criminal offences. The companies appeared to be aware of these difficulties for their standard forms, but nevertheless continued to use them.

Most of the companies consulted were not particularly sanguine about the enforceability of the exclusion clauses in their agreements. While they would, as a matter of policy, always be relied upon, their insertion seemed to be largely a question of psychology. One representative of a finance company stated that the presence of exclusions is more likely to secure compliance with the agreement, and far more likely to secure payment before the court hearings should the debt turn bad, since it left the customer with the (frequently erroneous) view that he had few enforceable contractual rights against the finance company.[8]

The main purpose of the exclusion clause in the standard form contract was therefore to increase the bargaining power of the business against the consumer in post-breach negotiations.

The use of adhesion contracts has often been analysed as the product of inequality of bargaining power:

The terms of this kind of standard form contract have not been the subject of negotiation between the parties to it, or any approved organisation representing the interests of the weaker party. They have been dictated by that party whose

---

[8] Yates, D., *Exclusion Clauses in Contracts*, 2nd edn. (London: Sweet & Maxwell, 1982) 29.

bargaining power, either exercised alone or in conjunction with others providing similar goods or services, enables him to say: 'If you want these goods or services at all, these are the only terms on which they are obtainable. Take it or leave it.' To be in a position to adopt this attitude towards a party desirous of entering into a contract to obtain goods or services provides a classic instance of superior bargaining power.[9]

This analysis suggests that the disparity of wealth and strong market position explains the use of adhesion contracts. These printed forms are used on this view as a means for regulating unilaterally the economic relation, usually to the considerable advantage of the regulator. As Kessler once observed:

Freedom of contract enables entrepreneurs to legislate by contract and, what is even more important, to legislate in a substantially authoritarian manner without using the appearance of authoritarian forms.[10]

The difficulty with this analysis is that adhesion contracts are used far more widely than the theory of inequality of bargaining power might suggest. They occur, for instance, in highly competitive markets, where it might be supposed that competitive pressures would force businesses to offer attractive terms.[11] Small businesses also use standard form contracts, even though the ordinary shopkeeper may have no greater wealth than the consumer. Standard form contracts are also routinely employed in commercial transactions between businesses with roughly equivalent bargaining power, though here the 'battle of forms' between businesses suggests that there is competition to win the opportunity for unilateral regulation of the transaction. These examples demonstrate that although adhesion contracts may be the product of superior wealth and bargaining power in many instances, their use in markets extends well beyond such instances.

It may be more precise to explain the presence of standard form contracts as the product not so much of superior bargaining power as of market failure. The type of market failure considered here concerns the market for contract terms. In consumer markets, for instance, consumers are unlikely to extend their search for goods beyond price and quality comparisons. They are unlikely to demand to see specimen standard form sales contracts in order to make comparisons. Businesses can then take advantage of this market failure by promulgating a standard form containing small print exclusions and disclaimers of liability, which, if

[9] Lord Diplock, in *Schroeder Publishing Co. Ltd v Macaulay* [1974] 1 WLR 1308, 1316, HL.
[10] Kessler, F., 'Contracts of Adhesion—Some Thoughts About Freedom of Contract', *Columbia Law Review* 43 (1943) 629.
[11] Trebilcock, M. J., *The Limits of Freedom of Contract* (Cambridge, Mass.: Harvard University Press, 1993) 118.

interpreted literally, almost relieve them of any obligations under the contract at all. In effect, the business retains a discretion under the contract over whether or not to perform the contract and over the level of quality which it will provide. This market failure can occasionally apply between businesses, as for example when there is no time to examine the terms in detail.

Another important reason for the use of standard form contracts concerns the reduction of transaction costs. Where a large business is likely to enter into numerous similar contracts, both internal to the organization in employment relations, and external to the organization with customers, then it can reduce the costs of this contracting process by using a printed standard form contract. The economies of mass production of consumer goods and services are therefore matched by mass contracts, that is, the production of a standard contractual package under which the goods and services are sold.

By insisting upon the use of the same terms for all transactions, the large organization can also control the operations of its own bureaucratic organization. When hiring employees, managers cannot offer special deals or promises to new recruits, but must observe the normal terms of employment which fit the employee into the rules of the organization. Similarly, the insistence upon standard form contracts controls how the sales force completes transactions with customers, so that no special promises that might prove expensive to fulfil can be offered. From this perspective, standard form contracts permit the organization to regulate efficiently its internal and external relations.[12]

Given this purpose for many standard form contracts, it becomes interesting to ask what happens when attempts are made to alter the standard form contract. If a consumer deletes some oppressive clauses from the contract before signing it, what effect does that have on the legal entitlements? The formal legal analysis suggests that the varied terms represent a counter-offer by the consumer, which is presumably accepted by the business supplying the goods or services. In Yates's study, however, it was revealed that this result was not the expectation of the businesses themselves, who believed that the striking out of clauses made no difference to the terms of the agreement.[13] Their business requirement for uniformity in consumer transactions was presumably perceived to amount to an overriding imperative, so that they expected a court to permit them to insist upon the imposition of their standard terms regardless of the consent of the individual consumer. This expectation reveals how much standard form contracts can be regarded as a matter of internal regulation of the business.

---

[12] Rakoff, T., 'Contracts of Adhesion: An Essay in Reconstruction', *Harvard Law Review* 96 (1983) 1174; Macneil, I., 'Bureaucracy and Contracts of Adhesion' *Osgoode Hall Law Journal* 22 (1984) 5. [13] Yates, D., n. 8 above, 27.

Standard form contracts therefore certainly economize on transaction costs, but they also provide the opportunity to exploit market failures. This opportunity can be taken up by businesses through employing lawyers to draft standard form contracts for repeat transactions, which are then presented to individuals, usually without any opportunity for negotiation. The publishers of this book, for instance, offer a standard form contract to authors which specifies exhaustively the obligations of the author to deliver the manuscript on time, in excellent condition, with various warranties against risks such as breach of copyright. In contrast, the contract imposes only an obligation on the publisher to publish the work at its discretion and at a time of its choosing. Wishful thinking suggests that there may be strong competition between publishers to get hold of my work, but this will only affect the level of royalties, not the power structure of the standard form contract, which is common throughout the industry.

My analysis of mass contracts therefore confirms the interpretation that presents them as an efficient governance structure. These contracts permit organizations to regulate themselves and to regulate their business relations with others in ways which economize on transactions costs. The consumer adhesion contract only becomes objectionable when it is placed in the context of the absence of a market for contract terms and the absence of competition for fair complaint mechanisms. In these instances, it becomes objectionable, because the standard form is used to redistribute power relations in ways which permit oppressive post-breach bargaining situations.

Private Law Regulation

Many legal systems have sought to regulate standard form contracts, particularly mass contracts issued to consumers. The purposes of this regulation usually comprise both efforts to reduce market failure in contract terms by making it possible for consumers to understand the meaning of the respective obligations, and also measures designed to reduce the power imbalance established by unilateral self-regulation. The form of this regulation is particularly interesting for our purposes, because it raises directly two central problems for the regulation of contracts.

The first problem concerns the effectiveness of the regulation. The dominant pattern in the regulation of adhesion contracts is to employ a private law regulatory strategy. A typical provision permits judges to invalidate unfair, unreasonable, or unconscionable terms.[14] If a dispute

---

[14] e.g. EC Directive 93/13, OJL 95/29, 5 April 1993; (USA) Uniform Commercial Code Art 2–302; (UK) Unfair Contract Terms Act 1977; (New South Wales) Contracts Review Act 1980.

with a consumer reaches court, therefore, there exists a strong chance that a fierce exclusion clause will be declared invalid and not binding on the consumer. It should be evident, however, that this style of private law regulation is unlikely to have any impact on the use and content of adhesion contracts. Since it is not unlawful in itself to use the oppressive terms in a standard form contract, there is no reason to leave them out. Even if the terms are of doubtful validity, there is in fact good reason for leaving them in as a source of bargaining strength in post-breach negotiations. Since the consumer is most unlikely to litigate the issue before a court because of the expense involved, the objectionable clauses will never be formally invalidated, and so they can be relied upon at least for the purposes of negotiating or imposing a settlement on the consumer. These considerations still apply even if a court determines that the clause is invalid, for there is no reason to refrain from using the clause as a bargaining counter in contracts with other consumers. These customers are most unlikely to be able to discover whether or not a court has declared a clause invalid, and the precedent may always be distinguished by introducing a minor alteration in the contract. If the purpose of this regulation includes an attempt to discourage the use of oppressive clauses in adhesion contracts, then plainly it is poorly designed to achieve compliance.

As well as being ineffective, this style of private law regulation also suffers from the weakness of creating an unsophisticated framework for the enquiry. It focuses attention on a particular clause in a contract, which excludes the evidence relevant to the operation of that clause. This closure rule ignores evidence about the balance of advantage in the contract as a whole. For example, the clause may be harsh, but the contract may contain some compensating advantage such as a low price or an onerous obligation with respect to quality on the business. More significantly, the court has difficulty in gaining access to information about the operation of the market within which this contract has been formed as a self-regulatory regime. The particular market conditions, the distinct qualities of the product or service supplied, or the structure of the business arrangements will not necessarily be regarded as relevant considerations when the court is merely instructed to consider whether the particular term is unfair, unreasonable, or unconscionable.

This private law regulation also suffers from the problem of lack of particularity. To some extent the vagueness of the tests for invalidity may serve the purposes of the regulation, for they discourage attempts at avoidance, and perhaps provide a reason for businesses and their legal advisors to be more cautious in formulating exclusion clauses. This uncertainty of the meaning of the regulation may equally be criticized by businesses, however, for it disables them from devising reliable planning mechanisms for the allocation of risks through contracts. Their costs and the need for insurance remain indeterminate, and these uncertainties may either discourage contracts or more likely drive up the price of goods and services to consumers.

Private law regulation can be improved in order to meet these objections to some extent. Some regulations include lists of terms, which will invariably or normally be regarded as being invalid. The European Directive on Unfair Terms in Consumer Contracts, for example, contains a long list in its Schedule of types of clauses for which there is a presumption of unfairness.[15] The list certainly addresses the problem of the lack of precision of the general clause, though the list cannot provide a complete guide as to the sorts of terms which courts will find objectionable.

The general weakness of compliance with private law regulation can also be tackled by procedural reforms to private law. As we have already noticed, private law has the capacity to introduce collective actors who represent victims of the abuse of mass contracts.[16] Consumer groups can be empowered to bring claims on behalf of a class of consumers. This collective action addresses the problem of the under-resourced nature of private law enforcement mechanisms. Yet the problem remains that in the absence of a competitive market for contract terms, the regulatory control promised by private law can effectively be evaded by businesses introducing minor variations in standard terms, so that the demonstration of the oppressive and impermissible content of the new terms requires fresh, expensive litigation.

Regulating Market Sectors

A more sophisticated regulatory framework for controlling unfair power relations in adhesion contracts needs to seek to regulate market sectors rather than individual contracts. This type of regulation requires the standard business terms in a particular sector to be tested for their fairness prior to being put into circulation in the market. One way to achieve this might be to require representatives of the two sides of the trade to negotiate the standard terms to be used, and to invalidate departures from the agreed model. Another method is to employ a government agency to negotiate and fix the standard terms of business in particular sectors. The advantage of collective negotiation over administrative regulation is likely to be the better information of the parties involved in these transactions as to the market conditions and how to structure the incentives under a contract to best advantage. Both of these methods remove competition for contract terms, but the justification for this strategy is precisely that no such competition at present exists. Either method is likely to achieve a much

---

[15] EC Directive 93/13, OJL 95/29, 5 April 1993.   [16] See above, Ch. 4, p. 88.

higher level of compliance, since breaches of the regulation will be immediately visible and are likely to be policed by rival businesses as well as consumers in order to prevent the gaining of an unlawful competitive advantage.

The regulatory framework under English law fails to match either of these models. There is an administrative agency, the Unfair Contract Terms Unit, which can investigate complaints of unfair terms and seek injunctions against the use of particular terms in a business's standard form contract. In practice, the agency exercises its power by means of a negotiation with a business about the deletion or modification of clauses in the standard form contract. But this agency cannot address a market sector as a whole except by exhortation, nor ensure compliance with its standards by all traders. There are also proposals following the German model to enable consumer groups to seek injunctions against the use of unfair terms by particular businesses, which greatly augments the policing of compliance with the regulation, but does not move towards market sector regulation.

Nevertheless, some evidence suggests that this administrative agency has greatly improved the effectiveness of the regulation in deterring the use of oppressive terms in adhesion contracts. This result is achieved in part by using the state's resources to pursue many more instances of oppressive terms than might be raised through private law litigation. In addition, the agency publishes its determinations on particular types of clause and issues reports on market sectors, so that lawyers can discover which clauses are likely to be disallowed in advance and rectify standard forms accordingly. There is some evidence of a reduction of the use of standard form contracts in consumer transactions.[17] Since the law provides an extensive set of default terms in ordinary consumer transactions such as sales and credit agreements, the only real advantage of a standard form in many instances was to gain the benefit of the oppressive clauses. Once this advantage is removed, then there is little reason to continue to insist that the consumer should sign on the dotted line. On the contrary, the retailer of products may consider it more advantageous to refrain from any formal contract and instead point the consumer in the direction of the manufacturer's guarantees. The consumer may then gain the mistaken impression that his or her only rights lie against the manufacturer rather than the retailer.

In order to achieve effective regulation of mass contracts for the purpose of the redistribution of power, the key lies in the development of regulatory schemes that are designed to analyse market sectors as collective actors. The failure of the market in contract terms and complaint mechanisms that

---

[17] Micklitz, H-W., 'Directive 93/13 In Action: A Report on a Research Project on Unfair Terms in Consumer Sales', in C. Willett (ed.), *Aspects of Fairness in Contract* (London: Blackstone, 1996) 77, 78.

provides the opportunity for the construction of objectionable power relations in mass contracts has to be addressed by removing this aspect of self-regulation altogether. In their business relations with outsiders to the organization, traders have to be required to conform to the approved terms for the market sector. These terms would amount to compulsory rules governing transactions with consumers in a particular line of trade or business. Private law might be adequate to monitor and enforce compliance with these compulsory terms in mass adhesion contracts for particular trading sectors, but it lacks the mechanism to introduce procedures for the compulsory negotiation of standard terms between collective actors on both sides.

Principal and Agent

In a simple, non-legal, analysis of the model of principal and agent, the principal employs the agent to perform indeterminate tasks. This contractual relation is chosen by the principal because the agent enjoys special skills and knowledge, which permit the agent to perform those tasks more efficiently than the principal. A client acquires the services of a lawyer, for example, without defining except in the broadest terms the task to be completed, because the client requires the lawyer to use professional skills and knowledge in order to achieve the client's objective. In this model of agency, the contract is incomplete by design in the sense that the client deliberately leaves all the detail to the exercise of discretion by the lawyer.

Supervisory Hierarchy

In order to obtain the advantage of this division of labour, therefore, discretion has to be vested in the agent. But then the question arises of how can the principal be sure that the agent performs the task in the best interests of the principal, or at least satisfactorily?

The primary response to this problem of monitoring of performance will be an incentive system. The agent's rewards will increase according to the benefit conferred on the principal. In effect, such a profit-sharing arrangement creates a form of partnership. In a typical case, an agent who is acting at a remote location will be rewarded by a commission on sales. Early records of international trade reveal how such profit-sharing arrangements dealt with the problem of providing incentives for agents in distant locations. The Genoese merchants of the twelfth century commenced their lucrative though risky trade in Syria by sharing with their agent, typically the captain of the ship who sold goods and purchased a return cargo, a quarter of the profits under a contract known as the *Accomendatio.*[18]

But an incentive system will rarely prove sufficient to achieve the objective of ensuring that the agent always acts in the best interests of the principal. Given the principal's lack of expertise and information, it will often be difficult to measure whether the agent has performed the contract in the principal's best interest. The nagging worry is whether the employee has worked as hard as possible, whether the professional has given the best advice, or whether the architect has kept the costs of construction to a minimum. Because of these problems of information and measurement, it is difficult for principals to ensure that incentive systems control the behaviour of agents. The solution lies in increasing the amount of information by means of the principal acquiring a supervisory or monitoring power through the contract.

The principal and agent relation therefore has at its heart a hierarchical power relation, in which the principal must obtain supervisory power over the agent in order to monitor the agent's exercise of discretion. This analysis may be applied, for instance to employment of workers and managers in a firm. Managers exercise a supervisory power over workers, and the owners of the firm enjoy supervisory power over the managers. Formal measures comprise such matters as works rules, staff handbooks, and the articles of association defining the powers of the board of directors. These might still be regarded as the rules established by the contractual relation, but their significant feature is that they are often open to unilateral change. The managers can revise the staff handbook, the shareholders can alter the articles of association, and the board of directors can steer the company in new business directions. Informal powers arise in the interstices of the hierarchies. The manager can direct the worker towards new tasks, and can manipulate behaviour by using the carrots and sticks of promotion and discipline. These bureaucratic powers may be created by a contract, but it places little constraint upon how they should be exercised. In some instances, the supervisory power will be exercised by neutral third parties, as in the case of the architect on a construction project, or a professional body supervising the work of lawyers and doctors.

In some cases, however, it will not be possible to devise an effective monitoring system of agents through supervisory hierarchical arrangements. This problem may occur when the agent acts at a distant location, as in the case of a foreign agent charged with the task of selling goods when they reach port. The problem is accentuated where no effective legal sanctions to punish cheating by agents are available. An appropriate incentive

---

[18] Byrne, E. H., 'Commercial Contracts of the Genoese in the Syrian Trade of the Twelfth Century' *Quarterly Journal of Economics* 31 (1916) 128.

system, such as a commission on sales, alleviates most of the risk of cheating, but there remains the difficulty of ensuring that the agent does not obtain secret collateral advantages such as bribes at the expense of the principal. An informal solution to this problem consists in the creation of a loose association or 'coalition' among traders, which involves a commitment to the dissemination of information among members about the trustworthiness of agents. The foreign agent will be observed by other members of the coalition and suspicions of cheating can be communicated to the principal. The principal may then take non-legal sanctions such as a refusal to trade in the future, which may also be emulated by other members of the coalition. Grief illustrates this pattern of informal monitoring which creates a reputation mechanism in repeated games in the context of Jewish traders in the Middle East during the eleventh century. The coalition itself seems to rest on ethnic ties and common interest.[19] A similar pattern of reciprocal monitoring of agents is revealed in another study of traders using agents in California in the early part of the nineteenth century.[20]

Apart from such cases where supervisory hierarchy is impracticable, we can expect this type of power relation to be constructed in most principal and agent relations for reasons of efficiency. The power of supervision will normally be backed up by the principal's right to terminate the agency relation on discovery or suspicion of facts suggesting inadequate effort or self-interested action on the part of the agent. The contractual right to terminate will be further supported by non-legal sanctions such as the refusal to engage the agent in the future and the imposition of damage to the agent's reputation through poor references and similar publicity of betrayal. The legal system often supports these powers by the imposition of compulsory fiduciary duties upon agents, which permit the principal to recover any 'secret profits' made by the agent.

The problem of unjust power relations then emerges in the vulnerability of agents to opportunism on the part of the principal. Having constructed this hierarchical relation in order to ensure the efficient operation of the agency relation and the maximum benefit to be derived from the division of labour, the principal has placed himself in a position where he might take advantage of the power structure for the purpose of escaping the obligation to reward the agent. A typical example might be the termination of the agency relation shortly before the agent becomes entitled to a substantial commission. Another worrying instance consists of the dismissal of an employee shortly before an entitlement to deferred pay in the form of a

[19] Grief, A., 'Contract Enforceability and Economic Institutions in Early Trade: The Maghribi Traders' Coalition', *American Economic Review* 83 (1993) 525.

[20] Clay, K., 'Trade Without Law: Private-Order Institutions in Mexican California', *Journal of Law, Economics & Organization* 13 (1997) 202.

pension matures under the terms of the contract. In these instances, the purpose of regulation could be conceived to be not the elimination of the efficient arrangements for a supervisory hierarchy within the principal and agent contract, but rather the prevention of the abuse of power in the form of opportunism by the principal.

Symbiotic Contracts

Before considering the problem of opportunism, however, we need to consider more closely the question of whether the simple principal and agent model provides an adequate analysis of the many types of business relations that are customarily collected together under that heading. In my view, the model proves too simple to provide an explanation of the efficient properties of many of these business relations. A more sophisticated explanation recognizes that in fact the business relation is better characterized by the presence of two principal and agent relations. These contracts have been dubbed 'symbiotic contracts' by Schanze.[21] In these contracts there is a crossed principal and agent relation: each party both acts as the agent for the other and as a principal in its own right.

A franchise can be analysed as a symbiotic contract. The franchisor is a principal which hires an agent, the franchisee, in the expectation that the franchisee will use its discretion in the performance of duties of exploiting the franchise in order to maximize the profits of the franchisor's business. Simultaneously, the franchisee uses the franchisor as an agent to conduct the business of promoting the franchise concept, such as the brand name through advertising, and in developing the product. On this analysis, the franchise relation maximizes the joint wealth of the parties by utilizing the division of labour in two directions at once. It establishes a contractual framework of crossed principal and agent relations, which gives an incentive to each party to utilize expertise to the maximum advantage of both parties.

More controversially, the same analysis can be applied to the employment relation. Instead of the employee being regarded merely as the agent of the employer, the employee can also be regarded as a principal, who uses the employer for such purposes as developing products and marketing them in order to supply the employee with highly remunerative work.

The difficulty encountered by this analysis of many business relations as symbiotic contracts is that the model apparently contains the prediction that both parties will require supervisory hierarchy over the other. The

[21] Schanze, E., 'Symbiotic Contracts: Exploring Long-Term Agency Structures between Contract and Corporation', in C. Joerges (ed.), *Franchising and the Law* (Baden Baden: Nomos, 1991).

franchisee will need to create a mechanism for judging whether or not the franchisor is promoting the brand name. Similarly, the employee will require a mechanism for monitoring the performance of management in developing worthwhile work opportunities. The striking feature of most of these contracts is, however, that the supervisory hierarchy is usually restricted to the benefit of one party alone. In a franchise contract, for instance, the franchisor invariably has the right to terminate the contract for almost any breach of the contract of the extensive operating instructions issued by the franchisor. Yet the franchisee will not enjoy any equivalent right to monitor and punish, if the franchisor fails to keep to any of its undertakings (which are usually rather vaguely defined by the franchisor in any case).[22] Similarly, in the case of employment, the employer normally enjoys considerable managerial discretion to control and discipline the workforce, but an equivalent power for the employees to control management's exercise of discretion in developing the business goals of the firm is often absent.

This observation of asymmetry in the supervisory hierarchical relations in symbiotic contracts suggests two possible conclusions. Either the complex analysis of crossed principal and agent relations is inaccurate, or the structures established by symbiotic contracts often fail to achieve the most efficient governance structure. The latter conclusion might suggest the presence of a social preference for hierarchy, even though the asymmetric relation fails to provide the most efficient governance structure. In other words, employers and franchisors prefer to be undisputed bosses than to share their power for the sake of improving the efficiency of the symbiotic relation.[23] Institutional economists prefer to play down this latter possibility, for they search exhaustively until they have discovered efficiency explanations for all contractual hierarchies. But evidence that market power is used to achieve inefficient structures which confer broader power upon the dominant party seems persuasive in examples ranging from employment to large-scale capital investments.[24]

No doubt the full potential power of these lop-sided systems of governance will not be exercised due to the presence of non-legal sanctions, such as harm to reputation.[25] An employer will wish to avoid a reputation for arbitrary dismissals, for instance, because that will discourage workers from joining the firm and cause existing employees to behave opportunis-

---

[22] Hadfield, G. K., 'Problematic Relations: Franchising and the Law of Incomplete Contracts', *Stanford Law Review* 42 (1990) 927, 944–5.

[23] Margalin, S. A. 'What Do Bosses Do? The Origins and Functions of Hierarchy in Capitalist Production', *Review of Radical Political Economics* 6 (1974) 33.

[24] Gompers, P., and Lerner, J., ' The Use of Covenants: An Empirical Analysis of Venture Partnership Agreements', *Journal of Law and Economics* 39 (1996) 463.

[25] Dnes, A. W., 'A Case-Study Analysis of Franchise Contracts', *Journal of Legal Studies* 22 (1993) 367.

tically.[26] The employer will use tools of Human Resources Management in order to give employees the impression of responsiveness to their concerns. But the harmful reputation effects can be avoided easily by covert action, leaving the full potential for disciplinary action. The principal also has an economic incentive to preserve good business relations with productive agents, so that the principal is likely to want to exercise discretion fairly with respect to those agents whom the monitoring process reveals as productive. Although these types of constraints upon the misuse of asymmetric power relations relieve the tension between the efficient model and social practice, they do not remove the need to consider the underlying issue.

The question is whether or not legal regulation should be introduced for the purpose of enhancing the efficient properties of symbiotic relation. Such regulation would counter the asymmetric supervisory hierarchy by granting the weaker party the right to a similar supervisory jurisdiction over its agent. This regulation might require, for instance, representatives of workers on the board of directors of companies, and for a council of franchisees to enjoy supervisory powers over a franchisor. This type of regulation differs from measures designed to address opportunism by principals, because it seeks to complete lop-sided governance structures.

Remedies against Opportunism

For legal regulation designed to discourage opportunism by principals, it is possible to construct mandatory rules of a private law character that place limits on the exercise of discretion by principals. Examples include legal rights against wrongful termination of employment, a distributor's right to a court hearing against the termination of a dealership in automobiles,[27] a retail franchisee of gasoline's right not to have the franchise terminated in bad faith,[28] and the right not to have a franchise terminated without good cause.[29] An additional purpose of this regulation is to provide the threat of publicity of the court process, in order to support the non-legal sanction of harm to reputation against the principal. The form of this regulation

---

[26] Epstein, R., 'In Defence of the Contract at Will', *University of Chicago Law Review* 57 (1984) 947.

[27] Automobile Dealers Day in Court Act, 15 U.S.C. ss. 1221–1225 (1988); Macaulay, S., 'Long-Term Continuing Relations: The American Experience Regulating Dealerships and Franchises', in C. Joerges (ed.), n. 21 above, 197. UK law lacks statutory regulation in this context, but there have been examples of the courts being unwilling to enforce harsh termination clauses in distributorships by means of imposing a narrow interpretation upon the contracts: *Schuler AG v Wickman Tool Sales Ltd* [1974] AC 235, [1973] 2 All ER 39, HL.

[28] Petroleum Marketing Practices Act 15 U.S.C. 2801–2806; Macaulay, S., n. 27 above, 204.

[29] Wisconsin Fair Dealership Law, Wisconsin Statutes 135.01–.07 (1988); California Franchise Act, California Business & Professions Code 20000; Macaulay, S., n. 27 above, 209.

therefore adheres closely to a private law model of regulation by the insertion of a mandatory term enforceable by the favoured party.

We must doubt, however, that this regulation significantly alters the distribution of power and thus deters opportunism in these principal and agent relations. If the agent experiences an abuse of power in the form of opportunistic behaviour by the principal, then this abuse sends a signal that the co-operative relations are breaking down, so that the agent may be best advised to look for alternative business opportunities with better prospects. If no such alternative is readily available, the agent's best interests may lie in suffering from the opportunism in order to keep the business relation alive. The issues are therefore only likely to reach an open dispute when the agency relation has been terminated. At this stage, the agent may claim a remedy based upon the regulation, such as compensation for unfair dismissal or termination of a franchise without good cause, though the costs of litigation may deter the pursuit of the remedy. An award of financial compensation alleviates some of the losses of the agent, but is unlikely to alter significantly the future contractual practices of the principal.

The effects of this regulation are likely to be discovered more in the administrative procedures of the principal. The principal is likely to be more cautious in hiring an agent by using more extensive searches for information about the agent's skills, motivation, and aptitude. The principal is also likely to intensify monitoring procedures, so that a decision to terminate an agency can be justified by documentary evidence of unsatisfactory performance. For example, one of the effects of a statutory right to claim unfair dismissal in the UK has been an increase in the bureaucratization of personnel management and the introduction of more careful hiring procedures.[30] These measures may be justified as enhancing the economic benefits of the transaction for both parties, though at some administrative cost. But they do little to counter any asymmetry in the original allocation of discretionary power.

A regulatory technique which departs from a private law model is to empower a government agency to examine the content of discretionary power relations within principal and agent relations with a view to altering the terms of the relation. French legislation on the employment relation, for instance, empowers a government labour inspector to examine works rules to check that they do not contain provisions which infringe the law, or the civil liberties of individual employees, or the *principes generaux* of the legal system. Unless such infringements can be demonstrated to be justifiable and proportionate to the business objectives of the employer, the labour inspector may require modifications of the works rules with ultimate

---

[30] Collins, H., *Justice in Dismissal*, (Oxford: Clarendon Press, 1992) 248–52.

sanction of criminal penalties.[31] What is interesting about this regulation is that it mandates an assessment of the principal's own rules governing the exercise of discretionary power prior to their application in a particular case. This method entails administrative review of unilateral self-regulation in contracts, with a view to ensuring concordance between the self-regulation and regulatory objectives. As a regulatory strategy, therefore, it improves on the private law model by offering some chance of altering the routine exercise of discretionary power in principal and agent relations.

The Indeterminacy of Opportunism

Although the regulatory objective in such cases is to remedy opportunism in principal and agent relations, the determination of when opportunism has taken place resists any straightforward analysis. The question for adjudication is when has the power granted under the contract been abused? How can we distinguish between such abusive exercises of hierarchical power and harsh but economically rational decisions? The legal issue in a private law context will present itself as an interpretation of the terms of the contract. A court will attempt to discover implicit constraints over the exercise of discretionary power from the implied undertakings of the parties. The contract may make provision, for example, for discretionary unilateral termination by one of the parties, but a court may be invited to discover an implied limitation upon the exercise of this power, such as a requirement that it should be exercised in good faith. Outside standard nominate contracts, where established default terms may provide the basis for such implied limitations on discretion, such as the requirement to give reasonable notice of termination in contracts of employment in English law, the court may discover that private law regulation offers little guidance on how such issues might be resolved.

The problem for legal regulation in such cases is that the distinction between opportunism and a permissible exercise of a contractual discretionary power cannot be delineated by formal tests. In a franchise relation, for instance, the franchisor may enjoy the power to terminate the franchise at its discretion. The reason for the insertion of such a clause is that the criteria by which the franchisor makes such a business decision cannot be reduced to simple formula. The franchisee may damage the reputation of the business format in a host of ways, the significance of which will depend considerably upon the extent to which they become notorious. At the same time, the franchisor will not wish to terminate a franchise for even a significant breach of contract, if in other respects the franchisee is a highly successful operator of the licence. The complexity of

---

[31] Code du Travail, L. 122–33–L. 122–39.

the business judgement combined with the paramount importance to the franchisor of protecting the reputation of the brand name drives the planning of the contract towards the allocation of a unilateral discretion to terminate. Once this unilateral power has been created, it becomes possible for the franchisor to abuse the right to terminate the contract by, for instance, using a pretext in order to replace a satisfactory franchisee with another who may perform even better. Such an exercise of discretionary power may be described as opportunism, because it may cause loss to the franchisee through the waste of investments in plant and training, and because the behaviour is contrary to the expectation of the franchisee based on the business relation (as opposed to the precise terms of the contract) of the longevity of the franchise provided that performance was satisfactory. Since the franchisee usually lacks any powerful non-legal sanctions, such as the ability to damage the reputation of the franchisor, the franchisee may seek to claim that the business expectation was incorporated implicitly into the contractual agreement. Without some type of legal protection, this type of opportunism would go unremedied, which in turn would either lead to a reduction in the number of people willing to become franchisees,[32] or provoke demands for more complex governance structures such as those inserted by statutes.

The problem at the heart of interpretation of this contractual relation is that two rival and incommensurable expectations supply its meaning. The franchisor expects to retain an unreviewable discretion in order to be able to make complex business judgements that serve the interests of the operation best. The franchisee expects the franchisor to exercise powers in ways that conform to the goal of maximizing joint wealth through long-term co-operation. The contract is not incomplete, but rather subject to incompatible priorities in determining the best way to maximize its productive qualities.

In the United States the courts have been frequently called upon to resolve issues of franchisor opportunism. As Hadfield argues, their decisions usually protect the franchisor's broad discretion to make business judgements in their own interests, subject only to restraints against 'arbitrary' decisions and improper motives.[33] This approach gives priority to the franchisor's expectations by confirming the discretionary power to make business judgements. The effect is to devalue the franchisee's expectation in the co-operative nature of the business relation. This result is illustrated in a case where Leyland Motors terminated a franchise to sell

---

[32] Klein, B., *et al.*, 'Vertical Integration, Appropriable Rents, and the Competitive Contracting Process,' *Journal of Law and Economics* 21 (1978) 297, 303; Hadfield, G. K., n. 22 above, 954.

[33] Hadfield, G. K., ibid. 927, 982. For instance, *Moody v Amoco Oil Co.*, 734 F. 2d 1200, 1217.

the Rover marque when the franchisee refused to sell through its distributorship an additional line of cars under the Triumph marque. From the perspective of Leyland Motors it made sense to amalgamate their dealerships, but the franchisee could not agree to this change, because the additional line of cars would present unfavourable competition to another line of cars sold by the franchisee. The court upheld the termination of the franchise by Leyland Motors since it was based on a legitimate business reason.[34] On this interpretation of the contract, the interest of the franchisee in protecting its investment in both existing franchises is ignored.

In a surprising comparison, the problem of franchisor opportunism has rarely surfaced in the courts in the UK. The leading study by Beale, Harris, and Sharpe only discovered one litigated dispute over termination of a dealership in cars in a period of twenty years.[35] There are many possible explanations for this absence of disputes. There may be another forum such as arbitration under the aegis of the trade association of manufacturers. The absence of any specific regulation of this kind of opportunism except the general principles of private law may discourage any challenges. But a better explanation may lie in the terms of the contract itself. These terms generally provide for termination only after a lengthy period of notice such as a year and after warnings, which reduces the potential for opportunism compared to the US contracts where termination is permitted almost at will. Beale, Harris, and Sharpe suggest that despite the one-sided character of these distribution contracts, in practice the parties are bound together by their sunk investments in the long-term commercial venture, so that opportunism by the franchisor will rarely be a problem.[36] This explanation certainly captures the symbiotic quality of these relations, but it leaves as a puzzle why these economic incentives to refrain from opportunism seem to have less force in the US.

This comparison calls into question the earlier hypothesis that the one-sided nature of many agency contracts produced an inefficient system of governance. The case for regulation was made on the basis that the self-regulation by the parties failed due to reasons of abuse of market power to achieve the optimal balance of reciprocal obligations and systems of monitoring of performance. If this hypothesis were correct, we should also expect regulation designed to correct this market failure to enhance the profitability of these kinds of commercial relations. Instead of regulation merely imposing a cost on business, this kind of regulation that completes an incomplete transaction should function to help these business

---

[34] *David R. McGeorge Car Co. v Leyland Motor Sales*, 504 F 2d 52, 56 (4th Cir. 1974), *cert. denied*, 420 U.S. 992 (1975).   [35] Beale, H., *et al.*, n. 5 above, 331.
[36] Ibid., 304.

transactions to become more profitable. Some evidence in the US from an examination of statistics regarding the prevalence of these types of symbiotic relations following regulation designed to afford protection against opportunism suggests that the regulation has reduced the amount of franchising, presumably by increasing the costs to franchisors of enforcing quality controls.[37] In the employment field which is regulated in the UK, the evidence from surveys and econometric studies about the economic effects of unfair dismissal laws on levels of employment is much more equivocal.[38] It may not be possible, therefore, to generalize with respect to the regulation of power relations formed in agency relations. The symbiotic qualities of these transactions may be obtained efficiently through one-sided contracts provided that the economic incentives to refrain from opportunism effectively govern contractual behaviour. Where those incentives are too weak, however, as may be the case with most employment relations, then regulation designed to reconstruct the contractual governance structure to bring it into concordance with the ideal set of economic incentives may prove an efficient regulatory intervention.

Contract and Organization

We have considered the two basic ways in which contracts establish relations of power: the unilateral, discretionary rule-making authority in adhesion contracts, and the supervisory hierarchies in principal and agent relations. The third principal way in which contracts are used to create power relations comprises multi-party associations. Here the basic structure of the agreement is that members join the association by means of a contract which incorporates the rules of the association. These rules establish governance structures over the members. A golf club provides a simple example. Members join the club, and in so doing consent to the rules. Under these rules a committee has the power to create further rules and to punish members for breach of the rules. A similar structure may be found in such diverse associations as trade unions, charities, political parties, and financial exchanges.

This model of a multi-party association becomes more complicated in the typical corporate business organization or firm. The members of the firm have different types of contracts of membership as shareholders, directors, and employees. The rules of the corporation contained in the memorandum and articles of association allocate powers between these

---

[37] Brickly, J. A., *et al.*, 'The Economic Effects of Franchise Termination Laws', *Journal of Law and Economics* 34 (1991) 101.　　　　[38] Collins, H., n. 30 above, 259–60.

different groups, and provide mechanisms for changing the rules. Usually the major powers to run the business are vested in the directors, with various constitutional safeguards to protect the interests of other members, especially those of the shareholders or investors of financial capital.

The common element in these multi-party associations is the adoption of a governance structure in order to achieve a purpose. This objective can only be successful if the association is constructed as an organization with power to control its members by means of rules and a disciplinary system. The presence of hierarchy within the organization is necessary to provide the co-ordination needed to achieve its objectives. For this reason, the presence of power relations within multi-party associations should not be regarded as objectionable in itself. The question is rather whether or not constraints should be placed on contracts of association in order to determine who should exercise power and how that power should be exercised.

It is tempting to answer this question in the negative. These contractual associations are voluntary, so if a member dislikes the way power is exercised, the member can always opt for exit. A shareholder can sell her shares, and a worker can quit the union. Moreover, the rules have been created by the members themselves, so that if they dislike the way in which the organization is being run, they can change the rules or the composition of the governing committee. The shareholder can vote for a new board of directors or a change in the articles of association, and the union member can vote for a new executive committee or seek to amend the rules of the union. The problem with these responses to problems of power within organizations is that they overlook both the presence of irretrievable investments and the problem of oligarchy. The option of exit may be extremely unattractive to a member because of the resulting economic loss. We noticed in our discussion of club markets or exchanges, for instance, how a broker would lose his source of livelihood if excluded from the trading floor. The problem of oligarchy is simply the familiar observation that those in power in organizations will be reluctant to relinquish that power, so they will manipulate the rules of the association to their advantage. Using their position, the incumbents may be able to defeat any challenge to their authority and enforce their will on the members.

For these reasons, amongst others, many powerful organizations have been subjected to mandatory rules governing the distribution and exercise of power. The private corporation is subject to mandatory rules that empower the shareholders to choose the directors and to constrain the actions of the directors. The trade union is subject to mandatory rules requiring the election of its governing officials by its members, and mandatory votes on aspects of its activities such as political action and strikes. Legal regulation also pays close attention to the ownership and use of the assets of the organization, so that those in power cannot appropriate its resources. A detailed scrutiny of these mandatory regulations is beyond the scope of the present study. Legal systems have differentiated their treatment of particular types of organizations such as corporations, trade unions, and charitable trusts, so that the law thinks about them in a different way from that of a mere association founded in contract.

What interests us here is rather those multi-party associations founded in contracts which have not been subjected to special mandatory rules to govern the exercise of power within the organization. Does legal regulation regard these associations as simply a contract where the law should uphold the self-regulation by the parties, or can the law recognize that the power relations of the organization require intervention to control the allocation and exercise of power? This question raises two issues. First, we need to examine the variety of multi-party associations which might be subject to regulation concerned with the abuse of power. Second, we examine the capacity of legal regulation to devise appropriate standards and to enforce compliance.

Hybrids

For the most part, multi-party associations that exercise power over their members will be easy to recognize. The model comprises an association formed by contracts of membership, where the rules of the association empower a group to make decisions to further the purposes of the organization. This power extends to the possibility of damaging the economic interests of members of the organization, and also to the exclusion of members. This model can be illustrated by trade associations, social and sports clubs, and learned societies. There are types of economic association, however, which do not fit this paradigm exactly, yet which seem to possess some of the features of an organization. These business relations do not fit easily into the contrast between contract and organization, so they have been called 'hybrids' or 'networks'.[39]

The analysis of hybrid business organizations began with studies in the discipline of new institutional economics. This work, commencing with Coase's seminal theory of the firm,[40] seeks to explain the economic causes of different industrial structures. The central question is why some productive and distributive activities are conducted through vertically integrated firms, whereas other similar activities occur through market transactions for the supply of goods and services. This is the 'make' or 'buy' decision. I find this way of posing the question in terms of an

[39] Powell, W. W., 'Neither Market nor Hierarchy: Network Forms of Organization', in G. Thompson *et al.* (eds.), *Markets, Hierarchies and Networks: The Coordination of Social Life* (London: Sage, 1991) 265.
[40] Coase, R. H., 'The Nature of the Firm', Economica NS 4 (1937) 386.

opposition between hierarchies and markets rather unsatisfactory, since it seems to suggest that hierarchies are not present in markets. A better way to analyse the issue is to compare the different kinds of hierarchy established through different types of contractual relations. The question then becomes why some forms of hierarchy are used to organize production as opposed to others.

In these terms of a contractual analysis, the simple question becomes why in some instances a contract of employment is chosen, whereas in others a market transaction of sale or the provision of services by another business occurs. An answer can then be devised by means of an examination of the attributes of the different types of contracts. Contrasts can be drawn regarding their incentive structures, their handling of problems of incomplete contracts including governance structures, their potential for adaptation and flexibility in response to changing market conditions, their techniques for protection of sunk investments, and so forth. Vertical integration in a firm using contracts of employment as the form of industrial structure can then be explained on the ground that this type of contract provides the most efficient solution to the problems presented by the economic relation of production or distribution, such as the prevention of opportunistic renegotiation of contracts,[41] the establishment of the optimum incentives for investment,[42] and a solution to the problem of the incompleteness of contracts.[43] A part of the intended message of this work is to suggest that the creation of large vertically integrated firms is not motivated by attempts to achieve anti-competitive market domination, but is rather a rational response to the problem of devising efficient contracts.[44]

Although focused on the issue of the optimum limits of vertical integration, this economic analysis of contractual structures can be applied as a tool for examining small differences in contractual arrangements. The analysis of some of the elementary economic problems of costs and incentives can suggest reasons why we might find a particular kind of contract term in one deal but not in another analogous transaction.[45] For example,

---

[41] Klein, B., *et al.*, n. 32 above, 297.

[42] Hart, O., and Moore, J., 'Incomplete Contracts and Renegotiation', *Econometrica* 56 (1988) 755.

[43] Hart, O. D., 'Incomplete Contracts and the Theory of the Firm', *Journal of Law, Economics, and Organization* 4 (1998) 119; Hart, O., *Firms, Contracts and Financial Structure* (Oxford: Clarendon Press, 1995).

[44] Williamson, O. E., *Markets and Hierarchies: Analysis and Antitrust Implications* (New York: Free Press, 1975).

[45] Shelanski, H. A., and Klein, P. G., 'Empirical Research in Transaction Cost Economics: A Review and Assessment', *Journal of Law, Economics and Organization* 11 (1995) 335; Wiggins, S. N., 'The Economics of the Firm and Contracts: A Selective Survey', *Journal of Institutional and Theoretical Economics* 147 (1991) 603; Lyons, B. R., 'Empirical Relevance of Efficient Contract Theory: Inter-Firm Contracts', *Oxford Review of Economic Policy* 12(4) (1996) 27.

Palay's study of rail freight contracts in the US reveals differences in the content of terms in superficially similar contracts under which a shipper hires the services of a contractor to move goods.[46] He links the difference primarily to the presence of 'idiosyncratic investments'. If the goods to be shipped can be put in ordinary box cars, then the contract simply prices the service. If the goods can only be shipped in specially constructed cars, such as special racks for a new model of automobile, then this specific investment in the transaction provokes a more elaborate 'governance structure', in this instance an agreement to share the risk that the cost of the investment in the special racks would be wasted in the event of insufficient volume of car sales in the form of an amortization agreement. When these kinds of specific investments become particularly heavy compared to the value of the transaction, then Palay discovers instances of partial vertical integration between shippers and carriers (such as ownership by the shipper of specialist wagons).

An unforeseen outcome of the work of new institutional economics has been to demonstrate that imaginative combinations of contractual obligations create business associations which straddle the divide between market and hierarchy. These business associations are founded in contractual relations between distinct units of capital. But their contractual relations become so elaborate in their governance structures, that they mimic many organizational aspects of a firm. These contractual relations occupy a terrain between organization and arms length contracting, so they have been described as hybrids:

Hybrids usually come in contractual disguises: just-in-time organizations and other satellite delivery networks, franchising systems and other distribution organizations, data processing contracts as a result of 'outsourcing', credit transfer networks in banking, subcontracting systems in the construction industry, networks in energy, transportation and telecommunication, strategic alliances in collective research, large scale consortia in collaborative reseach pacts.[47]

Major construction projects provide an example of this hybrid association. In these projects, the commissioner of a new building (known as the employer) enters contracts with several parties such as the main contractor, the architect, and a project manager. The main contractor enters further contracts with specialist suppliers of goods and services. The subcontracts may extend further down a long chain. Although each of these contracts represents a distinct market relation, the co-ordination of the construction

---

[46] Palay, T. M., 'Comparative Institutional Economics: The Governance of Rail Freight Contracting', *Journal of Legal Studies* 13 (1984) 265.

[47] Teubner, G., 'Piercing the Contractual Veil? The Social Responsibility of Contractual Networks', in T. Wilhelmsson (ed.), *Perspectives of Critical Contract Law* (Aldershot: Dartmouth, 1993) 211–12.

project as a whole requires elaborate organizational relations. The contracts create governance structures and hierarchies between the parties for the purposes of co-ordination, monitoring performance, and supervision. For example, the architect or a surveyor may have the power to determine whether or not some aspect of the work has been completed in conformity with the contract. The project manager may have the power to direct operations on the construction site. The contractors may have the power to direct the work of other sub-contractors in a manner similar to a contract of employment. If one examines only the form of the individual contracts, the construction project appears to be no more than a set of contractual arrangements. When one stands back and views the whole operation, however, it is plain that it has many features of an organizational hierarchy similar to those found within an integrated firm. It is a multi-party association, formed out of a series of contracts, but which can only achieve its purpose by the creation of governance structures beyond the formal contractual undertakings.

A similar analysis of a business format franchise suggests that it presents a hybrid type of economic association. The formal contractual arrangements comprise a series of licences granted by the franchisor to franchisees to run retail operations under the franchisee's name. A close examination of the terms of these contracts reveals, however, that the franchisor achieves a hierarchical relation with the franchisee analogous to a principal and agent relation. This hierarchy may be justified by the need to protect the value of the asset of the business format against damage to business reputation by errant franchisees. But the organizational qualities of such business format franchises extend beyond this hierarchy, because the business needs to adapt to changing conditions, to encourage innovation, and to co-ordinate its operations. Again the franchise operation begins to resemble the organizational features of a vertically integrated firm, except that there is no integration of ownership of the assets between franchisor and franchisees. In Teubner's phrase, it is a 'polycorporate actor'.[48]

The lesson drawn by the new institutional economics from this discovery is that as well as vertical integration of ownership, the interesting problem of explaining industrial structure must devote its energies to understanding the creation of governance structures designed to co-ordinate production without vertical integration. From our point of view, however, the discovery of hybrids suggests that the problem of regulating power in multi-party business associations needs to extend its focus beyond the simple paradigm of voluntary associations described above. We need to recognize that similar hierarchies can be created without formal badges of membership in a single organization. In particular, the sharp contrast drawn between

---

[48] Teubner, G., n. 47 above, 226–30.

employment in a vertically integrated organization and contracts between independent businesses can be misleading as a test for whether or not hierarchies of organizational power may be present.[49] Hybrids mimic the supervisory and monitoring powers of principal and agency relations, and achieve equivalent powers of unilateral regulation to those found in formal organizations.

Expectations of Membership

The final question is whether regulation designed to qualify or redistribute power in these multi-party associations is desirable and possible. The starting-point should be one of respect for the self-regulation achieved by the parties through their contractual relations. They have established their own governance structures for the sake of obtaining the benefits of the collective and co-ordinated pursuit of their interests. To interfere with the rules of the association risks upsetting the fragile balance of interests between members and the collective group, thereby jeopardizing the efficient pursuit of the purposes of the organization. Nevertheless, two forms of regulation are compatible with this respect for the autonomy of organizations.

The first type of regulation examines the procedures by which decisions of the organization have been reached. Legal regulation may not only require conformity to the procedural rules of the association, but may also supplement those rules by requirements designed to protect the interests of members in the operation of fair procedures. We considered this type of regulation before in the context of club markets.[50] The objective of the regulation was to import into the rules of the association procedures designed to achieve fair treatment of members, especially when the proposed decision might severely harm the economic interests of members, as in the case of an exclusion from membership of an exchange. I argued that private law has the capacity to import into organizational rules basic standards of fair procedures, such as requirements that a member should have the opportunity to hear the charges against him and to seek to rebut them. Although these procedural standards are more familiar in the context of public law, where the courts have imposed them upon institutions of the state, there are many instances where private law has demonstrated the capacity to introduce similar standards into voluntary associations. Pursuing that argument further, we can now suggest that in some instances this type of regulation would be appropriate for

[49] Collins, H., 'Independent Contractors and the Challenge of Vertical Disintegration to Employment Protection Laws', *Oxford Journal of Legal Studies* 10 (1990) 353; Lazerson, M. H., 'An Outcome of Markets and Hierarchies?', *American Sociological Review* 53 (1988) 330, 336–7.   [50] Above, Ch. 9.

hybrids. In the case of franchises, for instance, private law regulation might be developed to ensure that franchisors followed fair procedures before terminating licences of franchisees.

The second type of regulation seizes on the point that the multi-party association has been formed for a particular purpose. The organizational hierarchy has been created in order to co-ordinate collective actions for the achievement of that purpose. Legal regulation can be introduced to ensure that the organs of government in the association, such as the ruling committee, cannot exercise their powers for different types of purpose. In the distinct regulation of companies, this strand of requiring the directors to act always for the proper purposes or in the best interests of the company has become the crucial limit upon their powers. This style of regulation is also appropriate for unincorporated associations and hybrids. Private law has been slow, however, to develop this type of regulation. It can be created, however, through a combination of declarations that certain decisions were outside the powers of the governing committee (*ultra vires*), or that the decision was made in bad faith. The latter style of regulation develops the idea that there is a duty to perform contracts in good faith, which is common in many legal systems outside the United Kingdom.[51] In the case of an unincorporated association, for instance, the duty might preclude decisions based upon irrelevant considerations such as the sex or race of a member. In the example of hybrids, the duty would require the dominant member of the organization to make decisions based upon rational business considerations aimed at maximizing the joint profits of all members of the organization. The analogy is drawn in Germany between the position of the dominant partner in hybrids and the parent company in a group of companies, in order to invoke the law that the parent owes a type of fiduciary duty towards the business interests of its satellites.[52] In the United States this doctrine of good faith in performance has been applied frequently to hybrid types of contractual associations where one party has a discretionary power. In requirements contracts, for instance, the purchaser must determine its requirements in good faith, and not order goods for other purposes such as stockpiling or speculation.[53] Similarly, in a case involving the termination of a distributorship, a manufacturer was held to have breached the implied covenant of dealing in good faith

---

[51] Farnsworth, E. A., 'Good Faith in Contract Performance', in J. Beatson and D. Friedmann, *Good Faith in Contract Law* (Oxford: Clarendon Press, 1995) 153.

[52] Teubner, G., n. 47 above, 216 and 219, discussing the application of Aktiengesetz s. 17.

[53] *Homestake Mining Co. v Washington Public Power Supply System*, 476 F Supp 1162, aff'd 652 F 2d 28 (9th Cir 1981).

by failing to disclose information which would have saved the distributor from wasting an investment in the business.[54]

The justification for these types of regulatory intervention through private law into the internal governance of multi-party associations rests on a redistribution of power. But the objective of regulation is not to reallocate powers, but rather to control the exercise of power. In seeking to identify the abuse of power, this legal regulation recognizes that organizations consist of more than the contractual entitlements expressed in its rules. The organization has a social dimension, one of membership in the association, which creates expectations that go beyond the formal rules. The reluctance of private law to intervene in these associations may be explicable by the priority it attaches to the planning documents in contracts. But private law does have the capacity to integrate this social dimension of membership of the organization by giving effect to the reasonable expectations of its members through reviewing the procedures and purposes of the exercise of discretionary powers created within the organization.

Conclusion

Our discussion has supported the view that many instances of power in contractual relations have been constructed as an indispensable technique for achieving the economic goals of the parties. The use of governance structures to resolve the indeterminacy of contracts left incomplete by design is an example of an imaginative solution to a problem that might present sufficient grounds for distrust that the parties might otherwise decline to enter the transaction at all. Nevertheless, we have also observed many instances where bargaining strength and market failure combine to provide opportunities to create power structures which cannot be justified on the ground of their contribution to efficiency and trust. Indeed, it is arguable in many of these latter instances that a regulatory intervention designed to qualify or constrain the power structure might in fact enhance efficiency and trust.

But the regulatory task of redesigning power structures presents considerable difficulties for the legal system. The regulation needs to be tailored precisely to each type of economic relation, so that it can respond to the exigencies of efficiency in different types of transactions. Private law regulation of power structures has the advantage over public law regulation that it commences its analysis with respect for the self-regulation of the

---

[54] *Bak-A-Lum Corp of America v Alcoa Building Products*, 351 A 2d 349 (New Jersey Supreme Court, 1991).

parties, but this can also be a source of weakness when the regulatory task requires the imposition of new governance structures. For the most part, however, effective private law regulation designed to redistribute power can be achieved by means of qualifying the contractual arrangements by reference to such requirements as a duty to follow a fair procedure, a duty to refrain from opportunism or the abuse of power, and the duty to perform contracts in good faith. But these controls over private power require a sophisticated interpretation of contracts, which calls upon the courts not only to revise the planning documents in the light of the informal expectations of the parties, but also to accommodate the problem that these rational expectations may conflict in marginal instances of abuse of power.

With respect to the most common problem of power in contractual relations, the abuse of unilateral rule-making power in mass adhesion contracts, we concluded that the market failure in competition for contract terms justified the removal of the unilateral rule-making power. Regulation should instead induce market sector agreements on the standard terms to be offered to consumers, so that competition would be restricted to quality and price. Private law rules could support the outcome of such collective negotiations within trade sectors by declining to scrutinize the content of the collectively agreed power relations, but on its own this support would not provide a sufficient incentive to ensure conformity to those standards. In addition, public regulation that required a collective regulation of terms in mass adhesion contract would be necessary in order to remedy the market failure.

In this discussion of power, a rather narrow description of the problem raised by contracts has been adopted. We have concentrated attention on the relations between the parties to the contract. Much more might also be said about the power constructed by contracts that affects the interests of third parties, but who cannot mount an action in contract for redress or to challenge a decision. Similarly, contractual arrangements can restrict legal responsibilities to third parties or other members of the network, thereby creating a position of power to act unimpeded by social responsibilities. These issues mirror the discussion of the social responsibility of corporations, that is the requirement of collective groups to respect the objectives of democratic legislative institutions. These considerations apply to contracts which create looser kinds of organization without vertical integration. The legal problem of regulating power in such instances has to be addressed by granting third parties derivative rights under contracts and by attributing legal responsibilities to hybrids and other multi-party associations.[55]

---

[55] Collins, H., 'Ascription of Legal Responsibility to Groups in Complex Patterns of Economic Interaction', *Modern Law Review* 53 (1990) 731; Teubner, G., n. 47 above, 230.

11

Unfair Contracts

Should one of the purposes of regulating contracts be to deter unfairness? If so, how might that objective be achieved efficiently and efficaciously? Although there is an overlap between the problems of power relations and unfairness in contracts in practice, in principle these issues are distinct. The problem of power is concerned with the creation through private ordering of a discretionary power to determine unilaterally the content of legally enforceable contractual obligations. The issue of fairness examines the balance of the substantive obligations, that is the price of the stipulated performance. The overlap occurs when the contract contains a discretion to control the content of the obligations to be performed. This discretion can be exercised in order to reduce or augment the content of the stipulated performance, thereby altering the balance of the substantive obligations. In a consumer standard form contract, for instance, the seller's terms may include a discretion to substitute alternative and less valuable goods. Here the contract may be criticized both for the oppressive power relation, and, if the power is exercised to the detriment of the consumer, for the resulting substantive imbalance of the obligations.

The regulation of unfairness in contracts is usually perceived as an exceptional measure. The general principles of the private law of contract do not usually contain an express general power for the courts to upset contracts on the basis of the substantive imbalance of obligations. Courts employ many legal doctrines in order to tackle problems of perceived unfairness. They can apply doctrines such as mistake, duress, and fraud in an expansive way in order to invalidate contracts, since most bad bargains can be explained as the result of a mistake, strong pressure to accede to demands, or misrepresentations about the content of the deal. Yet the ostensible purpose of such doctrines is to grant relief from the consequences of involuntary consent to contracts, not relief from substantive unfairness as such. Statutory interventions do sometimes contain provisions which explicitly empower courts and agencies to regulate the fairness of terms of contracts. Common examples include laws on 'fair rents', minimum wage laws, and price setting by regulators for utilities such as water and electricity supplied to the public. In consumer sales, legislation frequently inhibits excessive interest rates in credit transactions, and it often imposes controls over the content of non-price terms contained in standard form contracts, in order to invalidate the substantive imbalance of obligations to the detriment of the consumer.

Yet it remains unclear whether these statutory interventions can be properly described as pursuing a policy objective of regulating substantive unfairness in contracts. The regulation of contracts in these instances may be explained by reference to other goals. The minimum wage laws do not require fair pay, but rather set a minimum rate per hour. The objective of the legislation appears to be concerned primarily with the social exclusion that results from trying to live on an income at little more than a subsistence level, together with a desire to relieve the taxpayer from the burden of providing additional support to the working poor through the social security system. In the case of fair rents, the objective may include a concern about substantive unfairness, but it also includes a desire to help tenants to keep their homes by protecting them against price increases that they cannot afford. The regulation of prices for utilities may include a concern for fairness, but its dominant motives are rather to force the utilities to become more efficient in their operations and to prevent social exclusion from these essential services by their price. Other types of price regulation of commodities, such as agricultural products, have as their objective the stabilization of prices and markets, in order to protect farmers against sharp swings in prices that might force them out of business. The regulation of consumer contracts is frequently justified not on the ground of unfairness, but rather as a remedy for market failure. Rules requiring disclosure of information and formal documents protect consumers against unwittingly entering into bad bargains due to a lack of information about the product or poor expertise in assessing the terms of the transaction.

Why is the legal system so reluctant to adopt as a central purpose of regulating contracts the provision of relief against unfair contracts? After all, it is difficult to justify the use of state power to enforce a harsh bargain that causes major financial misfortune to an individual. Such enforcement fits uneasily with the justification for enforcement of contracts in general that the facility to enter binding consensual transactions will augment the wealth of all the parties concerned. Although the enforcement of contracts normally assists the achievement of Pareto optimal exchanges, should legal regulation stick to a rule of unremitting enforcement of all agreements, even where the exchange under consideration plainly does not satisfy the Pareto optimal standard, because one party will be substantially worse off than before? Does the contribution of the law to the construction of markets require a rigid rule of enforcement of consensual transactions with no exceptions? Or could the law still provide all the necessary support for markets whilst creating exceptions in instances of hardship and substantive unfairness?

The rigid rule of enforcement of contracts without any direct regulation of substantive unfairness depends for its continued support in legal doctrine upon a series of propositions. The first proposition is that most alleged instances of unfairness in contracts turn out to be illusory on closer inspection. Harsh terms will in fact be balanced by commensurate reductions in price or other advantages, so that the transaction remains Pareto optimal on detailed examination. The second proposition is that any alternative to a rigid rule of enforcement will create serious damage to the basic objective of regulating contracts, which is to help to construct markets. In other words, any power granted to courts or other agencies to unravel transactions on the ground of substantive unfairness will seriously diminish the contribution of the legal system to the establishment of trust and sanctions. The third proposition is that insofar as the law attempts to regulate unfairness, it invariably backfires; regulation tends to worsen the predicament of those persons it purports to help. In the case of the regulation of interest rates in consumer credit transactions, for instance, this argument suggests that a cap on interest rates merely has the effect of excluding consumers who represent a poor credit risk from the market altogether, so that they cannot purchase expensive items at all. A fourth proposition is that insofar as a few instances of genuine substantive unfairness can be discovered, then an effective remedy will be to address problems of market failure. The unfair terms will almost certainly be the result of some type of market failure, such as a monopoly situation or asymmetries of information between the parties. The solution is to impose regulation which combats monopolies and informational asymmetries, not to regulate the ensuing unfairness as such. The question then to be considered is whether regulation of market practices does effectively remove problems of unfairness.

In this chapter, we shall consider these four propositions in turn. Each proposition rests upon a claim which might be tested empirically. The available evidence is sparse, however, so we will not be able to demonstrate the falsity of the propositions. But we can certainly cast doubt on their validity, which in turn creates the possibility for challenging the orthodox view of regulating contracts that rejects control over substantive unfairness.

The Illusion of Unfairness

'Qui dit contractuel, dit juste'; so the adage goes. A consensual agreement under conditions of fair competition, it is claimed, must comprise a fair set of obligations. Yet many contracts appear to include harsh terms. Is this appearance just an illusion, which, on closer inspection, will be dispelled? My argument will be that although we should be circumspect about jumping to hasty conclusions concerning the unfairness of trans-actions, the appearance of unfairness is not always illusory.

It is useful to make a preliminary distinction between three kinds of substantive unfairness in contracts. The first type comprises the paradigm case where the price paid for goods or services appears excessive or derisory. A typical example in litigated cases involves the sale of property for far less than its market value. We also see occasionally instances of prices charged for services greatly in excess of ordinary market rates. The second type of unfairness involves a one-sided allocation of risk. In a sale of a car to a consumer, for instance, the standard form contract might include a term that excludes the liability of the retailer in the event of the car proving defective, poor quality, or dangerous. In such a contract, the consumer has bought the physical item, but there is no warranty that the car will be functional, satisfactory, or safe. The consumer has to bear those risks. As a result, it can be argued that the consumer has entered an unfair contract, because in return for the price the consumer has only received a promise to supply a heap of metal and plastic, not a car that works and will serve its normal functions as a vehicle. The third type of unfairness concerns the agreed remedies for breach of contract. In the security rights constructed by the terms of a contract, for instance, the contract may ensure that one party has a strong or even punitive non-legal sanction available, so that breach is fiercely deterred and default is punished by a sanction that exceeds the plaintiff's loss. Although differing in appearance, all three types of unfairness can be analysed as concerned with the price of the transaction.

In the second type of unfairness, the issue is not whether one party bears all the risks, but rather whether the price adequately reflects that allocation of risk. In the example of the sale of the car to the consumer, the price might be so low that it might be regarded as reflecting accurately the balance of advantage. The consumer may have only purchased a wreck with no guarantees whatsoever, but the price paid was so minimal that it might be regarded as fair. (Of course, we might wish to regulate such a contract on other grounds such as the protection of the safety of the consumer and the public.) In the famous case of *Cutter v Powell*,[1] a seaman agreed to take the job of second mate on the ship 'Governor Parry' on its voyage from Kingston, Jamaica, to Liverpool in the summer of 1793 in return for a promise of thirty guineas payable ten days after arrival at Liverpool. Unfortunately the sailor died half way through the voyage, and his widow claimed his wages. Although the jury awarded the full sum, it deferred to the judgement of the court that nothing could be recovered, because the terms of the contract required the seaman to complete the

---

[1] (1795) 6 Term Rep 320.

voyage before any payment fell due. The court reasoned that since the normal rate of pay was about £8, the premium whereby the sailor obtained the chance nearly to quadruple his remuneration must have be purchased by an implicit agreement to accept all the risks of a hazardous voyage. On this reasoning, the harsh outcome for the widow was the result of a fair price being paid for the risk.

In the third type of unfairness, the fundamental issue also concerns the price paid. The terms of the contract may contain a swingeing penalty clause or a fierce security right. In the event of default the creditor can obtain a remedy that far exceeds any losses resulting from the breach of contract. But the question of whether such a term should be regarded as unfair must turn on the price paid for this remedial advantage. If the creditor has paid for these rights, perhaps by reducing the price in the light of the security rights or increasing the promise to gain the advantage of the penalty clause, then provided that the payment is adequate, again no question of unfairness arises. In a commercial contract, one party may appear to have bargained for the right to terminate the transaction on the slightest pretext even if it has suffered no real loss, but again the harshness of this termination clause may have been paid for by a higher price and may be necessary to protect certain types of 'sunk investments'.[2] Similarly, in commercial contracts the harsh term may create a non-legal sanction, such as the right to withdraw a licence or a lease on short notice, which the parties may consider to be necessary in order to provide an adequate sanction against default. It is suggested, for instance, that in franchise contracts, this power to terminate the use of intellectual property rights or the lease of premises is necessary to ensure that the franchisee complies assiduously with the standards of the franchise, for the possible legal sanction is weak compared to the threat of loss of livelihood and non-salvageable investments.[3] Economic analysis thus suggests that the power to exercise this non-legal sanction is paid for by way of a higher percentage of profits payable to the franchisee, so there is nothing unfair about the transaction at all.

These arguments insist that we cannot determine the issue of unfairness without investigating thoroughly the issue of whether advantages have been paid for in the price. Equally, we cannot determine that a price is unfair without examining all the terms of the contract. These elementary economic insights are illustrated in a study of sales of peas and sweet corn by farmers to canners in the USA.[4] Although the study indicated price variations of up to 68 per cent, which suggested that some farmers

---

[2] Klein, B., 'Transaction Cost Determinants of "Unfair" Contractual Arrangements', *American Economic Review Papers* 70 (1980) 356.   [3] Ibid.

[4] Jesse, E. V., and Johnson, A. C., 'An Analysis of Vegetable Contracts', *American Journal of Agricultural Economics* 52 (1970) 545.

had received poor prices for their crops, when other contract provisions were taken into account, the price variation was reduced to 10 per cent. Yet these economic models do not go far enough in reducing the illusion of unfairness.

Once we examine these contracts from a sociological perspective, we become aware that most are embedded in long-term business relations which provide the source of trust and non-legal sanctions that help to overcome the problem of first mover. The apparent unfairness of the price in a particular contract may be part of a rational decision about self-interest designed to sustain or enhance the long-term business relation. In business format franchises, for instance, the franchisor usually obtains from franchisees a major capital investment which may be entirely lost by abrupt termination of the contract. As we have already observed, however, this investment may serve as a necessary signal of trustworthiness on the part of the franchisee, without which the franchisee would not be willing to enter the transaction at all.[5] A similar interpretation that stresses the role of unfair terms in constructing trust may be placed on the events surrounding the decision in *Williams v Roffey Bros & Nicholls (Contractors) Ltd*.[6] In this case, a disadvantageous modification to a fixed price building contract was impugned on the ground of absence of consideration. The argument was that the employer received nothing in return for the price increase except a promise to perform the original agreement, which was of no value, since the employer already possessed that entitlement. On its face, therefore, the transaction was unfair, or in the language of the common law, the promise to pay more was unsupported by 'fresh consideration'. Yet we know from our empirical investigations that the employer may agree to a variation such as a price increase in a fixed price contract, because it recognizes that such an action will serve to sustain a long-term business relation. In this case there was evidence that the employer realized that the original price agreed with the contractor was based upon mistaken assumptions, so that the work could only have been performed at a loss. In order to sustain the deal for both parties, and perhaps to continue the long-term business relation, it would be rational for the employer to agree to a gratuitous price increase. We can therefore discover an unfair contract in the heart of a business relation, where the unfairness is designed to help to construct and sustain a commercial contract. For the court to strike down the modification of the price on the ground of unfairness would be for it to obstruct commercial relations by providing a facility for unscrupulous parties to escape their obligations based upon trust. Fortunately the court

---

[5] Dnes, A. W., '"Unfair" Contractual Practices and Hostages in Franchise Contracts', *Journal of Institutional and Theoretical Economics* 148 (1992) 484, 496. See above, Ch. 4.
[6] [1991] 1 QB 1, [1990] 1 All ER 512, CA.

was astute enough to perceive this problem. At the expense of some distortion of the doctrinal concept of consideration, it was able to uphold the contract on the ground that the employer had obtained various 'commercial advantages' from modification. The lesson to be drawn from this example is that even where the terms of a contract appear unfair in the sense of an excessive or derisory price, the unfairness may still be an illusion when the contract is placed in its context as part of a long-term business relation.

A similar lesson may be drawn from the apparent unfairness of some security rights in contracts. Non-legal sanctions provide a crucial ingredient for the construction of markets. In some instances that we have called security, the terms of the contract may help to construct the non-legal sanction by allocating proprietary interests. The parties will only use the contract to construct the non-legal sanction where this is necessary to achieve the appropriate balance of incentives to overcome the risks of betrayal and disappointment. In most instances, however, non-legal sanctions such as withdrawal of future business, loss of investments, or damage to business reputation can be achieved without the assistance of a contract. The effect of controlling or invalidating security rights might therefore be to prevent the parties from constructing a satisfactory balance of non-legal sanctions, in which security rights match the power of non-legal sanctions. By denying the parties the power to create such non-legal sanctions regulation would have the undesirable effect of discouraging the parties from entering the proposed transaction. In the case of franchises, for instance, the franchisee has considerable power to damage the business reputation of the franchisor by poor performance of the contract. In order to balance this power adequately, the contract creates various non-legal sanctions such as a right to terminate the contract abruptly and the forfeiture or loss of the franchisee's investments. The security rights established by the contract thus only represent the tip of the iceberg of the non-legal sanctions that sustain a transaction. To ignore the effect of these other non-legal sanctions and to examine for the purposes of regulation the security right in isolation might well create more unfairness than it relieves.

The arguments drawn from economic and sociological analysis demonstrate the strength of the case for suggesting that most examples of alleged substantive unfairness in contracts turn out to be illusory on closer inspection. Consider how these arguments apply to the celebrated US case of *Williams v Walker-Thomas Furniture Co.*,[7] which is often regarded as a paradigm instance of unfairness. Although the case report does not reveal all the details, we can be reasonably confident about most of the context by drawing on Greenberg's study of the business operations of the defendant

---

[7] 121 U.S. App. D.C. 315, 350F. 2d 445 (1965).

company.[8] The defendant company sold furniture and electrical goods on credit to poor consumers. The contract involved the doorstep sale of stereo record playing equipment under a credit arrangement constructed so that the purchaser was regarded as leasing the equipment until the full purchase price had been paid. Such transactions can be described as conditional sales or hire-purchase contracts. The price stated in the contract for the stereo set was $514.95, which we can be sure was far in excess of the price for the same goods in ordinary high street shops. The price contained the interest charges on the credit arrangement, which often approached 30 per cent,[9] so we may infer that the ordinary retail price was near $300. There is no evidence in the case or the empirical study about the content of the standard form contract with respect to the allocation of the risks of defective products. We may surmise that the standard form followed the typical pattern of the time of excluding any implied warranties as to quality, but it seems that it was also the practice of the company to give a warranty for six months against defects. The value of this guarantee may have been illusory, however, for the company apparently reserved the unilateral discretion to determine whether or not the goods had been defective.[10]

The litigation concerned the third type of unfairness with respect to the company's security rights under the conditional sale. The contract contained the normal term that if the customer failed to pay any monthly instalments, then the company was entitled to repossess the item. But in addition the contract provided that:

the amount of each periodical installment payment to be made by [purchaser] to the Company under this present lease shall be inclusive of and not in addition to the amount of each installment payment to be made by [purchaser] under such prior leases, bills or accounts; and all payments now and hereafter made by [purchaser] shall be credited pro rata on all outstanding leases, bills and accounts due the company by [purchaser] at the time each such payment is made.

The purpose of this term was to keep a balance due on every item purchased until the last item had been fully paid for, an event which might never occur if the customer continued to enter into transactions with the company. The company's security right under the contract therefore applied to all items ever purchased (or more precisely leased) from the company, not merely each new item, so that in the event of any default on instalments, the Company could repossess every item ever sold to the customer. In Williams's case, the plaintiff had defaulted on the monthly

---

[8] Greenberg, D. I., 'Easy Terms, Hard Times: Complaint Handling in the Ghetto', in L. Nader (ed.), *No Access to Law: Alternatives to the American Judicial System* (New York: Academic Press, 1980) 379, 384; see also above, Ch. 4.   [9] Ibid.
[10] Ibid. 388.

payments for the stereo equipment, and she now risked losing items purchased over a number of years to the total stated value of $1,800, even though she had already paid $1,400, because under the company's accounting system a small amount remained due on every item that she had purchased. The default was hardly surprising since appellant was a single parent with seven children living on a government benefits cheque for $218 each month.

Was this contract unfair? With respect to the price paid for the stereo equipment, this exceeds by far the ordinary market price, so it has the appearance of unfairness. Yet the price also includes the cost of credit, the interest to be charged on the submerged loan, so the correct comparison lies with the retail store price plus the rate of interest normally charged to people in Williams' position. One may surmise that she would have been regarded as a poor credit risk by most financial institutions. Either she would not have been able to obtain any credit at all, or she would have had to pay a high premium to compensate the bank for the risk of default. In these circumstances, where we know under ordinary market conditions that the 'poor pay more',[11] the credit charge of 30 per cent might not be regarded as unfair at all.

With respect to the second aspect of unfairness, we require further information about the price actually being paid for the guarantee, which is hidden in the total cost. It may be the case that only a small price was charged since the company did not expect to meet many claims out of its own pocket. There is a one-sided allocation of risk, but this may even be reflected in a lower price of the goods compared to stores that back their goods with reliable warranties (once the interest charge has been removed from the price charged).

It can also be argued that the 'catching bargain' aspect of the security provisions was a fair deal for the customer. An economic analysis can suggest that the terms were fair since they constituted the optimal efficient transaction.[12] During the period of repayments, the purchaser will only have a 'negative equity', that is the market value of the used goods will be less than the sum owed under the credit arrangement (except perhaps during the last few months of the repayment schedule). The seller therefore requires additional security in order to construct an adequate non-legal sanction in order to protect the price. The most convenient security comprises the goods which the seller normally deals in, namely goods previously sold to the debtor. These goods can easily be resold (perhaps as new goods) by the company using its regular sales force. Without this

---

[11] Williams, F. (ed.), *Why the Poor Pay More* (London: MacMillan/Child Poverty Action Group, 1974).

[12] Epstein, R., 'Unconscionability: A Critical Reappraisal', *Journal of Law and Economics* 18 (1975) 293.

additional security, the price of the credit arrangement (concealed in the inflated purchase price) would have been even higher. It seems to follow that not only is the catching bargain fair, but also it is in the best interests of the debtor. We cannot be sure on the basis of the available information whether or not we should regard this contract as unfair on the ground of excessive price. We would need to discover what interest rates might have been charged to the appellant in the open market and how the price of the goods was calculated. The point is rather that the contract has all the appearance of unfairness, but on closer inspection this appearance may turn out to be illusory.

Nevertheless, these beguiling arguments of economic analysis should not lead us to the conclusion that no unfair contracts exist, but rather the correct inference is that these contracts are much harder to detect than we might suppose. In the previous chapter it was argued in connection with hierarchies established by contract that although many hierarchies are essential for the construction of optimal contractual relations, there was evidence that the patterns of hierarchy deviated in many instances from the most efficient institutional arrangements. Similarly, in the case of apparent unfairness in contracts, though many instances of excessive price may prove justified on closer inspection, we can also find examples of prices that cannot be explained on the basis of optimal terms for the parties. In the *Williams* case, for instance, the security right over all the goods ever purchased clearly exceeded any conceivable risk of loss from default on the purchase of the stereo equipment. A harsh security right was justified in this high risk credit arrangement, but plainly the company inserted into the standard form contract a device which gave them a non-legal sanction that licensed substantial enrichment upon default without any compensating advantage to the customer. We can be less sure about the unfairness of the price and the allocation of risk. The price charged in the *Williams* case may have corresponded to the ordinary market price charge by doorstep sellers to welfare recipients in the ghetto. The unfairness of the price only emerges through a comparison with other markets, such as ordinary retail stores and their terms for credit transactions or doorstep sales to middle-class consumers. The problem here is to decide which market may be the appropriate comparison, and then to make some allowance for a normal variation of prices within markets. Nevertheless, these obstacles can be overcome by some rough estimates, which would probably demonstrate that the price charged was greatly at variance with any comparative market. With respect to the allocation of risk, we encounter a more formidable problem that the value of the promised warranty depended heavily on how the unilateral discretion in determining whether faults existed was exercised. The Greenberg study provides evidence that the company invariably avoided the obligation to repair or replace faulty items.[13] If we assume that the express warranty was presented as a valuable commitment and that the consumer paid something for this benefit, then we can conclude that the contract was also unfair in this respect, since the item purchased, the protection from the risk of faults, was valueless.

The lesson to be drawn from this analysis of alleged unfairness is the painful one that appearances are indeed deceptive. In order to judge substantive fairness, we need to engage in a detailed examination of the particular circumstances of the transaction. We need to consider not only all the terms of the transaction in order to determine whether harsh terms have been purchased by commensurate reciprocal advantages, but also the social and economic context of the transaction in order to estimate whether the substantive imbalance was necessary for the transaction to occur in the first place. In other words, fuller information may reveal that the transaction satisfies the test of Pareto optimality. Nevertheless, I have argued that once this information becomes available, we will discover some instances of real substantive unfairness.

Open Texture Rules

Regulating unfairness in contracts requires a contextual appreciation of the terms of contracts. In order to avoid the pitfalls of the illusion of unfairness, accurate determinations of when unfairness has occurred demand an examination of all the terms of the contract and the context in which agreement was reached. All the terms have to be considered in order to detect the latent trading in price adjustment. The circumstances have to be examined in order to understand both when unfair bargains rest upon further advantages from the business relation and preservation of the deal, and when the apparent commensurate advantages of the terms conceal a real practice of unfairness.

These considerations drive the legal form of regulation of contracts away from clear or bright-line rules towards open-ended standards such as the test of 'unconscionability' used in *Williams v Walker-Thomas*.[14] Statutes employ similar phrases such as 'good faith', 'fair and reasonable', and 'extortionate'. In the UK, the courts can decline to enforce exclusion clauses that allocate risks on the ground that in all the circumstances the term was 'unfair and unreasonable'.[15] The European Directive on Unfair

---

[13] Greenberg, D. I., n. 8 above, 379.

[14] Neither detailed consumer protection legislation nor the Uniform Commercial Code applied to the District of Columbia at the time of the transaction, so the Court had to rely upon general principles of private law as the source of regulation.

[15] Unfair Contract Terms Act 1977.

Terms in Consumer Contracts,[16] and its implementing legislation,[17] similarly confer on courts the power to invalidate a term in a consumer contract which 'contrary to the requirement of good faith causes a significant imbalance in the parties' rights and obligations under the contract to the detriment of the consumer'. This regulation expressly excludes the price term from the review, so that it applies only to ancillary terms such as exclusion clauses and security rights. In connection with consumer credit transactions, a court can refuse to enforce an 'extortionate credit bargain'.[18]

This use of general phrases with indeterminate meaning permits adjudication on the basis of an investigation of all the circumstances. Any simple test, such as a price less than half the normal market value as in the Roman doctrine of *laesio enormis*, will inevitably be vulnerable to the accusation that the test is both over- and under-inclusive: the test will catch bargains that are fair once all the circumstances are taken into account, and fail to detect unfairness when it appears in more subtle forms such as oppressive security rights. The only solution to devising regulation that has the potential to conform to its policy objectives must be one that employs standards that permit the adjudicator to consider all the circumstances of the impugned transaction. For this purpose, the regulation must provide the adjudicator with the capacity to justify a detailed examination of all the relevant circumstances. This capacity to consider all the circumstances of the case can only be achieved by conferring a discretion upon the adjudicator. This discretion can only be limited by a general standard that states the policy objective or principle. As a result, legal regulation framed in rules invariably prefers the use of general standards which state the requirement of fairness without further precision. Open texture in rules is the antidote to self-referential closure.

But this potential for greater accuracy in regulation of substantive unfairness provided by open-textured rules will be purchased at the price of weakened efficacy. The general standards require a type of private law adjudication mechanism for their application to the particular facts of a case. We have observed the probable impotence of such a regulatory strategy, especially when the protected group lack the information and resources to enforce the regulatory standards.[19] In some instances, we may therefore prefer a strict rule, such as a minimum wage law, on the ground that a clear public standard is likely to increase markedly the degree of compliance. The public standard can also be provided with better funded policing of compliance, such as labour inspectors, and punitive sanctions. These advantages of public regulation can, however, be exaggerated. As well

---

[16] Directive 93/13.
[17] Unfair Terms in Consumer Contracts Regulations 1994, SI 1994/3159.
[18] Consumer Credit Act 1974.   [19] See above, Ch. 3.

as the normal weaknesses of any poorly funded bureaucratic form of regulation, the effectiveness of this style of regulation can be undermined whenever the parties to the transaction share incentives to avoid the regulation and keep the terms of their transaction secret from public inspection. An employee may conceal information about wages fixed below the minimum level for fear of losing the job; or the tenant may collude in an excessive rent in order to avoid threats of dispossession; or the consumer may agree an informal arrangement to purchase goods at an exorbitant rate of interest when no other option for acquiring the goods appears to be available. Public enforcement does not necessarily overcome the structural weakness of under-resourced self-enforcement in private law. Furthermore, the formal standards normally required by public regulation immediately become vulnerable to the criticism that they lack sufficient precision in the determination of substantive unfairness. For this reason, even in public regulation, such as the requirement of 'fair rents', the regulation usually embraces an open textured standard.

The Risk of Uncertainty

The use of general open-ended standards for regulating unfairness immediately provokes a vitriolic criticism. It is asserted that such discretionary powers to invalidate or rewrite the terms of contracts undermine the utility of legal regulation as an institution for assisting in the construction of markets. The content of the law is rendered uncertain, and this incalculability prevents the parties to a transaction from relying upon it as a predictable source of support for their exchange. This appeal for the need for certainty in the law leads swiftly to the conclusion that the wise course is for the law to refrain from policing the fairness of transactions. Instead, legal regulation should stick to a rigid rule of the enforcement of consensual arrangements (though it can police the question of whether or not the transaction was consensual). The few instances of unfair transactions which will still be enforced under this regime are, on this view, a price worth paying for the greater benefits to be derived from the construction of reliable markets and the preservation of the legitimacy of the legal system.

Some further support for the enforcement of a rigid rule against interventions on the ground of substantive unfairness no doubt derives from its connection with the ideal of freedom of contract. When freedom of contract is justified as a necessary incident of the moral stance of respect for the dignity and autonomy of individuals, any interference with freedom of contract smacks of paternalism, a form of social control that implicitly reduces the worth of citizens. This criticism of any paternalism does seem extreme, however, for it leads to the conclusion that out of respect for the dignity and autonomy of individuals, we should respect their freedom to enter contracts which expropriate all their wealth, which force them to rely upon others for the means of subsistence, and which effectively remove them from the opportunity to participate in markets. Other interpretations of the requirements of respect for the dignity and autonomy of individuals do not lead to such unattractive conclusions. We can argue, for instance, that we should only respect autonomous choices to the extent that they do not destroy autonomy in the future. Alternatively, respect for autonomy might be limited to a broad range of worthwhile choices.[20] On either of these more instrumental interpretations of the principle of respect for the dignity and autonomy of individuals, it would be permissible to set limits to freedom of contract by invalidating at least some unfair contracts.

The defence of a rigid rule against regulation of substantive unfairness more commonly takes the instrumental form of the creation of the risk of uncertainty. If courts or other agencies are granted a general power to upset bargains on the ground that they perceive the terms to be unfair, this power threatens to undermine the utility of the law as the basis for support for market transactions. It is suggested that the parties to a contract will always be unsure whether or not their transaction might be impeached on the ground of unfairness. This uncertainty may draw them towards less optimal transactions or prevent them from reaching a deal at all. This argument suggests, for instance, in the context of doorstep sales to consumers at a high price, that the rational response will be either that businesses will demand an even higher price from consumers in order to compensate for taking the risk of legal unenforceability, or, more probably, that businesses will withdraw from the market altogether, thereby depriving consumers of what can be a valuable and convenient way of shopping.

The force of this argument depends upon certain empirical assumptions. The principal assumption is the one that we have already considered at length,[21] which is whether legal enforceability of contracts provides a significant source of either the trust or the sanctions that are required in order to overcome the problem of co-operation. By casting serious doubt on the significance of the law, especially with respect to legal sanctions, we have also undermined the contention that uncertainty in the law will harm the construction of markets. It was clear, for instance, in *Williams v Walker-Thomas*, that the possibility of legal enforcement was never a significant part of the calculations of either party. The strategy of the business was to avoid third parties altogether, and to secure the power to control all remedies for breach of contract. The consumer also was unlikely to contemplate legal sanctions, in part due to the threat of reprisals such as

---

[20] Smith, S. A., 'In Defence of Substantive Fairness', *Law Quarterly Review* 112 (1996) 138.
[21] See above, Ch. 4.

the enforcement of security rights, but no doubt mostly due to the usual reasons for consumers being denied access to justice such as cost and ignorance of rights. We have also noted before that the potential legal invalidity of terms in contracts apparently has no influence on the business decision whether or not to use them.[22] For these reasons, together with the other weaknesses of the private law system, we can be reasonably confident, for instance, that whatever the outcome of the *Williams v Walker-Thomas* litigation, the business practices and the standard form contract of the company would not have been altered. When contracts are primarily sustained by trust and non-legal sanctions, which they usually are, uncertainty about legal enforceability is unlikely to make any difference to the calculations of the parties whether or not to run the risks of betrayal and disappointment.

This conclusion may not apply to every instance of contractual practices. In particular, it may be argued that when lawyers negotiate a detailed planning document which allocates risks precisely, and which therefore implicitly allocates the burden of insurance costs, uncertainty about the enforceability of these planning documents will damage the utility of this practice. Of course, in these circumstances, few judges are likely to discover any substantive unfairness, for they will detect the intelligence behind the scheme for risk allocation, even if it does produce apparently unfair outcomes, such as the result of one party not being liable for negligently causing damage to property of the other. But even if the chance of mistakes in adjudication are minimal, it may be argued that any risk of invalidity is likely to harm the use of planning documents for the purpose of risk allocation. In my view, however, this view makes the error of confusing the lawyer's perspective with that of the business parties. We noted earlier how the planning documents are normally regarded by the parties to a transaction as peripheral, something to be settled by the lawyers in separate negotiations.[23] If this interpretation of contractual practice is correct, then we must conclude that uncertainty with respect to the enforceability of the planning documents is unlikely to affect the decision whether or not to enter into the contract. The lawyer's practice of precise risk allocation through planning documents may be rendered more difficult by having to ensure that they pass any test of substantive unfairness, but this uncertainty about legal enforceability is unlikely to affect the entry into contractual relations by the business parties.

We have also questioned already a second assumption expressed in this criticism of indeterminacy in law.[24] We contested the view that the type of calculability sought by businessmen can be described in terms of the

---

[22] e.g., Yates, D., *Exclusion Clauses in Contracts*, 2nd edn. (London: Sweet & Maxwell, 1982) 19–23 (standard forms). [23] See above, Ch. 6.
[24] See above, Ch. 7.

predictable application of known rules. The type of calculability that is preferred is one in which the outcomes of legal regulation conform to the expectations of businessmen. In particular, considerations of the long-term business relation, the customs of the trade, and the success of the deal for both parties will guide those expectations rather than any reference to the precise terms of the planning documents or the formal rules of law. Formalism in legal reasoning, which closes off the possibility of taking such expectations into account, can in fact subvert the calculations of business. We argued before, therefore, that the uncertainty in the legal regulation produced by open-textured standards contributed in an important way to the achievement of the necessary calculability desired by business. In a similar way, we can insist here that general clauses such as good faith and reasonableness enable regulation to achieve results in accordance with expectations regarding the validity of clauses in contracts. A rigid rule that prevents such interventions would in fact come as a surprise to most commercial parties, who would expect the legal system to decline to enforce terms in the planning documents that impose extremely harsh bargains.

The concern about indeterminacy in law should therefore be regarded with scepticism. A degree of indeterminacy is necessary for the legal system to adjust its regulation to the variety of market customs and the particular circumstances of transactions. This reduction of predictability is superior to the alternative of formalism, for the latter presents a serious threat to confidence in the law as an intelligent regulator of contractual practices. Uncertainty, up to a point, presents no risk to the constitution of markets. On the contrary, it is required if legal regulation is to provide respected support for transactions. Supporters of the rigid rule against substantive evaluation of contracts cannot therefore rely upon the instrumental arguments against open-textured standards. They must take their stand on an extravagant and uncritical respect for freedom of contract combined with an emphasis upon the illusion of unfairness.

Hybrid Reasoning

Yet there is a deeper criticism of the use of open-textured standards in the law of contract. This second criticism suggests that the requirement to engage in a detailed examination of all the circumstances and the economic logic of the deal is either beyond the capacity of legal institutions, or that if they attempt it, the incorporation of sociological and economic methods into legal reasoning will distort the law and undermine its legitimacy. This second criticism comprises a version of the 'regulatory trilemma'.[25]

---

[25] Teubner, G., 'After Legal Instrumentalism? Strategic Models of Post-Regulatory Law', in G. Teubner (ed.), *Dilemmas of Law in the Welfare State* (New York/Berlin: Walter de Gruyter, 1988) 299; see above.

By conducting a detailed enquiry into the economic justifications for all the terms of the contracts, the regulatory agency or court will engage in a practice similar to that conducted by institutional economists, who are concerned with such matters as transaction costs, efficiency considerations in contract design, and governance structures. The regulator will also have to assess sociologically how the non-legal sanctions sustain the contractual practices and be sensitive to the way in which contractual terms permit the parties to dispense with the need to rely upon judicial sanctions for breach of contract. As well as the risk of making crass mistakes in conducting such an unfamiliar enquiry,[26] adjudicators may weaken the integrity of legal doctrine by adopting a type of hybrid discourse, part legal and part socio-economic.[27]

With respect to the problem of mistakes in legal regulation of substantive unfairness, we have to admit that the problem is an inevitable side-effect of the closure of legal discourse. Mistakes will be generated by the inability of legal doctrine to examine all the relevant circumstances of the transaction. This inability derives from way in which the law thinks about contractual undertakings. The purpose of open-textured regulation is to combat the self-referential closure of legal doctrine, but this form of regulation cannot succeed without altering the nature of legal discourse itself. Open-textured rules may weaken the closure rules of the legal discourse, but in my view they never sunder legal discourse from its doctrinal roots. In the legal reasoning governing contracts, we have observed on several occasions that the reasoning emphasizes the precise transaction comprising the terms contained in the formal documents. This emphasis upon the superficial record in the self-referential legal discourse establishes two typical closure rules.

In the first place, the legal system does not examine the economic logic of the transaction in order to grasp the relative significance and interdependence of the terms of the contractual undertaking. One effect of this closure rule is that terms such as penalty clauses can be analysed in isolation without asking whether or not a commensurate price increase was exacted in return for liability to pay the penalty. When legal reasoning embarks on the application of open-textured rules, as in the case of the unconscionability of penalty clauses, it never seems to go far enough into an examination of the efficiency considerations that led to the creation of this particular contractual structure. Legal decisions are therefore always vulnerable to the criticism that they have not examined the circumstances with sufficient thoroughness.

[26] Trebilcock, M. J., 'An Economic Approach to the Doctrine of Unconscionability', in B. J. Reiter and J. Swan, *Studies in Contract Law* (Toronto: Butterworths, 1980) 379.
[27] Teubner, G., 'Altera pars Audiatur: Law in the Collision of Discourses', in R. Rawlings (ed.), *Law Society and Economy* (Oxford: Clarendon Press, 1997), 149.

A second closure rule tends to prevent the legal system from examining the market context in which the transaction occurs in order to understand how it is sustained and how competition may be working. In a case concerning an apparently harsh allocation of risks, for instance, in order to determine whether this term is unfair, a court would need to examine whether in fact alternative risk allocations at different prices were available, and even if they were not, whether this similarity of standard form contracts revealed the presence of a cartel or merely the discovery in private ordering of the most efficient technique of risk allocation. In *George Mitchell (Chesterhall) Ltd v Finney Lock Seeds Ltd,*[28] for instance, the House of Lords held that a term in a sale of seeds to a farmer, which limited liability for consequential economic damage to the price of the seeds, was unfair and unenforceable, because this term left the farmer grossly under-compensated. The court supported this conclusion by several further observations. It noted that the other seed merchants also used a similar limitation of liability clause, so that the farmer had no real opportunity to choose different terms. This analysis implied that the seed merchants operated a cartel, but of course the similarity of terms might have been explicable on the ground that the farmer could insure more cheaply against this risk of loss than the seed merchants, with the consequence that the parties had found from experience that limitation of liability for consequential damage was the most efficient (Pareto optimal) contractual arrangement. The court was also impressed by the fact that the seed merchants often paid substantial damages to farmers, despite the protection of the limitation clause. The court inferred that the seed merchants must have accepted themselves that the term was unfair. Such an inference is difficult to draw, however, for probably the most important motive for the payment of compensation was to preserve general business reputation and to keep a long-term business relation alive. The court may have mistaken rational action oriented towards the business relation as action amounting to an admission of substantive unfairness in the contract.

These tentative criticisms of such decisions go beyond the earlier point that the courts may succumb to the illusion of unfairness. The argument is rather that legal discourse programmes the courts to examine the evidence of the terms and the circumstances of the transaction in particular ways which disable them from reaching judgements about substantive unfairness that coincide with those verdicts suggested by economic and sociological analysis of contractual behaviour. The legal analysis still remains distinctive from those suggested by other disciplines or communicative systems.

It is at this point that we reach the fundamental problem posed by the regulation of substantive unfairness. In order to reach decisions that

[28] [1983] 2 AC 803, [1983] 2 All ER 737, HL.

conform to sophisticated assessments of substantive unfairness informed by sociology and economics, legal adjudication has to incorporate these frameworks of analysis into its reasoning. In so doing, however, the legal analysis corrupts or misreads those other discourses, so that it misses their full subtlety. In *George Mitchell v Finney Lock*, for instance, the court had incorporated into the legal analysis an assessment of whether the terms had been produced by a competitive market, but it failed to grasp the point that identical terms did not necessarily prove the lack of competition. Similar terms could also prove precisely the opposite conclusion, if they could be explained on the basis of efficient cost avoidance. The legal analysis always remains vulnerable to the criticism of other disciplines that it has failed to incorporate their insights fully. Yet the legal analysis refrains from transforming its reasoning into a complete simulation of economics or sociology, because its legitimacy and authority depends upon its commitment to the integrity of its principles and their links to a defensible scheme of justice. The intuitive decision of all the judges in the *George Mitchell v Finney Lock* case that the limitation of damages clause failed the 'fair and reasonable' test was founded on this scheme of justice. Although the court sought to justify its decision on the further grounds of market practices and business expectations, these arguments could not satisfy the sophisticated requirements of a convincing case within the discourses of economic and sociological analysis. The normative complexity of the sources of regulation presents an insuperable obstacle to such a complete transformation of legal doctrine.

The resultant hybrid reasoning employed in the application of open-textured rules regarding substantive unfairness is therefore unlikely to satisfy the policy objectives of regulation. The question then becomes whether legal reasoning should engage in such inaccurate analyses of substantive unfairness or should instead abandon such attempts and revert to the rigid rule against assessments of unfairness. My view is that hybrid reasoning based upon open-textured rules still provides a superior regulatory strategy to that of formalism and the rigid rule of enforcement.

Regulatory Backfiring

The criticisms of regulating unfairness voiced by economic analysis are on firmer ground when we consider the problem of the side effects of regulation. The general criticism is that this paternalist intervention invariably harms those groups that it is designed to protect:

In sum, redistributive regulation will have complex distributive consequences, and the group particularly disadvantaged by the regulation will typically consist of those who are already most disadvantaged.[29]

These harmful side-effects may be criticized either on the ground that the harm outweighs the benefits of the regulation, or that at least the protected group ought to make the choice between harms rather than the legislator. The former argument raises an empirical question, whereas the latter is an argument of principle against any form of paternalism where the state determines the best interests of individuals.

The objection to paternalism represents a variation on the theme that the law should not place any restraints upon the discretion of individuals to use the power of self-regulation through freedom of contract to create transactions and relations of their choice. Our objection to this position has been framed both in terms of the protection of the value of markets as creating the opportunity to make Pareto optimal exchanges and in terms of the need to set limits to the contractualization of social life. We will not reconsider those arguments here, but rather we will examine the empirical contention that on balance the regulation of unfairness invariably produces net harm to the groups which it is designed to protect.

The principal criticism of the regulation of unfairness insists that this interference with the pricing mechanism of the market inevitably backfires. This objection applies logically only to regulation designed to alter market prices. Most regulation of substantive unfairness attempts instead to bring the terms of the contract into conformity with a presumed ordinary market price under competitive conditions. Nevertheless, the argument is applied to most regulation of substantive unfairness, because it is believed that, due to the illusion of unfairness, these contracts do generally represent the competitive market price. It is suggested that the effect of regulation which interferes with the pricing mechanism of the market is that instead of the protected group paying lower prices for goods and services or receiving higher wages, in the long run they pay more or receive less. This argument can be applied to such examples as fair rent legislation and the minimum wage. In the case of fair rents, the regulation tries to lower rents. The effect of the reduction of rental income from the capital investment in property will be that investors will seek alternative economic sectors for their capital. The absence of investment in rental accommodation will eventually produce a shortage, which in turn will force up prices. The legislation will almost certainly be unable to resist this pressure to sanction an increase in prices for fear of destroying the availability of rental accommodation altogether. But the result will be that at the end of the cycle the

---

[29] Sunstein, C., 'Paradoxes of the Regulatory State', *University of Chicago Law Review* 57 (1990) 407, 423.

level of rents will be higher than would have been the case without regulation. The same argument can be made with respect to the minimum wage
legislation. By forcing up the price of labour to employers, employers will
reduce their demand for workers, thereby causing an increase in levels of
unemployment. The pool of unemployed people will then exert a down-
ward pressure on wages. The result at the end of the cycle will be some
unattractive combination of higher levels of unemployment and lower
wages than would have been achieved by an unregulated market. Similarly,
controls on interest rates charged to consumers are alleged to have the
effect of depriving poor consumers with no credit rating from obtaining
credit at all, since no lender will accept the risk of default within the
statutory maximum rate of interest.[30]

The same arguments can be applied to regulation of non-price terms,
such as restrictions on the construction of harsh security rights or the use
of sweeping exclusion clauses. The prohibition on unfair terms in consumer
contracts, for example, removes the potential for trade-offs between price
and other terms. In a sale of goods, the warranty of quality becomes
mandatory, so that the seller cannot bargain for a price reduction in return
for a waiver of the warranty. This restriction may obstruct optimal
transactions where perhaps a poor consumer prefers to pay a lower price
and accept the risk of poor quality. At its most extreme, the argument
becomes that these poor consumers will become excluded from the
market altogether.[31]

This economic message that 'you cannot buck the market' must be
treated warily. It assumes that the market functions without any inelasticity
in supply and demand.[32] In the case of fair rents, for instance, the model
assumes that the investors can withdraw into other sectors so that the
supply of rented accommodation will be reduced. In the example of the
minimum wage, it assumes that employers will reduce the demand for
labour rather than try to pass on the increased costs in their prices. The
effect of regulation of unfairness is in fact highly unpredictable. Any
reliable prediction requires a detailed examination of the operation of
the precise market subject to regulation. That observation suggests that
regulation of unfairness may be effective in achieving its goals in some
markets but not in others. It supports a regulatory approach that proceeds

---

[30] Cayne, D., and Trebilcock, M., 'Market Considerations in the Formulation of Consumer
Protection Policy', *University of Toronto Law Journal* 23 (1973) 396.
[31] Schwartz, A., 'A Reexamination of Nonsubstantive Unconscionability', *Virginia Law
Review* 63 (1977) 1053.
[32] Leff, A., 'Economic Analysis of Law: Some Realism about Nominalism', *Virginia Law
Review* 60 (1974) 451; Kennedy, D., 'Distributive and Paternalist Motives in Contract and Tort
Law, With Special Reference to Compulsory Terms and Unequal Bargaining Power',
Maryland Law Review 41 (1982) 563.

cautiously, through trial and error, in order to discover when unfairness can be relieved without incurring the price of disadvantageous backfiring.

Minimum wage law is one field where the actual effects of regulation have been closely studied. Here the predictions of the backfiring of regulation have been particularly strident. The simple market model suggests that a minimum wage has a direct unemployment effect in those sectors of the economy where the rate of pay set by market forces lies significantly below the level set by the statutory minimum wage. This unemployment effect is therefore likely to be most noticeable in particular sectors of the economy such as agriculture, catering, and cleaning, and in relation to particular groups such as young people and unskilled women and ethnic minorities. In addition, it is predicted that other groups of workers will insist on the preservation of wage differentials by demanding proportionate increases. If acceded to, these wage demands could greatly increase labour costs for most firms due to a ripple effect, with consequent damage to profitability or levels of employment, and with the possible further consequence of setting off an inflationary wage and price spiral. The effect of price inflation would be to wipe out the gains in wages for all workers.

But the empirical studies of the impact of minimum wage laws tend on the whole to refute this economic model. In the United States a study of the effects of an increase in the New Jersey minimum wage in 1992 on employment in fast food restaurants demonstrated an expansion in the amount of employment.[33] This result is puzzling because many workers in such restaurants are young, taking part-time, temporary jobs at the minimum wage. The study was controlled by a comparison with eastern Pennsylvania, where similar general economic conditions pertained, but where there was no increase in the minimum wage and less growth in this sector of employment. Even more puzzling was the finding that employment growth was higher at restaurants that were forced to increase their wages than at restaurants that already paid the new minimum wage. This is not an isolated study, and though other results in the United States provide more ambiguous support for the positive employment effects of a minimum wage, they confirm the absence of detectable negative effects. The net effect of the minimum wage was therefore a modest transfer of wealth from shareholders in companies to low paid workers. The explanation for these results lies probably in the theory that employers have a discretionary range within which wage rates may be fixed. At some point, no doubt, the wages become too high for the employer to be able to employ the worker so that the marginal product exceeds the cost. Beneath that level, however, the employer has to balance savings in direct wage costs

---

[33] Card, D., and Krueger, A. B., *Myth and Measurement: The New Economics of the Minimum Wage* (New Jersey: Princeton University Press, 1995).

against other considerations regarding productivity, such as the reduction of staff turnover, the filling of vacancies quickly, and the encouragement of co-operation by paying above market rates. The raising of the minimum wage may have the effect of compelling the employer to give greater weight in the setting of wages to these productivity considerations. The positive employment effect may occur first through the filling of all vacancies, and in the longer term through the greater productivity of workers which increases the incentive to hire more employees.

This one example, of course, does not demonstrate that regulation of substantive unfairness never has the predicted backfiring effect. But it does support the view that each market must be examined closely and the effects of price regulation assessed empirically before we can judge whether regulation may be effective in its goals. What is striking about such empirical investigations of the effects of price regulation is that they invariably present a picture which differs from the predictions of the market model in significant respects. In the case of fair rent regulation, the evidence suggests that the market is sufficiently inelastic for a moderate system of rent controls to be imposed without adverse effects in terms of a reduction in the supply and quality of rental accommodation,[34] and indeed there may be benefits in promoting the improvement of the quality of the housing stock.[35] Similarly, the predicted adverse effects on the availability of credit due to legal regulation of the contractual construction of harsh security rights such as the catching bargain in *Williams* are also hard to discover in fact.[36]

A more general criticism of the market model suggested by economics insists that an unregulated market may not achieve the most optimal level and type of transactions. In the consumer credit context, for instance, the availability of 'easy money', albeit at high rates of interest, may create an 'oversupply' of credit. The judgement that the market outcome represents an 'oversupply' may represent a paternalist view that poor creditors may be unduly tempted to exacerbate their poverty by taking loans, so that eventually the state's welfare system has to cope with a much greater degree of hardship. Alternatively, it may be argued that this increase in the money supply has adverse macro-economic effects on inflation. Similarly, the

---

[34] Lee, R., 'Rent Control The Economic Impact of Social Legislation', *Oxford Journal of Legal Studies* 12 (1992) 543; Ackerman, B., 'Regulating Slum Housing Markets On Behalf of the Poor: Of Housing Codes, Housing Subsidies and Income Redistribution Policy', *Yale Law Journal* 80 (1971) 1093.

[35] Note, 'Reassessing Rent Control: Its Economic Impact in a Gentrifying Market' (1987–88) 101 *Harvard Law Review* 1835.

[36] Schill, M. 'An Economic Analysis of Mortgagor Protection Laws', *Virginia Law Review* 77 (1990) 489; Whitford, W. C., and Laufer, H., 'The Impact of Denying Self-Help Repossession of Automobiles: A Case Study of the Wisconsin Consumer Act', *Wisconsin Law Review* [1975] 607.

availability of cheap labour may be criticized as steering employers towards low capital investment and low productivity from the workforce, whereas in the long term employment and wealth are best served by an economic system which competes on the basis of high productivity and high levels of capital investment. These broader economic arguments insist that the legal and institutional structures of markets are themselves controversial, so that an unregulated market does not always produce the best wealth or welfare outcomes even on the assumption that backfiring is an invariable outcome of price regulation.[37]

A final observation with respect to the problem of backfiring regulation is that the application of mandatory rules to a system built on self-regulation has the effect that one pattern of self-regulation becomes excluded as a possible legally enforceable form of transaction. The response of participants in markets to this restraint is likely to involve the creation of alternative structures of self-regulation that can achieve a similar result. In the history of consumer credit for instance, the creditors devised alternative structures such as hire purchase or forms of negotiable instruments in order to escape controls over usury and sharp practice. In commercial transactions, the obstruction to the development of penalty damages clauses can be avoided by such techniques as incentive pricing structures and agreed set-offs. These new forms of self-regulation may of course be equally objectionable on the ground of substantive unfairness, but in many instances they may avoid the worst excesses of the original contractual structure. The effect of regulation of substantive unfairness is therefore rarely likely to prove to be an impediment to market transactions, but rather the contractual form of these transactions will assume a different shape. In most instances, the real challenge for regulating unfairness lies not in the problem of backfiring but rather in channelling the form of transactions in directions which tend to avoid the worst instances of substantive unfairness.

The Adequacy of Regulating Market Failure

Legal regulation can certainly improve the competitiveness of markets. It can break up monopolies, deter fraud and misleading trading practices, and redistribute information more evenly among participants in the market by the imposition of compulsory duties of disclosure. This regulation will not achieve the ideal conditions of perfect competition of economic theory, but it will certainly contribute to fairer competitive conditions

---

[37] Ramsay, I., 'Consumer Credit Law, Distributive Justice and the Welfare State', *Oxford Journal of Legal Studies* 15 (1995) 177.

in the market. A fourth proposition that provides an argument against regulating substantive unfairness in contracts insists that regulation of non-competitive conditions in markets, that is market failures, will eliminate all or nearly all instances of substantive unfairness. The regulation of market failures permits the preservation of a rigid rule of enforcement of all consensual transactions, for they will now comply with the Pareto optimal standard. In addition, the regulation of market failures appears to be compatible with respect for the principle of freedom of contract, for the regulation can be presented as a protection of freedom rather than a form of paternalist intervention.

In the strategy of regulating market failure, the object of regulation becomes market practices rather than the self-regulation of the parties to the contract. Market practices are objectionable in so far as they contribute to market failures. The two principal sources of market failure are asymmetries of information and monopolies. Consumer purchases are frequently made under conditions of asymmetric information. The manufacturer or retailer usually enjoys superior information and expertise both with respect to the nature of the product and with respect to the content and meaning of the terms of a standard form contract. Consumers cannot easily distinguish high quality goods from poor ones, so they tend to select on the basis of price, which may drive down the quality of all goods and impede competition.[38] Even price comparisons can be seriously obstructed by such devices as creating superficial differences between products sold at competing shops. At the same time, consumers are unlikely to study or understand the small print of a standard form contract, so that there is no competition between traders in the market for contract terms such as warranties, with the predicted effect of a 'race to the bottom', that is the widespread use of swingeing exclusion clauses and oppressive security rights in favour of the trader. Striking evidence of the way retailers take advantage of the lack of information and expertise of consumers comes from studies of discriminatory pricing practices. In the United States, it has been shown that retail sellers of cars discriminate in their pricing in some instances on the basis of factors which have no economic rationale, such as race and sex.[39] A possible explanation of this behaviour is that traders use these characteristics as proxies for criteria for estimating the consumer's information, expertise and bargaining power. When the retailer is dealing with a black woman, the retailer assumes inexperience and poor ability to evaluate the deal and then presses for a harder bargain.

[38] Akerlof, G. A. 'The Market for "Lemons": Qualitative Uncertainty and the Market Mechanism', *Quarterly Journal of Economics* 84 (1970) 488.

[39] Ayres, I., 'Fair Driving: Gender and Race Discrimination in Retail Car Negotiations', *Harvard Law Review* 104 (1991) 817.

The presence of monopolies is rarer in markets, though can be found in some public utilities and government services. But market conditions can frequently resemble monopolies. Doorstep selling takes advantage of the consumer's inability to make price comparisons and seeks to use subtle pressure to conclude the deal before such comparisons can be made. The buyer's urgent need for essential goods or services can be exploited by charging a high price when no alternative supplier can be found in time. We have also observed that long-term business relations can develop significant elements of bilateral monopoly where sunk investments cannot be exploited other than by continuing the relation. An example is an employee's development of firm-specific skills which cannot be used to obtain a good job with another employer, so the employee is effectively confined to remain with the present employer or sacrifice a significant proportion of income.

Regulation can tackle these market failures by many devices. Asymmetries of information can be countered by compulsory duties of disclosure of information or requirements of formalities designed to draw unfavourable terms to the attention of the consumer.[40] By selecting carefully the information to be disclosed, the regulation can also direct consumers towards more expert comparisons. For example, consumer credit regulation requires information about interest rates to be presented uniformly (the APR), which not only permits meaningful comparisons, but also discourages consumers from making the misleading comparison between the actual cost of weekly or monthly repayments.[41] Misleading information can be countered by the imposition of criminal penalties against such trading practices.[42] The exploitation of near monopolies can be deterred by granting consumers a 'cooling-off' period, during which they can cancel the agreement once the pressure has been removed.[43] Regulation can also invalidate contracts concluded as a result of false or misleading information, inadequate information, or the misuse of superior expertise. Private law has developed its doctrines respecting the adequacy of consent to contracts in order to supply such regulation through the rules of duress, undue influence, unconscionability, misrepresentation, and mistake. These doctrines provoke a careful examination of the events leading up to a particular transaction such as a secured loan agreement between a bank

---

[40] EC Directive 87/102; Consumer Credit Act 1974, ss. 60–65; Consumer Credit (Agreements) Regulations 1983, SI 1553.
[41] Whitford, W. C., 'The Functions of Disclosure Regulation in Consumer Transactions', *Wisconsin Law Review* (1973) 400, 423–5.
[42] Trade Descriptions Act 1968 (misleading descriptions of products and services); Consumer Protection Act 1987, ss. 20–21 (misleading price description); EC Directive 84/450; Control of Misleading Advertisements Regulations 1988, SI 915.
[43] European Doorstep Sales Directive 85/557; Consumer Protection (Cancellation of Contracts Concluded away from Business Premises) Regulations 1987, SI 2117.

and its customer, in order to determine whether the bank will be prevented from enforcing its security on such grounds as its failure to provide an adequate explanation of the terms of the transaction,[44] or to ensure that the customer received independent advice about the merits of the transaction.[45]

How effective is this regulation of market practices? To answer this question we need to be careful about defining the objectives of the regulation. The purpose of the regulation is usually described as enhancing the competitiveness of the market rather than the elimination of substantively unfair contracts. Thus the continuing presence of substantively unfair contracts does not necessarily point to the failure of the regulation. Nor is the purpose of the regulation to secure perfect competition in markets, for this is an unobtainable theoretical ideal. The objective is merely to enhance competitive conditions by deterring those market practices which are believed to produce significant market failures.

Yet even this narrow description of the objective of regulation remains opaque, because the market system depends for its success on the preservation of the value of inequalities in bargaining position. The market can only provide a superior mechanism for the supply of goods and services if it also offers incentives for the participants to acquire information and expertise. The crucial incentive is that the participants can use this information and expertise to enter transactions at prices which reward their work in obtaining the information and expertise. There would be no point, for example, in studying hard to become a lawyer if the law required the lawyer to disclose all this knowledge prior to entering into a transaction with a client. The transaction would never take place if the client could obtain the information freely. Moreover, there would be no incentive to study to become a lawyer, and the supply of lawyers would dry up. Thus asymmetries of information and expertise must be protected for the purpose of securing the market mechanism. The problem which confronts the regulation of market practices is to draw a distinction between, on the one hand, asymmetries of information and expertise which must be protected, and, on the other hand, those which create an undesirable market failure.

The general direction of a solution to this problem lies in an analysis of when the asymmetries of information or other types of bargaining disadvantage accrue to the benefit of the weaker party in the long run by sustaining a market for a valued service or product. In general, this principle will permit those participants in markets who gain a bargaining

---

[44] *Cornish v Midland Bank plc* [1985] 3 All ER 513, CA.
[45] *Lloyds Bank Ltd v Bundy* [1975] QB 326, [1974] 3 All ER 757, CA; *Barclays Bank plc v O'Brien* [1994] 1 AC 180, [1993] 4 All ER 417, HL.

advantage through work such as research and study to obtain the benefit of advantageous transactions as a reward for diligence.[46] On the other hand, where the bargaining superiority arises simply from taking advantage of the weakness of another, which is due to infirmity, gullibility, ignorance of business matters, or a temporary state of necessity, then the general principle suggests that no benefits will accrue to the weaker party in the long run by permitting such transactions, so the contract should be unenforceable. Between these two clear ends of a spectrum, however, the application of the principle to many familiar market practices remains indeterminate.

Consider, for example, the practice of retailing goods without clearly identifying prices. The retailer may calculate that the high prices charged for luxury goods might deter purchases, but that once a consumer has taken the time to select an item, he or she may be reluctant to withdraw from the deal on the basis of price alone. This is a marketing device designed to suppress price comparisons in favour of quality comparisons. The practice impedes the competitiveness of markets, but does it amount to a sufficiently grave instance of market failure to justify intervention? If we apply the test that the asymmetry of information must accrue to the benefit of the consumer in the long run, then we cannot be sure whether or not this marketing practice is necessary for sustaining retail outlets for luxury items. On balance, the need for this marking practice seems unlikely, so regulation requiring clear price marking seems to be justified.[47] Nevertheless, the application of the test requires an investigation of the consequences of regulation, which cannot be predicted with certainty in advance.

Although we cannot determine clear tests for when market failures are sufficiently serious to justify regulation, it is plain that such regulation can contribute to the reduction of imperfections in markets that provoke unfair contracts. A brief visit to the highly regulated arena of the modern supermarket can show the beneficial impact of regulation. The market becomes more competitive due to the requirements of clear price and quantity labelling, combined with the informational labelling of contents of items. All this disclosure of information may indeed compel supermarkets to be placed in remote locations, so that the costs of shopping around for different items exceed the benefits of the cheaper prices to be obtained. The questions that interest us here are whether the regulation, by deterring selected market practices, has the desired outcome of eliminating those market practices and has the further consequence of the expected reduction in the incidence of unfair contracts?

---

[46] Kronman, A. T., 'Mistake, Disclosure, Information, and the Law of Contracts', *Journal of Legal Studies* 7 (1978) 1.

[47] Price Marking Order 1991, SI 1382, implementing EC Directives 88/314 and 88/315.

The distinction between private law regulation and public law regulation is important in this context. Private law regulation usually provides the remedy of permitting the weaker party who is harmed by a market practice to escape from a transaction. In most instances, the costs of invoking this remedy will exceed the potential benefits. For example, if a consumer is induced to enter a contract for the purchase of a cleaning powder on the basis of statements that it possesses superior cleansing powers, but that in fact this information is false or misleading, then the consumer might be able to rescind the contract. But the costs of such legal action are so great that the consumer is much more likely to put up with the deception and merely use the non-legal sanction of selecting another brand next time. The private law remedy of rescission only becomes powerful when it has the potential to defeat the trader's security rights constructed by the contract. By threatening rescission of the transaction, the consumer can deprive the trader of the security right which was the principal sanction that supported the transaction. For this reason, most private law regulation has been developed in the context of either transactions of great value or the enforcement of security rights.

The field of ordinary consumer transactions has been occupied largely by public regulation. The effectiveness of this regulation is also open to doubt.[48] It has proved extremely difficult to provide reliable assessments of the benefits of such regulation.[49] By requiring manufacturers and retailers to supply information to consumers about products and services, we may certainly increase the amount of information available to consumers, but the ordinary consumer has only a limited capacity to understand and assimilate such information, which limitation, when combined with the expense of searching for alternatives in the market, is likely to diminish the benefits to market competition.[50] Disclosure of information may reduce the costs of acquiring information, but it remains a substantial transaction cost for most consumers to assimilate and use this information, so the impact on the operation of markets may be negligible, or even counter-productive.[51] This pessimistic conclusion is resisted by the argument that provided some proportion of consumers use the information, then the benefits of competition will be extended to all consumers because traders will not wish to lose the informed segment of its customer base.[52] At the same time, the requirement that information supplied such as descriptions

---

[48] Burrows, P., 'Contract Discipline: in Search of Principles in the Control of Contracting Power', *European Journal of Law and Economics* 2 (1995) 127.

[49] Ramsay, I., *Consumer Protection: Text and Materials* (London: Weidenfeld and Nicholson, 1989), 257–9.   [50] Whitford, W. C., n. 41 above, 400.

[51] Sunstein, C., 'Paradoxes of the Regulatory State', *University of Chicago Law Review* 57 (1990) 407, 424–5.

[52] Schwartz, A., and Wilde, L., 'Intervening in Markets on the Basis of Imperfect Information: A Legal and Economic Analysis', *University of Pennsylvania Law Review* 127 (1979) 630.

of products and price indications should be accurate and not misleading presents a converse incentive for traders to reduce the amount of information which they supply to consumers.

Critics of this regulation may therefore point to the possibility that the increasing density of regulation is caused by the need to combat the undesired side effects of earlier regulation, and may draw the conclusion that we end up with a complex regime which differs little in outcome from the kinds of market practices which would have survived in an unregulated market. The difference between the two is merely that firms have to incur substantial compliance costs in order to fit within the details of the regulations, and public authorities expend substantial resources in policing and enforcement costs. These costs will often be passed on to consumers, so that we have a price increase without better competitive conditions. Although these arguments are exaggerated for effect, they certainly cast doubt on the unalloyed benefits of this regulation in terms of redressing market failures.

The final question to be asked is whether the reduction in market failure achieved by this regulation also serves to reduce the incidence of substantively unfair contracts. Again some scepticism about the beneficial effects seems to be the appropriate conclusion. Because the avoidance of unfair contracts is merely a desired side effect of the regulation rather than its purpose, it is not constructed to achieve the elimination of unfair contracts. Regulation sets the standards for trading behaviour, and provided that these standards are followed, then the contract produced remains immune from criticism. In the context of doorstep consumer credit transaction, as in the *Williams v Walker Thomas* example, provided the seller complies with the relevant procedural requirements such as a written statement of a 'cooling-off period', a clear statement of the interest rate, the delivery of a contract written in plain legible English, the transaction cannot be challenged on the ground of market failure. If we add to this observation the worry that most consumers will be unable to take advantage of this information and protection from misleading statements, then we must doubt whether many cases of unfair contracts are effectively deterred.

Conclusion

Perhaps no other topic divides legal scholars so sharply as those who favour regulation on the ground of fairness or distributive justice and those who reject it as unnecessary, undesirable, impracticable, or more commonly all three. My argument has rebutted the view that regulation of unfair contracts is unnecessary and undesirable. Unfair contracts are not entirely illusory. Interventions in markets designed to redress unfairness are not undesirable on the ground that they create uncertainty or invariably back-fire by harming those whom the regulation is designed to help. The alleged problem of uncertainty misunderstands how markets are constructed and sustained. The real problem is rather that the legal system encounters problems of legitimacy and accuracy in its regulation as it develops sophisticated tests of unfairness. Nor does this type of regulation inevitably backfire, but on the contrary the evidence suggests that in many markets the costs of compliance cannot be passed on to the protected group. It has also be argued tentatively that the regulation of market failures by deterring practices which subvert the operation of competitive markets can only make a small contribution to the reduction of substantive unfairness in contracts.

Regulating substantive unfairness in contracts should therefore in my view comprise an important ingredient of the legal system. The open textured rules devised by private law appear to be the most adept at handling the complex issues which this task raises, though there is certainly room for specific public regulation in particular market sectors in order to obtain the advantages of tailored, precise regulation, and more resources for enforcement of standards.

12

Quality

The problem of quality in contractual relations relates to both the constitution of markets and distributive issues. The source of difficulties presented by quality concerns information. In most transactions, the purchaser of goods and services cannot be sure of their qualities in advance. Goods may have latent defects, and services may not prove as competent or reliable as expected. This uncertainty with respect to quality provokes a reluctance to enter transactions, which must be countered by the construction of trust or sanctions. In addition, the risk of defects in quality presents three distinct distributive tasks for regulating contracts. First, poor quality may raise the problem of unfairness in contracts, for the purchaser may have paid far more than the market value of the goods and services taking into account their defects. Second, poor quality may raise issues of externalities, as in the case of unsafe products such as cars that may damage not only the purchaser but also other people. Third, the difficulty of detection of poor quality in advance creates the opportunity for free riders to obtain an undesirable distributive advantage in markets. When most goods and services comply with a standard of satisfactory or acceptable quality, unscrupulous traders have the opportunity to supply poorer quality goods and services at the same price provided that the differences cannot be detected. These free riders pose the threat of a version of Gresham's law that bad goods will eventually drive out high quality goods from the market,[1] unless regulation can help to overcome the information problem by enabling purchasers to detect the difference in quality.

Many of the strategies for the construction of trust that we have observed are directed towards the task of overcoming the problem of information about quality. A business reputation for supplying goods and services of satisfactory quality is a crucial element in competitive markets. Businesses promote this reputation so that their name or the name of the product functions as a reliable signal to purchasers of good quality. Having established the reputation for quality, the business then demands a price premium, which can only be preserved as long as the

---

[1] Akerlof, G. A. 'The Market for "Lemons": Qualitative Uncertainty and the Market Mechanism', *Quarterly Journal of Economics* 84 (1970) 488.

reputation persists.[2] The absence of any regulation of quality would therefore not lead to the widespread supply of defective products and shoddy
services. The interest of sellers in establishing long-term business relations
with consumers in the form of regular purchases from a shop provides a
strong incentive to ensure that customers are satisfied by their purchases.
Hence many retailers proclaim in their promotion literature that 'satisfaction' is guaranteed.[3] In other words, they are content to give redress to any
customer who is dissatisfied by a product in order to preserve the business
relation. For this reason, surveys of redress of consumer problems with
respect to faulty goods invariably discover a high rate of success (perhaps
two-thirds) for consumers who complain and seek redress by informal
means.[4] Since business reputation is vital to sustain quality in markets,
we can predict that one important task of regulation is the protection of
these signals such as brand names and consumer guarantees from misuse
by others. The trade name becomes an item of property that can be
protected from use by others through registration as a trade mark and
injunctions can be issued against 'passing off' goods and services as those
supplied by a reputable trader. This regulation serves to assist the construction of trust in markets. But some limits are placed upon contractual
devices designed to protect business reputation, for some devices such as
resale price maintenance agreements between manufacturers and retailers
will be regarded as damaging to competition between retailers.[5]

The question to be considered in this chapter is how regulation might
best assist the construction of markets and the prevention of undesirable
distributive effects in markets in addition to the protection of business
names. Should quality issues be left to the parties to a transaction, so
that they define by their self-regulation in the terms of the contract their
expectations with respect to the quality of goods or services? Will this self-
regulation achieve what may be described as an 'efficient level of quality'?
Is this standard of an 'efficient level of quality' acceptable, if it fails to
tackle the distributive problems described above? Assuming that further
regulation is required, what form should this regulation take, and how
should it be enforced?

These rather abstract questions can be rendered more concrete by considering the task of regulation in a particular context such as a consumer
purchase of a washing machine. Here the problem of quality is that the

[2] Klein, B., and Leffler, K. B., 'The Role of Market Forces in Assuring Contractual
Performance', *Journal of Political Economy* 89 (1981) 615.
[3] Ramsay, I., 'Consumer Redress Mechanisms for Poor-Quality and Defective Products',
University of Toronto Law Journal 31 (1981) 117, 126; Ross, H. L., and Littlefield, N. O.,
'Complaint as a Problem-Solving Mechanism', *Law and Society Review* 12 (1977–78) 199.
[4] Ramsay, I., *Consumer Protection: Text and Materials* (London: Weidenfeld and
Nicholson, 1989) 420.
[5] Chafee, Z., 'Equitable Servitudes on Chattels', *Harvard Law Review* 41 (1928) 945.

consumer lacks reliable information to distinguish between the qualities of washing machines offered on the market. The standard of quality which the consumer expects is also hard to define except in general terms such as that the machine should work, not break down, not wear out, and have a satisfactory appearance. These expectations will be qualified by the price, so that the expectations increase or diminish in line with the price paid. The first question for regulation is whether the quality standards should be determined by the parties through the terms of the contract, or should legal regulation provide standards either as default rules or as mandatory requirements? The next question is how should these standards be formulated? For example, should the standards employ vague terms such as 'satisfactory quality', or should the standards attempt precise specifications such as a requirement that the machine be constructed in a sufficiently robust way that none of its parts wear out within three years. Assuming that regulation imposes some form of standards, should the monitoring and enforcement of those standards be left to the parties to the transaction in the private law strategy of self-enforcement or should the task be allocated to a regulatory agency? In other words, should the purchaser have the task of monitoring and enforcing the quality standards applicable to the washing machine, or should regulation supply a system of inspection and public enforcement of quality standards?

Efficient Level of Quality

When consumers purchase products and services, they seek value for money. This standard represents a function of price and quality. Since quality can vary and still be acceptable, the standard of value for money has to be a sliding scale of reasonable quality in view of the price being charged for the goods. The efficient level of quality is reached when the cost of further improvements to quality exceeds the value of those benefits to consumers.

This description of the efficient level of quality suggests strongly that regulation should be left to the parties to the transaction. They should determine the particular function of price and quality which satisfies their interests. For one consumer, a lower price may be preferred even at the cost of some defects, whereas another might be prepared to pay a premium for top quality goods. To impose a uniform standard of quality on these transactions would produce an inefficient level of quality in one, or even both.

In order to achieve an efficient level of quality that responds to variables in the price/quality ratio, regulation has to be confined to default rules that apply in the absence of express determinations of quality standards.

Furthermore, in order to comply with the efficient level of quality, these default rules have to present a sliding scale of quality, so that the requirement of quality can be adjusted according to the price paid and therefore according to the expectations of the parties with respect to quality. Private law regulation provides such an efficiency standard in most jurisdictions. In English law, the Sale of Goods Act s. 14 requires the goods to be of 'satisfactory quality', which is defined in s. 14(2A):

For the purposes of this Act, goods are of satisfactory quality if they meet the standard that a reasonable person would regard as satisfactory, taking account of any description of the goods, the price (if relevant) and all the other relevant circumstances.

The equivalent default rule for contracts for services requires the service to be performed with 'reasonable care and skill'.[6] The standard of reasonable care is not defined, but presumably also reflects the price paid for the service.

Private law regulation normally takes a further step beyond the provision of a default rule in order to support the standard of the efficient level of quality. In consumer transactions, the default rule usually becomes a compulsory term of the contract. In other words, the consumer is not permitted to agree to self-regulation which excludes this standard. In Europe this result is achieved by legislative intervention,[7] though it also possible to achieve this result as in the United States by invalidating exclusion clauses on the ground of unconscionability or some other broad standard of fairness.[8] The case for such compulsory terms may be put in terms of market failure. Since most consumers do not read the small print of standard form contracts, manufacturers and retailers often take advantage of this absence of competitiveness in the market for contract terms by inserting sweeping exclusion clauses designed to remove any obligation to supply goods of satisfactory quality. Due to the absence of a competitive market for contract terms in consumer markets, the potential advantage of permitting self-regulation to fix an efficient standard of quality is likely to be absent. The insertion of a compulsory term that enforces an efficient standard of quality merely redresses this market failure.

Priest argues that the content of a business standard form contract corresponds nevertheless to an efficient allocation of the risk of poor quality.[9] He suggests that in practice the exclusion or reduction of quality

---

[6] Supply of Goods and Services Act 1982, s. 13.
[7] EC Directive 93/13 and its implementing national legislation such as the UK Unfair Terms in Consumer Contracts Regulations 1994, SI 3159. Other national legislation may deal with the issue specifically, e.g. Unfair Contract Terms Act 1977, s. 6.
[8] *Henningsen v Bloomfield Motors, Inc.*, 32 N.J. 358, 161 A.2d 69 (1960).
[9] Priest, G., 'A Theory of the Consumer Product Warranty', *Yale Law Journal* 90 (1980–81) 1297.

standards by contractual agreement corresponds to those instances, such as the sale of automobiles, where consumers may use the product in a variety of unpredictable ways and may suffer unpredictable levels of consequential losses. Under those conditions, the consumer is in a better position than the manufacturer to estimate the risk of loss and to insure against it individually, for the manufacturer would have to charge higher prices to all consumers to cover the risk of unusual consequential losses. It seems to follow that the disclaimers in standard form contracts describe the efficient level of quality. But this argument seems unconvincing. The warranty of quality supplied as a default term by private law only applies to ordinary uses of goods. Unforeseeable losses are not recoverable under the liability rule on the ground of remoteness. To exclude the warranty of satisfactory quality on these grounds is therefore to protect the retailer and manufacturer against non-existent liability. The purpose of the exclusion clause must therefore be to evade the quality standard even where this is the efficient standard. In practice, as well, the evidence in the UK tends to support the finding of widespread use of exclusion clauses without differentiation according to efficient risk allocation.[10] The effect of self-regulation turns out to be a systematic failure to achieve an efficient standard of quality, that is, one to which the parties would have agreed with full information. The common response of private law to this failure of self-regulation has been to impose a mandatory regulation in consumer standard form contracts that requires the supply of goods of satisfactory quality.

Because the problem of quality in transactions is created by informational asymmetries, we must doubt, however, that self-regulation can achieve the efficiency standard. The difficulty for self-regulation is that one party will not have sufficient information to bargain for terms that express all aspects of the efficiency standard. When the consumer purchases a washing machine, for instance, an important dimension of the price of the goods consists in the cost of post-sale repairs. The cost to a consumer of a product can be described as the sum of the product price and the cost of repairs designed to remedy defects in quality. The best value for the consumer occurs when this sum is at its lowest. This may occur typically when the price is high, the defects are few, and therefore the cost of repairs is small. Product warranties include the cost of repairs, though usually only for certain kinds of defects for a limited period of time, within the price of the product. The consumer usually lacks information about either the statistical likelihood of the need for repairs or the probable cost of those repairs. Under those conditions, the consumer is unable to

---

[10] Yates, D., *Exclusion Clauses in Contracts,* 2nd edn., (London: Sweet & Maxwell, 1982) 19–23.

bargain for the efficiency standard. Either the consumer will assume the risk of those costs being greater than expected, or the consumer will purchase insurance or a product warranty, which may provide excessive or expensive coverage against those risks. A similar problem of informational asymmetry also obstructs bargaining for an efficiency standard in relation to other aspects of the purchase of the washing machine, such as the energy consumption of the machine and any personal safety risks presented by the machine.

The obvious solution to this problem created by informational asymmetries is to require manufacturers and retailers to supply detailed and reliable information about these hidden costs and risks. In other words, regulation would require extensive duties of disclosure about such matters as safety risks, costs of repairs, and energy consumption. Armed with this information, the consumer could choose a product that more close approximated to the efficiency standard. The main objection to this kind of regulation is that most consumers are unlikely to spend the time to read and understand all this information, so that most contracts will continue to deviate from the efficiency standard. The alternative regulatory approach is to set mandatory quality standards with respect to certain hidden costs and risks. With respect to safety standards or energy consumption, for instance, regulation might impose minimum standards across the market. This intervention will inevitably deviate from the efficient level of quality for any particular transaction, but it may achieve an approximation to an average efficiency level. Whereas specification of information requirements requires detailed public regulation with respect to each type of product, private law has the capacity to set general mandatory quality standards. In the case of product safety, for instance, the standard of 'satisfactory quality' can be interpreted to mean that the goods should always be perfectly safe in their ordinary uses. Similarly, with respect to the supply of services, the duty to take reasonable care could be interpreted to require sufficient care to avoid the risk of personal injuries.

Although we have focused on the regulation of quality in order to achieve an efficiency standard, regulation might also seek to address externalities, that is, considerations that the parties to the transaction do not value. Such considerations might include in the sale of the washing machine, for instance, a measure of pollution produced by the machine. The efficiency standard may therefore be altered in some instances, in order to compel the parties to internalize the costs of externalities in their transaction. Although private law may have the capacity to introduce these externalities into its standard setting, there is plainly a danger that in the enforcement of standards private parties will have no incentive to monitor compliance and to compel conformity.

Form of Standards

The private law standards which we have described above follow the general pattern of private law regulation in that the compulsory terms and default rules describe open-textured standards such as 'satisfactory quality'. Any greater specificity must be supplied through the facility of self-regulation in the terms of the contract. The public law standards that we have encountered, such as disclosure requirements, have been on the contrary extremely detailed and specific. These detailed standards can also apply to the components of products, such as a requirement that all washing machines should include pipes made from a particular rubber compound with durable qualities when exposed to hot water. The next question which I shall consider is what form of standards seem to be the most effective and efficient in achieving compliance with the desired quality standard. This manner of posing the question emphasizes two dimensions of the regulatory task, for a balance has to be struck between achieving an efficient level of quality and the costs of the regulatory regime which serves that purpose.

The principal cost of setting quality standards lies in the expense of determining them with a requisite degree of particularity for the purpose of ascertaining whether goods or services fall short of the standard of efficient levels of quality. In addition, regulation imposes the cost of publicizing those standards.

In the private law system, this cost of regulation is incurred by examining the evidence of faults presented in a particular case, and by the court interpreting the general standard of 'satisfactory quality' in this particular context. We have already observed that the private law system does not incur the cost of disseminating its standards. Leff has led a sustained attack on the costs and ineffectiveness of private law regulation of quality:

One cannot think of a more expensive and frustrating course than to seek to regulate goods or 'contract' quality through repeated lawsuits against inventive 'wrongdoers'.[11]

Leff highlights one weakness of private law regulation with respect to its generality. The standard is either too general or too specific to provide adequate guidance to participants in markets. The general standard cannot inform participants in market of what is required, so it proves an inapt tool of guidance. The general standard of 'satisfactory quality' becomes particularized to an individual case during a trial. It is always arguable that another case on slightly different facts should receive a different treatment.

---

[11] Leff, A. A., 'Unconscionability and the Crowd—Consumers and the Common Law Tradition', *University of Pittsburgh Law Review* 31 (1970) 349, 356.

The standard now becomes so detailed in its application that it still cannot serve as a guide to market behaviour.

This argument may exaggerate this weakness of private law regulation of quality standards, for it is possible to obtain guidance by reasoning by analogy from decided cases. Nevertheless, it is true that private law regulation provides indeterminate guidance in borderline cases. For example, the law may clarify the point that the durability of goods is an aspect of satisfactory quality,[12] but it remains for the courts in isolated and unpublicized decisions to specify what this requirement may mean in practice. Does it mean, for instance, that the goods should remain in working order for a reasonable time after purchase? In the view of Goode, an expert in the field,

If the goods are at that time [i.e. time of delivery] in such condition that with proper usage and in normal circumstances they will remain of satisfactory quality for a reasonable time, then they will satisfy the implied term of quality even if in the event they occur (*sic*), they develop a malfunction earlier than would ordinarily be expected for goods of the kind in question.[13]

This statement, which no doubt attempts to summarize the 'curiously little authority on the point',[14] surely provides no guidance at all to someone faced with the simple problem of the goods ceasing to function a few months after purchase. These general standards therefore seem unlikely to provide an effective regulatory instrument that guides participants in markets.

Leff's additional point that private law regulation is the most expensive kind should also be treated with circumspection. The costs of litigation are certainly high, but the issue is whether the alternative styles of standard setting are less expensive. In the alternative method of public regulation, the standards have to be set and publicized prior to any particular fault emerging. This task requires the regulatory agency to acquire expertise in the available technology and the relative costs of different product components. Not only is such a process likely to be expensive, but it appears to risk a high degree of error in setting standards which are either too high or too low. The cost to the state or taxpayer in standard setting is therefore likely to be much higher than the method of private law regulation. Given the probable costs of agency formulation of standards in advance compared to private law regulation by courts in the occasional instances

---

[12] Sale of Goods Act 1979, s. 14(2B), as amended by the Sale and Supply of Goods Act 1994.   [13] Goode, R., *Commercial Law*, 2nd edn., (London: Penguin, 1995) 325.
[14] Ibid. 324; the main authority is *Business Application Specialists Ltd v Nationwide Credit Corp. Ltd* [1988] RTR 332, CA, in which the court found that a second-hand Mercedes sold for £5000 which broke down after 500 miles and required £635 of repairs due to burnt-out valves was of 'merchantable quality', even though an independent expert said it would be unusual for defects of this kind to occur after only 38,000 on the odometer.

of litigation, it seems likely that private law will be able to render its standard with the requisite level of particularity at much less expense.[15] Leff may be correct to point to the relative ineffectiveness of private law standard setting for the quality of goods, but it seems unlikely that its total costs exceed other forms of regulation.

Regulation by general standards, applied through particularized adjudication, seems to provide the least expensive form of regulation. But it is also likely to be ineffective, because it fails to provide determinate standards that can guide participants in markets. The alternative of more elaborate and detailed standards is certainly more expensive and runs the serious risk of deviating from an efficiency standard. But the detailed guidance it provides is likely to be more effective in discouraging defects in quality. Is there a way in which more detailed standards can be produced without great expense and with minimal risk of deviations from the efficiency standard?

Regulation has the possibility of encouraging each industrial sector to set its own quality standards through technical specifications, and then to adopt these standards. This approach promises the great advantage of drawing upon the superior knowledge of the industry with respect to such matters as the cost of improvements in quality and the benefits of technological changes. This information places the industry in a superior position to either a public regulator or a court in devising an efficient standard for quality. Of course, one has to be suspicious that this style of self-regulation may lead to low standards. But this outcome does not necessarily follow, for the major sellers in the market may prefer to insist upon high standards in order to exclude low cost, low quality competition.

This pattern of industrial self-regulation is in fact widespread in the UK, and is increasingly common throughout Europe.[16] The British Standards Institution and other private trade organizations devise standards and then products are marketed on the basis that they conform to these quality standards. This system of self-regulation, however, remains outside the UK system of public regulation of product quality, for the standards are not endorsed, monitored, or enforced by a regulatory agency. The standards are, however, frequently incorporated as express or implied terms of the contract, so that they form an important technical ingredient in fixing quality standards in commercial contracts. In contrast, in Germany, the technical standards produced by trade associations will be regarded as mandatory quality standards in contracts.

---

[15] This is Shavell's argument in the different context of safety and personal injuries: Shavell, S., 'Liability for Harm Versus Regulation of Safety', *Journal of Legal Studies* 13 (1984) 357.

[16] Collins, H., and Scott, C., 'United Kingdom', in G. Bruggermeier (ed.), *Rechtprobleme von Qualitätsmanagementvereinbarungen und EG-Binnenmarkt* (Baden-Baden: Nomos, 1997) 239.

The practice of industrial self-regulation of technical standards appears to provide a substantial solution both to this problem of avoiding inefficient regulation and to the problem of dissemination of standards which are capable of guiding conduct. We need to consider, however, the cost of the development of these quality standards to the industry concerned. It is also possible that detailed technical standards might have undesirable side effects, such as the inhibition of foreign competition and innovation in design.[17] The development of European or international standards may reduce the obstacle presented by technical standards to competition. These standards may still be questioned, however, as a form of self-interested self-regulation that fails to take adequate account of the interests of consumers or externalities such as the environment.[18]

Assuming, however, that industrial self-regulation provides more efficacious and efficient guidance on quality, the question becomes whether it is cheaper to impose these industrial self-regulatory standards on the market through a regulatory agency or through private law. The intervention of a regulatory agency seems unnecessary in this process. The courts can incorporate the industrial self-regulation as part of their standard-setting function, so that satisfactory quality is always defined in part as compliance with industry technical standards. In other words, private law regulation seeks to become reflexive by incorporating within its standards the norms established by government and participants in the market. The reflexive standard becomes an international standard to regulate world markets to the extent that industrial self-regulation achieves global coverage. Since these standards are the product of self-regulation, however, a court should always be empowered to require a higher standard, or at least to insist that mere compliance with the industry standard does not guarantee that satisfactory goods have been supplied to the consumer.[19]

In the discussion so far, it has been assumed that the standard seeks to fix particular attributes of the goods or services to be supplied. The variable dimensions of regulation have been concerned with the degree of specificity of the attribute and the source of the efficient quality standard. In the context of contracts for services, a distinction emerges between the specification of inputs and outputs. Instead of trying to define how the service should be performed (inputs), the regulation may attempt merely to

---

[17] These considerations, combined with the difficulty of achieving clear technical specifications, led the Molony Committee to reject this regulatory approach: Board of Trade, *Final Report of the Committee on Consumer Protection*, Cmnd 1781 (London, 1962), paras. 254–6.

[18] Spindler, G., 'Market Processes, Standardization, and Tort Law', in C. Joerges and O. Gerstenberg (eds.), *Private Governance, Democratic Constitutionalism, and Supranationalism*, EUR 18340 (Luxembourg: European Communities, 1998) 145.

[19] *Handrigan v Apex Warwick, Inc.*, 108 R.I. 319, 275 A.2d 262 (1971)—compliance with American Standard Safety Code did not bar claim that goods (a ladder) were not of merchantable quality.

describe the desired outcome (outputs). One potential advantage of the regulation of outputs is that it can avoid expensive, detailed regulation. It might be expected, however, that the description of outcomes would become too vague to provide an effective instrument for measuring quality.

Suppose the contract provides for cleaning service for a school. The inputs could be described in detail, such as the employment of ten cleaners for one hour each evening, equipped with three vacuum cleaners, four mops and pails, and five dusters. The output would be described in necessarily vague terms, such as a requirement that the premises be kept to a reasonable standard of cleanliness and hygiene. This simple example reveals, however, that despite the precision of the inputs, the regulation may not achieve the required standard of quality even with full compliance, for it omits the crucial element of the intelligent employment of the inputs towards the desired goal. It is true that the regulation in terms of outputs is vague, but it may prove more effective in achieving compliance with the quality standard, because the parties will negotiate conventional understandings of when the output standard has been met. There is evidence that the product of this negotiation is ultimately more predictable and certain than the use of detailed regulation of inputs.[20]

Another technique for setting standards for products and services eschews any substantive standards altogether. It concentrates on the process of production rather than its outcomes. This method is widespread in commercial contracts between manufacturing business in the system known as quality assurance and total quality management.[21] Instead of the contract specifying in detail the quality of the required product such as a component, the contract requires the supplier of the component to conform to a particular management system which is oriented towards continuous improvements in quality, design, and efficiency. The objective of this approach is both to avoid any defects at all and to establish a trajectory of constant improvements in quality. This regulatory scheme is created, of course, by self-regulation through elaborate long-term commercial contracts, such as requirements contracts. Enforcement of these standards by private law is unnecessary, because the non-legal sanction of discontinuance of the business relation on failure to comply with the system of total quality management (signalled by the loss of certification by an independent consultant agency) is effective to compel compliance. The regulatory issue becomes rather whether the law should intervene to regulate the practice of certification of compliance with total quality

---

[20] Braithwaite, J., and Braithwaite V., 'The Politics of Legalism: Rules versus Standard in Nursing-Home Regulation', *Social and Legal Studies* 4 (1995) 307.

[21] Collins, H., 'Quality Assurance in Subcontracting', in S. Deakin and J. Mitchie (eds.), *Contracts, Co-operation, and Competition* (Oxford: Oxford University Press, 1997) 285.

management systems for fear that these private sector systems of certification might be open to abuse through economic pressure.

Monitoring and Enforcement

The cost of monitoring compliance with regulation points to a general advantage to the private law system of inspection. Consumers and business purchasers are allocated the task of inspecting their purchases for quality defects, which is usually inexpensive and adequate. The alternative system of public regulation might require the considerable expense of a team of inspectors examining samples from manufacturers of their products in order to determine whether they meet the quality standard. Presumably, the inspectors would also be required to handle complaints from individual consumers as well. A substantial administrative apparatus would be required for all types of products put on the market. The advantages in terms of cost of a private law system of monitoring therefore appear incontrovertible.

One reservation concerns the kinds of latent defects which might only be detected as a result of inspection by persons with technical expertise. The inexpensive monitoring system of private law can only achieve blunt determinations of whether the goods achieve satisfactory or acceptable standards, because either it lacks the sophistication to police detailed technical standards or the monitoring costs for complex standards are prohibitive.[22] If, for example, as part of the design of a washing machine, a component is used which will inevitably wear out quickly and require a repair, then the first that the consumer will know of this defect in quality is when the machine breaks down. If this breakdown occurs some time after purchase, then the consumer may believe that the fault is the result of 'ordinary wear and tear' rather than an initial defect in quality. It requires expensive technical expertise to demonstrate the design fault, which is unlikely to be employed in ordinary consumer litigation owing to its cost and the lack of access to such expertise.[23] In this area, therefore, public regulation, despite its expense, may be the only efficacious method to monitor conformity to an efficient level of quality. This argument suggests a role for selective regulation of potential design faults by a requirement that some components conform to detailed technical specifications monitored by a regulatory agency.

An enforcement mechanism should provide the least expensive way of

---

[22] Wilson, J. A., 'Adaptation to Uncertainty and Small Numbers Exchange: the New England Fresh Fish Market', *Bell Journal of Economics*, 11 (1980) 491, 503–4.

[23] National Consumer Council, *Buying Problems: Consumers, Unsatisfactory Goods and the Law* (London: National Consumer Council, 1984) 22.

ensuring adequate incentives for manufacturers and retailers to comply with the standard of efficient quality. Public regulation certainly has at its disposal fierce sanctions, which can ensure compliance with the standard. When breaches of the standards are detected by the inspectors, then the regulatory agency may be empowered to issue warnings, and to commence criminal proceedings. The escalating system of sanctions may lead ultimately to the compulsory withdrawal of products from the market or the exclusion of a particular business from the market altogether by means of a licensing system.[24] In practice, these strong sanctions will be held in reserve for persistent offenders, and lesser sanctions such as warnings or fines will be imposed in the first instance, as a type of signal that greater punishments will be imposed on recalcitrant manufacturers and retailers. The principal weakness of public enforcement is that the risk of being detected in breach of quality standards is fairly low owing to the limited resources granted to inspection. To render the incentive for compliance substantial, therefore, public regulation usually has to be in a position to impose deterrent levels of sanction when deviance is detected.

Compared to this range of sanctions, the threats offered by the private law system of liability to pay compensation for the cost of cure of defects appear minimal. Although monitoring by consumers may pick up a much greater number of defects than an inspection system, the sanction imposed by a court in the form of a liability rule provides little incentive to manufacturers and retailers to reduce defects in quality. We have already observed, however, that private law can produce some interesting alternative sanctions to the compensatory liability rule. For instance, the rejection of goods and the recovery of the price almost certainly loses a sale altogether, and the goods cannot subsequently be marketed (honestly) as new, thereby effectively losing all the profit element in that transaction for both retailer and manufacturer. The law can enhance the non-legal sanction of rejection of goods by lowering the threshold of quality defects that permit rejection.[25] A compulsory duty to repair faulty goods might also improve the incentives for compliance. An obligation might be placed upon the manufacturer to repair or replace any defective goods for a period of time after purchase, with this obligation enforceable by a court order of compulsory performance backed up by the threat of deterrent sanctions such as fines or *astreintes* (punitive damages).[26]

---

[24] Such a licensing system has been proposed for the sale of used cars, though safety issues are also present in that example: Office of Fair Trading, *Buying a Used Car—Consumers' Problems—A Consultative Paper* (London: 1979) ch. VII.

[25] Sale of Goods Act 1979, ss. 34–35A, as amended by Sale and Supply of Goods Act 1994 ss. 2–3.

[26] Reynolds, F., 'The Applicability of General Rules of Private Law to Consumer Disputes', in S. Anderman *et al.* (eds.), *Law and the Weaker Party* (London: Professional Books, 1982) ii. 93, 105, discussing Swedish consumer sales law.

Private ordering or self-regulation can also achieve a similar result by the consumer's purchase of an insurance policy. This policy recompenses the consumer for the costs of repair and replacement of a defective washing machine. The consumer therefore obtains a right to have the machine repaired and effective control over those repairs being carried out.

Although these new types of private law remedies for defects in quality might provide better incentives for compliance (at no additional administrative cost for the private law system of regulation), they may well still fall short of providing the kind of deterrent level sanction that supplies the appropriate level of incentive for compliance with an efficient standard of quality. The private law system therefore perhaps requires the innovation of the flexibility of a punitive damages measure for quality defects, in order to be able to adjust its sanction to provide sufficient incentive for manufacturers and retailers to achieve an efficient level of compliance with quality standards. A deterrent level of compensation which exceeds the actual loss to the consumer could be imposed.[27]

We have also observed that the private law system possesses certain structural weaknesses connected to the under-resourced nature of its system of enforcement. In this context of consumer transactions, the major problem is of course the reluctance of the consumer to incur the expense of litigation in order to obtain the small benefit of compensation or return of the price. In practice consumer redress for goods of poor quality operates almost entirely outside the legal system.[28] It is handled usually by complaints procedures of manufacturers and retailers, which differ in their likelihood of producing redress for the consumer. When third party adjudication becomes involved, this is also unlikely to be provided by an ordinary court. The consumer may have access to an ombudsman (more commonly in services), or the contract may provide for arbitration by an informal tribunal created by a trade association. In Chapter 14, we shall consider how these complaint mechanisms can be improved in order to achieve an adequate level of enforcement.

A final problem with the incentive system provided by private law regulation especially worth noting in this context concerns the ability of defendants to render themselves proof against judgement. The problem is not as severe here as in the context of claims for personal injuries in the absence of insurance,[29] for the level of compensation required by private law for defects in quality will usually be well within the means of the defendant business. Apart from the case of small retailers selling expensive

---

[27] There are some statutory examples; e.g. US, Uniform Consumer Credit Code, Art. 5.201 (adopted in many States) provides for punitive damages with a minimum and a maximum.

[28] National Consumer Council, n. 23 above; id., Seeking Civil Justice—A Survey of People's Needs and Experiences (London: National Consumer Council, 1995).

[29] Shavell, S., n. 15 above.

items, therefore, the major difficulty that is likely to arise is with sheltering behind the corporate veil by the frequent creation and dissolution of corporate entities, which leaves the consumer with no legal person against whom redress may be sought. This problem can perhaps be partially overcome by the expedient of expanding the range of liability to include manufacturers as well as retailers.

Contrary to the supposition of most consumers,[30] the doctrine of privity of contract (or the principle of relative effect) usually confines the plaintiff to a suit against the immediate retailer. At first sight, this restriction on the range of liability removes the incentive for the manufacturer to produce an efficient level of quality. The problem may be addressed by the possibility of liability rules along the chain of production. When the retailer becomes liable to the consumer for defective quality, then the retailer can pass on this cost by a claim against the manufacturer, and the manufacturer in turn passes on the cost to the component supplier. In this way, the liability is transferred, though only by adding to the administrative costs of private law liability. On the other hand, the retailer may be in a more powerful position than the consumer to threaten the use of non-legal sanctions, such as an unwillingness to stock a particular product in future, so that the liability rule has a powerful supplement. Indeed, the presence of non-legal sanctions may even raise the quality standard above an efficient level, for the retailer may insist upon superior performance and cosmetic standards than the average consumer would. But the privity rule is not cast in stone, and has been removed in some jurisdictions in order to enable a direct action between the consumer and the manufacturer for defective quality.[31] This result is often achieved also through private ordering in the form of manufacturer's guarantees, which in effect promise the cost of repairs directly to the consumer.

Conclusion

This investigation of the efficient form of regulation of product quality suggests that private law regulation possesses considerable capacities to achieve an efficiency standard, qualified by other distributive considerations.

---

[30] Cranston, R., *Regulating Business: Law and Consumer Agencies* (London: MacMillan, 1979) 58, quoting 'Product Liability', *Which?* (January, 1975) 5; id., *Consumers and the Law*, 2nd edn., (London: Weidenfeld and Nicholson, 1984) 146.

[31] Cranston, R., n. 30 above, 146–7, gives examples of the reversal of the privity rule in this context in Australia and California. In the USA, a patchwork of legislation and developments in the common law have been reversing the privity rule in respect of claims for pure economic loss in respect of claims for defects in quality against manufacturers: e.g. *Morrow v New Moon Homes, Inc.* 548 P.2d 279 (1976) (Supreme Court of Alaska); Virginia Code Ann. S.8–654.3 (Supp. 1964); Uniform Commercial Code s. 2–318, Alternative C.

In general, private law also offers a less costly mode of regulation than public regulation. In order to maximize its capacity to regulate quality, however, private law needs to adopt a reflexive strategy with respect to industrial self-regulation, so that it derives its quality standards from the sectoral product specifications and quality assurance processes. Whilst endorsing these standards, however, private law must retain the capacity to supervise these standards in order to redress the predictable problems of self-regulation such as the failure to take into account externalities. At the same time, private law needs to develop its capacity to provide a flexible range of remedies that extend beyond liability to pay a cost of cure measure of damages. Such remedies might include a strong rejection remedy for consumers, the potential to claim punitive damages against manufacturers of defective products, and injunctions against placing particular products on the market.

13

Government by Contract

In providing services to the public, the modern state has the choice between either using its own organization and employees or entering into contractual relations with external organizations for the supply of the service. The balance between these methods has varied, but the state has always purchased some services from independent private businesses. As part of a drive to improve the efficiency and effectiveness of government services in recent years, however, there has been a marked shift towards experimentation with forms of contractual relations. This phenomenon has occurred in most Western style of governments, but to some extent has been led by the United Kingdom, from where I shall take most of my illustrations.[1]

The simple idea behind government by contract is that formal agreements render explicit the required performance standards and the acceptable level of costs, so that performance can be monitored, and those responsible for default can be held accountable. The state thus appropriates the meaning of contractual relations described in Chapter 2, by choosing to narrow the obligations to specific tasks and to measure and value performance in monetary terms. Government through contracts therefore represents a change in the culture of public administration, from a stance of benevolent and responsive hierarchy to one of precise, delimited, delivery of efficient services.

This contractual culture in government appears in a variety of forms, ranging from almost ordinary commercial contracts to mere contractual metaphors that describe the relations between different parts of the government's own organization. The closest relations to commercial contracts occur when the state purchases supplies or services from a private sector business. Although the state has for centuries used external contractors for such tasks as road-building, construction, and armaments, this use of commercial contracts can be extended to all government functions, including the supply of management services to government and social services to the public. A similar degree of approximation to commercial contracts occurs through 'franchising' or in Civil Law countries 'concessions'.[2] Here the state claims a basic property right to control the economic

---

[1] Harden, I., *The Contracting State* (Milton Keynes: Open University Press, 1992).

[2] Daintith, T., 'Regulation', *International Encyclopedia of Comparative Law*, (1995) xvii, ch. 10, 53.

activity, such as television or railways, but grants through contract the right to supply such a service for a limited period of time to a private business. The terms of the contract, the franchise, contain most of the detailed regulation for the public provision of the service, so that public regulation assumes the form of self-regulation through contract. The process of 'market testing' involves the selection of a government task which can be put out to tender with a view to purchasing performance from the cheapest provider.[3] The contract may be won either by an external private business or by the existing public sectors workers re-organized within a new autonomous operational unit. When the public sector unit wins the contract, some modifications to the ordinary commercial contract become necessary. A more innovative management technique has been to revise the internal structures of the public admin-istration, so that the provision of services occurs through a 'quasi-market' between decentralized suppliers and purchaser departments within government. For example, an agency may be hived off from its parent government department, and under a 'Framework Document' have its functions, goals, and budget defined, and then its performance can be monitored by the parent department. This 'quasi-market' does not appar-ently produce legally enforceable contracts, since both parties are part of the same legal entity, but in many other respects the administrative relation mirrors a commercial contract.[4]

The principal issue presented to the legal system by these contractual relations is whether the legal discourse of the private law of contract should provide the applicable sub-system of regulation, or whether the special character of government contracts requires the introduction of a public law perspective that emphasizes such values as procedural fair-ness, individual inalienable rights, the rational conduct of government, and the importance of collective interests and public goods.[5] The system of public law has traditionally refrained from supervising government contracts through the process of judicial review, except to determine whether or not the power to enter a binding contract was within the powers of the state agency concerned. Even in Civil Law systems which possess a special public law jurisdiction such as France, the legal regula-tion of such contracts usually tracks closely the ordinary private law. But private law regulation may not prove adequate to address such matters as abuse of the monopoly power of the state and the need to protect the interests of third parties who are the public for whom the services are

---

[3] Jenkinson, T., and Mayer, C., 'The Assessment: Contracts and Competition', *Oxford Review of Economic Policy* 12(4) (1997) 1.
[4] Freedland, M., 'Government by Contract and Public Law', *Public Law* (1994) 86.
[5] Ibid.

provided.[6] More fundamentally, we can detect considerable structural problems in devising adequate self-regulation of contractual relations for the purpose of the provision of public services.

Public Services and the Market Mechanism

Although the most significant change in the presentation of government policies for the provision of services has been an insistence upon using markets and contracts as much as possible, it is important to recognize the limitations of this transition. Contracts involved in the provision of public services retain distinct characteristics, which separate them from ordinary commercial and consumer transactions.

The most attractive feature of markets is the way in which purchasers can choose between products and services according to their needs, price, and quality. The market mechanism tends to ensure that goods and services of the desired type and costs are produced in the right quantity. Legal regulation of these markets relies heavily upon self-regulation and self-enforcement, which add to the flexibility and responsiveness of markets. When this model of the market mechanism is applied to the government's provision of services, however, we encounter a structural problem.

In a government contract with an external provider, the government determines what service or goods are required. Owing to its virtual monopoly demand for various kinds of services, such as prisons, roads, and armaments, the government has the power to determine the content of the self-regulation contained in the contract. The terms of the standard form contract therefore not only settle the respective obligations of the parties, but also fix the content of the public service to be provided in much the same way as this function was achieved formerly by administrative rules, circulars, and decisions. The difference between self-regulation through contracts and self-regulation through administrative rules seems negligible. The government presents itself as a customer for services to be provided through a contract, but in reality it chooses merely to provide those services to the public through an agent, the external contractor. But in creating a market to supply the public service, the government uses the device of standard contractual terms to regulate how that market operates.[7]

The true assimilation of a market mechanism for the provision of public services requires the consumer of the services, the general public, to be

---

[6] Fredman, S., and Morris, G., 'The Costs of Exclusivity: Public and Private Re-examined', *Public Law* (1994) 69; Harlow, C., and Rawlings, R., *Law and Administration*, 2nd edn, (London: Butterworths, 1997), 138–41.

[7] Daintith, T. 'Regulation by Contract: the New Prerogative', *Current Legal Problems* (1979) 41.

empowered to participate in self-regulation and self-enforcement. In other words, the public needs to be able to participate in setting the standards for the provision of services, and to be able to apply legal and non-legal sanctions in order to ensure compliance with those standards. Under the ordinary private law of contracts, however, the citizen is not a party to government contracts, and therefore has no legal right either to negotiate the terms of the agreement or to enforce compliance with its terms. The only avenue for challenge will be one of judicial review in order to test whether the minister, government agency, or regulator has entered into contracts within the scope of its powers.[8] Nor are there satisfactory non-legal sanctions available to the citizen. The threat not to use a dirty hospital, to refuse to eat school dinners, to avoid an unreliable public transport system is hardly likely to affect the contractor's performance. At best, the citizen has the political power to vote for a change of government and to try to affect performance standards through adverse publicity.

One potential solution to the problem of making the provision of public services function in ways more like a market mechanism has been developed in the Citizens Charter programme in the UK.[9] Here there is a commitment to regular consultation with representatives of the consumers of the service in order to set standards. It would also be consistent with this policy to permit consumers of the service to bring claims for breach of these standards. In the Charter programme so far, however, these enforcement rights have been confined to the ability to register complaints with regulatory watchdogs, who have the possibility of awarding some financial compensation in a few instances such as rail services. The citizen as consumer has not been given the legal right to sue either for breach of the Charter standards or for breach of the terms of contracts which implement those standards through the agency of an external contractor. This programme therefore balks at assimilating public services with the market mechanism, preferring instead to preserve largely intact the government's unilateral power to determine both standards and compliance.

A much more powerful strategy for assimilating public services to the market mechanism uses an independent regulatory agency that supervises the direct provision of services to the public by private businesses. In the case of utilities such as gas, electricity, and water, for instance, the suppliers become private businesses through the technique of privatization. These businesses enter into contracts with customers, but a regulatory agency controls the terms of these contracts in respect of price and quality of service. The mission of the regulatory agency is to ensure an efficient and

---

[8] *R v Director of Passenger Rail Franchising, ex p Save Our Railways*, *The Independent*, 20 December 1995.

[9] Scott, C., and Barron, A., 'The Citizens' Charter Programme', *Modern Law Review* 55 (1992) 526.

reliable supply of the utility, at the least cost to the consumer. The regulator has the power to set standards, to monitor compliance, and to impose sanctions for breach of the standards. The need for a regulator springs in part from the monopoly position of many providers of utilities. But in addition, the regulator addresses the structural weakness of private law enforcement mechanisms under which an individual consumer would usually lack the resources to mount an effective legal challenge to defaults by a utility.

The price of introducing a regulator is that the market mechanism is heavily modified, for the regulator can usually insist unilaterally upon particular standards and controls the enforcement mechanisms. Indeed, this leads to doubts about whether or not the consumer enters into a legally binding contract at all with the utility, since all the terms may have been determined by negotiation between the regulator and the utility, leaving the consumer with merely information about the rules under which the service will be provided.[10] At the same time, the utility can usually control to a considerable extent the supply of information on which the regulator acts, so there is no guarantee that the regulatory regime operates in the best interests of the consumer.

The presence of the regulatory regime changes, however, the meaning of these contracts. The atomization which is characteristic of ordinary contractual relations is replaced by a collective perspective on the terms of the relations between provider and customer. As a result, the legal system in its observation of these contractual relations becomes unsure whether the private law of contract provides the appropriate regulatory scheme. A form of public law control such as judicial review of the action of the regulator in determining the content and interpretation of the contract becomes attractive as a method for testing the rational exercise of the regulator's powers. This power of review enables the court to respond to the public interest dimension of the dispute, whereas the contractual framework confines it to an assessment of whether any explicit undertakings by the regulator or the commercial operator have been broken. If a private law analysis is applied, then it may be possible to introduce the public law perspective through the back door by means of implied terms and controls over harsh terms justified by reference to the regulatory context. This technique was recognized as a possibility by the Court of Appeal in the context of a dispute between a telephone company and a commercial customer in order to provide a basis for challenging the express contractual term which entitled the telephone company to terminate any

---

[10] *Norweb v Dixon* [1995] 3 All ER 952, finding electricity supply to be non-contractual, but each utility has to be examined separately: Harden, I., n. 1 above, 38–41; Scott, C., 'The Juridification of Relations in the UK Utilities Sector', in J. Black, *et al.* (eds.), *Commercial Regulation and Judicial Review* (Oxford: Hart Publishing, 1998) 19, 50.

service by one month's notice.[11] The insertion of public standards into the legal reasoning with respect to these contracts reveals how the ordinary private law that defers to the self-regulation of the parties becomes inappropriate as a form of regulation of the commercial relations of these public utilities, because these commercial relations have been constituted within a confined space set by considerations of the public interest. The meaning of these contractual relations differs fundamentally from ordinary commercial transactions, so that if private law regulation is adopted as the legal framework of analysis, it has to achieve a novel differentiation in its classification system that permits the reinsertion of public interest standards into its reasoning.

The Problem of Co-operation

The government cannot escape political accountability to the public for the provision of services by merely entering into contracts which are designed to provide the required level of service. The need to remain responsive to public needs leads governments to seek to obtain in their contracts both flexibility in redefining the tasks to be performed and a discretionary power to monitor and direct the performance of the external contractor. An example in a local government authority's contract for grounds maintenance contained the following discretionary powers to require the contractor to:

omit or cease to provide any part of the service for such period as the Authorising Officer may determine; provide the service or any part thereof in such manner as the Authorising Officer may reasonably require; provide such services additional to the service as the Authorising Officer may reasonably require, provided that such services shall be the same as or similar to the service; provide at any time or at any location such emergency services as are required by the Authorising Officer; permanently to vary the service to be provided at any location.[12]

In addition, many large contracts involve a high degree of uncertainty with respect to the performance required even from the outset. In a contract to design and build an aircraft, for instance, the plans are likely to evolve during performance. Government contracts therefore tend to be incomplete by design, with institutional configurations of hierarchy in

---

[11] *Timeload Ltd v British Telecommunications Plc* [1995] EMLR 459, CA. Scott, C., n. 10 above, 19, 46–49.

[12] Walsh, K., *et al.*, 'Contracts for Public Services: A Comparative Perspective', in D. Campbell and P. Vincent-Jones (eds.), *Contract and Economic Organisation* (Aldershot: Dartmouth, 1996) 212, 222.

order to provide a mechanism to supplement and adapt the contractual undertakings.

This contractual form of institutional hierarchy creates a tension with the policy objective of market testing. Competitive contract tendering can control costs and provoke improvements in efficiency, provided that the tasks to be performed can be specified in advance. Task specificity permits pricing and market comparisons to be drawn. When the task becomes subject to discretionary adjustments, however, the pricing mechanism functions less satisfactorily, for the bidders have to include the uncertain cost of responses to adaptations. In order to ensure responsiveness to policy considerations, it is normal practice for the UK Government to include in its contracts a power of unilateral variation, as in the standard term that the public authority has the right 'to alter from time to time' the specifications and 'as from a date and to the extent specified by the Authority after consultation, where appropriate, with the Contractor on the effect of such proposed alterations, the Articles shall be in accordance with the . . . specifications, plans, drawings or other documents as so altered.'[13] Unless the contractual relation contains further incentives to support co-operation by the external contractor, the contractual framework contains a tension which is bound to provoke frequent disputes.

In the past, government contracts in the UK were frequently negotiated on a costs plus basis in order to resolve this problem of co-operation. The contractor received costs of performance plus a percentage for profit. Even in fixed price contracts, the standard terms normally contain price variations in respect of rates of wages paid by the contractor and prices of materials acquired for the purposes of the contract.[14] This method of price variation that provides an incentive to co-operate with alterations in contractual specifications has been increasingly discredited, because it provides insufficient incentive to keep total costs under control. But in the absence of such price variability, the external contractor will naturally resist alterations in contractual specifications which raise costs, even though the contract may contain mechanisms which permit unilateral alterations. We therefore discover a structural problem with government contracts, for the fixed price provides an incentive not to co-operate, even though responsiveness to alterations in conditions is a vital part of the government's objectives.

This structural problem has been partially addressed in the UK by a governance structure established by an agreement in 1968 between the government and the Confederation of British Industry (a representative organization of business).[15] The agreement establishes a Review Board for

---

[13] Turpin, C., *Government Procurement and Contracts* (Harlow: Longman, 1989), 189.
[14] Ibid. 168.
[15] The text of the memorandum of agreement is reprinted in Turpin, C., n. 13 above, 278–87.

Government Contracts which can resolve disputes about price, when the price payable under the contract was based upon a formula relating to costs and percentage profits. The Board can consider instances where there was a 10 per cent difference or more between the estimated and actual costs of performance, or where the achievement of a fair and reasonable price was frustrated because the information on which it was based has proved to be inaccurate or incomplete. This arrangement creates a mechanism for retrospective price variations in the light of variations and better information which is by implication inserted as a term into contracts containing major elements of uncertainty regarding the required performance. Although the Review Board is rarely called upon to reach a determination, (only eight cases between 1969 and 1986),[16] its presence plainly influences the conduct of the parties towards settlements of price variations, so that 'excessive profits' may be clawed back routinely by government and contractors can obtain retrospective price increases.

A significant feature of this governance structure is the way in which it removes private law regulation of major government contracts. The traditional private law stance of holding the parties to their agreement had to be replaced by an alternative dispute mechanism designed to solve a problem of co-operation. The mechanism supplies a neutral third party to impose price adjustments in the light of alterations in the required performance and the true costs of performance. The legal system could have supplied a solution to the problem of co-operation either by the creation of a separate jurisdiction of administrative courts empowered to impose retrospective price adjustments, as in France, or by developing a power of judicial revision of price terms in government contracts, as has occurred to a limited extent in the US federal courts.[17] In the absence of these possibilities, it is extremely rare for government contracts to be litigated in the ordinary courts in the UK. This reluctance to litigate must be explained in part by the unwillingness of the parties to damage long-term business relations by aggressive litigation, and also in part by the routine insertion of arbitration clauses in the standard form contracts. But more fundamentally this reluctance indicates that the normative framework supplied by the contract itself is incompatible with the way in which the traditional private law thinks about contractual undertakings.

The underlying problem here is that the meaning of contractual relations has to be distorted in order to serve as an instrument of government. Selznick perceived that contract can never provide an adequate articulation of the nature of associations with a structure of government, an observation that applies both to public and private associations:

---

[16] The text of the memorandum of agreement is reprinted in Turpin, C., n. 13 above, 179.
[17] *National Presto Industries, Inc. v United States,* 338 F.2d 99 (1964).

The authority of an agent may be as narrowly defined as the principal may wish, but governmental authority has an irreducibly comprehensive character. That is so because government has inherent responsibility, and at least a minimum of implied authority, to protect the welfare of the corporate group, taking account of its changing circumstances and adaptive needs. As a corollary, there is always some open-endedness in a government's claim upon the commitments of citizens or members.

For these reasons, the governmental model is difficult to square with the premises of the purposive contract. There may be mutuality, consensus, and limited commitment in a politically organized community. But the mutuality is not evenly balanced, the consensus is not specific, the commitments are, at best, only relatively limited.[18]

The Problem of Quality

The government must also address problems of satisfactory quality in the performance of contracts as part of its political accountability. In the absence of direct hierarchical control over performance by the contractor, the contract has to achieve quality by setting detailed standards in the terms of the contract and establishing appropriate incentive systems. The incentive system provides the contractor with an additional reward, or at least protects the government contractor against termination of the business, provided that it achieves compliance with the quality standards specified by the contract. In the absence of such incentive systems, there must be a suspicion that contractors will invariably be tempted to cut costs and chisel on quality once the contract has been awarded.[19]

Government contracts, therefore, typically contain extensive specifications of quality in the form of performance indicators running for hundreds of pages.[20]

Contracts for local authority services are typically extremely detailed, involving sometimes hundreds of pages of documentation. The number of contract conditions is also large, often 50 or more. The service to be provided is normally defined in input terms, though, as experience is gained, there is more focus on outputs.[21]

It is easier, for instance, to define how many times a week a street should be swept than to describe the level of cleanliness and tidiness that should

---

[18] Selznick, Philip, *Law, Society and Industrial Justice*, (New York; Russell Sage Foundation, 1969), 61.

[19] Dnes, A., and Rickman, N., 'Contracts for Legal Aid: A Critical Discussion of Government Policy Proposals', *European Journal of Law and Economics* 5 (1998) 247.

[20] Vincent-Jones, P., and Harries, A., 'Limits of Contract in Internal CCT Transactions: A Comparative Study of Buildings Cleaning and Refuse Collection in "Northern Metropolitan"', in D. Campbell and P. Vincent-Jones (eds.), n. 12 above, 180, 188.

[21] Walsh, K., *et al.*, n. 12 above, 220.

be achieved. In a contract for the provision of residential care a central and vital term was 'Staff should treat residents in a way which maintains their dignity, individual identity and self-respect.' This clause defines the appropriate output, but it is obviously hard to determine when the clause has been broken. The temptation then arises to provide greater specificity, such as determining a staff–patient ratio and agreeing rules on how the nursing home should be run. This detail, of course, cannot ever provide a complete specification of quality and performance standards. Perhaps the story of the contract for an aircraft that could not fly because that was not an express technical specification is apocryphal, but the general problem of incompleteness of contractual self-regulation can never be solved entirely by lengthy terms. The alternative of relying upon customary market standards as default rules appears to be often unavailable in this context due to the unfamiliarity of this type of transaction and the absence of developed regulatory models of default rules. No doubt this detailed specification increases the transaction costs of outsourcing compared to internal hierarchical controls, and this may prove a hidden cost which reduces the savings to be achieved by external contracting. In this respect, therefore, government by contract runs into the same impasse as direct public regulation in seeking to devise precise measures of the desired broad outcomes.[22]

Having attempted to set detailed quality standards, the government authority must then monitor performance and punish default. There seems to be a distinct lack of non-legal sanctions to discourage default. Although the government authority might terminate the contract for serious breach, the problem of quality is normally one of minor defects and chiselling, and in any case a change of contractor involves substantial costs and delays. One approach used extensively by local authorities is to allocate penalty points for minor failures to comply with the quality standard, and to reduce payment according to the number of accrued points. These provisions therefore construct a self-enforcing sanction, though there are doubts upon the validity of these penalty provisions under private law.[23] Another technique employed is to construct a performance bond, that is, a form of security provided by a bank's promise to pay compensation for defects in performance, which the local government authority may claim directly from the bank. But this security cannot assist much in securing quality, since the bond can only be claimed on proof of loss, which is hard to establish in these cases of poor performance of a public service. There is some evidence from surveys that these constructed non-legal sanctions are

---

[22] Braithwaite, J., and Braithwaite V., 'The Politics of Legalism: Rules versus Standard in Nursing-Home Regulation', *Social and Legal Studies* 4 (1995) 307.
[23] Walsh, K., *et al.*, n. 12 above, 223.

rarely employed, because to do so would undermine the co-operative relations between the parties which are vital to the public authority in securing the necessary flexibility in providing services to the public.[24]

Lawyers as planners pay great attention to the construction of non-legal sanctions and security in these contexts, because it is far from clear that the private law system of remedies offers any substantial sanctions against breach of quality standards. For a remedy of compensation, the courts normally require the aggrieved party to prove losses. Failure to comply with a quality standard may in fact lead to no losses, or, if there are losses then they will be in the form of psychological injury such as dissatisfaction with the service experienced by third parties, that is, the citizens who receive the services. An award of damages therefore encounters two major doctrinal obstacles: a reluctance to compensate non-pecuniary losses such as injury to feelings or anger provoked by breach of contract,[25] and the conceptual obstacle that the government as plaintiff has not suffered the loss, but rather the citizens who receive the service have the grievance.[26] The precision of the contract in specifying in detail the measurements of the service to be provided does create the possibility of arguing that compensation should be awarded by reference to the savings of the contractor by not complying with the requirements. For example, the breach of the contract to provide a fire service in New Orleans caused by hiring fewer firemen than specified in the contract led to an unsuccessful claim for damages measured by reference to the saving on salaries.[27] Private law tends to resist such claims for damages for breach of contract based upon the profits earned by the party in breach,[28] because they violate the principle that damages should compensate for the plaintiff's loss, and they tend to remove the wealth maximizing incentive to breach contracts when better economic opportunities are presented. The effect of these rules is to deprive the government as a plaintiff in a breach of contract suit of the ability to impose a sanction of a substantial claim for damages on the contractor for deviation from specific measurable requirements under the contract.

In the private industry sector, this problem of controlling the quality of performance has been addressed by the technique of controlling the management system of the supplier, so that it complies with the standards of Total Quality Management. For this control over management systems

---

[24] Ibid. 224.

[25] *Addis v Gramophone Co Ltd* [1909] AC 488, HL. There are exceptions that do not appear to extend this far: *Jarvis v Swans Tours Ltd* [1973] QB 233, [1973] 1 All ER 71, CA.

[26] There are only limited possibilities for recovery of damages for another's loss: *Jackson v Horizon Holidays* [1975] 3 All ER 92, [1975] 1 WLR 1468, CA.

[27] *City of New Orleans v Firemen's Charitable Association*, 9 So. 486 (1891).

[28] *Surrey County Council v Brodero Homes Ltd* [1993] 3 All ER 705, [1993] 1 WLR 1361, CA.

to be worthwhile in view of its added costs, however, the private sector contractual relations consciously construct a long-term business relation between the parties, known as a 'supplier partnership', which is designed to augment trust, protect against the loss of the investments in management systems, and provide economic incentives for compliance.[29] The supplier partnership, however, represents a long-term commitment often with a sole supplier of a component, which removes the possibility of frequent market testing on price. Under the Japanese system on which these supplier relations have been modelled, the formal contracts may be for a fixed period of time, but both parties expect the relation to be indefinite in duration.[30] Private sector businesses have therefore made the strategic decision to reduce competition on price in order to obtain reliable assurances of quality in performance of contracts. The assurances of quality from the supplier become more reliable in part due to compliance with the management system designed to guarantee good quality and in part to the presence of the substantial non-legal sanction of withdrawal from the long-term relation despite extensive sunk investments.[31] Although the government can modify its competitive tendering procedures in order to require bidders to have Total Quality Management systems (or their equivalent) in place, the insistence upon frequent market testing may obstruct the government from achieving the gains in quality afforded by long-term partnerships.

The existence of single supplier relations was discarded by government because of a suspicion that it eliminated price competition and raised costs. Such close, interdependent relations seemed to be incompatible with the idea of market testing. In its recent policy statements on procurement, however, the need to combine co-operation with competition for the purpose of continuous improvements in quality has been acknowledged.[32] The catch phrase is 'value for money', which obscures the tension between competitive prices and reliable assurances of quality in performance.

The structural problem here is that reliable assurance of quality in performance depends ultimately not on contract terms but on trust and non-legal sanctions. Relations of trust and powerful non-legal sanctions depend upon the establishment of long-term business relations and the confinement of competition to a known and trusted 'procurement commu-

---

[29] Collins, H., 'Quality Assurance in Subcontracting', in S. Deakin and J. Mitchie (eds.), *Contracts, Co-operation, and Competition* (Oxford: Oxford University Press, 1997) 285.

[30] Sako, M., *Prices, Quality and Trust: Inter-Firm Relations in Britain and Japan* (Cambridge: Cambridge University Press, 1992) 159, 170.

[31] Taylor, C. R., and Wiggins, S. N., 'Competition or Compensation: Supplier Incentives Under the American and Japanese Subcontracting Systems', *American Economic Review* 87 (1997) 598.

[32] White Paper, *Setting New Standards: A Strategy for Government Procurement*, Cm 2840 (London: HMSO, 1995), 1.

nity' of contractors.[33] These necessary conditions will be subverted by the policy of seeking to maximize competition through market testing.

The need for a governance structure and detailed monitoring in order to achieve co-operation and quality seems to lead towards the creation of conflictual relations between government and external contractors. This structural tension in government contracts results in many costly disputes between the parties, unless the parties can discover long-term economic interests to be derived from the preservation of a business relation.[34]

Quasi-Contract in Government

The contracts used as a management device within government in order to improve efficiency do not constitute legally binding agreements. Instead, the contractual form for expressing the administrative relation is designed to appropriate the meaning of contractual relations as a framework of reference by which the parties should orient their conduct. The purpose of moving from bureaucratic regulation towards a contractual framework is to obtain transparency in the tasks to be performed, to control the costs of the administrative operation, and to help to make the operational unit accountable for its expenditure and performance. If problems arise with these contracts, then the difficulty can be addressed by further administrative measures. The use of contracts should therefore be regarded as one technique used normally in combination with others such as audits, inspections, and grievance procedures through which one part of government seeks to regulate another.[35]

The metaphor of contract can be employed both within the organization of government and in the relations between government and citizens. In the case of the former, the state separates out distinct operational units, which then enter into formal written undertakings. In the National Health Service, for instance, different units of the system such as Hospital Trusts, General Practice partnerships, and Health Authorities, may enter agreements for the supply of a quantity of a particular aspect of medical care at a particular cost. This agreement then fixes the respective obligations of the different organizational units. Breach of the agreement, however, does not give rise to a private law action for compensation, but rather there is an

---

[33] Turpin, C., n. 13 above, 259.

[34] Vincent-Jones, P., 'Hybrid Organization, Contractual Governance, and Compulsory Competitive Tendering in the Provision of Local Authority Services', in S. Deakin and J. Michie (eds.), n. 29 above, 143; Vincent-Jones, P., 'The Limits of Contractual Order in Public Sector Transactions', *Legal Studies* 14 (1994) 364.

[35] Hood, C., *et al.*, 'Regulation Inside Government: Where New Public Management Meets the Audit Explosion' *Public Money and Management* (1998) 61.

administrative system for the resolution of disputes.[36] A similar quasi-contractual relation applies between local government authorities and their departments that win contracts to provide services under the competitive contract tendering system.[37] The justification for the exclusion of private law regulation is usually simply that the costs of litigation between organizational units should be avoided, though presumably the administrative costs of alternative dispute resolution are also not negligible.

The most recent deployment of the contractual metaphor as an instrument of bureaucratic control has occurred in the relation between different departments of central government in the UK. The Treasury department, which allocates resources to the other departments such as health, education, and defence, has insisted that the award of additional resources should be attached to 'contractual' commitments to comply with efficiency and quality targets, and also the implementation of particular agreed policy objectives, such as the reduction of waiting time for hospital treatment and the reduction of class sizes in primary schools.

Each department has reached a public service agreement with the Treasury, effectively a contract with the Treasury for the renewal of public services. It is a contract that in each service area requires reform in return for investment. So the new contract sets down the new departmental objectives and targets that have to be met, the stages by which they will be met, how departments intend to allocate resources to achieve these targets and the process that will monitor results. The Prime Minister has decided that this continuous scrutiny and audit will be overseen by a Cabinet committee, continuing the work of the existing public spending committee, and money will be released only if departments keep to their plans.[38]

Under this system of accountability, the non-legal sanction of withholding resources from departments can provide the sanction for breach of contract, but ministers have agreed a private system of adjudication, a cabinet committee, in order to determine whether the terms of the contract have been breached. This governance structure prevents opportunist re-negotiation of the contract by the Treasury. The use of the contractual metaphor signifies the narrowing of the criteria of measurement of the performance of ministers, so that achievement of negotiated performance targets becomes the official measure of success.

In the quasi-contractual relations between government and citizens, there is a similar exclusion of private law regulation. The objective of translating administrative regulation into contracts here remains in part one of imposing a discipline upon the bureaucracy to be precise about its

---

[36] National Health Service and Community Care Act 1990, s. 4.
[37] Vincent-Jones, P., n. 34 above.
[38] Gordon Brown, MP, Chancellor of the Exchequer addressing Parliament, *The Guardian*, Wednesday July 15 1998, p. 9.

obligations and their costs. In addition, by requiring the citizen to sign a written document, the state tries to ensure that the citizen becomes aware of his or her reciprocal obligations and the conditions under which assistance will be granted. For example, in order to be able to claim a job seekers allowance (formerly known as unemployment benefit), the agency can require the claimant to sign a document which renders explicit the details of the requirement that the applicant should be actively seeking employment.[39] The 'Job Seekers Agreement' might specify, for example, that the claimant should make a certain number of job applications over a period of time and attend any job interviews offered by potential employers. Disputes over the requirements and compliance with the requirements are referred merely to administrative tribunals within the government agency. The merits of the introduction of the contractual metaphor in this context are that, first, it forces the official to be specific about the actions required under the general clause of 'actively seeking employment', and secondly, it provides the opportunity for the applicant to negotiate about the details of this requirement in order to render them practicable in the circumstances. There arises a suspicion, of course, that the opportunities for negotiation will be slight, and that the requirements will be offered like an adhesion contract on a take it or leave it basis.[40]

The exclusion of private law regulation from these agreements may save legal costs, but the question arises whether administrative enforcement provides a sufficient sanction for these quasi-contracts to achieve their purposes. Private law sanctions are generally too weak to coerce performance, but they have two important effects that we have noticed. First, they help to make the commitment to the precise obligations undertaken more credible, and secondly, they provide an incentive to plan the transaction carefully in advance. Once the threat of a private law sanction is removed, the question is whether the administrative resolution of the dispute can have the same effects. These effects are certainly desired from the appropriation of the contractual metaphor, for the aim is to encourage organizational units to become careful to control their commitments and the associated costs, and to hold them responsible for deviations from their undertakings.

There is evidence from the contracts used within the UK National Health Service that these contracts lack clarity about the allocation of risk and the quality of performance expected.[41] These details of contractual planning may be absent owing to the transactions costs involved. But the reluctance to incur these transaction costs may be due in turn to the

---

[39] Jobseekers' Act 1995, ss. 1, 9.
[40] Fulbrook, J., 'The Jobseekers Act 1995: Consolidation with a Sting of Contractual Compliance', *Industrial Law Journal* 24 (1995) 395.
[41] Allen, P., 'Contracts in the National Health Service Internal Market', *Modern Law Review* 58 (1995) 321; Walsh, K., *et al.*, n. 12 above, 229.

absence of risk for which planning is necessary. If the administrative system of the Health Service makes retrospective adjustments to risk allocation during performance of the contract by varying the terms of the contract, then the incentive to plan with precision is removed. Similarly, with respect to the monitoring of the quality of the performance, if again the central administration continues to perform this function of standard setting and monitoring, then these costs of ensuring contract compliance can be avoided. The central administration retains these powers, of course, in order to ensure the responsiveness of the health service to public needs. The consequence is that this absence of detailed contractual provision on risk and quality tends to undermine the utility of contracts as a management device, for difficult questions of costs, risk allocation, and monitoring of quality can thereby be avoided. It may follow from this argument that these fictional contracts can rarely achieve the management objectives for which they are designed. Unless they become true commercial contracts subject to private law regulation, then they merely draw attention to some aspects of costs without compelling a more comprehensive assessment of costs, risks, and quality.

The employment of the metaphor of contract in public administration should therefore be understood as an appropriation of some aspects of the meaning of contract for the purpose of rendering the operations of the administration more transparent and potentially more accountable. By inserting the discourse of contract into bureaucratic relations, the parties are induced to provide more articulate descriptions of their requirements and to discover the costs of these requirements. In a context such as the National Health Service where rationing of health care is essential to control the total cost, the information produced by contractual practices can be monitored and used by central government for the purposes of steering the distribution of services. The price of acquiring this information includes the transactions costs of formulating and monitoring performance of contracts, but also, perhaps more importantly, the costs of obstructions to co-operation, flexibility, and innovation which the contractual valuation of conduct tends to introduce into social and economic relations. These costs would only be increased by the introduction of legal enforceability, with a consequent damage inflicted on the public service, and probably little further valuable information would be produced for the purposes of central control of the bureaucratic system. The utility of contractualization in public administration therefore has severe limitations.

Conclusion

In pursuing their objectives, governments have been attracted to contracts as a mechanism for the provision of services to the public, because contracts appear to combine the virtues of efficiency and transparency. Our observations of this practice have pointed to several structural problems that prevent the realization of these virtues. The need to preserve political responsibility for the outcomes of public services drives governments to balk at the full operation of the market mechanism for the setting of standards, and to refuse to make precise commitments about their requirements with contractors. As a consequence, the utility of contracts for achieving the efficient delivery of public services becomes significantly diminished. Thus we have doubted whether any worthwhile gains will be achieved by the insertion of contracts into public services.

The underlying problem here may be described as a special variant on the competing norms of rational contractual behaviour. Instead of the preservation of the requisite trust in the long-term business relation, the primary normative orientation of government remains its political responsibility to ensure the provision of satisfactory services to the public. The dominance of this normative orientation systematically undermines the attempt to restrict the normative orientation to the deal (value for money) and the contract (the precise undertakings of the contractual documents). In other words, the contractual frame of reference thinks about the provision of a public service in ways which create fixed entitlements and obligations, whereas in the last resort the government must always give priority to the normative framework of conformity to its political responsibilities and commitments. The use of contracts as an instrument of government tries to reverse these priorities for the sake of efficiency and transparency, but in so doing the practice creates considerable tensions which become revealed in the structural impediments to the achievement of co-operation and quality through contracts.

This tension between normative frameworks leads to considerable problems for the evolution of an appropriate regulatory capacity. In our earlier discussions of private law regulation of business transactions, my argument was that to provide the necessary support for the construction of markets and contracts, private law had to adopt a contextual approach which embraced the three normative dimensions of the business relation, the economic deal, and the contract. This task for regulation was difficult, because private law tends to be fixed upon the contractual framework of entitlements in the planning documents, but we noticed many ways in which contextualization could occur. The long-term business relation and the economic deal could be inserted, for instance, into the contractual framework by means of interpretation or supplementary terms of the contract. The task for regulating government contracts is similar in that it requires contextualization, but the problem is greater, because the dominant normative context of political responsibility tends not merely to qualify contractual commitments, but to require them to be overridden and rejected by mandatory standards that protect public interests. In adjudicating this collision between normative contexts, the courts need to develop further the capacity of legal reasoning to shape the principles of regulation in the light of the consequences of the implementation of government policy through contracts. A traditional private law approach of enforcing the planning documents with regard to the social consequences of so doing becomes even more plainly unsatisfactory in the case of government contracts, which themselves represent the implementation of policy through self-regulation.

14
Dispute Settlement

Disputes arising in connection with contracts take a bewildering variety of forms. If we adopt a broad concept of dispute, so that it includes all kinds of grievances and disagreements, as well as more formal claims and counter-claims, then we can usefully distinguish between three broad categories. The most numerous category of contractual dispute consists of the count-less dissatisfactions experienced by consumers with shoddy goods and services. A smaller number of disputes, though by far the largest category that enters the legal system, consists of claims for sums of money owed. The third category, which is probably tiny in comparison with the other two, though the sums of money at stake are likely to be far greater, consists of commercial disputes about the proper performance of contractual obligations. These three types of dispute present rather different challenges for regulation due to their variety in terms of numbers, character of the parties, the sums of money at stake, the use of lawyers, the likelihood of the use of the legal system, and the complexity of the dispute.

Regulation of contractual disputes also requires the articulation of its purpose or policy. The conventional legal view holds that the purpose of regulation should be to provide a reliable method for the vindication of contractual rights. The response of the legal system to contractual disputes should be to provide a mechanism, called litigation, by which the rights and obligations of the parties can be authoritatively determined without the use of violence, that is a judgment by a court, and those rights should be enforced by state power, which in the case of contractual disputes might involve an official seizure of the debtor's property. A narrower conception of the purpose of regulation might comprise the provision of access to justice, that is a procedural right to a fair hearing of a grievance. Against these purposes for regulation, it might be suggested more pragmatically that the dominant purpose should be the peaceful resolution of the dispute. Such a peaceful resolution can occur only by agreement between the parties, so the objective of regulation must be to establish mechanisms designed to facilitate an agreement or settlement. The tension between these purposes for regulation of contractual disputes provides the central problem to be addressed in this chapter.

The assertions of entitlement and correlative obligation which fuel the legal process of litigation and adjudication tend to exacerbate the conflict between the parties. They shift the discourse away from the normative framework of preserving the business relation and ensuring the mutual benefit to be derived from the deal towards the legalistic assertion of contractual rights. In endeavouring to provide access to justice and the vindication of contractual rights, the legal process therefore becomes an instrument for unravelling the ties of trust and confidence in commercial relations, and for preventing an accommodation which preserves the benefits expected from the transaction for both parties. Social order is only preserved at the cost of economic disintegration. This argument suggests the hypothesis that litigation before a court with respect to a contractual dispute will only occur by the choice of the parties when they perceive that economic disintegration has already occurred, so that they no longer put in jeopardy the potential economic benefits of relations of trust. We can test that proposition by an investigation of the incidence of litigation in contractual disputes.

We then turn our attention to the question of whether the legal system does achieve its goal of helping parties to contracts to vindicate their rights, even if it does so at the cost of economic disintegration. The central question is whether the legal process ensures that its outcome represents a fair determination of those rights. In our consideration of the important role of settlements, we will attempt to examine the truth and implications of the widespread suspicion that the legal system tends to produce distorted outcomes that deviate substantially from impartial determinations of contractual rights.

We then proceed to consider how alternative dispute processes have been constructed with the ambition of achieving a more accurate vindication of contractual rights whilst at the same type minimizing the economic disintegration effects of dispute settlement. These alternatives to litigation such as arbitration, mediation, and complaint-handling mechanisms in fact provide the institutional framework for the resolution of the vast majority of contractual disputes. For the most part these alternatives function outside the purview of legal regulation. We consider whether fresh legal regulation might assist the efficacy and efficiency of these methods of alternative dispute regulation.

My argument will be that the dominant goal in regulating contractual disputes should be one of promoting contractual settlements of disputes. This goal diminishes the conventional importance attached to the vindication of contractual rights and access to justice in the ordinary courts. Instead, the regulatory objective of settlement suggests that the law should aim to support and steer mechanisms that possess the capacity to produce or facilitate a fair resolution of disputes by agreement. I have two main reasons for preferring the goal of settlement. First, this objective fits closely with the aim of protecting business expectations, especially those expectations based upon the business relation and the deal. Secondly, the distributive outcome for poorer litigants such as consumers is likely to be superior to the alternative of improving access to courts and the vindication of contractual rights.

The Taste for Litigation

Litigation involves the use of the legal process in order to resolve a contractual dispute. If the dispute has not been resolved by informal means such as remedying a complaint by supplying a substitute, litigation is initiated by the plaintiff making a formal claim such as a writ under the powers of a court against the defendant. Pre-trial procedures then occur involving the 'discovery' or disclosure of documents and other evidence, the acceptance of uncontroversial evidence, sworn statements of evidence, expert reports, and the further specification of claims and counter-claims. Eventually the trial takes place, and the judge (and sometimes a jury in the USA) reaches a conclusion about the facts, the relevant law, and the final result. A court has the inherent power to award a wide range of remedies to the plaintiff, but the normal remedy for breach of contract today consists of an order to pay damages or financial compensation. Failure to obey the court's order will result in a further process for seizure of the defendant's property to the value of the goods. In nineteenth-century England, however, a common sanction for judgment debtors was imprisonment.[1]

Litigation is notoriously expensive and slow, especially in Common Law systems. The costs and delays will deter most potential litigants. We might predict, therefore, that litigation which proceeds to trial is mostly an activity of wealthy businesses or government. On this hypothesis, the incidence of litigation depends upon a cost/benefit analysis by the plaintiff, in which the costs of litigation such as lawyers' and courts' fees are weighed against the potential benefits from a successful outcome. These benefits need to be calculated by discounting a successful outcome by the risk of losing the case, the risk of the inability to enforce a judgment against an insolvent debtor, and the reduced value of the deferred award of compensation. Under this hypothetical cost/benefit analysis, we would predict that litigation would be selected by plaintiffs only when the potential benefit of a substantial award of damages is high, so that the risks of loss and inevitable costs are overshadowed.

Although this hypothesis provides an account of the incidence of litigation

[1] Rubin, G. R., 'Law, Poverty and Imprisonment for Debt, 1869–1914', in G. R. Rubin and D. Sugerman (eds.), *Law, Economy and Society: Essays in the History of English Law 1750–1920* (London: Professional Books, 1984) 192.

in general, it is not sensitive to the particular features of contractual disputes. In this field we can suggest an alternative hypothesis that litigation occurs when the business relation is perceived to have no future. Under this account, the cost/benefit calculation with respect to litigation in relation to contracts always contains the additional factor of preservation of the potential benefit from the continuation of the business relation by the avoidance of litigation. The loss of this benefit counts as a cost of litigation, and will often exceed the potential benefit from the vindication of contractual rights in relation to any particular contract between the parties. Under this hypothesis, therefore, the major determinant of litigation consists in the breakdown of long-term business relations of trust and confidence. It is not the size of the sums of money at stake that provides the crucial variable, but rather the calculation of the potential benefit from the preservation of the business relation.

This alternative hypothesis also places emphasis upon the variable of the methods of alternative dispute resolution. If the parties can use a mechanism that resolves their dispute without placing them in the aggressive posture of litigation, then whenever they wish to preserve their business relation they are likely to prefer this alternative to litigation. The alternative dispute resolution mechanism may also be preferred because it reduces the costs of pursuing a claim, but this factor will not be crucial in determining the rejection of a court process. The principal attraction of alternative dispute resolution is that it has the potential to resolve the dispute without placing the long-term business relation in jeopardy.

How well do these rival hypotheses fit the available evidence about the incidence of contractual litigation? The statistical evidence provided by governments about their court services is not gathered in categories that provide convenient measures for our purposes. For example, the category of a contractual dispute is not used in the English statistical service, but has to be constructed by eliding together other categories which may at the same time contain irrelevant material. Even worse, we have only rough estimates based upon random surveys of the incidence of contractual disputes as a whole, so that we cannot easily establish the proportion and characteristics of those disputes that end up before a court. Notwithstanding these reservations, I suggest that we can be reasonably confident that the second hypothesis better accounts for the incidence of litigation in contractual disputes.

The most numerous category of litigation about contractual disputes consists in the pursuit of debts by business organizations against an individual, either a consumer or a small trader such as a shopkeeper.[2] Here

---

[2] Ramsay, I., 'Consumer Redress Mechanisms for Poor-Quality and Defective Products', *University of Toronto Law Journal* 31 (1981) 117, 135; Wanner, C., 'The Public Ordering of

the legal process is invoked in order to claim money owed in circumstances where the business organization places a low value on the potential benefits of future trade with the other party. The business organization may even find the use of litigation helpful in establishing a reputation in the community of enforcing its claims in order to deter others from withholding payment. The legal process is being used here not to resolve the dispute, but rather to harness state power in order to obtain access to the debtor's property. The procedure selected by the creditor will attempt to truncate any enquiry into the merits of the dispute and proceed as directly as possible to judgement and seizure of goods:

We cannot escape the conclusion that in gross the courts in the United States are forums which are used by organizations to extract from and discipline individuals.[3]

This pattern of litigation has not altered since the nineteenth century:

The tallymen, the money-lenders, the flash jewellery touts, the sellers of costly Bibles in series, of gramophone and other luxuries of the mean streets, these are the knaves the State caters for.[4]

As well as the debt collection process, we discover a smaller amount of further litigation about contractual disputes. In these cases the dispute raises more complex issues about performance of the contracts, such as whether the goods supplied were of satisfactory quality, or whether the expected performance was a contractual obligation. Here it is possible to find support for the first hypothesis that emphasizes the deterrent effect of the cost of litigation. The players in the litigation are almost invariably large organizations with the resources that can accommodate the risks of loss. Ordinary consumers, employees, tenants, and so forth will only usually be able to muster the requisite resources if they can achieve some kind of collective support for the litigation, either through an insurance system for legal expenses, or by seeking the aid of a collective organization such as a trade union or consumer group. A study of litigants in local County Courts in the UK in the 1960s failed to turn up a single case of a

---

Private Relations', *Law and Society Review* 8 (1974) 421; Cranston, R., 'What do Courts Do?', *Civil Justice Quarterly* 5 (1986) 123, 128–9; Cain, M., 'Where are the Disputes? A Study of a First Instance Civil Court in the U.K.', in M. Cain and K. Kulcsar (eds.), *Disputes and the Law* (Budapest: Academiai Kiado, 1983) 119.

[3] Galanter, M., 'Afterword: Explaining Litigation', *Law and Society Review* 9 (1974–5) 347, 360.

[4] Parry, E. A., *The Law and the Poor* (London: Smith, Elder & Co., 1914), 61, quoted in Rubin, G. R., 'The County Courts and the Tally Trade, 1846–1914', in G. R. Rubin and D. Sugerman (eds.), n. 1 above, 321, 326. Tallymen were itinerant sellers of luxury goods to the poor on credit, operating in a similar manner to Walker-Thomas, though apparently prone to use the sanction of imprisonment for debt, no doubt by way of example to others.

consumer as a plaintiff.[5] Ordinary consumers and small traders have to opt for a less expensive dispute resolution mechanism than the ordinary courts.

When we examine the incidence of litigation over contractual disputes in the ordinary courts, can we discern a pattern in addition to the wealth of the parties? Is it possible to find the distinguishing characteristics of disputes that end up in court compared to those which are resolved by using other mechanisms such as arbitration? In particular, can we find support for the hypothesis that the long-term business relation provides the crucial variable in determining the taste for litigation? In the words of one manufacturer in an American survey:

So far, we have been quite successful in avoiding law suits, and believe other methods of adjustment are much more effective—and leave a better taste.[6]

Under this second hypothesis, litigation over contractual disputes should appear before the ordinary courts when either the transaction was discrete, that is, not embedded in any past or expected future dealings between the parties, or the plaintiff perceives that the business relation cannot be resuscitated. These instances should be rather unusual in an economy, if our arguments about the importance of trust and long-term business relations in constituting markets are correct.

One approach to these questions examines the features of contractual disputes before appellate courts. These will be unusual disputes, because the parties have expended considerable resources in order to assert their legal rights. But they may provide some insight into the taste for litigation. Macaulay describes the features of cases in appellate litigation over contractual disputes in the United States.[7] These disputes include the collapse of long-term business relations caused by major external shocks such as the oil crisis in the 1970s, claims brought by employees against their employers for abusive discharge and sexual harassment in the hope of obtaining the unusual remedy of punitive damages, and disappointments arising from the failure of new technologies to produce expected results. The disputes arising from the collapse of long-term business relations fit the hypothesis that litigation marks the rupture of the business relation. The employment cases similarly arise only after the breakdown of the employment relation, and, though the plaintiff usually lacks the resources needed for litigation, the potential prize of punitive damages alters the normal cost/benefit

---

[5] Consumer Council, *Justice Out of Reach* (London, HMSO, 1970) 14–15. Another study in 1980 does not distinguish this type of consumer claim, but reveals that about 1% of claims were brought by private citizens against private businesses for matters other than debt: Cain, M., n. 2 above, 127.

[6] Comment, 'The Statute of Frauds and the Business Community: A Re-Appraisal in Light of Prevailing Practices', *Yale Law Journal* 66 (1957) 1038, 1062 n. 66.

[7] Macaulay, S., 'An Empirical View of Contract', *Wisconsin Law Review* (1985) 465.

analysis. The cases involving new technologies seem to involve discrete trans-actions, without a long-term business relation to support co-operation.

A similar survey of English cases would reveal, I suggest, the most frequent disputes at appellate level to be concerned with test cases on the interpretation of standardized contracts governing international trade, the allocation of risks in major construction and property development projects after the transaction has been completed or collapsed, and aggressive litigation by banks to enforce security interests in test cases.[8] The litigation over test cases is pursued because of its potential effects on liabilities in many other cases, so that successful litigation can discourage future claims. The English banking cases arise from debt enforcement, and they represent test cases designed to preserve the facility of truncated enforcement of security against consumers. Apart from test cases, where relatively small sums may be at stake, the litigation which reaches court is likely to involve large sums of money, which renders the investment in litigation potentially worthwhile.[9] Appellate cases do not, of course, provide a reliable guide to the incidence of litigation in contractual disputes. These are the cases where the stakes are high and often the law is unclear. Even so, we can discern the pattern of a breakdown in long-term business relations in these cases, such as the problems caused by the oil crisis or the collapse of construction projects. The cases concerning international trade, though likely to fall within long-term business relations, do not present such a stark exception to this pattern, because the dispute will have invariably been handled in the first instance by arbitration outside the court system.

One American study attempts to examine more closely the incidence of commercial litigation more generally. It examines the types of contractual relations involved in litigation under the Uniform Commercial Code, which typically comprises sales and credit arrangements. This study uses Macneil's distinction between discrete and relational contracts, and finds

---

[8] This impression is supported by a study of the work of the Commercial Court in London, a court which handles a considerable proportion of business litigation: 'The study of the Commercial Court by Coopers and Lybrand found . . . that shipping cases accounted for 54 per cent. of writs in the sample, the most common cause of action here being breach of contract. Other important categories were non-marine insurance (9 per cent.), mercantile contracts (8 per cent.), road and land contracts (8 per cent.), banking (7 per cent.), and debt (6 per cent.)', reported in Vincent-Jones, P., 'Contract Litigation in England and Wales 1975–1991: Transformation of Business Disputing?', *Civil Justice Quarterly* 12 (1993) 337, 354, 20, referring to Coopers and Lybrand Associates, *Study of Commercial Court* (November 1986), para. 4.6. Cf. Reynolds, F., 'The Applicability of General Rules of Private Law to Consumer Disputes', in S. Anderman *et al.* (eds), *Law and the Weaker Party* (London: Professional Books, 1982) ii. 93–110.

[9] Vincent-Jones, P., n. 8 above, 340: 'In judgments for breach of contract in the same year [1985], 25 per cent of cases involved sums between £10,000 and £50,000, a remarkable 42.8 per cent involving sums of over £50,000.'

support for the proposition that litigation is more likely in discrete contracts such as a unique sale of machinery to another business or in a sale to a consumer or a small business.[10] Although this study provides some support for the hypothesis that litigation is linked to a breakdown of long-term business relations, the distinction between discrete and relational contracts does not match exactly the contrast that we have been drawing, for it is possible to have discrete contracts as part of a series within a long-term business relation, and also to have an inefficient relational contract without the support of co-operative business relations.

Other long-term studies of the incidence of contract disputes suggest that exogenous shocks to production systems can provoke an increase in litigation. In an American study of litigation between automobile manufacturers and their dealers or suppliers between 1970 and 1990, there is evidence of a marked increase in the early 1980s, followed by a decline in the late 1980s. The most probable explanation of this rise lies in the heightened competition experienced by American car manufacturers during the 1980s from Japanese manufacturers that caused instability and uncertainty in the long-term business relations with suppliers of components and distributors.[11] The subsequent decline in litigation might be attributed in part to the greater integration between suppliers and manufacturers under single supplier systems and thus a restoration of more cooperative business relations. But another interesting explanation is that in response to the costs of litigation and its disintegrative economic effects, the parties developed cheaper methods of alternative dispute resolution.[12] Even so, the incidence of litigation is extremely small given the numbers of contracts and their value. There is similar evidence of an increase in contractual litigation in all sectors in England and Wales in the 1980s, though the official statistics do not clearly distinguish contractual actions from other types of claims.[13]

The causes of the increase in litigation concerning contracts, which is part of a wider increase in the incidence of litigation, remain speculative. There may be a connection between the incidence of contractual litigation and business cycles.[14] Rights against insolvent parties have to be pursued through the courts and a formal legal process. Thus economic recession tends to increase the incidence of litigation about contracts. Another crucial variable may be the relative attraction of settlements and alternative

---

[10] Crystal, N. M., 'An Empirical View of Relational Contracts Under Article Two of the Uniform Commercial Code', *Annual Survey of American Law* (1988) 293.

[11] Kenworthy, L., *et al.*, '"The More Things Change . . .": Business Litigation and Governance in the American Automobile Industry', *Law and Social Inquiry* 21 (1996) 631.

[12] Ibid. 631, 675. [13] Vincent-Jones, P., n. 8 above, 337.

[14] Dunworth, T., and Roger, J., 'Corporations in Court: Big Business Litigation in U.S. Federal Courts, 1971–1991', *Law and Social Inquiry* 21 (1996) 497.

dispute resolution compared to litigation, which might depend heavily on the relative costs and flexibility of the procedures. But there may be many other factors that trigger an increase in litigation. A small alteration in the rules of civil procedure may suddenly give a group access to courts to an extent that was impracticable before. Accounting practices with regard to the placing of costs and potential benefits from litigation on the balance sheet may often be crucial in determining whether litigation is preferred to settlement.[15] The widespread availability of affordable insurance to cover the costs of litigation may prove the most vital factor for ordinary persons.

In addition to this statistical evidence, we also can draw upon the products of surveys of businesses to discover the incidence and motives for litigation. Here the pattern is clear that litigation is studiously avoided in business relations in favour of seeking an accommodation of interests. The findings of a recent survey of businesses in Seattle provide a representative sample that supports the second hypothesis.

The legal counsel for one large manufacturer stated that despite on-going disputes with all of their major suppliers, 'there was no litigation; no outside attorneys were consulted'. Even disputes with suppliers over warranty claims and disclaimers are 'never resolved by litigation' . . . Except in cases involving unpaid bills and dishonesty, lawsuits are extraordinarily rare. The reasons for not using the courts in resolving disputes were also notably similar. Business considerations—especially a concern that the relationship continue on amicable terms—as well as commitment to the terms of the bargain were the most common. The senior vice-president of a Seattle-based public relations firm, for example, in reply to the question of how problems with long-term clients are resolved, replied, 'We've eaten bills.' He explained: 'If, in fact, we think both sides are at fault, we say, "Hey, let's share the loss on this." And we talk about it. We do eat parts of the bills. We ask the client to pay extra sometimes. Sometimes that endangers the relationship, but generally speaking people are pretty reasonable.'[16]

Although each of these variables may affect the taste for litigation, the main hypothesis that the incidence of contractual litigation depends upon the presence of economic disintegration seems to be supported by the evidence available. The switch to the contractual discourse of rights occurs only when no long-term business relation seems to be practicable and the parties feel unable to achieve an accommodation that preserves some diminished benefits for both. Even when these conditions have been satisfied, however, the cost of litigation will exclude access to litigation as a dispute resolution mechanism for most consumers. The taste for litigation,

[15] Nelson, W. E., 'Contract Litigation and the Elite Bar in New York City, 1960–1980', *Emory Law Journal* 39 (1990) 413.
[16] Haley, J. O., 'Relational Contracting: Does Community Count?', in H. Baum (ed.), *Japan: Economic Success and Legal System* (Berlin/New York: Walter de Gruyter, 1997) 167, 172.

though it may vary between countries at the margins, must therefore be small. Parties to economic transactions will focus most of the time on the economic benefits to be achieved by preserving long-term business relations and on ensuring that a particular deal has successful outcomes.

Vindication of Contractual Rights

We consider next the question whether the legal system achieves an institutional framework through which contractual rights may be vindicated accurately. For this purpose, we shall assume that a judgment by a court will invariably produce the correct outcome, that is, it provides the benchmark for an accurate vindication of contractual rights. Of course, mistakes can be made by a judge, either due to the inadequacy of the evidence presented, or due to a misunderstanding of the law. But in principle these mistakes can be rectified by the operations of the legal system through the system of appeals to higher courts, and so for the purpose of this discussion we will assume that the determinations of contractual rights provided by the highest courts are conclusive, even though they may differ from the original expectations of the parties. What interests us here, however, are those cases where litigation is commenced, so that the formal institutional process of litigation is invoked, yet the final determination is not supplied by an ordinary court.

From this perspective, we discover that even when the plaintiff has decided to take the step of a formal assertion of contractual rights through litigation, it is most unlikely that the matter will come before an ordinary court. The parties will almost invariably settle their dispute prior to trial. The question that interests us here is whether the terms of the settlement correspond to the probable outcome of a judicial determination. Do the legal institutions provide the necessary structures and incentives for the parties to achieve the same result as a court would impose? If not, should we be concerned about this deviation from legal standards? Do settlements represent a systematic departure from the standards of legal justice, and if so, does this reveal a distortion of justice through a manipulation of the legal process by powerful players, or does it demonstrate rather that the standards of legal justice are incompatible with the expectations and interests of the parties to contractual disputes?

Incidence of Settlements

At any stage during the proceedings, the parties to the litigation may settle a dispute. A formal settlement comprises an agreement to terminate the litigation combined with any terms with respect to compensation. A settlement determines the outcome of the case in the vast majority of litigated disputes. We cannot be sure about the proportion of cases settled, because although courts keep statistics on the number of writs issued and the number of cases brought to trial, the difference between these two figures includes many other ways in which a case will not proceed to trial. For example, in the English High Court (Queen's Bench Division), in any year about 22,000 writs involving contractual disputes may be issued, but only about 200 cases proceed to trial and final judgment.[17] In the London Commercial Court that deals mostly with major contractual disputes, in a typical year about 2,500 writs may be issued, but less than 20 cases will be determined by a judgment after a trial.[18] The gap between these figures includes not only settlements but also cases struck out for not displaying a cause of action, cases not pursued or withdrawn (possibly indicating a settlement), and judgments obtained without a trial[19] (which does not preclude a subsequent divergent settlement). From the available evidence we may hazard a guess that at least 80 per cent of cases involving contractual disputes are settled, but it is likely that the proportion may be even higher.

There are plainly strong incentives to settle a dispute. In most civil litigation, one incentive is the desire to avoid the costs of litigation. A settlement can make both parties better off than if they continue to litigate, for the value of a potential victory before a court will be consumed by legal expenses. Through termination of the legal proceedings, these expenses are reduced, so that the plaintiff may be better off by accepting lower compensation than expected whilst saving the legal expense of a court hearing. Under a cost/benefit calculation, therefore, the predicted outcome of settlements will be that the plaintiff receives an amount less than a court would award, since the compensation offer will be reduced to reflect the risk of the plaintiff losing the case and the plaintiff's savings in legal costs. The practice of preferring settlements also hides one of the dark secrets of litigation. Victory in court provides no guarantee of obtaining compensation. The court process for seizure of goods to satisfy a judgment debt starts a game of cat and mouse where assets are hidden, moved, or simply dissolve into the abyss of insolvency. From a study of small claims courts in the UK, for instance, we learn that after six months from a judgment only half of the plaintiffs had received full payment.[20] Victory in court may have

---

[17] Lord Chancellor's Department, *Judicial Statistics*, 1996 Cm 3716, 27–9.
[18] Ibid. 33.
[19] These judgments might comprise 'consent judgments' where the court merely endorses a settlement, or a default judgment where the defendant has made no moves to defend a case; in the case of the former, the statistics disguise the presence of a settlement.
[20] Baldwin, J., *Small Claims in the County Courts in England and Wales: The Bargain Basement of Civil Justice* (Oxford: Clarendon Press, 1997) 133.

important symbolic functions and serve to restore certain kinds of business reputation, but if the plaintiff actually wants compensation, it is probably safer to accept a reduced amount of cash on the table in a settlement rather than await the outcome of the court process.

On the other hand, in commercial disputes, the debtor has incentives to avoid an early settlement. The delay in any payment has the value of borrowing money at the relatively low rates of interest required in legal proceedings.[21] The defendant may also have the opportunity to render itself 'judgment proof' by secreting assets, moving them outside the jurisdiction or, for corporate entities, entering voluntary insolvency.

In the case of contractual disputes, however, we must be alert to another possible motive for settlements. We may discover the motive of seeking to revive a business relation by reaching a friendly accommodation of interests, and thus avoiding further damage by terminating the litigation. In such cases, the terms of the settlement are likely to be driven not by the likely outcome of a court hearing, but rather by the need to restore a workable and satisfactory business relation for both parties. This motive remains a cost/benefit calculation, but includes the factor of the potential benefit of restoration of future trading relations. When this motive guides the settlement, the parties will not be seeking to track a court-imposed result, for they will be looking beyond the particular contractual dispute.

The Deviance of Settlements

Although litigation may generally occur when the long-term business relation has dissolved, we cannot infer that this second type of motive for settlements will not in fact generate many agreed settlements. It may be precisely in order to combat this breakdown in business relations that the parties desire to reach a settlement. If so, then the fact that the settlement does not approximate to a court judgment does not create the suspicion that the settlement is flawed. On the contrary, the deviant settlement may represent a subtle calculation by both parties as to their best long-term interests. They may choose to relinquish or abate claims in a particular case in an endeavour to restore harmonious business relations. Although we lack any hard evidence that enables us to compare settlements with probable judicial awards, even if this evidence were to demonstrate that settlements fail to provide plaintiffs with any approximation to their legal entitlements, we still could not be sure that the institutional arrangements are defective by reason of their presenting impediments to the successful assertion of contractual rights.

Nevertheless, some studies do reveal that settlements deviate consider-

---

[21] Cranston, R., n. 2 above, 134.

ably from putative contractual entitlements for reasons which appear to be unsatisfactory from a distributive point of view. One persuasive explanation of the variation between settlements and legal rights seizes upon the different bargaining strengths of the parties. A settlement is produced by a negotiation. The parties deploy their best available resources for this purpose. They will insist upon the strength of their legal position, and seek to minimize the validity of the claims of the other side. The legal entitlements will often not be beyond doubt. As Macaulay observes with only a little exaggeration:

> I often tell my classes that if lawyers of equal ability represent clients with equal resources and willingness to invest them in a case falling under Article II [of the Uniform Commercial Code governing transactions in goods], then the case will end in a tie.[22]

Lawyers are paid to generate uncertainty about legal entitlements. Even when the law appears clear, there will be further uncertainties generated by the inability of the parties to find evidence to support their contentions in court. In this context of negotiations under conditions of uncertainty about entitlements, there is evidence to support the view that bargaining resources have a significant impact on the outcome of settlements.

In Wheeler's study of negotiations regarding the enforcement of a type of security interest known as 'reservation of title clauses', she argues that the most valuable asset in the negotiations is the use of a lawyer who routinely handles the particular type of work, for that lawyer will be able to manipulate the law with confidence and conviction in order to intimidate the other side into a poor settlement.[23] In her study, the attempt to enforce the security interest by sellers was generally unsuccessful, despite their relatively strong though unclear legal position under the contract, for the defendants were typically larger businesses employing lawyers with experience in defending such claims. These 'repeat players' can be plaintiffs in debt collection cases, or defendants in claims against insurance companies.[24] Often, as Wheeler suggests, 'The repeat player, as the dominant actor, has no intention of reaching a settlement'.[25] The negotiations are conducted with a view to deterring the other side from asserting its legal entitlements altogether.

Settlements may also be pursued after a trial. Although the court will have provided a judgment about entitlements, there is usually the possibility of an appeal and the difficulties surrounding the court's collection process, so the parties can then engage in further negotiation about the

[22] Macaulay, S., n. 7 above, 465, 469.
[23] Wheeler, S., *Reservation of Title Clauses* (Oxford: Clarendon Press, 1991).
[24] Galanter, M., 'Why the "Haves" Come Out Ahead: Speculations on the Limits of Legal Change', *Law and Society Review* 9 (1974–5) 95.   [25] Wheeler, S., n. 23 above, 201.

extent to which the original court's decision will be observed. The court's decision becomes a bargaining chip in the negotiations, but its orders will not be observed where the economic interests of both parties point in other directions. For example, if the parties want to keep the deal alive rather than terminate it for breach, then the judicial decision to rescind the contract will be replaced by a settlement which establishes a new contractual relation on different terms. In the Westinghouse case,[26] the company was unable to fulfil long-term uranium supply contracts without suffering enormous financial losses due to major increases in the costs of all energy sources in the 1970s. The company failed to extract itself from the contracts on the basis of 'commercial impracticability'.[27] Having lost the case, however, the company then negotiated new supply contracts and restored the business relations.[28] The settlement therefore deviated substantially from strict legal entitlements, but to enforce these entitlements and to drive Westinghouse into liquidation was plainly not in the interests of any of the parties.[29] In a consumer context, where the dominant litigation concerns debt collection, after a court judgment, usually without trial, the creditor faces the problem of collection. Evidence from the USA again points to the importance of settlements. Although the creditor enjoys a strong bargaining position having won judgment, most of the debt will usually be collected through a voluntary agreement or settlement, which is cheaper than invoking the legal execution process. The debtor is induced to settle in the hope of protecting any credit rating and by the incentive of a reduced payment.[30]

The legal system perceives a public interest in promoting settlements, not least because the minimization of trials reduces the cost of the legal system to the taxpayer. But the process of negotiation behind settlements gives considerable advantage to the 'repeat players' or those with convincing bargaining power (including the threat of becoming insolvent), so that settlements routinely subvert the entitlements which the law of contract is designed to protect.[31] On the other hand, the legal system can only declare entitlements, it cannot always enforce them by way of remedies, so settlements may approach the goal of vindication of contractual entitlements to remedies rather closer than the court process.

---

[26] *In re Westinghouse Electric Corporation Uranium Litigation*, 405 F Supp 316 (1975); Joskow, P. L. 'Commercial Impossibility, The Uranium Market and the Westinghouse Case', *Journal of Legal Studies* 6 (1977) 119.   [27] Uniform Commercial Code 2–615.
[28] Dawson, J. P., 'Judicial Revision of Frustrated Contracts: The US', *Boston University Law Review* 64 (1984) 1, 26.
[29] Campbell, D., and Harris, D., 'Flexibility in Long-term Contractual Relationships', *Journal of Law and Society* 20 (1993) 166.
[30] Whitford, W. C., 'A Critique of the Consumer Credit Collection System', *Wisconsin Law Review* [1979] 1047, 1051.
[31] Coleman, J. L., *Markets, Morals and the Law* (Cambridge: Cambridge University Press, 1988), ch. 9; Fiss, O., 'Against Settlement', *Yale Law Journal* 93 (1984) 1074.

Regulating Settlements

This examination of settlements as the normal product of litigation suggests that they rarely represent an approximation to the requirements of legal justice. In some instances the parties deliberately set out to reach a different allocation of rights and obligations with a view to a restoration of long-term business relations. In other instances, the bargaining power of repeat players and those benefiting from superior legal advice during negotiations permits settlements which diminish the weaker party's rights or avoid them altogether. It is not easy, however, to distinguish between these two kinds of settlement for the purposes of regulation. Although one might be tempted to seek to control the process of negotiation towards a settlement through legal regulation in order to prevent undue influence being exercised by the stronger party, this regulation would also have to be able to identify those instances when the weaker party nevertheless perceives superior economic benefits to be available from a disadvantageous settlement having regard to the potential of the long-term business relation. Can we be sure, for instance, that long-term business interests did not affect the judgement of the subjects of Wheeler's study, so that a disadvantageous settlement was acceptable because it kept a valued customer?

The outcome of most litigated disputes about contracts is another contract, the settlement. The legal system devolves the power to the parties to determine their own valuation of their rights, and then to translate these entitlements into economic measurements of interests. The courts will recognize the validity of these contracts, subject to exceptions for fraud. The meaning of legal justice in contracts thus becomes appropriated by the meaning of contract itself. The valuation of conduct becomes narrowed to measurable economic benefits, and the interests of others in the outcome of the dispute is systematically disregarded. The legal institutions therefore seem to be structured to establish a process that encourages private settlement of disputes rather than a public vindication of rights. Fiss has led an attack on this institutional process in civil litigation as a whole, for he argues that it detracts too severely from the public interest in the assertion and enforcement of legal standards of justice.[32] In the context of litigated contractual disputes, however, there may be a different policy at work. In these commercial disputes, legal regulation takes the stance of encouraging self-regulation and self-enforcement in order to enable the parties to construct their relations of trust and forge beneficial deals. Within this policy, it also makes sense to grant the parties the power of self-regulation with respect to the outcomes of justice, so that they may forge their own standards and reach accommodations of interest. We must question

---

[32] Fiss, O., n. 31 above.

whether there is any independent value in the assertion and enforcement of the law of contract between parties to a commercial dispute in circumstances where they agree in the light of their interests to apply different standards. Just as the parties are free to remake their deal by agreed modifications in order to respond to changes in circumstances, so too they can be granted the facility to alter their legal entitlements retrospectively by a settlement in order to further their business interests.

In this context, legal regulation should be aimed at increasing the efficacy and efficiency of settlements. The question is whether the litigation process provides procedures and occasions when the parties to the dispute can negotiate a fair settlement. Many recent experiments with the annexation of compulsory mediation and arbitration to litigation procedures have the promotion of settlements as their principal objective. The difficulty that has to be confronted is that by making the litigation process more elaborate, there is a risk of increasing the costs of settlement without in fact increasing the number or fairness of settlements. On the other hand, the common experience of settlements forged at the door of the courtroom or even during the trial suggests that an earlier intervention designed to promote negotiation towards a settlement might have saved the parties considerable expense in preparation for trial. I think that we know too little about the motives for settlement during the litigation process to be sure how best to resolve the deadlock in a situation of the disintegration of economic ties. We know that the imminence of the trial tends to promote serious negotiations, but equally we can surmise that the sheer delays and expense of the litigation process provide a strong economic incentive to negotiate a settlement. We should be suspicious of any claims that reforms of civil procedure will facilitate more efficient settlements.

In England, Lord Woolf's plans for the reform of civil justice seek to increase efficient settlements by means of increased judicial control over litigation from its inception, combined with the provision of better information for the parties about the costs and risks of a continuation of the litigation.[33] These measures assume that lawyers present an obstacle to efficient settlements, that the judges will become motivated to try to engineer settlements through case management, and that better information will break the parties' resistance to settlement. The major technique employed is case management by the judge, which is aimed at narrowing down quickly the major issues in dispute. This technique may well shorten trials, but it may not assist settlements.

Modern negotiation theory tells us that settlement may often be more likely when there are more issues, rather than fewer. If there are numerous issues at stake,

---

[33] Lord Woolf, *Access to Justice: Interim Report to the Lord Chancellor on the Civil Justice System of England and Wales* (London: HMSO, 1995).

parties' complementary, and not necessarily competing, needs and interests can be traded off to increase the number of potential settlements in 'Pareto-optimal' terms, *i.e.* parties explore a number of possibilities until no-one can be made better off without some harm to the other side.[34]

Even if the new measures assist settlements, they may only do so by increasing their costs because of the 'front-loading' of litigation expenses in order to cope with the demands of case management.

At root, the problem here is that the regulatory system that governs litigation remains tied to the policy of facilitating an early and inexpensive trial. In the context of contractual disputes, however, where the primary objective should be the facilitation of fair settlements, these reforms of the litigation process may prove irrelevant to the facilitation of settlements or even harmful. As Palmer and Roberts astutely observe of the Woolf reforms:

The ills of lawyers' litigation strategies are bluntly identified; but the central problem—the historic conflation of settlement and trial—is endorsed and compounded. In permitting the continued use of the path towards the court for the pursuit of settlement strategies, having recognised so candidly how disadvantageous to the client such practices are, he leaves negotiation and adjudication harmfully entwined.[35]

Lord Woolf also suggests, however, that the parties should be encouraged to use alternative dispute resolution mechanisms, though he does not follow the US federal model of compulsory court annexed arbitration,[36] or similar techniques for early determination of issues by neutral umpires.[37] Here the proposals seem more circumspect and therefore more plausible. The choice of a mechanism for achieving a settlement remains with the parties, but the legal system may assist them by promoting and publicizing the availability of many different forms of dispute resolution, such as mediation, arbitration, and 'early neutral evaluation', so that an appropriate or preferred procedure is readily available. We should observe, however, that the parties' preferences may not be for any public service, but rather for a private procedure under their own control. The legal system needs to recognize in regulating the litigation process for the purpose of promoting the settlement of contractual disputes that an important dimension of the optimal strategy consists of abstention in deference to the parties' own construction of a dispute settlement procedure.

---

[34] Menkel-Meadow, C., 'Will Managed Care give us Access to Justice?', in R. Smith (ed.), *Achieving Civil Justice: Appropriate Dispute Resolution for the 1990s* (London: Legal Action Group, 1996), 94.

[35] Palmer, M., and Roberts, S., *Dispute Processes: ADR and the Primary Forms of Decision Making* (London: Butterworths, 1998) 192.   [36] Ibid. 277–87.

[37] Rosenberg, J. D., and Folberg, H. J., 'Alternative Dispute Resolution: An Empirical Analysis', *Stanford Law Review* 46 (1994) 1487.

Access to Justice

We have so far examined only those disputes about contracts that invoke the formal procedures of litigation. This collection of disputes represents the tip of the iceberg, because the vast majority of contractual disputes use different processes. The typical response of consumers to a disappointment is either to do nothing or to make a complaint to the business that supplied the goods or services rather than to invoke a formal procedure.

According to the most recent OFT consumer dissatisfaction survey, consumers in the United Kingdom experience some 90 million unsatisfactory transactions ('causes for complaint') a year. This means, on average, four instances of cause for complaint per household. In about 40% of these cases, or 36 million transactions, consumers take no action to register the complaint and obtain remedy for the problem.[38]

At the same time, as we have noted already, businesses exhibit a strong preference for avoiding the ordinary courts in favour of arbitration and other mechanisms of informal dispute resolution.

Should we be concerned that the ordinary courts and their procedures are not the location for the resolution of the vast majority of contractual disputes? What benefits might be obtained by securing better access to the courts for consumers and small businesses? Should legal regulation channel parties towards the institutions of the courts, or should it instead seek to encourage and regulate alternative dispute resolution? In other words, should legal regulation be designed to permit the institutions of the state to provide determinations over as many contractual disputes as possible, or should legal regulation concentrate upon ensuring the fairness of the processes that the parties construct or select? In short, in our response to calls for access to justice in the context of contractual disputes, should we promote public or private justice?

Complaint Mechanisms

When confronted by a disappointment or a betrayal in contractual relations, the injured party is most unlikely to invoke the procedures of litigation. The first step in commercial and consumer claims alike is to voice a complaint to the other party. For consumers, this is also likely to be the full extent of the procedure for redress.

We have already touched on the reasons why in commercial contracts it is rational for the parties to seek to resolve their dispute informally. In studies of disputes between business contractors, as in the Beale and

---

[38] Office of Fair Trading, *Raising Standards of Consumer Care: Progressing Beyond Codes of Practice* (London: OFT, 206,1998) 9.

Dugdale survey, in this pre-legal stage of the dispute, contractual behaviour is likely to be oriented principally towards the business relation and the deal. In order to preserve the business relation, the response to a complaint is likely to be one of concern and willingness to make redress if there is a problem. The form of the redress is also influenced by the need to keep the deal economically viable for both parties. The redress offered may be to rectify the defect or to make a price reduction. Beale and Dugdale report that it is rare for any money to be paid, and certainly compensation for consequential damages for loss of profits is not expected, presumably because this would prevent the deal from being profitable for the seller.[39] Financial compensation can take the form of giving credit in the long-term business relation, so that the price of the next order may be reduced or a credit note issued for spare parts. It is unlikely that the parties will seek to cancel the transaction entirely. Other studies of commercial practice reveal a similar pattern of a search for a financial accommodation, typically aimed at recompense only for wasted expenditure.[40] The complaint mechanism provides the solution to the problem as long as the parties share an interest in preserving the long-term business relation or can find a way to make the deal viable for both parties. There is little taste for litigation except as a last resort.

This option of litigation almost disappears entirely when the aggrieved party is a consumer. The handling of the complaint by the business will in practice constitute the sole remedy for most consumers. In surveys of consumers who perceived problems with a product, there is consistent evidence that less than half went for help to a third party such as a lawyer, an ombudsman, or a Consumer Advice Agency in order to take further legal action. A big survey in the United States in the 1970s put the number as low as 1.2 per cent.[41] These results were similar to those in the UK at about the same time.[42] The willingness of consumers to involve an external advisor may have increased in the last thirty years. A small survey in the UK in 1995 found that about 56 per cent sought some kind of third party help in respect of faulty goods, though only a tiny minority eventually had

[39] Beale, H., and Dugdale, T., 'Contracts Between Businessmen: Planning and the Use of Contractual Remedies', *British Journal of Law and Society* 2 (1975) 45.

[40] Comment, n. 6 above, 1061.

[41] Best, A., and Andreasen, A. R., 'Consumer Response to Unsatisfactory Purchase: A Survey of Perceiving Defects, Voicing Complaints, and Obtaining Redress', *Law and Society Review* 11 (1976–77) 701. A similar percentage was reported in Miller, R., and Sarat, A., 'Grievances, Claims and Disputes: Assessing the Adversary Culture', *Law and Society Review* 15 (1980–1) 525.

[42] Cranston, R., *Regulating Business: Law and Consumer Agencies* (London: MacMillan, 1979) 60, quoting from J. Walter Thompson Ltd, 'Housewives Attitudes to Marketing' (July 1974).

their dispute resolved by legal proceedings.[43] Even when advice about legal rights is sought from a third party, there is evidence that lawyers,[44] and Consumer Advice Bureaux,[45] steer clients back towards the complaint mechanism. Furthermore, if the consumer turns to a state agency with powers to enforce standards, the public officials usually attempt to negotiate a satisfactory outcome with the retailer, rather than immediately to bring a prosecution under the public regulation. This negotiation can be interpreted as a further invocation of the complaint mechanism. In Cranston's study of the work of Trading Standards Officers in the UK, he reveals that the officer is expected to make a diplomatic approach to the trader to explain the nature of the complaint, and then encourage the business to operate a fair mechanism to resolve the matter:

The overriding goal of negotiation is to obtain enough redress to satisfy consumers without appearing to favour them unduly in the eyes of a businessman. Within consumer agencies redress is an all-important consideration in evaluating the performance of consumer officers.[46]

Thus even in the context of public regulation, as well as private law regulation, the complaint mechanism constitutes the principal tool for resolution of the dispute. The complaint mechanism operated by the business provides the dispute resolution system for most consumers, and its product is their remedy.

At first sight, this provision of private justice appears inherently suspect. It comprises an institutional process under which the defendant determines the validity of the plaintiff's claim and what remedy, if any, will be granted. It is chosen by the consumer because it is cheap and the consumer may not be aware of the possibility or procedures for using any other kind of process. It is chosen by public officials charged with enforcement of public regulation again because it is cheap (compared to prosecutions), and because it is likely to produce some resolution of the dispute quickly. One might expect, however, that the justice dispensed by the complaint mechanisms of businesses would systematically deprive the consumer of any rights or expectations generated by the contract.

Yet a closer examination of complaint mechanisms suggests a more equivocal judgement about the kind of justice they dispense. It is true that the complaint mechanism often pays scant regard to the probable legal entitlements of the parties, but this deviation is not always to the

---

[43] National Consumer Council, *Seeking Civil Justice—A Survey of People's Needs and Experiences* (London: National Consumer Council, 1995), 25, 41.

[44] Macaulay, S., 'Lawyers and Consumer Protection Laws', *Law and Society Review* 14 (1979) 115.

[45] Cranston, R., *Consumers and the Law*, 2nd edn. (London: Weidenfeld and Nicholson, 1984) 85.   [46] Cranston, R., n. 42 above, 90.

disadvantage of the consumer. Business strategy towards complaint handling is dominated by considerations of long-term business relations and
competitive advantage. Observations of responses to complaints reveal
different types of reactions by businesses according to the market context,
especially the importance of business reputation and customer relations.
Where the retailer relies upon volume sales as in the case of supermarkets
or operates a store in the more expensive end of the market, these considerations of reputation and not contractual entitlements are likely to
dominate responses to complaints.[47] The response to a complaint in these
cases follows the pattern of 'the customer is always right', so that even if
the retailer doubts that the goods sold are unsuitable or defective, the
consumer will be offered a full refund or substitute goods. Another study
of retailers' policies in Edmonton, Alberta, revealed that only one out of
106 stores would accept no returns of goods at all, and the overwhelming
majority gave cash refunds, store credits, or exchanges.[48] Another reason
stressed by businesses for generous responses to complaints is that investigation is expensive, so it usually cheaper to take the customer's word and
pay a refund or supply substitute goods.[49] This response provides the
dominant pattern of complaint handling by retailers, though of course
there are exceptions where the retailer manipulates the complaint-handling
mechanism for its own advantage.

We have already examined an example of this aberrant behaviour in the
study of Walker-Thomas Furniture Co. by Greenberg. The general strategy
of salespersons was to achieve a costless response to a complaint whilst
preserving the long-term credit arrangement. He describes how various
tactics are employed to achieve this end.[50] First, the complaint about the
quality of the product is linked to the repayments under the credit arrangements, so the issue is turned into one about whether repayments have been
made, not the right to reject unsatisfactory goods. Second, the sales representative seeks to persuade the consumer that the product was not faulty
by suggesting that it was damaged by carelessness of the consumer, and
that therefore the customer should pay for the repairs. Third, the sales
representative takes care to preserve his personal good relations with the
customer by expressing concern and filling out paperwork, but then
explains (falsely) that he can do nothing without the approval of the store
manager. When the complaint is rejected by this apparently remote person,

---

[47] Ross, H. L., and Littlefield, N. O., 'Complaint as a Problem-Solving Mechanism', *Law
and Society Review* 12 (1977–78) 199–216.   [48] Ramsay, I., n. 2 above, 127.
[49] Cranston, R., n. 42 above, 162; Whitford, W. C., and Kimball, S. L., 'Why Process
Consumer Complaints? A Case Study of the Office of the Commissioner of Insurance of
Wisconsin', *Wisconsin Law Review* (1974) 639, 675.
[50] Greenberg, D. I., 'Easy Terms, Hard Times: Complaint Handling in the Ghetto', in
L. Nader (ed.), *No Access to Law: Alternatives to the American Judicial System* (New York:
Academic Press, 1980) 379, 387–89.

the business relation between customer and salesperson is nevertheless preserved and perhaps even strengthened by the representative claiming to have used his advocacy skills on behalf of the client. Finally, if the customer seems intent upon taking the complaint to an external agency, the salesperson offers to pay for the repair himself. This beneficence is probably illusory, since the cost can be hidden in the repayment schedule, but it prevents external intervention in the relation that might acquaint the consumer with his or her legal rights, and again tends to cement the long-term business relation. At all times during this complaint-handling mechanism, the sales representative wants to persuade the customer to maintain the business relation through which commissions will be earned and the employer will prosper. In the words of one sales representative speaking to a customer with a complaint:

Hey, you don't want to do something stupid like complaining and ruin all I've done for you, do you? Why make your credit worse that it already is? If you start making trouble and we have to cut you off, then where are going to go? Look's like that living room set is beginning to come apart—where you gonna get a replacement except from me? You don't want to spoil all this for yourself, now, do you?[51]

By controlling information, locking the consumer into a long-term business relation based upon credit, and by exploiting the personal relation between the company's representative and the customer, the retailer can usually achieve costless resolution of disputes. The customer can be persuaded to withdraw the claim as unfounded, as endangering the credit relation, as harmful to the customer's reputation in the community, or even as jeopardizing the customer's source of income. The complaints mechanism for resolving consumer grievances therefore seems to provide a much weaker avenue for redress for faulty goods for economically disadvantaged consumers than for consumers who make cash purchases at regular stores.[52]

Insurance against defects is an important feature of consumer markets for durable goods. The insurance may either take the form of a manufacturer's warranty against defects which is included in the price of the product, or a separate insurance policy purchased by the consumer to cover the cost of repairs. In either case, the document which defines the limits of the insurer's obligations will be treated as determinative of the scope of the redress available. The manufacturer or insurance company has a bureaucratic apparatus designed to ensure that no false claims or claims outside the scope of the warranty or policy will be met. In Whitford's study of the disposition of claims under automobile warranties in the United

---

[51] Greenberg, D. I., n. 50 above, 389.
[52] Ross, H. L., and Littlefield, N. O., n. 47 above, 212–13.

States, for instance, the firms use elaborate rigid procedures outlined in the small print of the warranty for determining the validity of claims.[53] There is a high degree of formalism and attention to the details of the terms of the policy, and considerations of customer good-will rarely influence the outcome. A similar legalistic approach to complaints or appeals has been found in connection with claims under insurance policies.[54] I suspect that a study of the insurance policies frequently bought by consumers at the time of purchase of a durable good would also reveal a close attention to the detail of the claim by the insurance company, unless perhaps the retailer issues the insurance policy in its own name and therefore risks its reputation.

We have paid close attention to these complaint mechanisms, because they represent the principal mode of redress for most breaches of consumer contracts. Within these complaint mechanisms, private law regulation is often treated by the parties as entirely irrelevant. It only becomes significant when a business has constructed a particular remedial scheme of insurance against faulty products and services, as in the case of warranties and insurance, when the business will insist upon the contractual frame of reference to guide contractual behaviour in order to confine its additional obligations to the insured risk. The complaint mechanism does not therefore entail 'bargaining in the shadow of the law',[55] for the contractual frame of reference is usually rejected for the other frameworks of the business relation and the long-term economic interest of the business.

As a generalization, we may say that the response of consumer complaint mechanisms is either that the customer is always right or is always wrong. The mechanism is usually designed to preserve long-term business relations, that is repeated sales.[56] It requires, however, rather more sophistication to manage the system of declaring the customer always to be wrong and yet preserving the economic relation. The mechanisms to achieve this end involve the construction of third parties who determine the outcome of disputes, the store manager, the manufacturer, or the insurer, combined with the control of information, the construction of dependent credit relations, and attempts to construct the issue as the responsibility of the consumer. The frame of reference of the complaint mechanism is therefore aimed towards long-term business relations and

---

[53] Whitford, W. C., 'Law and the Consumer Transaction: A Case Study of the Automobile Warranty', *Wisconsin Law Review* (1968) 1006.

[54] Ross, H. L., 'Insurance Claims Complaints: A Private Appeals Procedure', *Law and Society Review* 9 (1975) 275–92.

[55] Mnookin, R., 'Bargaining in the Shadow of the Law: The Case of Divorce', *Yale Law Journal* 88 (1979) 950; Ramsay, I., n. 2 above, 129.

[56] There are exceptions to this when there is no expectation of repeat sales, notoriously in the second hand car market and double glazing, where we are unlikely to find any complaint mechanism at all.

reputation. The contractual discourse of rights, let alone the private law discourse, is seldom invoked except as a tactic in the discursive strategies of managing the system that the customer is always wrong.

Small Claims

The systematic disregard for legal entitlements displayed by complaint mechanisms has provoked a regulatory policy of seeking to improve access to justice for consumers. It is believed that a combination of the costs of litigation and ignorance of legal entitlements prevents consumers from going to court in order to obtain their contractual rights. The obvious remedy appears to be one of creating a simplified and inexpensive judicial procedure, a 'consumer friendly' legal process.

Since the early part of the twentieth century most jurisdictions in the United States have experimented with the introduction of small claims courts. Subsequently this movement to provide better access to justice in the form of minor courts, tribunals, or public arbitration has spread to the UK, Australasia, and parts of Europe.[57] These tribunals differ from ordinary courts in their procedures and limited jurisdiction. Their purpose was to create a forum for individuals to claim their legal rights without the need for legal representation and advice. It was believed that the creation of an informal tribunal, which dealt with disputes expeditiously, could offer consumers in particular the opportunity for access to justice in order to enforce private law rights. The jurisdiction is usually limited to small sums of money (since 1996 £3,000 in the UK). How far have these small claims courts enabled consumers to vindicate their contractual rights?

Despite recent amendments to the schemes, the summary of the US experience of small claims courts provided by Yngvesson and Hennessey in 1975 still seems appropriate:

> From the point of view of the average citizen, and particularly one who is poor, they are much more likely to be used against him than by him; they are not easily accessible; the atmosphere is alien and confusing; and the range of procedures is limited and is geared more to efficiency for those administering justice than to effectiveness for the individual with a grievance.[58]

Baldwin reaches a similar verdict with regard to the small claims 'arbitration' system (of the county courts) in England and Wales:

---

[57] Administration of Justice Act 1973, and Order 19 of County Court Rules. Cranston, R., n. 45 above, 88–94; Ison, T. G., 'Small Claims', *Modern Law Review* 35 (1972) 18; Yngvesson, B., and Hennessey, P., 'Small Claims, Complex Disputes: A Review of the Small Claims Literature', *Law and Society Review* 9 (1975) 219. European Commission Recommendation of 30/3/98 on the principles applicable to the bodies responsible for out-of-court settlement of common disputes OJ L 115/31, 17/4/98.

[58] Yngvesson, B. and Hennessey, P., n. 57 above, 268.

The evidence in this and other studies shows instead that, while such mechanisms provide a means whereby access to justice might be extended, in practice they continue to be used by very limited sectors of the population, particularly by professional people or those representing business interests. And any hopes that the small claims context might provide an avenue through which the poor might find redress for their grievances seem to have no empirical support whatever.[59]

In practice, these courts have often been used by businesses to claim small debts cheaply.[60] Recent statistics in the UK show that a majority of plaintiffs are now individuals, though in relation to contractual disputes the clear majority remain small businesses.[61] Although the UK small claims courts certainly act expeditiously, with the average length of hearing timed at 48 minutes, there seems to be a trend towards the use of legal representation even though there is no evidence that representation improves chances of success.[62] A part of the explanation for the use of lawyers is surely the fact that the issues raised by claims for small amounts are not necessarily any less complicated in legal reasoning or in the assessment of evidence than those for large sums of money.[63]

Nevertheless, the most significant feature of small claims courts is the way in which they have quickly become the court in which the vast majority of contractual disputes are resolved by the legal system. The official statistics in England and Wales do not classify the type of claim in a manner suitable for ascertaining precisely the location of contractual litigation by the type of court. It is possible, however, to discern a broad picture. In respect of cases involving a contractual dispute resolved by a trial, the higher courts (including the Commercial Court[64] and Official Referee's Court[65]) process about

---

[59] Baldwin, J., n. 20 above, 15.

[60] Appleby, G., 'Small Claims in England and Wales', in M. Cappelletti, and J. Weisner (eds.), *Access to Justice*, (Alphenandenrij: Sijthoff, 1978) ii.1. 736.; Yngvesson, B., and Hennessey, P., n. 57 above, 237–8, which shows most courts have about 80% plaintiffs that are either business or government; cf. Weller, S., *et al.*, 'American Small Claims Courts', in C. J. Whelan (ed.), *Small Claims Courts: A Comparative Study* (Oxford: Clarendon Press, 1990) 5, 10. In the UK, about 60% of cases are small businesses collecting debts: Baldwin, J., n. 20 above, 16, 26. There is a similar pattern in Canada: Ramsay, I., 'Small Claims Courts in Canada: A Socio-Legal Appraisal', in C. J. Whelan (ed.), above, 25, 29.

[61] Lord Chancellor's Department, n. 17 above, 40; Baldwin, J., 'Increasing the Small Claims Limit', *New Law Journal* (1998) 274, 275.

[62] Baldwin, J., ibid., 275–6. There is some support in the US for the view that when only one side has legal representation this increases the chance of success: Yngvesson, B., and Hennessey, P., n. 57 above, 250–51; Weller, S., *et al.*, n. 60 above 5, 12 (defendants without legal representation more likely to lose). Some jurisdictions in Australia ban legal representation.

[63] Yngvesson, B., and Hennessey, P., *et al.*, n. 57 above, 258–9.

[64] The Commercial Court is really part of the ordinary court system, but contains judges who specialize in disputes related to ships, insurance, carriage of goods, international transactions, banking and finance, the purchase and sale of commodities, and legal supervision of arbitration: Lord Chancellor's Department, n. 17 above, 33.

[65] For a discussion of this hybrid form of court and arbitration, Fay, E., *Official Referees' Business* (London: Sweet & Maxwell, 1983).

300 cases a year. The local court system, the county courts, deal with about 5,500 contractual claims in a year. But the small claims arbitration system deals with about 75,000 a year.[66] Litigants and court administrators therefore show a strong preference for avoiding the costs of litigation before an ordinary court. The reduction of formalism and expense, however, has probably not led to a substantial increase in over-all levels of contractual litigation in the UK, but merely changed the selection of the forum in favour of the small claims system.[67] For small businesses, sole traders, shopkeepers, and small professional firms, however, the small claims system may have proved beneficial in reducing the costs of debt collection and minor contractual disputes. At the same time, it seems that the private individual defendants in such cases continue with their perennial disadvantages stemming from the lack of legal representation and unfamiliarity with legal procedures.[68]

The ambition of providing a customer-friendly legal procedure that permits consumers to assert their contractual rights seems therefore to have largely failed. Instead, the small claims courts have assisted business in asserting contractual discipline against consumers by providing a less expensive method of debt collection. These insights have now provoked a different regulatory response. The solution proposed is to provide alternative dispute mechanisms.[69] These avoid the unilateral determinations provided by complaint-handling mechanisms yet also eschew the forms and expenses of legal adjudication.

The concept of alternative dispute resolution has no precise meaning, but encompasses methods and procedures for bringing conflict to a conclusion without the use of courts to provide a final determination of the issues. Here we shall focus on arbitration and mediation. Arbitration consists of adjudication about rights in a similar discourse to that employed by a court, but differs by using an adjudicator selected by the parties and a procedure devised by self-regulation. The practice of mediation seeks to provide a neutral third party to assist the parties in dispute to reach a negotiated settlement.

---

[66] Lord Chancellor's Department, n. 17 above, 32, 33, 41. The picture is different if one examines the initiation of litigation, for a very high proportion of disputes in the higher courts are resolved by settlement. About 9,000 writs involving contractual disputes might be issued by the higher courts in a year.

[67] In New South Wales, Australia, with the exclusion of business plaintiffs and lawyers, and an emphasis upon mediation, there does seem to be an increase in contractual claims: Yin, C. N., and Cranston, R., 'Small Claims Tribunals in Australia', in C. J. Whelan (ed.), n. 60 above, 49, 64.

[68] Whelan, C. J., 'Small Claims in England and Wales: Redefining Justice', in C. J. Whelan (ed.), n. 60 above, 99, 118.

[69] See generally Palmer, M., and Roberts, S., *Dispute Processes: ADR and the Primary Forms of Decision Making* (London: Butterworths, 1998).

Arbitration

Businesses favour the use of arbitration in order to reduce costs and delays of dispute settlement through litigation in the courts. It may also have the attraction of being a private process, so that the potential damage to business reputation by a public declaration of default can be avoided. Yet arbitration remains fundamentally a structure provoking discourses of claims of contractual rights, so that it shares the same feature as litigation of imposing damage on the other normative contexts of the deal and the long-term business relation. As one American businessman put it:

If you win the arbitration, you lose the customer . . . you only arbitrate where you can afford the loss.[70]

The use of arbitration can work to the advantage of both parties in commercial contracts, but when imposed upon a consumer through an adhesion contract there is a real danger of the arbitration effectively waiving the consumer's rights to the procedural evidential safeguards of a court trial.[71]

A striking feature of commercial disputes in the United Kingdom has been the prevalence of arbitration as the dominant system of formal dispute resolution. The use of the courts for disputes over commercial contracts has always been low compared to European civil law jurisdictions, no doubt in part due to the relative costs of litigation. We have already considered in Chapter 8 why the 'substantive rationality' of arbitrators fits the needs of business better than the formal rationality of private law systems administered by ordinary courts.

In consumer transactions as well, businesses favour the use of arbitration and often insert this option as a term in the standard form contract. These private adjudication systems obviously create the risk that the industry or trade will devise procedures which deprive a consumer of a chance to have a complaint considered impartially. Special regulation of consumer arbitration agreements is therefore appropriate in order to ensure procedural fairness.[72] In practice, however, such is the economic interest of businesses in avoiding the expense of litigation in ordinary consumer disputes (as opposed to test cases) that they may be willing to adopt procedures which will attract consumers to the forum. In the United Kingdom, for instance, many insurance companies have agreed to use an arbitration system which

---

[70] Bonn, R. L., 'The Predictability of Nonlegalistic Adjudication', *Law and Society Review* 6 (1972) 563, 573.

[71] Schwartz, D. S., 'Enforcing Small Print to Protect Big Business: Employee and Consumer Rights Claims in an Age of Compelled Arbitration', *Wisconsin Law Review* (1997) 33.

[72] Consumer Arbitration Agreements Act 1988, replaced by Unfair Terms in Consumer Contracts Regulations 1994, Schedule 3, para. (q), by Arbitration Act 1996.

follows tighter regulatory standards than private law, namely those laid down in the industry's own Codes of Practice, and where the arbitrator's award is binding on the insurance company but not on the consumer, who therefore remains free to pursue a claim in the ordinary courts.[73] All the costs of the arbitration are also borne by the defendant insurance company, win or lose. Although this Personal Insurance Arbitration Service is un-usually favourable to consumers,[74] its existence reveals the strength of the preference by business to avoid litigation before the ordinary courts.

Similar considerations have led many business sectors, especially those supplying services, to create their own ombudsmen for the purpose of investigating consumer complaints and to recommend redress. Crucially, these ombudsmen are not tied to the self-regulation provided by the standard form contract supplemented by private law, but can consider the merits of a case more broadly. This discretion to employ substantive rationality permits ombudsmen both to deploy specialist expertise in rela-tion to the industry, and simultaneously to give weight to the reasonable expectations of the consumer. These ombudsmen have proved popular with relatively sophisticated consumers, in many instances becoming the first port of call after a business has rejected a claim.[75]

Mediation

More recent developments have sought to channel commercial disputes into mediation[76] and informal adjudication.[77] These measures seek to reduce the cost of dispute settlement and expedite outcomes compared to litigation and arbitration. One of the important reasons for the costs and delays of litigation and arbitration lies in the unwillingness of the parties to disclose full information about the strengths and weaknesses of their case in the hope of achieving a better settlement. A mediation system prior to trial may increase disclosure at an early stage, thereby enabling the parties to agree to an early settlement.[78] There is also evidence to support the hypothesis that compliance with mediated settlements is higher than adjudication over small claims, thereby improving the efficacy of dispute resolution.[79]

---

[73] Bridges-Adams, N., 'Too Good to Be True?', *New Law Journal* (1998) 755.

[74] Thomas, R., 'Consumer Arbitration Agreements Act 1998', *Arbitration* (1991) 48.

[75] Wilkinson, H. W., 'Complaining to Ombudsmen', *New Law Journal* (1992) 1348.

[76] Practice Note (Commercial Court Alternative Dispute Resolution) [1994] 1 All ER 34.

[77] e.g. the statutory adjudicator in construction disputes: Housing Grants, Construction and Regeneration Act 1996, Part II.

[78] Leff, A., A., 'Injury, Ignorance and Spite: The Dynamics of Coercive Collection', *Yale Law Journal* 80 (1970) 1.

[79] McEwen, C. A., and Maiman, R. J., 'Small Claims in Maine: An Empirical Assessment', *Maine Law Review* 33 (1983) 237.

More fundamentally, the emphasis upon mediation and specialist adjudication seems to be designed to change the frame of reference for the normative standards to be applied. Instead of the dispute being resolved by reference solely to the way in which the formal private regulation has established rights and obligation, some of the informal procedures such as mediation create the opportunity for the parties to invoke the economic rationality or 'deal' aspect of the transaction. This change of normative framework turns the dispute resolution mechanism into a form of assisted negotiation towards a settlement, in which the mediator improves communication between the parties, helps to crystallize the issues, and can indicate possible structures for solutions to the dispute that fit into the possibility of preserving the benefits of the deal insofar as possible.

Although these developments are still in their early stages in the UK, these techniques of mediation and conciliation appear not to be popular for the participants in some industries such as construction. This dislike of mediation arises perhaps because they have always attempted a negotiated settlement prior to the invocation of a more formal dispute procedure, so that further negotiation with the assistance of a mediator may appear to be a waste of time and money.[80] In other words, once the normative framework for contractual behaviour switches from the business deal to the contractual system of entitlements, it proves hard for the parties to reverse this transition, especially perhaps if the issue is now in the hands of lawyers.

Similar moves towards the introduction of mediation as the best technique for the resolution of private law consumer complaints have also been attempted.[81] Mediation has been presented as a process that overcomes many of the weaknesses of small claims courts for the poor litigant.[82] The courts have also promoted the possibility of mediation in order to reduce the backlog of cases. But individual litigants do not appear to have been attracted to mediation in contractual disputes. They may perceive that the process is still conducted by lawyers, so that they may prefer to stick with the court system with its reputation for impartiality.[83] Individuals may also believe that their disadvantages in terms of expertise with respect to negotiations will be less harmful to their interests if they can obtain impartial adjudication.

Given that the vast majority of consumer problems are dealt with by the complaint mechanisms of retailers and manufacturers, it must be doubted

---

[80] Gould, N., and Cohen, M., 'ADR: Appropriate Dispute Resolution in the U.K. Construction Industry', *Civil Justice Quarterly* 17 (1998) 103. Genn, H. *The Central London County Court Pilot Mediation Scheme* (London: Lord Chancellor's Department, 1988).

[81] e.g. Saskatchewan Consumer Products Warranties Act, R.S.S. 1978 c c-30.

[82] Yngvesson, B. and Hennessey, P., n. 57 above, 260, 264–5.

[83] Auerbach, J. *Justice Without Law? Resolving Disputes Without Lawyers* (Oxford: Oxford University Press, 1983) 131–3.

whether for those few cases which proceed towards trial a further mediation process will resolve the matter. On the contrary, by placing an additional obstacle in front of the consumer seeking redress, it weakens her bargaining power even further with respect to a settlement, and may deter the commencement of litigation altogether.[84] We must also be concerned that the 'repeat player', the business used to handling complaints, may be able to manipulate such an informal process to its advantage. By steering these few cases away from the courts, the mediation procedure also prevents the courts from engaging in the weak form of private law regulation of clarifying the meaning of the legal standards in particular contexts.[85] Mediation and other forms of alternative dispute resolution do not therefore provide a solution to the problems of lack of resources of consumer plaintiffs, and may further weaken the efficacy of private law regulation in achieving satisfactory quality.

With respect to consumer complaints, there is another established pattern of mediation. When the consumer turns to a consumer agency charged with the responsibility for enforcing public regulation, then the official commonly assumes the role of mediator between consumer and retailer. The officer does not threaten prosecution, but rather tries to achieve a settlement as a mediator by explaining the facts as described by the consumer and the relevant legal obligations of the business, without stating what outcome might be required by the law. The fact that the mediator also possesses powers of prosecution in the last resort seems to expedite the resolution of the disputes,[86] and it must certainly encourage the trader to listen attentively to the complaint and to provide a justified response. Although this role of mediator for public officials is not of course contemplated or described in the relevant legislation, it may represent the most successful instance of mediation in contractual disputes.

For Settlement

My examination of the systems of dispute resolution in connection with contracts has emphasized the point that legal regulation tends to be oriented towards a solution through litigation and adjudication by courts whereas the preferences of the parties are usually to avoid these mechanisms. For the vast majority of disputes, which concern minor grievances of consumers, the parties seek a settlement through the operations of the retailer's complaints mechanism. The bulk of cases which enter the legal system consist of claims for debts, where the creditor usually pursues

---

[84] Ramsay, I., n. 2 above, 149.   [85] Ibid. 142.
[86] Cranston, R., n. 42 above, 95.

successfully a truncated procedure which establishes an authoritative bureaucratic decision that a precise sum of money is owed by the debtor, but then the creditor often has to seek a settlement for part of that debt. In the complex and high value commercial disputes, the parties prefer to avoid litigation in order to preserve the long-term business relation and the profitability of the deal for both parties by reaching a settlement. On those rare occasions when the incentives to settle are insufficiently compelling, then the commercial parties will normally prefer to use private arbitration for the determination of rights. This divergence between the objectives of regulation and the practices of the parties in dispute leads me to question whether the objectives of the regulation need to be revised.

The contemporary emphasis of public policy to provide access to justice seems to be aimed at redistributing a 'good' that parties to contractual disputes do not want. Consumers probably do not want to be bothered by formal dispute processes, and retailers certainly wish to avoid the costs of litigation in resolving complaints. Commercial contractors will continue to prefer to use private arbitration for their disputes. Improved access to justice appears only to benefit businesses seeking to enforce debts against individuals, by reducing the costs of the enforcement process, though not necessarily increasing the chances of recovery of the money.

Nor do I think that the parties to contractual disputes generally want a mechanism which provides strict vindication of contractual rights. As I have argued throughout this book, the dominant considerations in contractual behaviour are likely to be provided by the framework of the business relation and the success of a particular deal. Strict enforcement of contractual rights, by reversing the priority in favour of the contractual frame of reference, is likely to subvert those considerations which usually point in the direction of accommodation and settlement. In the case of retailers, for instance, when they adopt the policy that the customer is always right, obsessive attention to the strict entitlements of the consumer under private law and the terms of the contract would subvert their policy objective of maintaining the relation and achieving future sales. Similarly, businessmen are reluctant to introduce lawyers into the dispute settlement process, for they fear that a similar reversal of priorities will occur by the lawyers' appropriation of the dispute.

Settlement is the preferred outcome of the parties in most contractual disputes, not some formal vindication of contractual rights based upon a narrow and partial interpretation of expectations. The important question for regulation is whether settlements can be facilitated, without providing the opportunity for oppressive or one-sided settlements, in which expectations of one party are as roundly destroyed as by losing in litigation. The key to achieving a settlement is to accord priority to the broad range of expectations of the parties, not to permit the reduction of discursive framework to the contractual set of entitlements. In the context of commercial disputes, this policy objective may amount to little more than respecting the choice of the parties as to the mechanism for the resolution of the dispute. Regulation may perhaps assist by creating a variety of institutions, such as arbitration, mediation, and conciliation, on which the parties may draw according to their perceptions of how best to achieve a satisfactory settlement. With respect to debt collection, the courts and their judgments appear to serve as a bargaining counter in achieving a more advantageous settlement for the creditor compared to other creditors. There may be a case for making it harder to achieve such an advantage, at least to the extent of assisting the debtor in preventing truncated judgment procedures where there is a genuine dispute about the sum of money owed.

Perhaps regulation can make its most important contribution to resolution of disputes in connection with consumer grievances. But the objective of regulation should not be to improve access to justice and easier vindication of contractual rights. Although the reasoning behind the creation of small claims courts of improving access to justice as a real alternative to the costs and frustrations of making complaints remains as popular today as when it was first initiated,[87] these adjustments to the operations of the legal system have made little difference to the plight of consumers in practice. We should instead learn from the behaviour of the parties to such disputes, who usually channel the dispute into a complaints mechanism. In complaint handling, from the perspective of business, contractual entitlements are unimportant compared to such matters as business reputation and the preservation of long-term trading relations in the form of repeat purchases. At the same time, the consumer with a complaint is naturally reluctant to devote the time and energy to engage in any type of external dispute resolution mechanism, whether it comprises an informal court, arbitration, or even a mediation service. We may surmise that in general this is a rational response on the part of consumers, because they expect the retailer to be concerned about the long-term business relation, and count on this potential non-legal sanction as the driving force in the complaint-handling mechanism. The rationality of this response is confirmed when we discover that many consumers obtain superior rights under the complaint-handling mechanism than their strict legal entitlements.

A better way to view regulatory policy is therefore to concentrate on the non-legal sanctions that support complaint-handling mechanisms which favour the interests of consumers. Can these sanctions be strengthened in such a way that those complaint-handling processes which systematically repress the interests of consumers can be eliminated or at least reduced? These deceptive complaint-handling mechanisms are vulnerable to

---

[87] Nader, L., 'Disputing Without the Force of Law', *Yale Law Journal* 88 (1979) 998, 1020.

exposure and adverse publicity. Once it is publicized that a business never responds to complaints, then it cannot hope to establish the repeated pattern of trading on which its prosperity depends. Yet it is difficult to discover the information that exposes these companies without expensive investigations and media exposure through investigative journalism. Any legal procedure for exposing systematic practices designed to prevent consumers from obtaining redress seems to be necessarily cumbersome, for eventually a court must be provided with ample proof of these practices before it can be persuaded to close a business down.[88]

In the United Kingdom, the method of self-regulation by retail sector has been attempted. The trade association designs a set of standards for consumer redress mechanisms, seeks approval of those standards from the Office of Fair Trading, and then encourages its members to conform to the standards.[89] But this system fails to establish reliable complaint mechanisms for consumers. Retailers have no incentive to comply with the standards, for they lack publicity, so that reliable complaint mechanisms do not sufficiently influence consumer decisions. Trade associations have no incentive to police members and to impose sanctions against deviant members, for the association relies upon members for its subscriptions and survival. The complaint mechanisms that trade associations establish also can be designed to discourage complaints (and therefore costs to the association) by their elaborate requirements, so that consumers will often be best advised to turn to the ordinary courts.[90]

A better approach to the encouragement of satisfactory complaint mechanisms must adopt as its priority the conferral of commercial advantage to the retailer. Such an advantage can only be produced by a system of certification through which a business obtains the right to display a logo or badge that functions as a signal of reliability and fairness to consumers. A system of independent certification by reference to a model code would be required in order to render the certificate commercially valuable. Businesses which enjoy a good reputation as a result of prior investments would not need the logo, but new business and those which seek to improve their market share would have the economic incentive to incur the expense of certification. It would be necessary both to have periodic appraisals of the retailer's performance and the possibility of a criminal sanction for fraudulent use of the logo (as a false trade description). Proposals along these lines have been developed in the United Kingdom by the Office of Fair Trading.[91] These proposals differ from my own, however, because they permit the possibility of self-certification by a trader (in order to reduce

---

[88] Fair Trading Act 1973 part III contains such a mechanism which appears to be virtually unenforceable.   [89] Fair Trading Act 1973, s. 124(3).
[90] Office of Fair Trading, n. 38 above, 15.   [91] n. 38 above.

costs) and of a divergence in standards between sectors, and they appear to contemplate an arbitration system as the normal part of an approved complaint mechanism. In my view, self-certification by a retailer would undermine the credibility of the logo, thereby removing the economic incentive of the trader to acquire it in the first place. The possibility of divergence between market sectors seems to me to add an unnecessary complexity, for the proposed certification process considers business procedures in detail without imposing a fixed organizational model, so that it can be adjusted to the structure of the business. The recommendation for the need for an independent adjudication when the complaint mechanism fails, either in the form of arbitration or an ombudsman, may be harmless since it is unlikely to be used very much by consumers, but there is a danger that this final stage will encourage a more legalistic or contractual approach to the complaint-handling mechanism. I would be tempted rather to give the trader an incentive to acquire the logo by providing substantial protection against formal adjudication of legal rights, either by courts or arbitrators, where the certified complaint-handling mechanism has been followed.

This approach to legal regulation follows the pattern of reflexive regulation. It does not seek to force major changes of behaviour by trying to channel people towards novel institutions. It takes instead as its starting point the institutions which people have already constructed for themselves. It then seeks to understand the forces that sustain those practices, in this case the retailer's complaint-handling mechanism based upon long-term business relations and reputation. The regulatory intervention then takes the form of shifting the incentives slightly in order to encourage the participants to revise their practices in favoured directions. We provide the carrot of certification to encourage the practice of fair complaint handling, and the stick of adverse publicity and damage to economic interests to provide a further incentive to assimilate the regulatory objectives.

Our goal should not be one of access to justice, but rather the satisfactory and fair resolution of complaints for consumers. The parties do not want their contractual rights enforced. The consumer wants a solution to a disappointment, and the business wants to preserve its customer base. For this purpose, we should endeavour to revise existing social institutions, rather than to create new legal institutions that will confine their examination of the issues to the discourse of legal rights. The most important target of such a regulatory policy will be the retailer's complaint-handling mechanism. The vogue for policy initiatives designed to improve access to justice has been a distraction. We should recognize that the vast majority of contractual disputes are resolved by complaint-handling mechanisms. What is so striking about the law of contract and regulation of contractual practices is its almost complete absence in this field. The legal system presents itself as an institutional mechanism for channelling and resolving disputes, but in fact it has nothing to say about the process by which most contractual disputes will be resolved. Dispute settlement is left to market forces, those considerations of long-term business relations and reputation that provide retailers with incentives to devise complaint-handling mechanisms. What is needed for fair dispute resolution in a contractual context is legal intervention designed to adjust those market forces.

15
Conclusion

Markets and contracts are not natural phenomena. They only occur as a result of calculated human interaction. This social interaction establishes the trust and sanctions needed to establish the possibility of moving from taking to trading. The role of the law is not essential in this process: there are markets without a state. Nevertheless, legal regulation can have a significant impact on contracts and markets. Our discussion has been divided roughly into the two principal tasks for regulating contracts, that is, first, the assistance provided by the law to the construction of markets, and secondly, the effects of legal regulation designed to adjust the distributive outcomes of markets.

With respect to the construction of contracts and markets, I have argued that legal sanctions for breach of contract only make a marginal contribution. Other features of the legal process, such as the system of adjudication and support for security rights, are more important, because they reinforce non-legal sanctions such as collective reputation mechanisms and the credibility of commitments established by hostage-taking in the form of security rights. In regulating contractual agreements, the legal system often misunderstands the rationality of contractual practices, by emphasizing the significance of formal contractual commitments, especially if they are contained in planning documents, at the expense of supporting the priority given by the parties to the transaction to the long-term business relation and the success of the particular deal for both parties. Lawyers can make a valuable contribution to the formation of contractual agreements by clarifying the parties' objectives and the allocation of risks through planning documents, but there are limits to the utility of these written contracts, especially in contracts left incomplete by design. When seeking to enforce contracts, courts should recognize the tangential relevance of planning documents and their inevitable partial expression of the expectations of the parties.

In seeking to pursue the objective of supporting contracts and markets, legal regulation should regard its task as one of protecting the expectations of the parties. This task requires legal regulation to examine the discrete agreement in its embedded context of a business relation and market conventions, which is a process that we described as recontextualizing contractual agreements. This approach provides a method for reconciling the competing normative contexts of contractual agreements, which is vital if the law is to provide effective support for the establishment of the necessary trust and sanctions on which contracts and markets rest. The form of legal regulation which best enables the legal system to enhance this type of calculability of transactions oriented towards the full range of expectations of the parties is not a formal set of entitlements but rather open-textured rules and interpretative strategies which deprivilege the position of planning documents. In addition, the legal system needs to respect the autonomy of the parties' own systems of collective self-regulation, as in the case of arbitration, because these systems can usually achieve the task of contextualization more satisfactorily.

These conclusions may be regarded as controversial. They contain a sustained attack on a conventional theory of contractual regulation, which regards legal sanctions for breach of contract as the essential bedrock of civil society, and which insists that a formal system of strict legal entitlements, including those established by the planning documents, is necessary for markets to function. The basis for this attack has been an examination of the available empirical evidence about the successful operation of markets. The conventional view has troubled itself very little with this evidence, relying instead upon philosophical principles and simple economic models.

Turning to the second task for legal regulation of contracts, we have examined a number of discrete topics that may loosely be described as raising problems with respect to the distributive effects of markets. These discussions have sometimes commenced with an investigation of the evidence regarding the incidence of such problems as oppressive power relations, unfair contracts, and lack of access to justice, since even the existence and nature of the problems to be addressed by regulation is controversial. We have considered carefully what should be the principal objective of regulation in each context. Again this discussion has been based upon the available empirical evidence about the causes of these distributive problems, for by understanding the source of these problems we can produce a more differentiated response than a simple and probably ineffectual attempt to stop the incidence of the distributive problem. In relation to power relations established by contracts, for instance, the objective proposed was to insert regulation designed to establish structures that enhance the efficiency of these transactions, since the source of the relations of subordination was usually found in the development of incomplete governance structures designed to solve problems of coordination. Similarly, in the case of dispute settlement, the argument was that fair procedures designed to achieve settlements should be the principal goal of regulation, since the major problem was identified not as lack of access to justice but as the incomplete development of satisfactory complaint-handling mechanisms. In tackling these distributive questions, a crucial concern has been with respect to the development of efficient and effective regulatory systems. We have accordingly paid particular attention to the form of regulatory standards, and the monitoring and enforcement mechanisms.

This examination of the forms of regulatory systems has produced what may be regarded as an unconventional support for the use of private law. Instead of the tasks of regulating contracts being passed to new public regulatory systems, which has been the predominant response in the twentieth century to distributive problems in contracts, I have argued that private law has the capacity to provide a more sophisticated, contextualized, and efficient system of regulation in many instances. It is true that private law, especially in Europe, has failed to evolve its capacities adequately to address the whole range of regulatory tasks. Part of my argument has been, however, that with minor adjustments, often at the level of procedure rather than substantive law, such a capacity can be developed. The underlying advantage of private law regulation is the way it commences with a respect for the self-enforced, self-regulation of the parties to the contract, so that every intervention has to be justified as either one which better achieves their objectives or one which pursues important distributive objectives. This style of reflexive regulation ensures that interventions confront the context of transactions and provide regulation tailored to the particular circumstances of the transaction. Although public law regulation in the form of command and control strategies may sometimes be more effective in achieving compliance with its objectives, it creates the problem described as the 'regulatory trilemma', which the more subtle mechanisms of private law tend to avoid by methods for assessing the competing discourses surrounding contracts.

In order to support these conclusions, my method has departed from both conventional legal accounts of contract law and social science descriptions of markets. By viewing all legal intervention in markets, including private law, as types of regulation, we have been able to launch an investigation into the comparative advantages of different regulatory strategies with respect to the objectives of the legal regulation of contracts. We have therefore not followed the sharp distinctions drawn in political science, legal discourse, and economics between regulation and private law. Every effort has been made to ground an assessment of the comparative advantages of regulatory techniques in the available empirical evidence about the operation of markets and the effects of different types of regulation. It would be disingenuous, however, to pretend that the method employed simply entails a confrontation between legal regulation and the facts about its operations and effects.

In order to grasp the relation between regulation and the regulated sphere of social life, I have employed two principal methodologies in order to understand the facts revealed by empirical research. One method has been that of economics, which assumes social conduct can be explained by rational self-interested behaviour. In the context of contractual behaviour, we have been especially interested in models of rational conduct in the context of repeated non-co-operative games of indefinite duration. At first sight, this is an unlikely model, for contracts seem to represent the paradigm of co-operative one-off games. But the reason why this model is appropriate is that in contractual relations the problem is precisely to create co-operation in the form of exchange under conditions where short-term interest might often discourage a transaction owing to lack of trust and sanctions. The key to understanding how co-operation is established is to realize that the exchange is unlikely to represent an isolated transaction, but should rather be understood to be embedded in a business relation and other market conventions. Under this model, for instance, we have been particularly interested in how signals of trustworthiness or credible commitments serve to assist self-interested individuals in entering success-ful transactions.

A second method employed has been the insight of systems theory that the relation between contractual behaviour and regulation can best be understood as representing a problem of communication between two self-referential communication systems. Indeed, we extended this argument by the insistence that the social system of contracting needs to be divided into three distinct communication systems: the business relation, the deal, and the contract. The importance of stressing the gulf between these com-munication systems and legal regulation is that it alerts us to the many difficulties of achieving what I have described as contextualized regulation.

The use of these methods, and others, helps us to interpret the available evidence about the effects of legal regulation of markets and contracts. It must be admitted, however, that this evidence is patchy and susceptible to rival interpretations. The field of contractual behaviour is vast, and we have only been able to dip into the rich seam of research into its diverse manifestations from simple exchanges of fruit for fish in tribal societies to the operation of futures and derivative markets in complex financial markets. I am conscious too that I have also been unable to do justice to the variety of regulatory systems practised in comparative legal systems. The collective reputation mechanism provided by the courts differs radically, for example, between Japan and the United States, but these practices have been more or less lumped together. Different legal systems respond to their cultural context and local economic conventions, so that their regulation assumes different forms and institutions. In the endeavour to generalize about the performance of regulatory tasks, we have no doubt obliterated the significance of these local differences.

Interesting as these variations may prove to be, I do not think, however, that they represent the crucial task for further research and analysis. My view is that more valuable insights are likely to obtained by studying the problems for regulating markets and contracts posed by the globalization of markets. These problems commence with the formidable task of constructing trust and sanctions in a global marketplace. The distributive tasks of regulation will also become more complex as markets can relocate in order to take advantage of favourable regulation. Perhaps most interesting from a legal point of view will be the evolution of regulation as national legal traditions collide with transnational regulatory endeavours. This collision will certainly provoke disintegration of national legal systems, but perhaps it will create the conditions for the necessary evolution of the capacities of private law.

Disintegration in the law of contract will arise as regulation seeks to establish uniform rules for particular types of transactions across nation state boundaries. In order to achieve adequate contextual understanding of transactions, the regulatory and adjudicatory bodies will become established on the basis of market sectors rather than the political demarcations of nation states. At the same time, as these markets expand regionally or globally, the regulatory authority will need to establish co-ordination at a supra-national level. In the case of consumer transactions, for instance, as large trading blocks such as the European Union become a single consumer market, then regulation of these transactions for the purposes of assisting in the construction of trust and the reversal of distributive outcomes will become both supra-national in character, but also more precisely oriented to the normative expectations of the parties in retail trading. It may also become necessary for adequate contextualization of regulation to subdivide this regulatory field of consumer transactions by recognizing discrete market sectors, such as electronic trading through the Internet. The same process of disintegration of national regulatory systems over contracts will occur in commercial transactions, as indeed is already foreshadowed in such areas as international shipping, where the system of private arbitration provides the dominant regulatory and adjudicative approach.

At the same time, I suggest that the techniques of legal regulation of contracts will evolve new capacities. The need to establish reasoning about contracts which enables the contextualization of rational market behaviour pushes regulation towards greater differentiation between types of contract and the use of more open-textured standards. The tradition of private law can evolve that capacity, but it needs to develop the further capacity to orient its regulation towards entire market sectors rather than individual contracts. In particular, in order to escape its weaknesses with respect to the recognition of public goods and collective interests such as externalities, the reasoning of private law needs to realize a capacity to steer standard form contracts and dispute-handling processes for a particular market sector as a whole.

An optimism pervades this book about the potential of legal regulation to evolve these capacities. I have suggested that we have reached an interesting historical moment. The great nineteenth-century systems of private law were demonstrated to be defective instruments of regulation in many respects, particularly in achieving the distributive objectives of regulating contracts. I have added to those criticisms by attacking the effectiveness of formal logical reasoning in serving the most basic task of providing support for the construction of trust and sanctions in markets. Yet the solution to these regulatory problems adopted in the twentieth century, the welfare or public regulation that uses a command and control approach, has also been demonstrated to suffer equally from comparable weakness in efficiency and efficacy. Despite this record of failure in the tasks of regulating contracts, I have argued that the collision between private law and public law regulation of contracts creates a fresh productive capacity for regulation. The insights of the reflexive capacity of private law combined with the collective policy orientation of public regulation can provide the springboard for more productive regulation.

Bibliography

Ackerman, B., 'Regulating Slum Housing Markets On Behalf of the Poor: Of Housing Codes, Housing Subsidies and Income Redistribution Policy', *Yale Law Journal* 80 (1971) 1093.

Adams, J. N., 'Unconscionability and the Standard Form Contract', in R. Brownsword, G. Howells, and T. Wilhelmsson (eds.), *Welfarism in Contract Law* (Aldershot: Dartmouth, 1994) 230.

—— and Brownsword, R., 'The Ideologies of Contract', *Legal Studies* 7 (1987) 205.

Aivazian, V. A., Trebilcock, M. J., and Penny, M., 'The Law of Contract Modifications: The Uncertain Question for a Benchmark of Enforceability', *Osgoode Hall Law Journal* 22 (1984) 173.

Akerlof, G. A. 'The Market for "Lemons": Qualitative Uncertainty and the Market Mechanism', *Quarterly Journal of Economics* 84 (1970) 488.

Alexander, L., and Wang, W., 'Natural Advantages and Contractual Justice', *Law and Philosophy* 3 (1984) 281.

Allen, P., 'Contracts in the National Health Service Internal Market', *Modern Law Review* 58 (1995) 321.

Appleby, G., 'Small Claims in England and Wales', in M. Cappelletti and J. Weisner, (eds.), *Access to Justice*, (Alphenandenrij: Sijthoff, 1978) ii. 1. 736.

Arrighetti, A., Bachmann, R., and Deakin, S., 'Contract Law, Social Norms and Inter-Firm Co-operation', *Cambridge Journal of Economics* 21 (1997) 171.

Arrow, K. J., 'The Economics of Moral Hazard: Further Comment', *American Economic Review* 58 (1968) 537.

Arthurs, H. W., 'Special Courts, Special Law: Legal Pluralism in Nineteenth Century England', in G. R. Rubin and D. Sugerman (eds.), below, 380.

Atiyah, P. S. *The Rise and Fall of Freedom of Contract* (Oxford: Clarendon Press, 1979).

—— *Essays on Contract* (Oxford: Clarendon Press, 1990).

Auerbach, J., *Justice Without Law? Resolving Disputes Without Lawyers* (Oxford: Oxford University Press, 1983).

Axelrod, R. M., *The Complexity of Cooperation*, (Princeton: Princeton University Press, 1997).

Ayres, I., 'Fair Driving: Gender and Race Discrimination in Retail Car Negotiations', *Harvard Law Review* 104 (1991) 817.

—— and Braithwaite, J., *Responsive Regulation: Transcending the Deregulation Debate* (New York: Oxford University Press,1992).

Baldwin, J., *Small Claims in the County Courts in England and Wales: The Bargain Basement of Civil Justice* (Oxford: Clarendon Press, 1997).

—— 'Increasing the Small Claims Limit', *New Law Journal* (1998) 274–6.

Baldwin, R., *Rules and Government* (Oxford: Clarendon Press, 1995).

Baker, J. H., *An Introduction to English Legal History* 2nd edition (London: Butterworths, 1979).

Barbour, V., *Capitalism in Amsterdam in the Seventeenth Century* (Baltimore: John Hopkins Press, 1950).

Beale, H., and Dugdale, T., 'Contracts between Businessmen: Planning and the Use of Contractual Remedies', *British Journal of Law and Society* 2 (1975) 45.

—— Harris, D., and Sharpe, T., 'The Distribution of Cars: A Complex Contractual Technique', in D. Harris and D. Tallon (eds.), *Contract Law Today: Anglo-French Comparisons* (Oxford: Oxford University Press, 1989) 301.

Belobaba, E. P., 'The Resolution of Common Law Contract Doctrinal Problems Through Legislative and Administrative Intervention', in B. J. Reiter and J. Swan (eds.), *Studies in Contract Law* (Toronto: Butterworths, 1980) 423.

Bendor, J., and Mookherjee, D., 'Norms, Third-party Sanctions, and Co-operation', *Journal of Law, Economics and Organization* 6 (1990) 33.

Bernstein, E. A., 'Law and Economics and the Structure of Value Adding Contracts: A Contract Lawyer's View of the Law and Economics Literature', *Oregon Law Review* 74 (1995) 189.

Bernstein, L., 'Opting Out of the Legal System: Extralegal Contractual Relations in the Diamond Industry', *Journal of Legal Studies* 21 (1992) 115.

Bernstein, Lisa, 'The Silicon Valley Lawyer as Transaction Cost Engineer?', *Oregon Law Review* 74 (1995) 239.

Best, A., and Andreasen, A. R., 'Consumer Response to Unsatisfactory Purchase: A Survey of Perceiving Defects, Voicing Complaints, and Obtaining Redress', *Law and Society Review* 11 (1976–7) 701.

Birks, P., 'Definition and Division: A Meditation on Institutes 3.13', in P. Birks (ed.), *The Classification of Obligations* (Oxford: Clarendon Press, 1997) 1.

Black, J., 'Constitutionalising Self-regulation', *Modern Law Review* 59 (1996) 24.

Blau, P. M., *Exchange and Power in Social Life* (New York: Wiley, 1964).

Blegvad, B., 'Commercial Relations, Contract, and Litigation in Denmark: A Discussion of Macaulay's Theories', *Law and Society Review* 24 (1990) 397.

Board of Trade, *Final Report of the Committee on Consumer Protection*, Cmnd 1781 (London: 1962).

Bonn, R. L., 'The Predictability of Nonlegalistic Adjudication', *Law and Society Review* 6 (1972) 563.

Braithwaite, J., and Braithwaite, V., 'The Politics of Legalism: Rules versus Standard in Nursing-Home Regulation', *Social and Legal Studies* 4 (1995) 307.

Braudel, F., *Civilization and Capitalism*, ii, *The Wheels of Commerce*, trans. S. Reynolds, (London: 1982).

Brickly, J. A., Dark, F. H., and Weisbach, M. S., 'The Economic Effects of Franchise Termination Laws', *Journal of Law and Economics* 34 (1991) 101.

Bridges-Adams, N., 'Too Good to Be True?', *New Law Journal* (1998) 755.

Buckley, P., and Mitchie, J. (eds.), *Firms, Organizations and Contracts: A Reader in Industrial Organization* (Oxford: Oxford University Press, 1996).

Burrows, P., 'Contract Discipline: in Search of Principles in the Control of Contracting Power', *European Journal of Law and Economics* 2 (1995) 127.

Byrne, E. H., 'Commercial Contracts of the Genoese in the Syrian Trade of the Twelfth Century', *Quarterly Journal of Economics* 31 (1916) 128.

Cain, M., 'Where are the Disputes? A Study of a First Instance Civil Court in the

U.K.', in M. Cain and K. Kulcsar (eds.), *Disputes and the Law* (Budapest: Academiai Kiado, 1983) 119.

Campbell, D., ' The Social Theory of Relational Contract: Macneil as the Modern Proudhon', *International Journal of Sociology of Law* 18 (1990) 75.

—— 'Socio-Legal Analysis of Contract', in P. A. Thomas (ed.), *Socio-Legal Studies* (Aldershot: Dartmouth, 1997) 239.

—— and Harris, D., 'Flexibility in Long-term Contractual Relationships', *Journal of Law and Society* 20 (1993) 166.

—— and Vincent-Jones, P. (eds.), *Contract and Economic Organisation: Socio-legal Initiatives* (Aldershot: Dartmouth, 1996).

Card, D., and Krueger, A. B., *Myth and Measurement: The New Economics of the Minimum Wage* (New Jersey: Princeton University Press, 1995).

Cayne, D., and Trebilcock, M., 'Market Considerations in the Formulation of Consumer Protection Policy', *University of Toronto Law Journal* 23 (1973) 396.

Chafee, Z., 'Equitable Servitudes on Chattels', *Harvard Law Review* 41 (1928) 945.

Charney, D., 'Hypothetical Bargains: The Normative Structure of Contract Interpretation', *Michigan Law Review* 89 (1991) 1815.

—— 'Non-legal Sanctions in Commercial Relationships', *Harvard Law Review* 104 (1990) 373.

Chorley, R. S. T., 'The Conflict of Law and Commerce', *Law Quarterly Review* CLXXXIX (1932) 51.

Clarkson, K. W., Miller, R. L., and Muris, T. J., 'Liquidated Damages v Penalties: Sense or Nonsense', *Wisconsin Law Review* (1978) 351.

Clay, K., 'Trade Without Law: Private-Order Institutions in Mexican California', *Journal of Law, Economics and Organization* 13 (1997) 202.

Coase, R. H., 'The Nature of the Firm', *Economica* NS 4 (1937) 386.

Coleman, J. L., *Markets, Morals and the Law* (Cambridge: Cambridge University Press, 1988).

Collins, H., 'Independent Contractors and the Challenge of Vertical Disintegration to Employment Protection laws', *Oxford Journal of Legal Studies* 10 (1990) 353.

—— 'Ascription of Legal Responsibility to Groups in Complex Patterns of Economic Interaction', *Modern Law Review* 53 (1990) 731.

—— 'Distributive Justice Through Contracts', *Current Legal Problems* 45(2) (1992) 49.

—— *Justice in Dismissal: The Law of Termination of Employment* (Oxford: Clarendon Press, 1992).

—— *The Law of Contract,* 3rd edn. (London: Butterworths, 1997).

—— 'Productive Learning from the Collision Between the Doctrinal Subsystems of Contract and Tort', *Acta Juridica* (1997) 55.

—— 'Legal Classifications as the Production of Knowledge Systems', in P. Birks (ed.), *The Classification of Obligations* (Oxford: Clarendon Press, 1997) 57.

—— 'The Sanctimony of Contract', in R. Rawlings (ed.), *Law, Society and Economy* (Oxford: Oxford University Press, 1997) 63.

—— 'Quality Assurance in Subcontracting', in S. Deakin and J. Mitchie (eds.), below, 285.

Collins, H., 'The Voice of the Community in Private Law', *European Law Journal 3* (1997) 407.

—— and Scott, C., 'United Kingdom', in G. Bruggermeier (ed.), *Rechtprobleme von Qualitätsmanagementvereinbarungen und EG-Binnenmarkt* (Baden-Baden: Nomos, 1997) 239.

Comment, 'The Statute of Frauds and the Business Community: A Re-Appraisal in Light of Prevailing Practices', *Yale Law Journal* 66 (1957) 1038.

Consumer Council, *Justice Out of Reach* (London, HMSO, 1970).

Cornish, W. R., and Clark, G. de N., *Law and Society in England 1750–1950* (London: Sweet & Maxwell, 1989).

Cotterell, R., 'The Development of Capitalism and the Formalisation of Contract Law', in B. Fryer *et al.* (eds.), *Law, State and Society* (London: Croom Helm, 1981) 54.

Cranston, R., *Regulating Business: Law and Consumer Agencies* (London: MacMillan, 1979).

—— *Consumers and the Law*, 2nd edn. (London: Weidenfeld and Nicholson, 1984).

—— 'What do Courts Do?', *Civil Justice Quarterly* 5 (1986) 123.

—— 'The Green Paper on Consumer Guarantees', *Consumer Law Journal* 3 (1995) 110.

Crocker, K. S., and Masten, S. E., 'Pretia Ex Machina? Prices and Process in Long-Term Contracts', *Journal of Law and Economics* 34 (1991) 69.

Crow, I., Howells, G., and Moroney, M., 'Credit and Debt: Choices for Poorer Consumers', in G. Howells, I. Crow, and M. Moroney (eds.), *Aspects of Credit and Debt* (London: Sweet and Maxwell, 1993) ch. 2.

Crystal, N. M., 'An Empirical View of Relational Contracts Under Article Two of the Uniform Commercial Code', *Annual Survey of American Law* (1988) 293.

Daintith, T., 'Regulation by Contract: the New Prerogative', *Current Legal Problems* (1979) 41.

—— 'The Design and Performance of Long-term Contracts', in T. Daintith and G. Teubner (eds.), *Contract and Organisation* (Berlin: Walter de Gruyter, 1986) 164.

—— 'Law as a Policy Instrument: A Comparative Perspective', in T. Daintith (ed.), *Law as an Instrument of Economic Policy: Comparative and Critical Approaches* (Berlin/New York: Walter de Gruyter, 1988) 3.

—— 'Vital Fluids: Beer and Petroleum Distribution in English Law', in C. Joerges (ed.), below, 143.

—— 'Regulation', *International Encyclopedia of Comparative Law*, (Dordrecht: Martinus Nijhoff, 1995) xvii, ch. 10.

Dalton, C., 'An Essay in the Deconstruction of Contract Doctrine', *Yale Law Journal* 94 (1985) 997.

Danzig, R., 'Hadley v. Baxendale: A Study in the Industrialization of the Law', *Journal of Legal Studies* 4 (1975) 249.

Dasgupta, P., 'Trust as a Commodity', in D. Gambetta (ed.), below.

Dawson, J. P., 'Judicial Revision of Frustrated Contracts: The US', *Boston University Law Review* 64 (1984) 1.

Deakin, S., Lane, C., and Wilkinson, F., 'Trust or Law? Towards an Integrated

Theory of Contractual Relations between Firms', *Journal of Law and Society* 21 (1994) 329.

—— —— —— 'Contract Law, Trust Relations, and Incentives for Co-operation: A Comparative Study', in S. Deakin and J. Michie, (eds.), below, 105.

—— and Michie, J. (eds.), *Contracts, Co-operation, and Competition* (Oxford: Oxford University Press, 1997).

Devlin, P., 'The Relation between Commercial Law and Commercial Practice', *Modern Law Review* 14 (1951) 249.

Dezalay, Y., 'Between the State, Law, and the Market: The Social and Professional Stakes in the Construction and Definition of a Regulatory Arena', in W. Bratton, J. McCahery, S. Picciotto, and C. Scott, *International Regulatory Competition and Coordination* (Oxford: Clarendon Press, 1996) 59.

—— and Garth, B. G., *Dealing In Virtue: International Commercial Arbitration and the Construction of a Transnational Legal Order* (Chicago: University of Chicago Press, 1996).

Diver, C. S., 'The Optimal Precision of Administrative Rules', *Yale Law Journal* 93 (1983) 65.

Dnes, A. W., '"Unfair" Contractual Practices and Hostages in Franchise Contracts', *Journal of Institutional and Theoretical Economics* 148 (1992) 484.

—— 'A Case-Study Analysis of Franchise Contracts', *Journal of Legal Studies* 22 (1993) 367.

—— and Rickman, N., 'Contracts for Legal Aid: A Critical Discussion of Government Policy Proposals', *European Journal of Law and Economics* 5 (1998) 247.

Dunworth, T., and Roger, J., 'Corporations in Court: Big Business Litigation in U.S. Federal Courts, 1971–1991', *Law and Social Inquiry* 21 (1996) 497.

Durkheim, E., *The Division of Labor in Society* (New York: Free Press, 1933) (originally published 1893).

Duxbury, N., 'Do Markets Degrade?', *Modern Law Review* 59 (1996) 331.

Eccles, R., 'The Quasifirm in the Construction Industry', *Journal of Economic Behaviour and Organization* 2 (1981) 335.

Epstein, R., 'Unconscionability: A Critical Reappraisal', *Journal of Law and Economics* 18 (1975) 293.

—— 'The Social Consequences of Common Law Rules', *Harvard Law Review* 95 (1982) 1717.

—— 'In Defence of the Contract at Will', *University of Chicago Law Review* 57 (1984) 947.

Esser, J. P., 'Institutionalizing Industry: The Changing Forms of Contract', *Law and Social Inquiry* 21 (1996) 593.

Farber, D., 'Contract Law and Modern Economic Theory', *Northwestern University Law Review* 78 (1983) 303.

Farnsworth, E. A., 'Good Faith in Contract Performance', in J. Beatson and D. Friedmann, *Good Faith in Contract Law* (Oxford: Clarendon Press, 1995) 153.

Fay, E., *Official Referees' Business* (London: Sweet and Maxwell, 1983).

Feinman, J. M., 'Promissory Estoppel and Judicial Method', *Harvard Law Review* 97 (1984) 678.

Felsted, A., 'The Social Organization of the Franchise: A Case of "Controlled Self-Employment"', *Work, Employment and Society* 5 (1991) 37.

Ferguson, R. B., 'Commercial Expectations and the Guarantee of the Law: Sales Transactions in Mid-Nineteenth Century England', in G. R. Rubin and D. Sugerman (eds.), below, 192.

—— 'The Adjudication of Commercial Disputes and the Legal System in Modern England', *British Journal of Law and Society* 7 (1980) 141.

Fiss, O., 'Against Settlement' *Yale Law Journal* 93 (1984) 1074.

Flood, J., and Caiger, A., 'Lawyers and Arbitration: The Juridification of Construction Disputes', *Modern Law Review* 56 (1993) 412.

Fox, A., *Beyond Contract: Work, Power and Trust Relations* (London: Faber, 1974).

Frase, A. R. G., 'The Role of the Exchange', in H. Parry, E. C. Bettelheim, and W. Rees, *Futures Trading: Law and Regulation* (London: Longman, 1993) 73.

Fredman, S., and Morris, G., 'The Costs of Exclusivity: Public and Private Re-examined', *Public Law* (1994) 69.

Freedland, M., 'Government by Contract and Public Law', *Public Law* (1994) 86.

Fried, C., *Contract as Promise* (Cambridge, Mass.: Harvard University Press, 1981).

Friedman, D., 'The Efficient Breach Fallacy', *Journal of Legal Studies* 18 (1989) 1.

Friedman, L. M., *Contract Law in America* (Madison: University of Wisconsin Press, 1965).

Friedmann, W., *Law in a Changing Society*, 2nd edn. (Harmondsworth: Penguin, 1972).

Fulbrook, J., 'The Jobseekers Act 1995: Consolidation with a Sting of Contractual Compliance', *Industrial Law Journal* 24 (1995) 395.

Galanter, M., 'Why the "Haves" Come Out Ahead: Speculations on the Limits of Legal Change', *Law and Society Review* 9 (1974–5) 95.

—— 'Afterword: Explaining Litigation', *Law and Society Review* 9 (1974–5) 347.

Gambetta, D. (ed.), *Trust: Making and Breaking Cooperative Relations* (Oxford: Blackwell, 1988).

Gava, J., and Kincaid, P., 'Contract and Conventionalism: Professional Attitudes to Changes in Contract Law in Australia', *Journal of Contract Law* 10 (1996) 141.

Genn, H., *The Central London County Court Pilot Mediation Scheme* (London: Lord Chancellor's Department, 1988).

Ghestin, J., *Traité de Droit Civil, ii. Les Obligations: Le Contrat* (Paris: L.G.D.J., 1980).

Giddens, A., *The Consequences of Modernity* (Cambridge: Polity Press, 1991).

Gilmore, G., *The Death of Contract* (Columbus, Ohio: Ohio State University Press, 1974).

Goff, Sir Robert, 'Commercial Contracts and the Commercial Court', *Lloyds Maritime and Commercial Law Quarterly* [1984] 382.

Goldberg, V., 'Relational Exchange: Economics and Complex Contracts', *American Behavioral Scientist* 23 (1980) 337.

—— *Readings in the Economics of Contract Law* (Cambridge: Cambridge University Press, 1989).

—— and Erickson, J. R., 'Quantity and Price Adjustment in Long-Term Contracts: A Case Study of Petroleum Coke', *Journal of Law and Economics* 30 (1987) 369.

Goetz, C., and Scott, R., 'Liquidated Damages, Penalties and the Just Compensation Principle', *Columbia Law Review* 77 (1977) 55.

Goode, R., 'The Concept and Implications of a Market in Commercial Law', *Israel Law Review* 24 (1990) 185.

—— *Commercial Law*, 2nd edn., (London: Penguin, 1995).

Goodrich, P., *Languages of Law* (London: Weidenfeld, 1990).

Gordley, J., *The Philosophical Origins of Modern Contract Doctrine* (Oxford: Clarendon Press, 1991).

Gordon, R., 'Macaulay, Macneil, and the Discovery of Solidarity and Power in Contract Law', *Wisconsin Law Review* (1985) 565.

Gompers, P., and Lerner, J., 'The Use of Covenants: An Empirical Analysis of Venture Partnership Agreements', *Journal of Law and Economics* 39 (1996) 463.

Gould, N., and Cohen, M., 'ADR: Appropriate Dispute Resolution in the U.K. Construction Industry', *Civil Justice Quarterly* 17 (1998) 103.

Granovetter, M., 'Economic Action and Social Structure: The Problem of Embeddedness', *American Journal of Sociology* 91 (1985) 481.

Greeley, H. T., 'Contracts as Commodities: The Influence of Secondary Purchasers on the Form of Contracts', *Vanderbilt Law Review* 42 (1989) 133.

Greenberg, D. I., 'Easy Terms, Hard Times: Complaint Handling in the Ghetto', in L. Nader (ed.), *No Access to Law: Alternatives to the American Judicial System* (New York: Academic Press, 1980) 379.

Grief, A., 'Institutions and International Trade: Lessons from the Commercial Revolution', *American Economic Review, Papers and Proceedings* 82 (1992) 128.

—— 'Contract Enforceability and Economic Institutions in Early Trade: The Maghribi Traders' Coalition', *American Economic Review* 83 (1993) 525.

Grossman, S. J., and Hart, O. D., 'The Costs and Benefits of Ownership: A Theory of Vertical and Lateral Integration', *Journal of Political Economy* 94 (1986) 691.

Habermas, J., *Between Facts and Norms* (Cambridge: Cambridge University Press, 1996).

Hadfield, G. K., 'Problematic Relations: Franchising and the Law of Incomplete Contracts', *Stanford Law Review* 42 (1990) 927.

Haley, J. O., 'Relational Contracting: Does Community Count?', in H. Baum (ed.), *Japan: Economic Success and Legal System* (Berlin/New York: Walter de Gruyter, 1997) 167.

Harden, I., *The Contracting State* (Milton Keynes: Open University Press, 1992).

Harlow, C., and Rawlings, R., *Law and Administration*, 2nd edn, (London: Butterworths, 1997).

Harris, D., 'Incentives to Perform, or Break Contracts', *Current Legal Problems* 45(2) (1992) 29.

Hart, H. L. A., *The Concept of Law*, 2nd edn. (Oxford: Clarendon Press, 1994).

Hart, K., 'Kinship, Contract, Trust: The Economic Organization of Migrants in an African City Slum', in D. Gambetta (ed.), above, 176.

Hart, O., 'Incomplete Contracts and the Theory of the Firm', *Journal of Law, Economics and Organization* 4 (1998) 119.

—— *Firms, Contracts and Financial Structure* (Oxford: Clarendon Press, 1995).

Hart, O., and Moore, J., 'Incomplete Contracts and Renegotiation', *Econometrica* 56 (1988) 755.

Hayek, F. von, *The Constitution of Liberty* (London: Routledge, 1960).

—— *Law, Legislation and Liberty*, ii (London: Routledge and Kegan Paul, 1982).

Henderson, J. 'Judicial Review of Manufacturers Conscious Design Choices: The Limits of Adjudication', *Columbia Law Review* 73 (1973) 1531.

Hermalin, B., and Katz, M., 'Judicial Modification of Contracts between Sophisticated Parties: A More Complete View of Incomplete Contracts and their Breach', *Journal of Law, Economics and Organization* 9 (1993) 230.

Hillman, R. A., 'Court Adjustment of Long-term Contracts: An Analysis Under Modern Contract Law', *Duke Law Journal* (1987) 1.

Hobbes, T., *Leviathan* (Oxford: Oxford University Press, 1955) (first published 1651).

Holden, J. M., *The History of Negotiable Instruments in English Law* (London: University of London, Athlone Press, 1955).

Hood, C., James, O., Jones, G., Scott, C., and Travers, T., 'Regulation Inside Government: Where New Public Management Meets the Audit Explosion', *Public Money and Management* (1998) 61.

Horwitz, M. J., *The Transformation of American Law, 1780–1860* (Cambridge, Mass.: Harvard University Press, 1977).

Howarth, W., 'Contract, Reliance and Business Transactions', *Journal of Business Law* (1987) 122.

Huszach, S. M., and Huszach, F. W., 'Lawyers as Exchange Engineers in Commerce: An Empirical Overview', *Oregon Law Review* 74 (1995) 147.

Hviid, M., 'Relational Contracts, Repeated Interaction and Contract Modification', *European Journal of Law and Economics* 5 (1998) 179.

Ison, T. G., 'Small Claims', *Modern Law Review* 35 (1972) 18.

Jenkinson, T., and Mayer, C., 'The Assessment: Contracts and Competition', *Oxford Review of Economic Policy* 12(4) (1997) 1.

Jesse, E. V. and Johnson, A. C., 'An Analysis of Vegetable Contracts', *American Journal of Agricultural Economics* 52 (1970) 545.

Joerges, C., 'Quality Regulation in Consumer Goods Markets: Theoretical Concepts and Practical Examples', in T. Daintith and G. Teubner (eds.), *Contract and Organisation* (Berlin/New York: Walter de Gruyter, 1986) 142.

—— (ed.) *Franchising and the Law: Theoretical and Comparative Approaches in Europe and the United States* (Baden-Baden: Nomos Verlagsgesellschaft, 1991).

—— *The Market Without the State?*, EUI Working Paper Law No. 96/2, (Florence: European University Institute, 1996).

—— 'The Impact of European Integration on Private Law: Reductionist Perceptions, True Conflicts and a New Constitutionalist Perspective', *European Law Journal* 3 (1997), 378.

Joskow, P. L. 'Commercial Impossibility, The Uranium Market and the Westinghouse Case', *Journal of Legal Studies* 6 (1977) 119.

—— 'Contract Duration and Relationship Specific Investments: Empirical Evidence from Coal Markets', *American Economic Review* 77 (1987) 168.

—— 'Price Adjustment in Long-Term Contracts: The Case of Coal', *Journal of Law & Economics* 31 (1988) 47.

Kamkas, A., and Rosenwasser, R., 'Department Store Complaint Management', in L. Nader (ed.), *No Access to Law: Alternatives to the American Judicial System* (New York: Academic Press, 1980) 283.

Katz, A., 'When Should an Offer Stick? The Economics of Promissory Estoppel in Preliminary Negotiations', *Yale Law Journal* 105 (1996) 1249.

Kennedy, D., 'Form and Substance in Private Law Adjudication', *Harvard Law Review* 89 (1976) 1685.

—— 'Distributive and Paternalist Motives in Contract and Tort Law, With Special Reference to Compulsory Terms and Unequal Bargaining Power', *Maryland Law Review* 41 (1982) 563.

Kenney, R. W. and Klein, B., 'The Economics of Block Booking', *Journal of Law and Economics* 24 (1983) 497.

Kenworthy, L., Macaulay, S., and Rogers, J., '"The More Things Change . . .": Business Litigation and Governance in the American Automobile Industry', *Law and Social Inquiry* 21 (1996) 631.

Kessler, F., 'Contracts of Adhesion—Some Thoughts About Freedom of Contract', *Columbia Law Review* 43 (1943) 629.

—— 'Automobile Dealer Franchises: Vertical Integration by Contract', *Yale Law Journal* 66 (1957) 1135.

Kitagawa, Z., ' Use and Non-Use of Contracts in Japanese Business Relations: A Comparative Analysis', in H. Baum (ed.), *Japan: Economic Success and Legal System* (Berlin/New York: Walter de Gruyter, 1997) 145.

Klein, B., 'Transaction Cost Determinants of "Unfair" Contractual Arrangements', *American Economic Review Papers* 70 (1980) 356.

—— 'Self-Enforcing Contracts', *Journal of Institutional and Theoretical Economics* 141 (1985) 594.

—— Crawford, R. G., Alchian, Armen A., 'Vertical Integration, Appropriable Rents, and the Competitive Contracting Process', *Journal of Law and Economics* 21 (1978) 297.

—— and Leffler, K. B., 'The Role of Market Forces in Assuring Contractual Performance', *Journal of Political Economy* 89 (1981) 615.

Kronman, A. T., 'Specific Performance', *University of Chicago Law Review* 45 (1978) 351.

—— 'Mistake, Disclosure, Information, and the Law of Contracts', *Journal of Legal Studies* 7 (1978) 1.

—— 'Contract Law and Distributive Justice', *Yale Law Journal* 89 (1980) 472.

—— 'Paternalism and the Law of Contracts', *Yale Law Journal* 92 (1983) 763.

—— 'Contract Law and the State of Nature' *Journal of Law, Economics and Organisation* 1 (1985) 5.

—— and Posner, R. A., *The Economics of Contract Law* (Boston: Little Brown, 1979).

Kull, A., 'Reconsidering Gratuitous Promises', *Journal of Legal Studies* 21 (1992) 39.

Landa, J. T., 'A Theory of the Ethnically Homogeneous Middleman Group: An Institutional Alternative to Contract Law', *Journal of Legal Studies* 10 (1981) 349.

Landes, W. M., and Posner, R. A., 'The Private Enforcement of Law', *Journal of Legal Studies* 4 (1975) 1.

Lane, C., 'The Social Regulation of Inter-Firm Relations in Britain and Germany: Market Rules, Legal Norms, and Technical Standards', *Cambridge Journal of Economics* 21 (1997) 214.

—— and Bachmann, R., 'The Social Construction of Trust: Supplier Relations in Britain and Germany', *Organisation Studies* 17 (1996) 365.

Langbein, J. H., 'The Contractarian Basis of the Law of Trusts', *Yale Law Journal* 105 (1995) 625.

Law Commission, *Law of Contract: The Parol Evidence Rule*, Report No. 154, Cmnd. 9700 (1986).

Lazerson, M. H., 'An Outcome of Markets and Hierarchies?', *American Sociological Review* 53 (1988) 330.

Lee, R. G., 'Rent Control—The Economic Impact of Social Legislation', *Oxford Journal of Legal Studies* 12 (1992) 543.

Leff, A., 'Economic Analysis of Law: Some Realism about Nominalism', *Virginia Law Review* 60 (1974) 451.

—— 'Contract as Thing', *American University Law Review* 19 (1970) 131.

—— 'Unconscionability and the Crowd—Consumers and the Common Law Tradition', *University of Pittsburgh Law Review* 31 (1970) 349.

—— 'Injury, Ignorance and Spite—The Dynamics of Coercive Collection', *Yale Law Journal* 80 (1970) 1.

Lewis, R., 'Contracts between Businessmen: Reform of the Law of Firm Offers and an Empirical Study of Tendering Practices in the Building Industry', *British Journal of Law and Society* 9 (1982) 153.

—— 'Criticisms of the Traditional Contract Course', *The Law Teacher* 16 (1982) 111.

Livermore, J., 'Exemption Clauses in Inter-Business Contracts', *Journal of Business Law* [1986] 90.

Llewellyn, K. N., 'What Price Contract? An Essay in Perspective', *Yale Law Journal* 40 (1931) 704.

—— *The Common Law Tradition: Deciding Appeals* (Boston: Little, Brown, 1960).

Lord Chancellor's Department, *Judicial Statistics 1996* Cm 3716 (London: HMSO, 1997).

Lorenz, E. H., 'Neither Friends nor Strangers: Informal Networks of Subcontracting in French Industry, in D. Gambetta (ed.), above, 194.

Luhmann, N., *Trust and Power* (Chichester: Wiley, 1979).

Lutz, N. A., 'Warranties as Signals Under Consumer Moral Hazard', *Rand Journal of Economics* 20 (Summer 1989) 239.

Lyons, B. R., 'Empirical Relevance of Efficient Contract Theory: Inter-Firm Contracts', *Oxford Review of Economic Policy* 12(4) (1996) 27.

—— and Mehta, J., 'Private Sector Business Contracts: The Text Between the Lines', in S. Deakin and J. Mitchie (eds.), above, 43.

Macaulay, S., 'Non-Contractual Relations in Business', *American Sociological Review* 28 (1963) 45.

Macaulay, S., 'The Use and Non-use of Contracts in the Manufacturing Industry', *Practical Lawyer* 9(7) (1963) 13.

—— 'Private Legislation and the Duty to Read—Business by IBM Machine, the Law of Contracts and Credit Cards', *Vanderbilt Law Review* 19 (1966) 1051.

—— 'The Standardized Contracts of United States Automobile Manufacturers', *International Encyclopedia of Comparative Law* 7 (1973) 3.

—— 'Elegant Models, Empirical Pictures, and the Complexities of Contract', *Law and Society Review* 11 (1977) 507.

—— 'Lawyers and Consumer Protection Laws', *Law and Society Review* 14 (1979) 115.

—— 'An Empirical View of Contract', *Wisconsin Law Review* (1985) 465.

—— 'Long-Term Continuing Relations: The American Experience Regulating Dealerships and Franchises', in C. Joerges (ed.), above, 179.

—— 'Organic Transactions: Contract, Frank Lloyd Wright and the Johnson Building', *Wisconsin Law Review* (1996) 75.

—— Kidwell, J., Whitford, W., and Galanter, M., *Contracts: Law in Action* (Charlottesville: Michie Co.,1995).

McEwen, C. A. and Maiman, R. J., 'Small Claims in Maine: An Empirical Assessment', *Maine Law Review* 33 (1983) 237–64.

Mack, E., 'Dominos and the Fear of Commodification', in, J. W. Chapman and J. R. Pennock (eds.), *Markets and Justice* (New York: Nomos 31, New York University Press, 1989) 198.

Macneil, I, 'Contracts: Adjustment of Long-term Economic Relations under Classical, Neoclassical, and Relational Contract Law', *Northwestern University Law Review* 72 (1978) 854.

—— *The New Social Contract: An Inquiry Into Modern Contractual Relations* (New Haven: Yale University Press, 1980).

—— 'Values in Contract: Internal and External', *Northwestern University Law Review* 78 (1983) 340.

—— 'Bureaucracy and Contracts of Adhesion', *Osgoode Hall Law Journal* 22 (1984) 5.

—— 'Contract Remedies: A Need for Better Efficiency Analysis', *Journal of Institutional and Theoretical Economics* 144 (1988) 6.

Maher, M. E., 'Transaction Cost Economics and Contractual Relations', *Cambridge Journal of Economics* 21 (1997) 147.

Maine, H. S., *Ancient Law* (London: John Murray, 1861).

Malinowski, B., *Crime and Custom in Savage Society* (London: Routledge & Kegan Paul, 1926).

Mann, R. J., 'Explaining the Pattern of Secured Credit', *Harvard Law Review* 110 (1997) 625.

Margalin, S. A. 'What Do Bosses Do? The Origins and Functions of Hierarchy in Capitalist Production', *Review of Radical Political Economics* 6 (1974) 33.

Marx, K., 'Economic and Philosophical Manuscripts', in L. Colletti (ed.), *Early Writings* (Harmondsworth: Penguin/New Left Books, 1975).

—— *Capital,* i (Harmondsworth: Penguin/New Left Review, 1976).

Menkel-Meadow, C., 'Will Managed Care give us Access to Justice?', in R. Smith (ed.), *Achieving Civil Justice: Appropriate Dispute Resolution for the 1990s* (London: Legal Action Group, 1996) 94.

Mertens, L., 'Lex Mercatoria: A Self-applying System Beyond National Law?', in G. Teubner (ed.), *Global Law Without a State* (Aldershot: Gower, 1997) 31.

Micklitz, Hans-W., 'Directive 93/13 In Action: A Report on a Research Project on Unfair Terms in Consumer Sales', in C. Willett (ed.), *Aspects of Fairness in Contract* (London: Blackstone, 1996) 77.

Milgrom, P. R., North, D. C., and Weingast, B. R., 'The Role of Institutions in the Revival of Trade: The Law Merchant, Private Judges, and the Champagne Fairs', *Economics and Politics* 2 (1990) 1.

Miller, R., and Sarat, A., 'Grievances, Claims and Disputes: Assessing the Adversary Culture', *Law and Society Review* 15 (1980–1) 525.

Mnookin, R., 'Bargaining in the Shadow of the Law: The Case of Divorce', *Yale Law Journal* 88 (1979) 950.

Mueller, A. 'Contract Remedies: Business Fact and Legal Fantasy', *Wisconsin Law Review* [1967] 833.

Mulherin, J. H., Netter, J. M., and Overdahl, J. A., 'Prices are Property: The Organization of Financial Exchanges from a Transaction Cost Perspective', *Journal of Law and Economics* 34 (1991) 591.

Muris, T. J., 'Opportunistic Behaviour and the Law of Contracts', *Minnesota Law Review* 65 (1981) 521.

Nader, L., 'Disputing Without the Force of Law', *Yale Law Journal* 88 (1979) 998.

National Consumer Council, *Buying Problems: Consumers, Unsatisfactory Goods and the Law* (London: National Consumer Council, 1984).

—— *Seeking Civil Justice—A Survey of People's Needs and Experiences* (London: National Consumer Council, 1995).

Nelken, D., 'The Use of "Contracts" as a Social Work Technique', *Current Legal Problems* 40 (1987) 207.

Nelson, W. E., 'Contract Litigation and the Elite Bar in New York City, 1960–1980', *Emory Law Journal* 39 (1990) 413.

Nicholas, B., 'Rules and Terms—Civil Law and Common Law', *Tulane Law Review* 48 (1974) 946.

Note, 'Another Look at Construction Building and Contracts at Formation', *Virginia Law Review* 53 (1967) 1720.

Note, 'Reassessing Rent Control: Its Economic Impact in a Gentrifying Market', *Harvard Law Review* 101 (1987–8) 1835.

Nottage, L., 'Bargaining in the Shadow of the Law and the Law in the Light of Bargaining: Contract Planning and Renegotiation in the US, New Zealand and Japan,' in J. Feest and V. Gessner (eds.), *Interaction of Legal Cultures* (Onati: Onati International Institute of Sociology of Law, 1997).

Nozick, R., *Anarchy, State, and Utopia* (Oxford: Blackwell, 1974).

Office of Fair Trading, *Buying a Used Car—Consumers' Problems—A Consultative Paper* (London: OFT, 1979).

—— *Unfair Contract Terms*, Issue No. 3, (London: OFT, March 1997).

—— *Raising Standards of Consumer Care: Progressing Beyond Codes of Practice* (London: OFT, 206, 1998).

Oliver, D., 'Common Values in Public and Private Law and the Public/Private Divide', *Public Law* (1997) 630.

Olsen, F. E., 'The Family and the Market: A Study of Ideology and Legal Reform', *Harvard Law Review* 96 (1983) 1497.

Palay, T. M., 'Comparative Institutional Economics: The Governance of Rail Freight Contracting', *Journal of Legal Studies* 13 (1984) 265.

Palmer, M., and Roberts, S., *Dispute Processes: ADR and the Primary Forms of Decision Making* (London: Butterworths, 1998).

Patterson, E. 'Constructive Conditions in Contracts', *Columbia Law Review* 42 (1942) 903.

Phillips, L. T., 'Contractual Relationships in the Deregulated Transportation Marketplace', *Journal of Law and Economics* 34 (1991) 535.

Pirrong, S. C., 'The Efficient Scope of Private Transactions-Cost-Reducing Institutions: The Success and Failures of Commodity Exchanges', *Journal of Legal Studies* 24 (1995) 229.

Pittman, R., 'Specific Investments, Contracts, and Opportunism: The Evolution of Railroad Sidetrack Agreements', *Journal of Law and Economics* 34 (1991) 565.

Posner, E., 'Altruism, Status and Trust in the Law of Gifts and Gratuitous Promises', *Wisconsin Law Review* (1997) 567.

Posner, R., *Economic Analysis of Law*, 4th edn. (Boston: Little Brown, 1992).

Postan, M. M., *Medieval Trade and Finance* (Cambridge: Cambridge University Press, 1973).

Powell, W. W., 'Neither Market nor Hierarchy: Network Forms of Organization', *Research in Organizational Behaviour* 12 (1990) 295; also in G. Thompson, J. Frances, R. Levačić, and J. Mitchell (eds.), *Markets, Hierarchies and Networks: The Coordination of Social Life* (London: Sage, 1991) 265.

Powers, M. J., 'Effects of Contract Provisions on the Success of a Futures Contract', *Journal of Farm Economics* 49 (1967) 833.

Priest, G., 'A Theory of the Consumer Product Warranty', *Yale Law Journal* 90 (1980–81) 1297.

Radin, M. 'Market-Inalienability', *Harvard Law Review* 100 (1987) 1849.

Rakoff, T., 'Contracts of Adhesion: An Essay in Reconstruction', *Harvard Law Review* 96 (1983) 1174.

—— 'The Implied Terms of Contracts: Of "Default Rules" and "Situation-Sense"', in J. Beatson and D. Friedmann (eds.), *Good Faith and Fault in Contract Law* (Oxford: Clarendon Press, 1995) 191.

Ramsay, I., 'Consumer Redress Mechanisms for Poor-Quality and Defective Products', *University of Toronto Law Journal* 31 (1981) 117.

—— *Consumer Protection: Text and Materials* (London: Weidenfeld and Nicholson, 1989).

—— 'Small Claims Courts in Canada: A Socio-Legal Appraisal', in C. J. Whelan (ed.), below, 25.

—— 'Consumer Credit Law, Distributive Justice and the Welfare State', *Oxford Journal of Legal Studies* 15 (1995) 177.

Raz, J., 'Promises in Morality and Law', *Harvard Law Review* 95 (1982) 916.

Rea, C. 'Efficiency Implications of Penalties and Liquidated Damages', *Journal of Legal Studies* 13 (1984) 147.

Renner, K., *The Institutions of Private Law and their Social Functions*, O. Kahn-Freund (ed.) (London: Routledge, 1949).

Reynolds, F., 'The Applicability of General Rules of Private Law to Consumer Disputes', in S. Anderman *et al.* (eds.), *Law and the Weaker Party* (London: Professional Books, 1982) ii. 93.

Rice, D. A., 'Remedies, Enforcement Procedures and the Duality of Consumer Transaction Problems', *Boston University Law Review* 48 (1968) 559.

Rose, C., 'Giving, Trading, Thieving, and Trusting: How and Why Gifts Become Exchanges, and (More Importantly) Vice Versa', *Florida Law Review* 44 (1992) 295.

Rosenberg, J. D. and Folberg, H. J., 'Alternative Dispute Resolution: An Empirical Analysis', *Stanford Law Review* 46 (1994) 1487.

Ross, H. L., 'Insurance Claims Complaints: A Private Appeals Procedure', *Law and Society Review* 9 (1975) 275.

—— and Littlefield, N. O., 'Complaint as a Problem-Solving Mechanism', *Law and Society Review* 12 (1977–78) 199.

Rubin, G. R., 'Law, Poverty and Imprisonment for Debt, 1869–1914', in G. R. Rubin and D. Sugerman (eds.), below, 192.

—— 'The County Courts and the Tally Trade, 1846–1914', in G. R. Rubin and D. Sugerman (eds.), below, 321.

—— and Sugerman, D. (eds.), *Law, Economy and Society: Essays in the History of English Law 1750–1920* (London: Professional Books, 1984).

Sako, M., *Prices, Quality and Trust: Inter-Firm Relations in Britain and Japan* (Cambridge: Cambridge University Press, 1992).

Sander, F. E. A., 'Alternative Methods of Dispute Resolution: An Overview', *University of Florida Law Review* 37 (1985) 1.

Schanze, E., 'Symbiotic Contracts: Exploring Long-Term Agency Structures between Contract and Corporation', in C. Joerges (ed.), above, 67.

—— 'Regulation by Consensus: The Practice of International Investment Agreements', *Journal of Institutional and Theoretical Economics* 152 (1988) 144.

Schill, M. 'An Economic Analysis of Mortgagor Protection Laws', *Virginia Law Review* 77 (1990) 489.

Schlicht, E., 'On Custom', *Journal of Institutional and Theoretical Economics* 149 (1993) 178.

Schultz, F., 'The Firm Offer Puzzle: A Study of Business Practice in the Construction Industry', *University of Chicago Law Review* 19 (1952) 237.

Schwartz, A., 'A Reexamination of Nonsubstantive Unconscionability', *Virginia Law Review* 63 (1977) 1053.

—— 'The Case for Specific Performance', *Yale Law Journal* 89 (1979) 271.

—— 'Relational Contracts in the Courts: An Analysis of Incomplete Agreements and Judicial Strategies', *Journal of Legal Studies* 21 (1992) 271.

—— and Wilde, L., 'Intervening in Markets on the Basis of Imperfect Information: A Legal and Economic Analysis', *University of Pennsylvania Law Review* 127 (1979) 630.

Schwartz, D. S., 'Enforcing Small Print to Protect Big Business: Employee and Consumer Rights Claims in an Age of Compelled Arbitration', *Wisconsin Law Review* (1997) 33.

Scott, C., 'The Juridification of Relations in the UK Utilities Sector', in J. Black, P. Muchlinski, and P. Walker (eds.), *Commercial Regulation and Judicial Review* (Oxford: Hart Publishing, 1998) 19.

—— and Barron, A., 'The Citizens' Charter Programme', *Modern Law Review* 55 (1992) 526.

Scott, J., 'Empirical Studies Strike Back Against the Force of Contract Theory', *U.C.L. Jurisprudence Review* (1997) 256.

Selznick, P., *Law, Society and Industrial Justice* (New York: Russell Sage Foundation, 1969).

Shavell, S., 'The Design of Contracts and Remedies for Breach', *Quarterly Journal of Economics* 99 (1984) 121.

—— 'Liability for Harm Versus Regulation of Safety', *Journal of Legal Studies* 13 (1984) 357.

Shearing, C. D., 'A Constitutive Conception of Regulation', in P. Grabosky and J. Braithwaite (eds.), *Business Regulation and Australia's Future* (Canberra: Australian Institute of Criminology, 1993) 67.

Shelanski, H. A., and Klein, P. G., 'Empirical Research in Transaction Cost Economics: A Review and Assessment', *Journal of Law, Economics and Organization* 11 (1995) 335.

Shell, G. R., 'Opportunism and Trust in the Negotiation of Commercial Contracts: Toward a New Cause of Action', *Vanderbilt Law Review* 44 (1991) 221.

Simpson, A. W. B., 'Innovation in Nineteenth Century Contract Law', *Law Quarterly Review* 91 (1975) 247.

—— 'The Origin of Futures Trading in the Liverpool Cotton Market', in P. Cane and J. Stapleton (eds.), *Essays for Patrick Atiyah* (Oxford: Clarendon Press, 1991) ch. 8.

Slawson, D., 'Standard Form Contracts and Democratic Control of Lawmaking Power', *Harvard Law Review* 84 (1971) 529.

Smith, L., 'Disgorgement of the Profits of Breach of Contract: Property, Contract and "Efficient Breach"', *Canadian Business Law Journal*, 24 (1994–5) 121.

Smith, S. A., 'In Defence of Substantive Fairness', *Law Quarterly Review* 112 (1996) 138.

Speidel, R. E. 'Court-Imposed Price Adjustments under Long-term Supply Contracts', *Northwestern University Law Review* 76 (1981) 369.

Spindler, G., 'Market Processes, Standardization, and Tort Law', in C. Joerges and O. Gerstenberg (eds.), *Private Governance, Democratic Constitutionalism, and Supranationalism*, EUR 18340 (Luxembourg: European Communities, 1998) 145.

Steyn, Lord, 'Contract Law and the Reasonable Expectations of Honest Men', *Law Quarterly Review* 113 (1997) 433.

Stigler, G. 'The Economic Theory of Regulation', *Bell Journal of Economics and Management Science* 2 (1971) 1.

Stinchcombe, A. L., 'Contracts as Hierarchical Documents', in A. L. Stinchcombe and C. A. Heimer (eds.), *Organization Theory and Project Management:*

Administering Uncertainty in Norwegian Offshore Oil (Oslo: Norwegian University Press, 1985,) ch. 2.

Suchman, M. C., 'Translation Costs: A Comment on Sociology and Economics', *Oregon Law Review* 74 (1995) 257.

—— and Cahill, M., 'The Hired Gun as Facilitator: Lawyers and the Support of Business Disputes in Silicon Valley', *Law and Social Inquiry* 21 (1996) 679.

Sugerman, D., 'Legal Theory, the Common Law Mind and the Making of the Textbook Tradition', in W. Twining (ed.), *Legal Theory and Common Law* (Oxford: Blackwell, 1986) 26.

—— and Rubin, G. R., 'Towards a New History of Law and Material Society in England, 1750–1914', in G. R. Rubin and D. Sugerman (eds.), above, 1.

Sunstein, C., 'Paradoxes of the Regulatory State', *University of Chicago Law Review* 57 (1990) 407.

Talley, E. L., 'Contract Renegotiation, Mechanism Design, and the Liquidated Damages Rule', *Stanford Law Review* 46 (1994) 1195.

Taylor, C. R., and Wiggins, S. N., 'Competition or Compensation: Supplier Incentives Under the American and Japanese Subcontracting Systems', *American Economic Review* 87 (1997) 598.

Telser, L. G., 'A Theory of Self-enforcing Agreements', *Journal of Business* 53 (1980) 27.

—— 'Why There are Organized Futures Markets', *Journal of Law and Economics* 24 (1981) 1.

—— and Higginbottom, H. N., 'Organised Futures Markets: Costs and Benefits', *Journal of Political Economy* 85 (1977) 969.

Teubner, G., 'Substantive and Reflexive Elements in Modern Law', *Law and Society Review* 17 (1983) 239.

—— 'Juridification: Concepts, Aspects, Limits, Solutions', in G. Teubner (ed.), *Juridification of Social Spheres: A Comparative Analysis in the Areas of Labour, Corporate, Antitrust and Social Welfare Law* (Berlin: Walter de Gruyter, 1987) 1.

—— 'After Legal Instrumentalism? Strategic Models of Post-Regulatory Law', in G. Teubner (ed.), *Dilemmas of Law in the Welfare State* (New York/Berlin: Walter de Gruyter, 1988) 299.

—— 'How the Law Thinks: Toward A Constructivist Epistemology of Law', *Law and Society Review* 23 (1989) 727.

—— 'Piercing the Contractual Veil? The Social Responsibility of Contractual Networks', in T. Wilhelmsson (ed.), *Perspectives of Critical Contract Law* (Aldershot: Dartmouth, 1993) 211.

—— *Law as an Autopoietic System* (Oxford: Blackwell, 1993).

—— 'Global Bukovina: Legal Pluralism in the World Society', in G. Teubner (ed.), *Global Law Without a State* (Aldershot: Gower, 1997) 3.

—— 'Altera pars Audiatur: Law in the Collision of Discourses', in R. Rawlings (ed.), *Law Society and Economy* (Oxford: Clarendon Press, 1997), 149.

Thomas, D. R., 'Consumer Arbitration Agreements Act 1988', *Arbitration* 57 (1991) 48.

Trakman, L. E., *The Law Merchant: The Evolution of Commercial Law* (Colorado: Rothman, 1983).

Trebilcock, M. J., 'Private Law Remedies for Misleading Advertising', *University of Toronto Law Journal* 22 (1972) 1.

—— 'An Economic Approach to the Doctrine of Unconsionability', in B. J. Reiter and J. Swan, *Studies in Contract Law* (Toronto: Butterworths, 1980) 379.

—— *The Limits of Freedom of Contract* (Cambridge, Mass.: Harvard University Press, 1993).

Treitel, G. H., *The Law of Contract*, 9th edn. (London: Sweet & Maxwell, 1995).

Trubeck, D. M., 'Max Weber on Law and the Rise of Capitalism', *Wisconsin Law Review* (1972) 720.

—— Sarat, A., Felstiner, W. L. F., Kritzer, H. M., and Groosman, J. B., 'The Costs of Ordinary Litigation', *UCLA Law Review* 31 (1983) 72.

Turpin, C., *Government Procurement and Contracts* (Harlow: Longman, 1989).

Twining, W., *Karl Llewellyn and the Realist Movement* (London: Weidenfeld & Nicholson, 1973).

Umbeck, J., 'A Theory of Contract Choice and the California Gold Rush', *Journal of Law and Economics* 20 (1978) 421.

Veljanovski, C. G., 'An Institutional Analysis of Futures Contracting', in B. A. Goss (ed.), *Futures Markets: Their Establishment and Performance* (London and Sydney: Croom Helm, 1986) 13.

Vincent-Jones, Peter, 'Contract and Business Transactions: A Socio-Legal Analysis', *Journal of Law and Society* 16 (1989) 166.

—— 'Contract Litigation in England and Wales 1975–1991: Transformation of Business Disputing?', *Civil Justice Quarterly* 12 (1993) 337.

—— 'The Limits of Contractual Order in Public Sector Transactions', *Legal Studies* 14 (1994) 364.

—— 'Hybrid Organization, Contractual Governance, and Compulsory Competitive Tendering in the Provision of Local Authority Services', in S. Deakin and J. Michie (eds.), above, 143.

—— and Harries, A., 'Limits of Contract in Internal CCT Transactions: A Comparative Study of Buildings Cleaning and Refuse Collection in "Northern Metropolitan"', in D. Campbell and P. Vincent-Jones (eds.), *Contract and Economic Organisation* (Aldershot: Dartmouth, 1996) 180.

Walsh, K., Deakin, N., Spurgeon, P., Smith, P., and Thomas, N., 'Contracts for Public Services: A Comparative Perspective', in D. Campbell and P. Vincent-Jones (eds.), *Contract and Economic Organisation* (Aldershot: Dartmouth, 1996) 212.

Walzer, M., *Spheres of Justice: A Defence of Pluralism and Equality* (Oxford: Blackwell, 1983).

Wanner, C., 'The Public Ordering of Private Relations', *Law and Society Review* 8 (1974) 421.

Weber, M., *Economy and Society* (G. Roth and C. Wittich, eds.), (Berkeley: University of California Press, 1978) i and ii.

Weintraub, R. J., 'A Survey of Contract Practice and Policy', *Wisconsin Law Review* (1992) 1.

Weller, P., *The Theory of Futures Markets* (Oxford: Blackwell, 1992).

Weller, S., Ruhnka, J. C., and Martin, J. A., 'American Small Claims Courts', in C. J. Whelan (ed.), below, 5.

Wheeler, S., *Reservation of Title Clauses* (Oxford: Clarendon Press, 1991).

—— 'Lawyer Involvement in Commercial Disputes', *Journal of Law and Society* 18 (1991) 241.

Whelan, C. J., (ed.), *Small Claims Courts: A Comparative Study* (Oxford: Clarendon Press, 1990).

—— 'Small Claims in England and Wales: Redefining Justice', ibid. 99.

White Paper, *Setting New Standards: A Strategy for Government Procurement*, Cm 2840 (London: HMSO, 1995).

Whitford, W. C., 'Law and the Consumer Transaction: A Case Study of the Automobile Warranty', *Wisconsin Law Review* (1968) 1006.

—— 'The Functions of Disclosure Regulation in Consumer Transactions', *Wisconsin Law Review* (1973) 400.

—— 'A Critique of the Consumer Credit Collection System', *Wisconsin Law Review* (1979) 1047.

—— and Kimball, S. L., 'Why Process Consumer Complaints? A Case Study of the Office of the Commissioner of Insurance of Wisconsin', *Wisconsin Law Review* (1974) 639.

—— and Laufer, H., 'The Impact of Denying Self-Help Repossession of Automobiles: A Case Study of the Wisconsin Consumer Act', *Wisconsin Law Review* (1975) 607.

Whitley, R., Henderson, J., Czaban, L., Lengyel, G., 'Trust and Contractual Relations in an Emerging Capitalist Economy: The Changing Trading Relationships of Ten Large Hungarian Enterprises', *Organization Studies* 17(3) (1996) 397.

Wiggins, S. N., 'The Economics of the Firm and Contracts: A Selective Survey', *Journal of Institutional and Theoretical Economics* 147 (1991) 603.

Wilkinson, H. W., 'Complaining to Ombudsmen', *New Law Journal* (1992) 1348.

Williams, F. (ed.), *Why the Poor Pay More* (London: MacMillan/Child Poverty Action Group, 1974).

Williams, G. A., 'Reservation of Title in the Construction Industry: Who Wants It?—Some Economic Perspectives on Risk-Allocation', *Current Legal Problems* (1987) 233.

Williams, J., *The Economic Function of Futures Markets* (Cambridge: Cambridge University Press, 1986).

Williamson, O. E., *Markets and Hierarchies: Analysis and Antitrust Implications* (New York: Free Press, 1975).

—— 'Transaction Cost Economics: The Governance of Contractual Relations', *Journal of Law and Economics* 22 (1979) 233.

—— 'Credible Commitments: Using Hostages to Support Exchange', *American Economic Review* 73 (1983) 519.

—— 'Assessing Contract', *Journal of Law, Economics and Organization* 1 (1985) 177.

—— *The Economic Institutions of Capitalism* (New York: Free Press, 1985).

—— 'Calculativeness, Trust, and Economic Organization', *Journal of Law and Economics* 36 (1993) 453.

Wilson, J. A., 'Adaptation to Uncertainty and Small Numbers Exchange: the New England Fresh Fish Market', *Bell Journal of Economics* 11 (1980) 491, 503–4.

Winn, J. K., 'Relational Practices and the Marginalization of Law: Informal Financial Practices of Small Businesses in Taiwan', *Law and Society Review* 28 (1994) 193.

Wiseman, Z. B., 'The Limits of Vision: Karl Llewellyn and the Merchant Rules', *Harvard Law Review* 100 (1987) 465.

Woolf, Lord, *Access to Justice: Interim Report to the Lord Chancellor on the Civil Justice System of England and Wales* (London: HMSO, 1995).

World Bank, *World Development Report 1997: The State in a Changing World* (Oxford: Oxford University Press, 1997).

Yates, D., *Exclusion Clauses in Contracts*, 2nd edn. (London: Sweet & Maxwell, 1982).

Yin, C. N., and Cranston, R., 'Small Claims Tribunals in Australia', in C. J. Whelan (ed.), above, 49.

Yngvesson, B., and Hennessey, P., 'Small Claims, Complex Disputes: A Review of the Small Claims Literature', *Law and Society Review* 9 (1975) 219.

Zucker, L. G., 'Production of Trust: Institutional Sources of Economic Structure, 1840–1920', *Research in Organizational Behavior* 8 (1986) 53.

Zweigert, K., and Kotz, H., *An Introduction to Comparative Law*, 2nd edn. (Oxford: Clarendon Press, 1987) 2.

Index

Printed in the United Kingdom
by Lightning Source UK Ltd.
123844UK00001B/62/A

9 780199 258017